Norfolk Record Society
Volume LXXVIII for 2014

The First World War Letters
of
Philip and Ruth Hewetson

Edited by
Frank Meeres

Norfolk Record Society
Volume LXXVIII
2014

First published in 2014
by the Norfolk Record Society

ISBN 978-0-9556357-7-9

Typeset by Carnegie Book Production, Lancaster
Printed and bound by Jellyfish Solutions

Contents

The Hewetson Letters

Illustrations

Maps

Abbreviations

ARC	Army Reserve Centre
ASC	Army Service Corps
Battn; Bn	Battalion
BEF	British Expeditionary Force
BIP	Brigade Instructional Platoon
BRCS	British Red Cross Society
CA	Church Army
CFN	*Church Family Newspaper*
CO	Commanding Officer.
Coy	Company
DACG	Deputy Assistant Commissary General
DDMS	Deputy Director Medical Services
DRLS	Despatch Rider Letter Service
DSO	Distinguished Service Order
F	[usually] Felixstowe
FMH	Fargo Military Hospital
FSP	Field Service Postcard
GS	General Service
GSM	General Service Member (of a Voluntary Aid Detachment)
HC	Holy Communion
HQ	Head Quarters
HS	Home Service [but also used for Hugh Strong]
IBD	Infantry Base Depot
Liv St	Liverpool Street station, London, from where trains run to Cambridge and to Norfolk
LNLR	Loyal North Lancashire Regiment
LRB	London Rifle Brigade
Lt; 2nd Lt	Lieutenant; Second Lieutenant
MC	Military Cross
MFO	Military Forwarding Officer

MO	Medical Officer
NCO	Non-Commissioned Officer
OR	Used by Philip for Old Reptonian.
PC	Postcard
PJ	[Lionel] Powys Jones
PMC	President of the Messing Committee
PO	Postal order
RAMC	Royal Army Medical Corps
RE	Royal Engineers
Regt	Regiment
RFA	Royal Field Artillery
RFC	Royal Flying Corps, created in May 1912. Merged with RNAS on 1 April 1918 to form the Royal Air Force.
RNAS	Royal Naval Air Service: its responsibilities included, but were not limited to, the air defence of Britain. Merged with the RFC to form the Royal Air Force 1 April 1918.
RTO	Rail Transport Officer
SA	South Africa
Sergt	Sergeant
SR	Special Reserve
VAD	Voluntary Aid Detachment
VC	Victoria Cross
WAAC	Women's Auxiliary Army Corps
WF	Western Front
WRN [S]	Women's Royal Navy [Service]
YMCA	Young Men's Christian Association

Glossary

Adjutant	An officer who acts as an administrative assistant to a more senior officer
Battalion	The basic tactical unit of the infantry of the British Army in the Great War of 1914–1918. At full establishment it consisted of 1,007 men of whom 30 were officers. It comprised a Battalion Headquarters and four Companies.
Billets	A term for living quarters to which a soldier is assigned to sleep: officers would normally sleep in private houses, other ranks usually in barns
Brigade	A military formation of fighting units together with support arms and services. It is smaller than a division and is usually headed and commanded by a brigadier.
Budget	Used by both Philip and Ruth to mean a quantity or bundle of letters
Captain	The army rank immediately above Lieutenant
Coalboxes	Army slang for very large shells
Company	A military unit, typically consisting of 80–250 soldiers and usually commanded by a captain or a major. They are named alphabetically: 'A' Coy; 'B' Coy etc.
Corps	A large military formation, composed of two or more divisions
Division	A large military unit or formation, usually consisting of between 10,000 and 30,000 soldiers: made up of several regiments or brigades
Lieutenant	The lowest commissioned officer rank. Philip enters the Army as a Second Lieutenant (2nd Lt), and is later promoted to Lieutenant
Mess	Where military personnel socialise, eat, and live
New Army	After war broke out in August 1914, many thousands of men volunteered to serve, well over 2.5 million by

	February 1916. Conscription was introduced under the Military Service Act of 1916 for men between 18 and 41, and in 1918 the age limit was raised to 51.
Orderly Officer	A military officer who, for a given day, assumes responsibility for security, order, and supervision of the guard.
Platoon	A company of soldiers, usually led by a lieutenant and consisting of two to three sections or squads of ten to twelve people
Puttees	Legging or gaiter that covers the lower leg
Regiment	A military unit, consisting of at least two battalions, usually commanded by a colonel
Regular Army	The pre-war Army, recruited entirely from volunteers, the usual period being seven years with the colours and five with the reserve
Sap	A small trench extending forward from a front-line trench
Sergeant	A noncommissioned officer of a rank above corporal
Shell	A payload-carrying projectile which, as opposed to shot, contains an explosive or other filling
Shrapnel	Metal balls or fragments within an artillery shell, which scatter when the shell explodes
Subaltern	A junior army officer, having a rank below that of Captain.
Territorials [Terriers]	The Territorial Army, created in 1908: a volunteer army of men enrolled for four years, attending a training camp each: intended primarily for home defence.
Valise	A small overnight travelling case

Editorial note

The importance of Philip Hewetson's letters was recognised by his parents after the war had ended, and an attempt was made to publish them in the early 1920s, which came to nothing. The letters passed into his sister Ruth's hands on the deaths of her parents and became her most treasured possession. When she had to go into hospital in what proved to be her final illness, Ruth gave the collection to her vicar, Revd Norman Jeffery, with the request that the letters be used to give inspiration to others. She died in hospital, leaving her house to the use of the diocese of St Alban's. Revd Jeffery passed the letters onto the Bishop of St Albans who donated them to the Norfolk Record Office in 1995. This was at a time when the Record Office was in temporary premises after the fire in Norwich Central Library in August 1994, but they were carefully stored and moved to the new Record Office when it opened in 2003.

The archive consists of almost 250 letters written by Philip to one or both his parents, and occasional letters to his sister Ruth. They were written between 1914 and 1918, either from the Western Front or while he was training or recovering from wounds at Felixstowe. The letters were then passed around the family, including Ruth if she was away from home. Philip's mother has added the occasional comment to a letter before passing it on: these are noted in the transcription. The collection also comprises sixty letters written from Ruth to her parents while she was serving at Fargo Hospital in Wiltshire between March and October 1918.

Philip's letters are almost all dated: a few from Felixstowe are undated, but can be fitted into the sequence from their internal context. He writes in a clear hand, with very few deletions and alterations. His main idiosyncrasy is that his capitals are very similar to his lower case letters, so that words like 'God' and 'German', and the first words of sentences could be either: I have assumed the conventional capitalisations, except after exclamation marks, which he clearly does not regard as being the end of sentences.

On several occasions Philip made use of the standard Field Army Postcard provided by the Army. These are indicated in the text by the addition of the initials FSP.

Ruth's letters are dated only by day, and often a letter will be started one day and continued on another. Several are on cards with postmark dates and the remainder can be fitted into sequence by reference to events such as Easter, her birthday, Philip's being reported missing. As she explains in one letter, she adopted a convention of using \ to mean 'the' and / to mean 'of': however she often forgot and wrote the word in full. She also adopted the language of mathematics, using triangles of dots to mean 'because' and 'therefore'. In all these cases, the words have been transcribed in full.

The Hewetson letters are held at the Norfolk Record Office, with the overall reference number of MC 643. Each document has an individual sub-number: this is given at the end of each transcribed letter.

In publishing this text, Ruth's wishes for Philip's letters will finally have been fulfilled. In a time when the part played by women in the First World War is better appreciated than it was, her own letters will also bring alive what that war meant for a young woman such as Ruth.

Editorial Conventions

* *	Words inserted
< >	Words deleted
[*italics*]	Editorial addition within the text
<word illegible>	Indicates deleted word which cannot be read

Acknowledgements

I am grateful to the Norfolk Record Office for giving permission to transcribe the documents in this book, and to the present County Archivist, Gary Tuson, and the former County Archivist, Dr John Alban, for their help and support.

Many people have helped along the way: I am especially grateful to the series editor, Anthony Howe, to Dick Rayner, who took the photograph of Philip's grave, and to Elizabeth Budd and Louise Watling for their contributions and comments.

Introduction

The letters transcribed in this book are those written to their parents by Philip and Ruth Hewetson, brother and sister, brought up at Salhouse Vicarage in Norfolk. Philip was in the army from the outbreak of the First World War, and served on the Western Front, while Ruth worked in a war hospital in 1918: the letters show what everyday life was like for men and women during the First World War. The idea of publishing Philip's letters from the front was first mooted in the 1920s, when William Temple,[1] his former headmaster at Repton School, wrote to Philip's mother that: 'the interest attaching to the letters and to the story which they partly tell lies precisely in the fact that this story is not exceptional. It is one in which the record of many others may be read.'[2]

Philip and Ruth Hewetson

Philip and Ruth were the only two children of Revd William Hewetson and his wife Kathleen, who had married on 9 September 1890. Philip was born Richard John Philip Hewetson in Birmingham on 14 August 1893, Kathleen Ruth L'Estrange Hewetson in Chesterton, Cambridgeshire, on 21 July 1897. As was common in middle class families they were not called by their first given name but by a later one, hence they are always known as 'Philip' and 'Ruth'.

Philip was educated at The Knoll, Woburn Sands, from 1902 and went on to Repton Public School in Derbyshire (which his father and uncles had attended) in 1906. He became head of his house, but in many ways was just a typical schoolboy. Temple wrote of him: 'it was immediately clear that he was not specially clever or a boy with the gifts that easily lead to prominence

---

1. William Temple (1881–1944), headmaster of Repton School, Derbyshire, 1910–14; Bishop of Manchester, 1920–29; Archbishop of York, 1929–42; Archbishop of Canterbury, 1942–44.

2. Norfolk Record Office (hereafter NRO), MC 643/18/7. Temple was writing in 1919.

at school ... he was very specially straight-forward and absolutely, almost ruthlessly, conscientious.'[3] He made many friends, some of whom are mentioned in his letters, such as Jack Marriott of Cromer. As his later letters suggest, Philip was keen on sport: he won cups for running and played in his house football team every year from 1908: in his final year he played in the school first eleven, culminating in a match against Charterhouse school played at Leyton, Essex on 20 December 1911. *The Reptonian* reported that he 'reserved his best game for the Charterhouse match, when he made plenty of ground and centred with great accuracy, which had not been always the case'. His school work was steady rather than spectacular: he finished seventh in a form of eleven in the autumn term of 1911. In his report for that term, his classics master commented: 'An excellent worker who may always be trusted to do his best. He is not a very good scholar, but he is improving. His housemaster thought him 'a great help in the House', and Temple noted: 'A most reliable boy'.[4]

Philip was also in the Repton Officer's Training Corps: the O.T.C. was founded in 1908 as part of the Territorial Forces, the reorganised reserve to the Army. It had a junior section at public schools and a senior section at universities. Those trained in it, like Philip, would enter the Army at the lowest rank of commissioned officer, Second Lieutenant [2nd Lt]. Philip gained Certificate A, the highest award, at Repton in 1911.

Philip went to Oriel College, Oxford in autumn 1912, playing in the freshers' football match of that year. He completed two years at Oxford, taking a keen interest in University sport, renewing acquaintance with old Reptonians and making new friends at University. The two most often referred to in the letters are Hugh Strong, with whom he first joined up [who is referred to as 'Hugh', 'Hugo' or 'H. S.'], and Reggie Weber, the son of Frederick and Emily Weber; in 1911, the family were living in Southampton where Frederick worked in the Ordnance Survey, but later they moved to Bromley in Kent. Others are known, in the custom of the time, only by their surnames: two who recur in the letters are [Lionel] 'Powys-Jones', known in the letters as 'P.J.', whose family lived in Rhodesia, and [Gordon James] 'Bleistein', from a London Jewish family.[5]

In the summer of 1914, Philip was on holiday with the family in Bude, Cornwall: they were there on 4 August 1914 when war broke out. This was the end of his university career.

---

3. Ibid.

4. NRO, MC 643/1/42, 52.

5. Biographical details of these men, and all the soldiers that Philip mentions in his letters, are given in Appendix 2.

1.   Philip Hewetson

Ruth was educated at Norwich High School for Girls, then in the Assembly House in Norwich, and one of the foremost schools for girls in East Anglia. The headmistress was Miss Gertrude Mary Wise, a graduate of Newnham College, Cambridge who had taught science at the school between 1891 and 1900 and had been headmistress at Shrewsbury School between 1891 and 1900. Clearly a great influence on Ruth, she is mentioned several times in the letters. Ruth's closest friends also went to the school. Her best friend was Amie Evershed, born 24 July 1898, the daughter of a brewer: Amie's widowed mother, Alice, rented the house known as the Plantation on

2.   Ruth Hewetson

Earlham Road in Norwich. (It was actually owned by the Cozens-Hardy family, who gave the family notice to quit in 1918, causing a crisis reflected in several of Ruth's letters: this was perhaps a family dispute as Amie's mother was herself a Cozens-Hardy before her marriage.) Her other close friend was Xenia Muriel: born on 30 March 1898, she was the daughter of a Norwich doctor, Cecil Muriel, who lived at 42 St Giles Street, a short walk from the school, which she had attended since she was five years old.

All three were good at games, playing for their Companies (which in other schools would be called Houses) in tennis, netball and hockey. All three played netball for their Companies in 1914, and they were together in the school's First Seven. In the idyllic summer of 1914 all represented their companies in running: the space around the school was too small for a Sports Day and the Sports that year was held at the Haldinstein family garden at Thorpe Lodge.[6]

Ruth was sixteen at the outbreak of war and remained at school: she and her two friends played in the school netball team in spring 1915 and in a mixed-doubles tennis tournament in the summer. In that summer term, both Amie and Ruth took part in a series of races held in the Evershed's family home, the Plantation Garden. When lacrosse was introduced in 1915, Ruth was at first doubtful but soon became one of the school's best players. They were bright girls too, Ruth and Amie both winning Fourth Form prizes in 1913, and all three passing the Oxford senior examination in July 1915. Characteristically Amie, although the youngest, obtained a Class I, the others a class II: Ruth had been let down by a failure in her chosen specialist book – Bunyan's *Pilgrim's Progress*. Amie's success led to a share in the Senior Trust Scholarship. At art, Xenia excelled, obtaining a full certificate from the Royal Drawing Society: the other two achieving lesser distinctions for their work. Ruth was to treasure a painting given to her by Xenia. Ruth was perhaps the most musical, as reflected in her letters, and won a singing prize in February 1918.

It was a typical pre-war childhood for middle-class girls. However, the war was closing in on the three of them: after Zeppelins had bombed Norfolk in January 1915, Zeppelin drills were held in the school. The school adopted a soldier who was a prisoner of war in Germany and in November 1915 held a party for wounded Tommies, the school magazine commenting that the soldiers deserved VCs for facing something worse than Huns – a room full of schoolgirls! When the Bishop of Thetford spoke at the school's prize-giving in December 1915, he prophesied: 'These High School girls may possibly soon be working at the plough, or delivering letters, or collecting railway tickets, or doing any of a hundred other things that two years ago they would never have dreamed of.'[7] All the girls in the school must have wondered what roles they would play: Ruth was one of them. Girls were soon leaving school and taking up professions as diverse as nursing, aeronautical draughtsmanship, bank work and farm work. Xenia left school at Easter 1916, when she was eighteen years old, and was soon working for Components Ltd: one of

---

6. The family, which was headed by Alfred Haldinstein, son of Philip, founder of the Norwich shoe-making firm, were Jewish: one of the Haldinstein girls, Joyce, married a member of the Dutch community and lived there at the time of the Second World War: she escaped to Switzerland but her husband and son perished at Auschwitz.

7. *Eastern Daily Press* 18 December 1915.

several girls sent to London by the firm to be trained as a tool-setter, she then returned to work in Norwich making munitions.

Ruth and Amie stayed on. In the summer of 1916 it was the Hewetsons' turn to act as hosts: an 'American tournament' of tennis was played at Salhouse Vicarage and 'was much enjoyed'. The two girls had other interests too. Ruth was praised in the summer of 1916 for her keenness in gardening: this is reflected in her letters. Both were in the Literary Society, and Ruth read a paper to the group on R. L. Stevenson in November 1916, this interest no doubt explaining why Philip was sent a book by this author while he was at the Front.[8] Ruth acted as editor of the school magazine in 1916, an achievement mentioned by Philip: she was assisted by Amie in this. She tried to gather up accounts by ex-pupils of their war work, but, like many an editor, she found contributions slow and could publish only two, one on Red Cross work, the other (perhaps by Xenia) on making munitions.

Living with her parents at Salhouse, Ruth took an interest in local village life as well as school life, being especially involved with the Girl Guides: the Salhouse group was first founded in September 1917 with Ruth as their Captain: sixteen girls were enrolled. Several of the Girl Guides are mentioned in Ruth's letters.

The Hewetson and Burges families

The Hewetsons' parents were William and Kathleen: both came from clerical families. William Hewetson, their father, was born in 1862, and came from a large family, being one of eight children of John and Ruth Hewetson. John was vicar of Measham in Leicestershire from 1852 to 1893: he sent all his sons to Repton. William went on to Worcester College, Oxford, was ordained in 1888, and served his curacy at St Paul's, Birmingham under Revd Richard Burges. He married Kathleen Burges, one of the vicar's many children, in 1890; she had received a First Class certificate for the national Froebel Union examination in 1888, after two years study in London. The couple moved several times as William's clerical career developed. He was curate of Aston 1890–94, assistant secretary of the Church Pastoral Aid Society 1894–98, vicar of Thame 1898–1905, curate of St Paul Penge 1905–07, and vicar of Salhouse and Wroxham from 1907. Both William and Kathleen had a large number of brothers and sisters, the 'uncles' and 'aunts' that are frequently mentioned in the letters. Most frequently mentioned is 'Gobagger' (real name Julia), a sister of Kathleen's,

---

8. See letter 121.

who ran a girls' school in Folkestone.[9] Naturally, several of the uncles and aunts had families, their children being cousins and contemporaries of Philip and Ruth. The most frequently mentioned is Julian Tyndale-Biscoe. Julian was something of a 'wag', as it would have been described at the time. Philip notes a joke postcard he was sent by him, and Julian's memoirs tell of a time when 'Aunt Ethel' organised a family lunch at the Savoy Hotel in London, which he and Philip both attended. On a whim, Julian bought a wig and went dressed as a woman, successfully deceiving members of his own family! He was also a brave man, winning the Military Cross in an incident he is too modest to mention in his own memoirs. Julian was a gunner: his brother, Harold, who was in the Royal Flying Corps, is also occasionally mentioned.[10]

Another set of cousins were the Langdale-Smiths. The family lived in Holton, very close to Oxford, and Philip often cycled to visit them when he was at University. It was here that the danger of life in the armed forces was first brought home to him. His cousin, Frederick, was in the Royal Navy serving in the *Vanguard* when he drowned in an accident off Scapa Flow on 25 April 1913. When Philip attended his funeral in Holton, he noted that it was the first he had ever been to: there were to be plenty more deaths to come.[11] Another Holton cousin was Julia Langdale-Smith, a beauty according to Julian: on one occasion mentioned in the letters she visited Salhouse Vicarage.

Salhouse and Wroxham in the years before the First World War

Wroxham and Salhouse, two adjoining villages north east of Norwich, were usually served by the same vicar. In 1845, the then vicar, John Collyer, built a new Vicarage near Salhouse church at a cost of £1,000. This building (now *The Lodge Inn*, Salhouse) is conveniently situated for both Salhouse and Wroxham churches, and is where the Hewetsons lived from their arrival in 1907 until after the end of the war.

Salhouse was, and is, a scattered village: the church is well to the north of the village centre, and the Vicarage has a large garden, still surrounded by fields. The population in 1911 was 650. Wroxham was also a small village: its 1911 population was 729. Wroxham church is tucked away off the main road to Salhouse and Norwich. Wroxham is today famous as a holiday centre on

---

9. For further details of the family, see Appendix 3.
10. Julian Tyndale-Biscoe, *Gunner Subaltern* (London, 1971).
11. NRO, MC 643/2/18

the Norfolk Broads and this character was just beginning to emerge in the years before the Hewetsons arrived. John Loynes began to hire out craft, at first for fishing, in 1877, and in 1901 Ernest Collins built the first cabin yachts for hire in the village.

Each of the two villages had its own elementary school, and also its own railway station on the line between Cromer and Norwich. There was a doctor in Wroxham, but not in Salhouse. For William Hewetson the joint net income of the two parishes was £220, with fourteen acres of glebe – and a handsome vicarage house.

William Hewetson was keen to make his own contribution to the war effort. Too old to join up, he spent periods in France, 1917–1919, as a padre with the Church Army, running recreation huts where soldiers could read newspapers, write letters and purchase hot drinks, chocolate and cigarettes, as well as attend religious services. This is mentioned several times in Philip's letters although father and son managed to meet just once while they were both on the Western Front.

The British Army in the First World War

At the start of the First World War, the British Army was made up of volunteers, who signed up for seven years followed by five years in reserve: it consisted of about a quarter of a million men. Six divisions of the men were organised into the British Expeditionary Force, a tiny force by Continental standards, but well-equipped and organised. Much of this regular expeditionary force was destroyed in the battles of autumn 1914: more than half of the men were casualties, with one in ten men dead. The reserves had been reorganised in 1908 into the Territorials (affectionately known as 'Terriers'), out of the old volunteer army, militia and yeomanry. They could not be compelled to serve outside this country – but they could volunteer to do so and most did. These were the men who held the line while a new army was being created. Lord Kitchener, the Minister of War, created this new army, his campaign for volunteers being characterised by the well-known posters and slogans: 'Kitchener Wants You'; 'Your Country Needs You!' By the end of September, 750,000 men had volunteered, and by March 1916, there were 2½ million volunteers, 'by far the greatest volunteer force to go into battle.'[12] Philip was one of these men.

This huge number of men was still not enough. After some attempts at voluntary attestation, compulsory conscription of adult males was introduced

12. A. J. P. Taylor, *English History 1914–1945* (Oxford, 1975) p. 21.

in early 1916: men aged between 18 and 41 were called up. Men in essential industries such as engineering were not called up, indeed were no longer allowed to volunteer, and a very small number of men refused to serve ('conscientious objectors'), but by the end of the war a total of five million men had served in the forces. Most of the men Philip served with in 1918 would have been conscripts, and he mentions conscientious objectors on a few occasions, once commenting on one who has gone on hunger strike after being forcibly enlisted.[13]

Philip's war

Philip volunteered for service on 25 August 1914, the day after his 21st birthday. His first choice was the London Rifle Brigade, but, as the letters indicate, there was a muddle about his commission and he in fact joined the Loyal North Lancashire Regiment: he was appointed second lieutenant in the 3rd (Reserve) Battalion backdated to 15 August. This battalion was for recruitment and training, and was also where men gradually recuperated after being wounded before going out again to the battle front. Originally based in Preston, the 3rd Battalion moved to Felixstowe, Suffolk, where it had two functions, training and coastal defence.

Felixstowe had a population of 4,440 in 1911, but this was swelled during the war by men of the armed forces: Philip mentions men from reserve battalions of the Norfolk, Suffolk, Bedfordshire and Northamptonshire regiments. The town's most popular hotel was the *Felix*, on the cliff edge, which Philip mentions on several occasions. It had two Anglican churches, both of which Philip attended. Philip spent about six months training at Felixstowe before going out to the front: this was typical in the First World War. He later spent two further stints at Felixstowe, while recovering from wounds and illness, going through special courses of 'hardening', including training in trenches, before returning to the front line. During his three stays in the town, Philip got to know several local families with people of his age with whom he played tennis or danced. They included the Havells, the Maynes, the Liddells and the Cobbolds. He also got to know the Banks family at nearby Trimley, where the father was rector.

While Philip and the new intake of junior officers were in training, the regular army battalions had been mobilised. 1 Bn, LNLR was mobilised on 5 August 1914, and went abroad on the 12th, disembarking at Havre on the following day. Officers included Captain B. J. Wakley, Lts G. H. Goldie,

---

13. Letter 85.

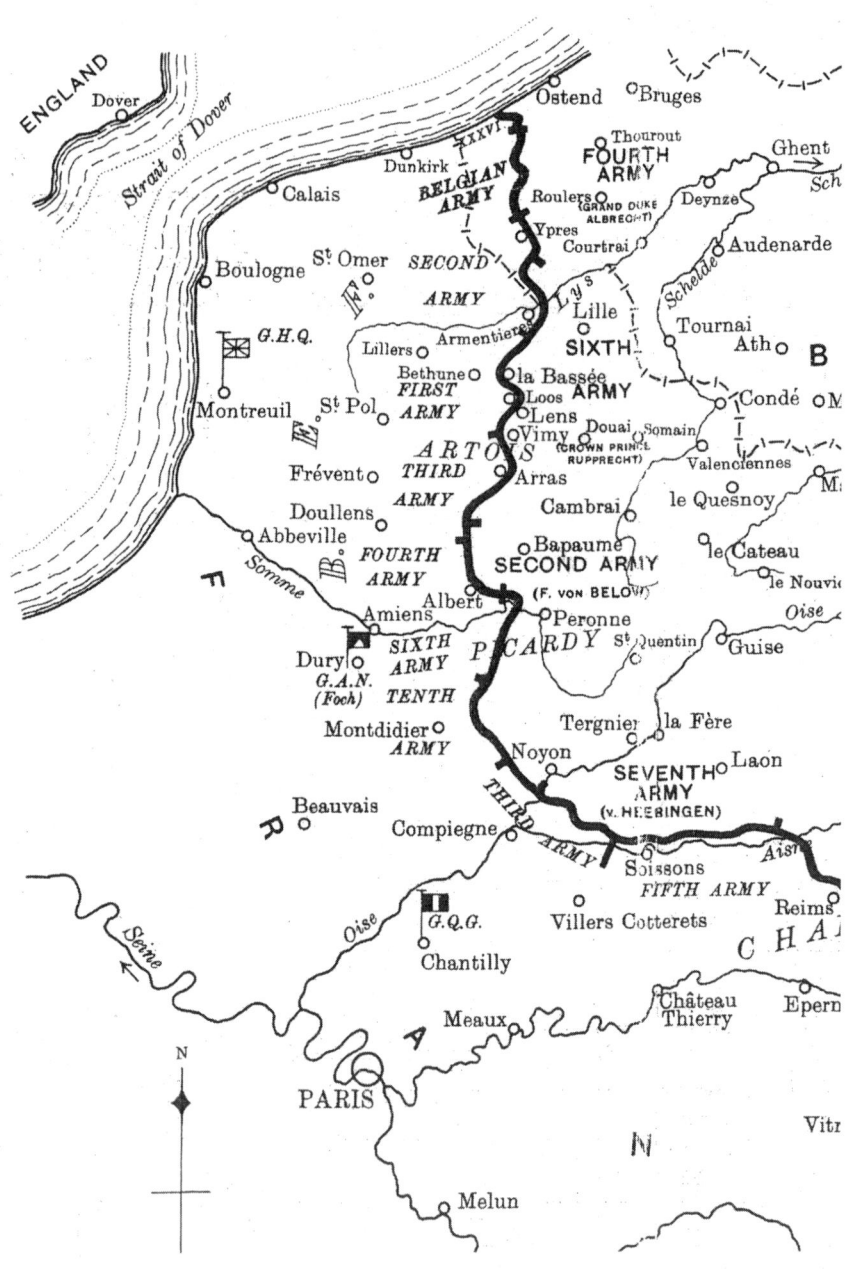

Map 1: The Western Front

and J. G. Halsted. The battalion fought in the battles of autumn 1914 in Belgium and France, while Philip was still training in England. It suffered many casualties: by January, its strength was down to 14 officers and 385 other ranks. A draft of new men was brought in, taking the strength up to 22 officers and 740 NCOs and other ranks. The battalion suffered more losses in the spring, balanced by new intakes of men. In June 1915, 340 new men arrived at Battalion Headquarters in France with thirteen officers: Major E. Monteagle-Browne, Captain R. S. J. Faulknor, and eleven 2nd Lieutenants – including Philip. Philip joined the battalion on 7 June, when they were at Bethune: he was posted to 'C' Company. The Regimental Diary shows what life was like for a reserve battalion in reserve: 'the very next day, a glorious June one, Bethune was shelled by enemy artillery but there was little damage and no one was hurt. The whole battalion bathed in the local swimming bath. The following days were spent in training, including bomb throwing'. This was an important skill: the diary records that 'there is a bombing officer in each Coy. who is responsible for the training of bomb-throwers in his Coy.'[14]

On 11 June, Philip was posted to 'B' Company. His commanding officer was Major Monteagle-Browne; his fellow second lieutenants were H. C. Maule, V. W. Newman, and S. Blythen: they commanded 34 NCOs and 150 men. There were several rapid changes in personnel: Monteagle-Browne was promoted to Headquarters and replaced on 3 July by Captain N. C. Phillips. Blythen was replaced by P. F. Goldie on 17 June (his cousin Robert Goldie arrived on the same day and was posted to 'C' company: both are mentioned in Philip's letters). The battalion spent time in reserve positions and time in the front line trenches. More men followed in August. Colonel H. C. Wylly, the historian of the regiment, wrote: 'It was consequently a strong battalion at the beginning of September, a month in which hostilities of an active character were to recommence, for during the previous weeks the casualties at the hands of the enemy had been few, though an officer and several men had been injured – one indeed killed – while practising with the bombs issued to the troops.'[15]

---

14. TNA, WO/95/1270. These 'war diaries' are now available on line.

15. Colonel H. C. Wylly, *The Loyal North Lancashire Regiment volume 2: 1914–1919* (London, Royal United Services Institution, 1933; republished by the Naval and Military Press, Uckfield 2007).

The Battle of Loos, 25 September 1915

Philip's first set-piece battle was at Loos in the autumn of 1915: this was also the first real battle for many of the volunteers of Kitchener's army. Loos [pronounced Loss] is in a coal-mining area, and the battle was set against a background of slag heaps, pit-heads and machinery. In September 1915, the British tried to break through the German lines with six divisions and a new weapon – gas. Chlorine gas had been used by the Germans at Ypres in April 1915, and the British wanted to make use of the weapon themselves: over 5,000 gas cylinders, containing nearly 150 tons of chlorine, were brought up to the front line trenches. The cylinders were placed in the front trench and the gas was discharged through pipes fitted with a jet: all the operator had to do was to turn on a stopcock when instructed. The Germans might well also use gas, so troops had to carry gas masks into battle. The primitive masks in use were so uncomfortable to wear that most men preferred to go into battle without them and risk a gas attack.

On 16 September, Philip's battalion rehearsed their role in the forthcoming assault: 'the movement was practised twice and quite successfully.' On 22 September it left Marles-les-Mines at 8 pm and reached Minx Mine Verquin shortly before midnight: the men camped out in a brick field, making use of straw pailasses. They marched to their position in the trenches in the pouring rain at 3.30 the next morning. The gas was released at sunrise – 5.50 am – on 25 September: it was mixed with smoke shells as the supply of gas was insufficient. The wind was light and variable: the gas reached the German trenches at some places but elsewhere drifted back and affected the British attack. The gas was switched off: another attempt to use the gas at 6.20 am also saw the gas affect the British troops. The general infantry assault was launched at 6.30 am. Philip's battalion was in the 2nd Brigade of the First Division, itself part of the IV Corps. The Loyal North Lancashires were in the front line of the attack, and their objective was to capture trenches in the region of the village of Hulluch. The gas was released in front of Philip's division when the 2nd Divisional Commander ordered it: it had disastrous results and had to be turned off at once. Despite many attempts, the attack was a complete failure, and the battalion was eventually retired from the battle: many men were affected by the British gas including Gardner and Phillips, officers mentioned in Philip's letters.[16] Philip was among the wounded: he was shot in the hand and arm early in the day and lay out in No Man's land for nine hours.

---

16. Gardner is first mentioned in letter 3, Phillips in letter 55.

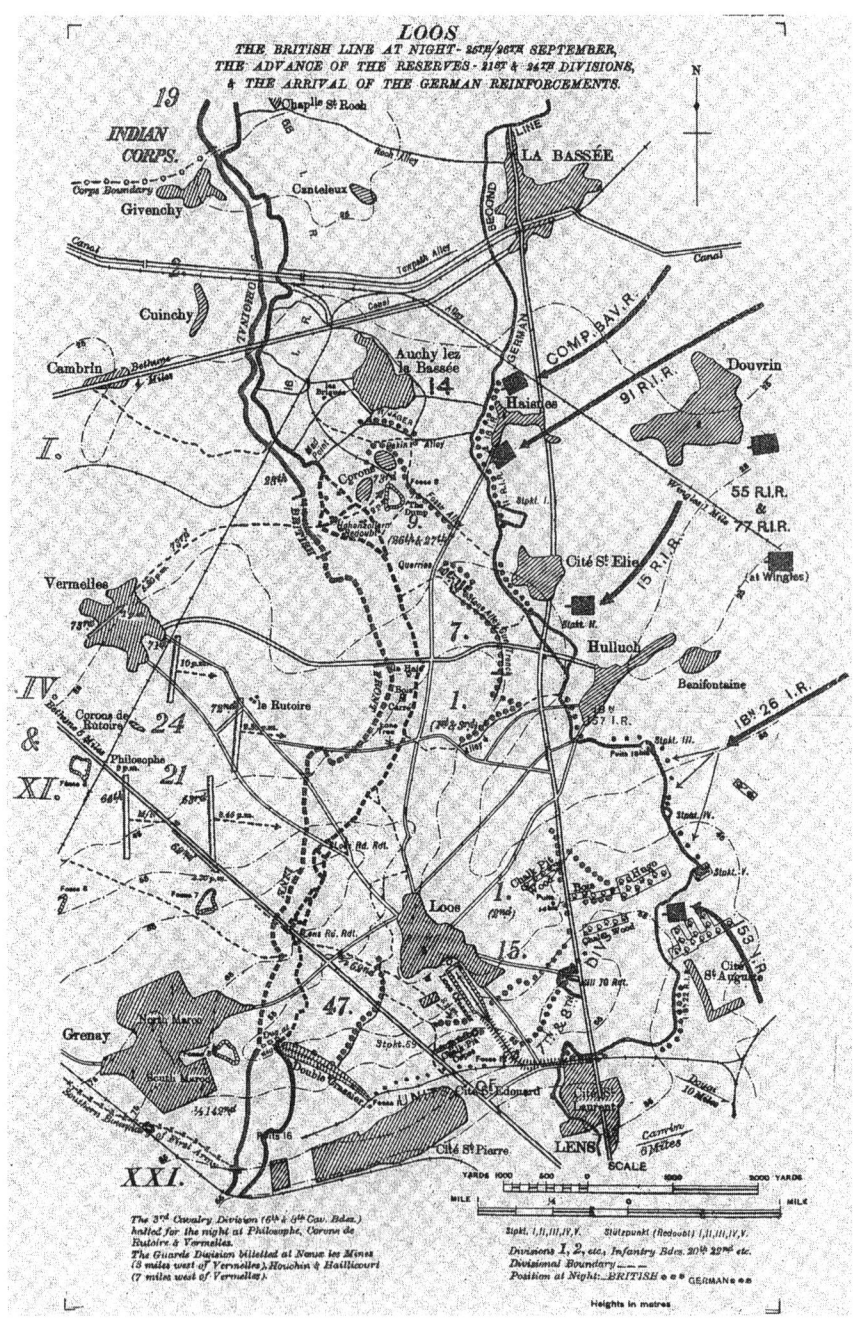

Map 2: The Battle of Loos, 25 September 1915

Philip's letters stopped for a time after he was wounded. The reminiscences of his cousin Julian Tyndale-Biscoe show what happened to a wounded soldier on the Western Front. He was hit in the shoulder during an attack. Unlike Philip, who had to lie out in the open until the stretcher bearers could get to him, Julian was able to struggle back the 300 yards to an aid post, with the help of some friends. Eventually, stretcher bearers took him to the dressing station. Here he was given morphine to take away his pain. Next morning, he was put in an ambulance for the long and bumpy journey to a rear dressing station: there were four wounded men in the ambulance, one of whom died on the way. Later he was put into another ambulance and taken to a casualty clearing station. Eventually he was taken to a Red Cross Hospital in Rouen, by this time having recovered enough to notice the beauty of the nurses! After two days there, he was taken by train to Havre and then a by hospital ship containing 2,500 wounded lying in cots strung from long poles. On arrival at Southampton he was taken by train to Somerville College in Oxford, then in use as a convalescent home.[17] Philip must have made a similar journey, eventually reaching a Military Hospital in Chelsea, and then spending some weeks in a convalescent hospital near Winchester, whence his next series of letters begins. As a result of his wound, he lost the use of his fingers for some months. Philip then returned to Salhouse to recuperate. When fit enough, he returned to Felixstowe while recovering from his wounds and for six months acted as assistant adjutant for the 3rd Battalion.

The Battle of Messines, 7 June 1917

Philip went to France for a second time on 16 March 1917, this time serving in the 9th Battalion, a Service Battalion, made up principally of conscripts. He was acting adjutant from 22 March until the Battle of Messines, when he acted as liaison office between a Canadian brigade and his own. The Battle of Messines took place on 7 June, after a long preliminary bombardment. At 03.10, nineteen mines which had been dug under the ridge on which the German front line was placed were set off: almost a million tons went up, the largest man-made explosion before the atomic bomb. The explosion was heard – and felt –in London as the top of the ridge simply disappeared, along with the German defenders. The British advanced, protected by a creeping barrage, and by 14 June had established a new front line.

On 13 June 1917, Philip took over command of 'C' Company. However,

17. Tyndale-Biscoe, *Gunner Subaltern*, pp. 97–101

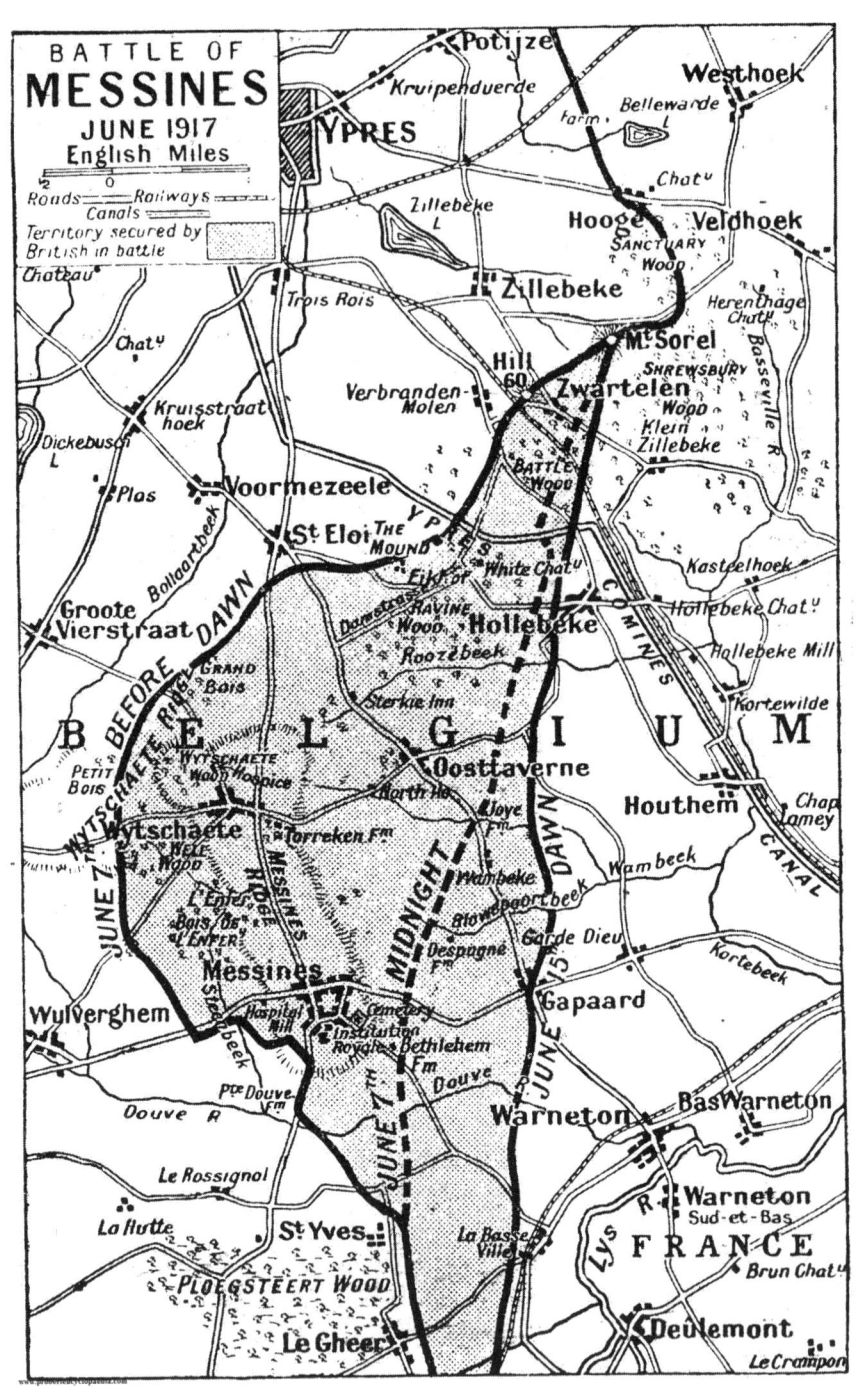

Map 3: Messines, June 1917

within a few months he was too ill for active service: he returned to England on leave on 15 October and was ordered to go before a Medical Board. This was held on 26 October and Philip was found 'Unfit for General Service' for a period of four months: his heart was overstrained. Philip now spent a third spell at Felixstowe, but felt that he was letting down his comrades at the front. In April 1918, although far from fit, he persuaded the authorities to send him to France for a third time. Leaving Felixstowe on 19 April, he rejoined the 9th Battalion, but was then given command of a Brigade Instructional Platoon. However, he was soon needed in battle.

The Second Battle of the Aisne, 27–28 May 1918

The general impression of the war is of German advances in 1914 followed by stalemate, with Germany occupied on the east by Russia and on the west by France and Britain. In the spring of 1918, however, the situation changed and the war became mobile once more. Two factors had brought this about. America had entered the war in April 1917, and her forces would eventually be bound to bring the Allies an overwhelming superiority on the Western Front. However, this would take a very long time, and in the meantime it was the Germans who had a chance to dominate. The campaign on the eastern front had come to a halt with the Russian Revolution and the Treaty of Brest-Litovsk on 3 March 1918 brought the war between Russia and Germany to an end. All the German troops serving on the Eastern Front could now be brought to the Western Front, in the hope that the Germans could break through before the American troops arrived in overwhelming numbers. This led to a series of German offensives in the spring of 1918. The one in which Philip was involved was on the river Aisne at the end of May. The line here was defended by four French divisions and one British Corps: it was regarded as a quiet sector of the Front, and the British troops included divisions mauled in earlier attacks, sent here for respite.

The Germans attacked on the Chemin des Dames with 42 divisions and 4,000 guns. The German bombardment opened at 1 am with ten minutes of gas, followed by 65 minutes of both gas and explosive, while trench mortars fired at the front line defences. The infantry began to advance at 3.40 am: it was successful. One German general recalled that 'whole platoons saw that resistance was hopeless and were reluctantly obliged to surrender'.[18] The guns of the 25th Division held twelve German battalions for more than

---

18. Major-General von Unruh, quoted in Martin Marix-Evans, *1918: The Year of Victories* (London, 2004) p. 91.

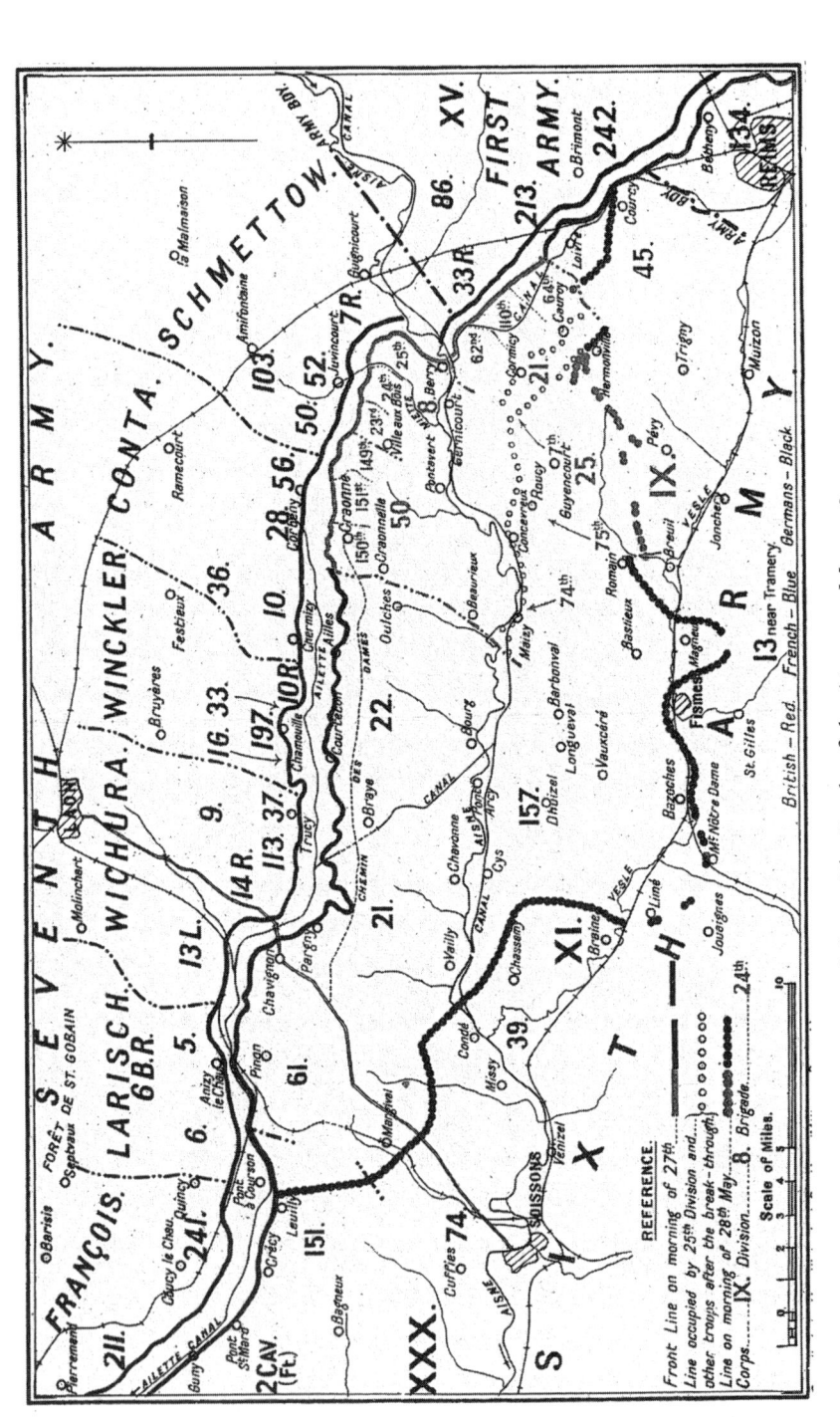

Map 4: The Battle of the Aisne, 27 May 1918

six hours before being overwhelmed at midday on 28 May. Reinforcements began to arrive on 29 May and the final attack on the British lines was on 6 June. The line held and the German advance was halted: but for Philip it was too late.

Philip's last letter home was dated 8 pm 19 May. This letter would have reached Salhouse on 24 or 25 May. Normally he wrote at least once a week, twice if he was not too busy: by the end of the month his parents would be desperately anxious. They would also have known of the great German attack on 27 May, and that thousands of British soldiers had been killed and many more taken prisoner. There was nothing that they could do but wait. The couple would have waited every day for the postman, hoping for a letter from Philip – and fearing a telegram from the War Office. This eventually came on 16 June: the news it contained was not as bad as they must have feared as they opened it:

Regret Capt R J P Hewetson North Lancashire Regt reported missing May twenty seventh. Further news when received.[19]

This could mean that he had been wounded and lost touch with his regiment, that he had been captured or that he was dead. Again, they could do nothing but wait.

The next news came from an army friend who had been with him at the time of the German attack on 27 May. This was Bill Loudon, who had seen Philip in action during the day: he had also been captured but had managed to escape. Arthur Langdale-Smith (Philip's uncle) saw Loudon on 28 June and was able to write to the Hewetsons that day with the good news that Philip was almost certainly a prisoner.[20] Loudon's report to the Hewetsons was reprinted in the Salhouse parish magazine for July: 'Your son's brigade unit did not move with the brigade into action, but was sent during the morning of the 27th to fill a gap which had occurred on the left flank. Your son, with two officers and one hundred men, went forward, but before reaching the place he was ordered to go to they encountered the enemy. His unit put up a splendid fight, which lasted about three-quarters of an hour. By that time they were almost surrounded. One officer and a few men managed to fight their way through. Your son was last seen alive by this officer, and there is every probability he was taken prisoner alive'.[21]

---

19. There is a copy of the telegram among Philip's papers at The National Archives: WO 339/16432.

20. NRO, MC 643/13/1

21. *Salhouse and Wroxham Church Magazine* July 1918, p. 2; NRO, MC 643/48/7

By the end of August, the Hewetsons knew that Philip had been taken prisoner, and also that he had lost a leg: this is clear from a letter from Philip's battalion commander, Colonel Craigie-Halkett, then in Cromer, wrote to William on 24 August.[22] Official confirmation that Philip was a prisoner of war in Germany came on 27 August, ten weeks after the War Office telegram. The parents tried to contact him. William was especially worried that Philip might not receive enough to eat: it was known that the Allied blockade had reduced Germany to a starvation diet and they could hardly be expected to treat their prisoners any better than their citizens. However, there might be hope, perhaps an exchange of prisoners through Switzerland. There were many weeks of worry ahead, but the Hewetsons could console themselves that at least their son was still alive, unlike so many other sons. When Ruth returned home after her six-month stint in the VAD in October there had been no further news. However it very soon came. The family received a letter, dated 14 October, from an English nurse, Constance Colt-Williams, who had herself been taken prisoner in the German advance at the end of May. Again, the family published the letter in the parish magazine:

> I have only just got back from Germany, where I have been a prisoner for 4½ months, and I am writing to you immediately to give you what news I can of your son, Capt. Hewetson, who was brought to our ambulance as a prisoner, seriously wounded in his leg. We had to amputate it immediately, and he was doing very well; then we were all sent to another ambulance about three weeks afterwards, and had to leave all our charge of the German doctors and, fortunately, English orderlies. About three weeks after that I saw one of the orderlies, who told me that your son had never done so well after the English surgeons and I – who was the only English nurse there – had left; and forgive me for having to tell you such painful news, but it appears that he died of septic pneumonia and dysentery about the end of June or beginning of July. The orderly told me that the Germans did everything possible for him, but he had had gas gangrene, and it was evidently too much for him.[23]

The letter appeared in the November edition, so the war would have been over by the time that many local people read the article: for the family, as

---

22. NRO, MC 643/13/6

23. The original letter, NRO, MC 643/13/8: the letter was written while Constance was still in Paris. *Salhouse and Wroxham Church Magazine*, November 1918, p. 2; NRO, MC 643/48/8

for so many others, joy at the end of the war was balanced by sadness and the loss of a loved one.

Further details emerged after the war. Sergeant Temple was with Philip on 27 May and wrote to his parents on 13 January 1919 with the full story. They had arrived at the front line about 1 am on 26 May: at 2 pm they ordered forward to fill a gap in the front line. They started forward at 2.30 but were almost immediately faced with the advancing Germans: they got into defensive positions. Eventually Hewetson ordered his men to retreat to a better defensive position, remaining at his post while the men did so: it was then that he was hit in the leg. Temple, himself wounded, crawled back to where Philip lay. The Germans then arrived, and their Red-Cross men attended the wounded, Philip characteristically insisting his men be cared for first. He lay out in the field for six hours, when he became delirious. He was taken down to the village of Glennes, where he and the other wounded spent the night in a barn. Next day he was taken by car to Beaurieux.[24]

The doctor who had operated on Philip was Major R. M. Handfield-Jones of the Royal Army Medical Corps, and he too was – many months later – able to give the family further details. Philip had been very badly wounded in the leg when he was captured: the leg was amputated in an operation in a cellar converted into a field hospital in Beaurieux, which itself fell into German hands soon afterwards, along with the patients and medical staff. Philip appeared to recover well from the operation. However, his health then showed an unfavourable change, which turned out to be typhoid. He was not able to take proper nourishment, and his constitution was greatly weakened. The hospital doctor was with him on the night of 2 July and asked him if wanted anything: he only asked to be given some water. Later, he became dazed and lost consciousness. Philip died at 6 pm on 3 July 1918: he was two months short of his 25th birthday.[25]

It is hard, in our present age of instant communications, to think of how long information took to be disseminated a century ago. Philip's friend Roly Barker was in India when the war ended. As late as 17 November he had heard (in a letter from Mrs Liddell) that Philip had lost a leg but had no idea of the rest of the story: he sent Philip a cheery letter but it was far too late: Philip had been dead for over four months.[26]

---

24. NRO, MC 643/13/13.
25. NRO, MC 643/13/11.
26. NRO, MC 643/41

Ruth's war

In 1917, Miss Wise drew the attention of her girls to the dangers of leaving school too early – this was 'misdirected patriotism for without a thorough education women cannot expect after the War to retain and improve their position in the fields of work suddenly thrown open to them by the War.' Amie stayed on at school to take exams in 1918 to go on to Cambridge University: Ruth mulled over various possibilities, reflected in Philip's letters – should she do canteen work in France, join an auxiliary force, whether army or navy, or go in for nursing? There was no compulsion for women to contribute to the war effort. In many cases, they were actively discouraged from participating: however, a large number of women were determined to show they could take their part in the country's struggle.

Ruth was faced with various choices as a woman wanting to 'do her bit'. The Women's Emergency Corps had been formed just two days after the outbreak of war. The Women's Legion followed, organised by Lady Londonderry, and recognised under an Army Council Instruction of February 1916 – it was divided into Canteen, Ambulance and Cookery sections, and there was also an agricultural section, working on the land. A report by General Lawson in 1917 recommended employing women in the Army in France due to the shortage of men. The Women's Auxiliary Army Corps (W.A.A.C.) was formed under an Army Council Instruction of 7 July 1917: there were no military ranks, the officers being controllers and administrators. By March 1918, there were 6,000 women in France. In the following month the name was changed to Queen Mary's Army Auxiliary Corps. A similar organisation for the navy, the Women's Royal Naval Service (W.R.N.S.), was set up in April 1918. When the Royal Air Force was established in that year, the Women's Royal Air Force (W.R.A.F.) was also created. Altogether, about 100,000 women joined auxiliary services of the armed forces. Many other women played their part by working in factories and farms, often replacing men and taking on these jobs for the first time in history. No less than 800,000 women worked in engineering, like Ruth's friend Xenia, many in making munitions, dirty and dangerous work. Another 250,000 worked on the land.

Nursing had always been a role for women in war time: the Red Cross and St John's Ambulance services provided voluntary service, as they still do today. In all, over 100,000 women served in nursing roles during the war. The First Aid Nursing Yeomanry (F.A.N.Y.) founded in 1907, ran field hospitals, canteens and soup kitchens. From 1908, Voluntary Aid Detachments (V.A.D.) were formed, including many members of the Red

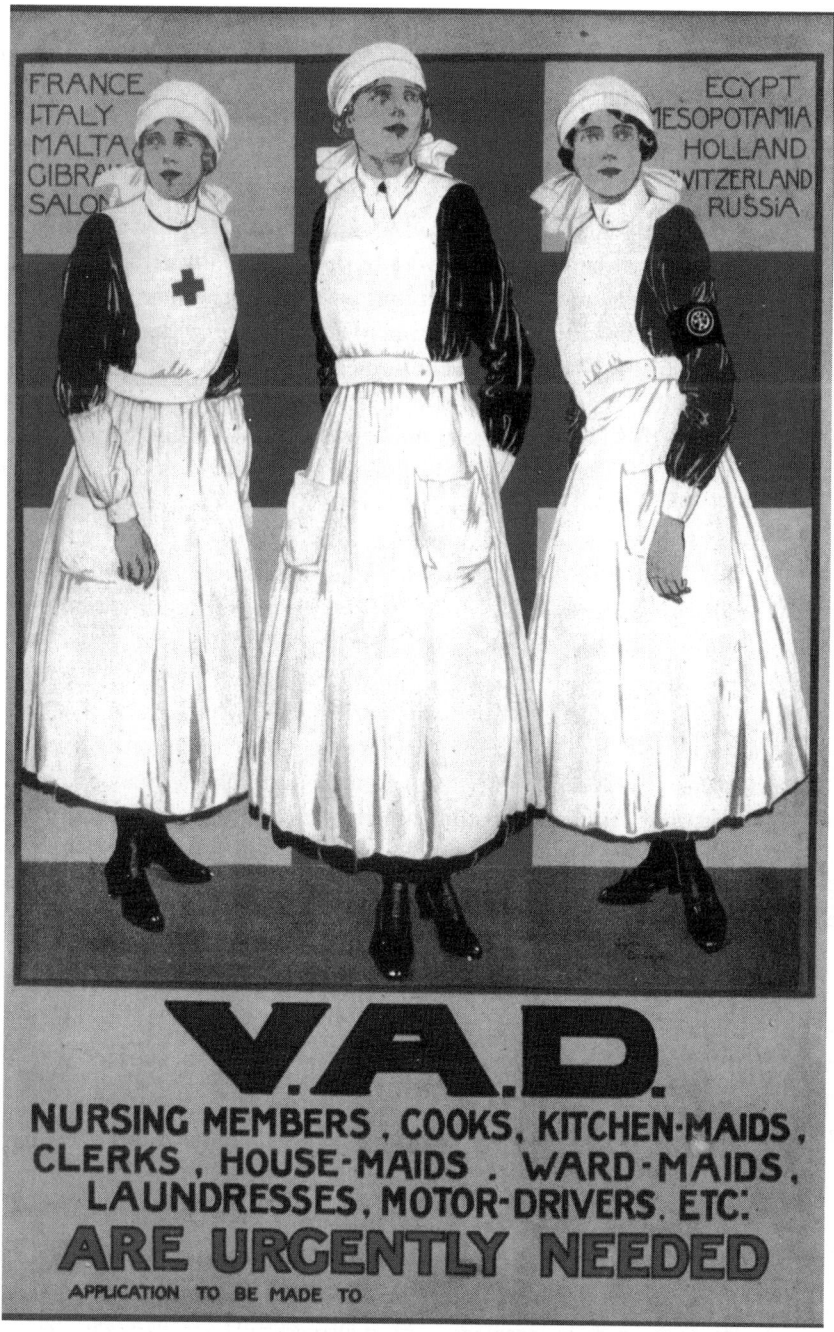

3. Poster for Voluntary Aid Detachment

Cross and St John's, and also many other people who were not qualified nurses but who could do vital ancillary work in war hospitals – including the basics like washing up, cooking and cleaning. There were 46,000 women serving at the outbreak of war and by the time of the Armistice over 90,000 women had registered. At first members of a Voluntary Aid Detachment had to undertake to learn nursing skills, and in theory were supposed to be over 22. However, from June 1916, they worked under a General Service scheme, with direct payment made by military authorities – they undertook cooking, clerical work, dispensing and storekeeping as well as nursing. In Norfolk, for example, they worked at the Lakenham Military Hospital and in over 60 auxiliary hospitals, really convalescent homes.

However, Ruth chose to work away from home as a General Service Member of the VAD. The letters make clear she initially hoped for a position in France, but, perhaps because she was not yet twenty-one, she was found a role in England, serving at the Fargo Military Hospital at Fargo in Larkhill, Wiltshire, very close to Stonehenge. This was in an area that was – and is – full of military establishments. Fargo opened as a camping ground for the artillery in 1904. In 1914 the Military Hospital was built – on the site of an older isolation hospital for horses. It was a very large institution, with more than a thousand beds. During the war, wounded men of all nationalities were there including Americans and many Australians – the latter were not impressed with the catering arrangements, referring to the Hospital as 'Starve-Oh'. It also had wards for wounded and sick German prisoners-of-war, who, the Australians complained, were better treated than the Allied soldiers![27] The hospital took in wounded soldiers from the Western Front, brought by ship into Southampton and then brought on by train to Amesbury station, and thence by ambulance to the Hospital.

Ruth's work was basic, but essential for the successful functioning of a hospital: she cleaned the nurses' accommodation and worked in the staff kitchens. Many women were doing the same: by 1918 there were 23,000 nurses and 18,000 nursing orderlies, a few serving in theatres of war all over the world, but most, like Ruth, working in the many Auxiliary War Hospitals that had been established in Britain.[28]

By late March 1918, Ruth was at Fargo. It was the first time in her life that she had been away from home for more than a few days: her letters well

---

27. T. S. Crawford, *Wiltshire and the Great War* (revd ed. Ramsbury, 2012) pp. 200–2

28. The Headquarters of the organisation was at Devonshire House, Piccadilly, London, which is mentioned in several of Ruth's letters. Thekla Bowser, *The Story of British V.A.D. work in the Great War* (London, 1917, republished 2003) pp. 43–52

reflect her growing independence of thought as she learned to cope with her new situation in life.

Ruth had been brought up in a clerical family and educated at a fee-paying school. Her letters make it clear that, for the first time in her life, her work at Fargo brought her into contact with women of all classes and backgrounds: she did not always find this easy. As the number and range of women volunteering for war work grew, there appears to have been a social dilution that caused some difficulties: Ruth's letters show that this was a concern to national figures in the Red Cross movement, such as Mrs Harker and Lady Ampthill.[29]

Afterwards: Ruth, the family, and her friends

Ruth's term of service was for an initial period of six months. Her letters show that she was undecided what to do afterwards, but Philip's capture made up her mind for her. She returned to Salhouse in October to support her parents: she was with them when her brother's death finally became known. Her mother, Kathleen Hewetson, spent the winter with her sisters in Folkestone. She did not like the kind of gravestone that was adopted by the Commonwealth War Graves Commission, writing a letter to the *Spectator* in December 1918 in which she referred to them as 'lumpy milestones': she wanted a cross to mark the grave of 'her beloved son' rather than a 'slab'.

William Hewetson returned to France: in 1919 he was appointed chaplain in Bordeaux and the family lived in France until 1922 when he became rector of St Cuthbert with Christchurch, Bedford. He was appointed an Honorary Canon of St Alban's Cathedral in 1935, celebrating fifty years as a priest in 1937. He remained at St Cuthbert's until he retired in 1938.

Ruth moved with her parents to Bedford, becoming a scripture mistress at Bedford High School. Like nursing, this was a traditional female occupation: there were over 200,000 women teachers in England and Wales at the time of the 1931 census. Their average pay of £254 was £80 less than a male teacher at the same level would receive and it was expected by most local authorities that women teachers would remain single: if they married their appointment was usually terminated. Ruth was also much involved in the Girl Guides Association, becoming Bedford Division Commissioner. William Hewetson died on 4 December 1940, three months after the couple's golden wedding: he was 78 years old. He was cremated in Cambridge. Ruth then lived with her widowed mother for twenty years before Katherine died in Bedford in

---

29. Letters 303 (Lady Ampthill), 279, 302, 303, 305 (Mrs Harker).

4.   Philip's grave

1960, at the age of 95. After her parents' deaths, Ruth lived at Great Barford in Bedfordshire, where she died in 1983.

Amie Evershed failed the scholarship exam for Girton College, Cambridge, in July 1918 but went on to the College in October anyway, presumably paid for by her family as Ruth suggests.[30] Village rumour linked Philip and Amie romantically: she never married, dying in Norfolk in 1984 at the age of 85. Xenia Muriel, whose humdrum life Ruth had come to despise,[31] continued working in Norwich. She married Captain Cedric Isham Curteis of the Royal Field Artillery in St Giles church, Norwich on 17 September 1919. She

---

30. Letter 280.
31. Letter 301.

moved with him to Great Hollesley, Suffolk, and, when his regiment went to India in 1926 she went with him. However, they divorced (in Britain) in 1936. Three years later, Xenia married another artillery man, Stuart Rudd-Clarke, ten years her junior, who was recommended for a D.S.O. in the Second World War. After the war they lived in the Rectory at Rollestone, very much on Ruth's old stamping ground. Rudd-Clarke died in Malta in 1971. Xenia continued to live in Wiltshire, dying there in 1987 at the age of 89.[32]

Women went through life-changing experiences during the war. Very few were near enough to the front line to be killed or captured, such as the nurse who tended Philip. Many thousands took on work that they would not have done, or been able to do before the war. Many suffered the loss of fathers, brothers, husbands and male friends. Newspapers picked up on the loss of males, referring in headlines in 1920 to 'A Million Surplus Women' and 'A Million Women Too Many': the 1921 census revealed that there were 1.75 million more women than men in England and Wales. Women who had been brought up to expect to find fulfilment in the roles of wife and mother found themselves having to pursue other lifestyle choices – and many did so extremely successfully, creating new roles for women in society. It can be argued that it was these independently-minded women who were the role models for the following generation, who surmounted many barriers to female equality in society. Ruth and her friends played their part in their own ways.[33]

---

32. Xenia's story was kindly researched for me by Elizabeth Budd.

33. Vanessa Nicholson, *Singled out: how two million women survived without men after the First World War* (London, 2007).

ERECTED

BY THE PARISHIONERS OF SALHOUSE
IN PROUD AND LOVING MEMORY OF THE
MEN WHO FELL DURING THE GREAT WAR
1914 TO 1919

GEORGE CATCHPOLE	Pte	EDWARD IVES	Pte
HERBERT CHAMBERS	Pte	HENRY LEGGETT	Pte
FRED CLARKE	L/Cpl	GEORGE PAGE	Sto
SAMUEL DEBBAGE	L/Cpl	JOHN POWLES	Pte
EDWARD FOX	Pte	WILLIAM RAYNOR	A.B.
ERNEST FOX	Pte	BERTIE THURTLE	Pte
WALTER FOX	Pte	ARTHUR WILEY	Gnr
ARCHIE GRIMES	Pte	JOHN WRIGHT	Pte
JAMES HARDESTY	L/Cpl	TIMOTHY WRIGHT	Pte
	PHILIP HEWETSON	Capt	

THEIR NAME LIVETH FOR EVERMORE

5.   Salhouse War Memorial

The Letters:
Philip Hewetson

1. The Union Society, Cambridge[1]

Sunday [*9 Aug. 1914*]

Dearest all

Yesterday was certainly a black day! HS[2] & I were going up to town as I had said to finish off on our kit but thought we might just drop in at the L.R.B. Headquarters to see that everything was alright as we had been told. Comber[3] & Carter[4] both advised us to do so so we did – We arrived Liv St. 12.40, and to 130 Burnhill Row S E, by curious small & dirty-ish streets. We went in and a sergeant directed us to a room upstairs where he said we should find the Colonel. We found him & 3 other officers surrounded by papers etc. I said we had come just to see that everything was alright, and when they had asked our names they just looked blank. They eventually found a paper with the names of about 8 recommended subalterns, H.S. among them. They <u>said</u> they knew nothing about me, and had got neither of our papers! The list had been sent through Oxford, which seems absurd as really Oxford can know nothing about us now.

---

1. On headed paper. Although Philip was at Oxford University, he was attending an O.T.C. camp at Cambridge on the weekend of 8/9 August. Cambridge was the most distinguished and experienced of the O.T.C.s, being the only one which had been awarded a battle honour (under its earlier name of the Cambridge University Rifle Volunteers its members had fought in the Boer War).

2. Hugh Strong; see Introduction and Appendix 2, which gives brief biographies of Philip's military acquaintances.

3. Captain, later Major, Henry G Comber, officer in the Cambridge University contingent of the Officers' Training Corps to whom Philip turned for help in getting a commission. He had graduated from Pembroke College, Cambridge, 1890.

4. Not otherwise identified.

The absurdity is that our papers were sent off from here together and Comber had a wire to say 'all recommended' – well I suppose somebody has lost the papers, or _ _ _ _!! I don't know what to think. They showed us the list and said that was all the Subalterns they would want, they were sorry as they supposed we wanted to keep together, still they were full so "good morning" and – we went! We went back to Liv St and ate a dejected lunch, H.S. advised me to return here and put myself in Comber's hands again, So I left at 2.30 & arrived Cam: 4. intending to see Comber & come on home by a 6.37. He was very annoyed at the unknown person who was responsible for my rejection, very sympathetic and utterly puzzled as to what could have happened. He promised he would get me <u>Some</u>thing <u>Some</u>time!

Well – this morning at breakfast I felt two hands on my shoulders, & looking up I saw Comber he said "It's alright, I've got you Something" my heart leapt, and I went to him later & he told me. Mind – its something quite indefinite yet but in a few days may be definite. A General, newly appointed over one of these new armies, has under him a <u>great</u> friend of Comber's. This friend I imagine is a big man himself, a Colonel, I think. Now the Gen: asked the friend if he could get him some subalterns, & the friend said yes, he would write to Comber. The General said that though of course the final choice rested with him he <u>would take Comber's recommendation;</u> now Comber is going to recommend me! among others! So the cloud of yesterday seems to be vanishing.

This means if all goes well a Commission in the New Army.[5] Of course it means I shan't get to the front so quickly as if I were in Terriers but I shall be in the Regular Army, and I suppose one simply can<u>not</u> choose. Its a pity Hugo & I are to be separated and instead of going through together we had to say "goodbye" on Liv St station yesterday. He'll go fighting before I do now after all!

I <u>shall</u> enjoy seeing you tomorrow! Today has been freezing and I shall rejoice in <u>warm</u> clothes. Some white flannel shirts, <u>tennis</u> ones, and a vest or two also I have no socks left now. I don't suppose really I shall be here many days longer but I must stay till <u>this</u> job or another (if this fails) is <u>sure</u>. Then I can come home & "wait till called for"

You get 5/ a day for food, and 5/3 a day pay; if under canvas 2/- a day extra and 1/- a day for your servant! not bad?!

I don't know about Lionel[6] but I think he's getting a Terrier job, in a Kent

---

5. See Introduction and Appendix 1. The New Army would need to be trained from scratch, so the Territorials would see service earlier.

6. Lionel Powys Jones; see Introduction and Appendix 2.

or Surrey regiment. Only about 60 left here now, rather dull in some ways. This camp nominally ends on Saturday but if enough men wish to continue it will go on. Looking forward to seeing you. Much love from Philip.

MC 643/3

2.   Headquarters Old Felixstowe

[Oct 9][7]

Dearest Mother

Here's the letter & photos at last! They'd been at Old Felixstowe post office here not Felixstowe. I think the photo marked I quite good but not the other.

   Hugh's not here yet! I can't think why not, I don't know what he can be waiting for. If I had been in his place I should have arrived here at once after waiting 9 or 10 weeks. This morning we started out for a route march at 8.45, & were to be out till 3 pm. However it was foggy and we had hardly been out ½ hour when we were summoned back, with orders that sentries etc: were to be placed as if it were night! So you see we're very much awake! Not safe to be out of the village on a foggy day.
Much love

Your very loving

Philip

MC 643/11/11

3.   3 Bn. Loyal North Lancs: Regt Old Felixstowe

Dec 13 [*1914*]

Dearest all

It has once more fallen to my lot to be on telephone duty all Sunday. However it is a pouring wet day so I don't mind really; and anyhow I think day duty is much better than night. It has saved me being up two days running. It is my turn to visit the sentries on the shore tonight & if I had been on telephone I should have had to go tomorrow night, as it is I can go tonight and so look forward to a proper night in bed tomorrow. I was very interested in the OR list of those serving which came with the photos this morning. I was interested too in the Egg letter in EDP, it's

---

7. Added in another hand.

very good. I hope slow moving Norfolk will take it up.[8] I got over my chill alright, though I think I will be honest and not say I am as fit as a fiddle. I get tired very easily and am not always well inside. I think all of us are quite ready for a move or change! 3 months of Old Felixstowe! You are really quite wrong when you say "I daresay you don't exactly want to be disturbed" we are all quite ready for 2 or 3 days leave but I don't think there's much chance of that, none in fact! I haven't been over to the Banks[9] for a long time, 3½ or 4 miles is a long way on a wintry night like we have now. but I've written to Mrs B. today to say I hope to get over soon. I had 3 curious letters yesterday. No 1 came first post from Srinagar Kashmir, a man in hospital there has apparently been being visited by Uncle C[10] who has told him I'm at "Trimley". This man lives in Felixstowe & wrote to me to say he's telling several friends that I am here. At tea time we had the sequel. One a letter from his mother asking me to tea on Wednes: which I've accepted. No 2. from a man named G. H. Hewetson[11] in Ipswich who says his vicar has told him I'm here & he wonders if we are any connection He does not think so but says he & his wife would very much like to meet me. He asked me over today but I could not go of course I am going to try and go today week. The good lady who has asked me to tea says she knows George T.B.[12] On the whole a very astonishing trio of letters I think. Yes, I do think everybody must be getting heartily sick of this war. I should say this is not at all the weather to go out in. However we all feel we want to be 'doing' something more exciting than we do here, though of course somebody must stop here. Still I daresay another big draft will go off before Xmas. I know the Felix is too ridiculously dear. Powys Jones cannot come

---

8. *Eastern Daily Press* (11 Dec. 1914). William Hewetson's letter stated that he was contributing to the National Egg Collection for wounded soldiers in hospitals: 'there is no more valuable a nutriment or recuperative food than a fresh egg'. He urged Norfolk poultry owners to do the same and contribute eggs for the cause. A second letter, published on 14 December 1914 showed that the response had been immediate: Hewetson had been able to send in a box of twelve dozen eggs donated by sixteen local producers on the previous Saturday.

9. Revd Samuel Banks was incumbent at Trimley St Martin, two miles from Felixstowe. His wife had the unusual name of Gratiana. They had two daughters, Dorothy and Sybil, respectively 17 and 15 in 1915: one member of the family had the nickname 'Nellie': see letter 29.

10. Cecil Tyndale-Biscoe, see Appendix 3.

11. George Henry Hewetson, aged 56 in 1911, bank manager, of King's Field, Park Road, Ipswich.

12. George Tyndale-Biscoe (born 1869), brother of Cecil and like him a Church of England clergyman.

here this end of the vac at any rate, he has to take Mrs P.J. back to Jersey. I am going out to supper at the Masons[13] tonight (where we play billiards). Gardner & Andrews are going too which will be nice. Certainly the new a[rrangement] has its advantages as far as leave goes. Gingerbreads would be very welcome. I think I'd better stick to the same old sort of razor I've always used. There seem a lot of warm things being brought out for service at the fronts. I'm getting off this telephone at 7pm instead of 8 tonight. Very much
love to all

Your very loving Philip

I see Mrs Torbett[14] occasionally. she's always V nice. There were rumours of a Germ submarine in Harwich (day of Dover raids)[15] but 'o' happened, though all destroyers & minesweepers bustled about as I hear they have again today.

MC 643/11/26

4. Old Felixstowe

Wednesday [*16 Dec.*]

Dearest Father

I thoroughly enjoyed as I always do the budget which came from home this morning; more especially as I am in bed! yes I'm afraid I've been bowled over this time, the doctor says it's jaundice! isn't that rotten luck – it started on Monday. I wasn't very well but went on morning parade however at lunch time I was very sick so the adjutant sent me to his room to get some Eno & told me to go & lie down which I did. I was better in the evening but didn't want my food. Same happened on Tuesday breakfast time when I was again evidently sick. I spent the day in bed chiefly sleeping, eating nothing but a little bread & milk at night. I slept well with a good fire and today the doctor said I'd got jaundice. He is going to get me moved into the White Horse[16] where I shall be more comfortable. Of course I'm not feeling

---

13. Frank Mason, JP, of Northcliffe, Maybank Lane, Felixstowe: he was a leading light in town affairs.

14. For Torbett, see Appendix 2. His wife's name was Ethel, and they had a son called James, born in 1911.

15. Dover was attacked several times by ships or aeroplanes – there was a raid on British ships there by German submarines on 10 December 1914.

16. Public house in Church Road, Felixstowe.

well but still I'm not exactly "ill" and uncomfortable feeling is confined to my inside. No headache. I have no appetite. I hope I shall be well before Xmas. I shall apply for "sick leave" when I'm better and with any luck this jaundice may be the means of getting me home for Xmasday! at any rate I'm sure I ought to get a week or 10 days somehow & sometime soon – you can't be convalescent here. I suppose you've heard today's news – Germans are bombarding Newcastle & Scarborough![17] I wonder if they'll come here tonight. I hope personally they wont come while I'm ill. Still I daresay I shall forget my jaundice if they come. The news has had no effect on the daily routine yet! Zeppelin attack on Scarboro' we hear! Very exciting – Thank Mother so much for Bp's Tons[18] I took 2 at once. Shall I go on with them while I have jaundice???

We had a very nice time at Masons on Sunday.

I am awfully glad the Egg Contribution went off so well. Congratulations on that and the letter you got. I did find some nice bits in C.F.N.[19] though I said nothing about it. Mrs Torbett lives at Highcliffe Cobbold Rd. I'm afraid none of the men will get Xmas leave from the Defences. They may have to sleep in the trenches tonight! I do hope they don't attack just now I'm ill.

Much love (don't worry) your very loving Philip.

MC 643/11/25

5.   3 Loyal North Lancs Regt. Old Felixstowe [20]

Jan 31 [*1915*]

Dearest Mother & Father

I've had a very jolly time yesterday and to-day. Unfortunately our footer match failed to come off. The Suffolks could not play us this week. The Sergeants were playing H.M.S. Daisy so they were no good, and the 11th Bn and F. Coy, both of whom I tried could not play! However the Suffolks are going to play us this week. We are going to try to get leave

17. In the days before radio, most people obtained information from newspapers: here Philip is relaying 'hot' news, presumably received via telephone. Like many rumours in wartime the information is only partly correct: Scarborough was bombarded by German navy ships on 16 December 1914: the other towns to suffer on the same day were Whitby and Hartlepool.

18. From its context, a stomach remedy.

19. The *Church Family Newspaper*, which the Hewetsons sent to both their children.

20. 'Just after I left him' added by Philip's mother.

to play on Thursday if so we can have the Town ground!! I have got a good side together, & we are going to have penalties every afternoon at 4. Two Captains & 2 full Lieuts: are going to play. I am looking forward to turning out in my nice sweater & blazer which came yesterday. The shirts you got me are excellent & I've got one on. Gamages[21] sent the waistcoat *(a leather under jacket, long over hips)* to Wellesley[22] & I've just fetched it up (6 pm) and have got it on. Thank you again so much, it will be most warm and serviceable I can see. I certainly am well fitted up. Well yesterday afternoon Hugh & Andrews & I went to tea with the Havells[23] where I met a girl[24] whom I had previously met when I went to tea with the adjutant[25] & Mrs T. once. I enjoyed myself "quite"! She's v. pretty. On the way back Hugh & I went & had a game of billiards at the Masons when I just managed to win by 100–89 scored in rather faster time than usual. Today I am orderly officer.[26] I did not get up very early & had breakfast at 9am, then I did some of my orderly duties before some after Church to which I went with Nichol. We had a splendid 'Sunday Lunch' as the adjutant called it. We sat on afterwards while the Doctor kept us in fits of laughter with story after story. He is a gifted mimic & raconteur. Satterthwaite (Uncle L.E.'s protégé)[27] is on telephone all day today so he answered for me during the afternoon & mounted my guard for me at 4pm thus enabling me to go down to the Band with Nichol and on to tea at the Felix with him afterwards. It was nice getting a peep of you on Friday, we had started out at 8.30 and did not get back till 1.45! So as it was pay day, & the men were tired & some had to be on night duty my lecture was cancelled – I am on telephone tomorrow (Monday) night. As the girls called Ruth "blooming" & somebody in Salhouse before I left called me "bonny" you needn't trouble about our health now!

On Friday we were practising an attack by sections right across that open

---

21. Department store in Holborn, London, founded in 1878: it advertised that it offered an international shipping service.

22. A large house in Gainsborough Road, Felixstowe, run as apartments by Mrs Rebecca Green, perhaps a family acquaintance.

23. Charles Havell, surgeon, lived at The Corner House, Cambridge Road, Felixstowe: like the Masons, the Havells sat on many local committees. His wife's name was Cicely: their daughter Joyce was 21 in 1915.

24. Miss Robinson see letter 8.

25. Torbett.

26. The officer who is in charge of the security and administration, duties taken in turn on a daily basis.

27. Revd. John Burges, see Appendix 3.

"gorsey" ground. I started my time in E Coy yesterday with a short route march.

Much love your very loving Philip.

We have again suffered in France.[28]

MC 643/4/1

6.   <31 Jan> 4th Feb Thursday evening

My dear Father

Just a hurried letter before post goes. We got our game this afternoon; we played on the Town ground, a splendid field, pavilion & good nets etc. We kicked off at 2.30, we had quite a good side – I played inside left and captained the side. I scored the first goal after about 10 minutes. At half we led 2–1. It was not a very scientific <goal> game but played with tremendous dash. There was no score in the second half so we won as stated. The game became harder & faster as it went on. Lots of hard knocks and give & take but no fouls. It was most enjoyable. I got on quite well on my telephone night. The bovril and digestive biscuits were an asset. I read the Coryston family[29] and kept awake well, taking a stroll occasionally – I had a good sleep next day and having no 'Dip' *all round cliffs* to do now – go to bed early 9.30 about each night. Mother's letter & parcel just came. Dawes & Barker[30] only went out with our past draft, so did Halstead[31] for the 2nd time. We are sending 19 (!) men out this week, our maximum possibility. My turn won't be far off now, but you never know. I keep very well and am enjoying life thoroughly. Much love your very loving Philip.

MC 643/4/2

---

28. The Germans attacked the British and French defenders at Cuinchy and Givenchy in the last week of January 1915.

29. A popular novel by Mrs Humphry Ward (1851–1920), published in 1913.

30. 'killed died of wounds' added by Philip's mother. Barker did not in fact die, so Philip's mother had heard a false rumour.

31. 'Missing' added by Philip's mother.

7.   3/ Loyal North Lancs Regt. Old Felixstowe. Feb: 8 1915

Dearest all

For some reason or other no letter has come today, so I expect it will turn up tomorrow first post. Really practically nothing has happened here this end of the week! I am writing this between 12–1; this morning I did not to go the Parish Church[32]. I bicycled down to Nichol who is with the Suffolks looking after the machine guns and we went to St. John's.[33] As the service there is at 10.20 I am back earlier than usual. There were 8 or 10 Blue jackets[34] just in front of us, looking so bronzed & weather beaten. We are sending out a small draft of 19 men tomorrow, they don't know what officer will go with them yet. The subalterns next in order in the army list to go are 1&2. the two Curwens; 3. Nichol; 4. de Blaby; 5. myself; 6. Wood. Of these apparently the two Curwens are just recovering from flu while Nichol is too young. People say it rests between de Blaby & Wood, so they seem to be missing me out at present. This next Thursday both Strong & Nichol go to Hythe[35] for a 3 weeks musketry course and if de Blaby goes out I shall be somewhat "left" – we find both Morris & Carr the other two subs in White Horse quite impossible. This afternoon I shall be going down to hear the band and then very likely Hugh & I will be biking over to the Banks. I am hoping that Gardner will be returning from Hythe when the other two go & if so he will be someone to go about with. I am keeping very fit and cinnamon & quinine & also all the other bottles help to keep away anything that threatens. The adjutant after holding out so long has at last got flu. I was orderly officer yesterday, it was a cold blowy rainy day and I wore the leather waistcoat – Just this minute I've read a 3 page foolscap letter written to Andrews from a subaltern who went out 3 or 4 weeks ago. Very interesting but it doesn't make you long to get out there. He says when you first come under fire you duck your head & pray for Felixstowe. He begins by saying he did not know what it was to be "in a funk" till he got out there. He's had some wonderfully narrow escapes. Several officers have had letters from our officers at the front just lately. I quite like my new Company. I am on parade 9–10 then 10–11 I

---

32. The parish church in Felixstowe is St Peter and Paul: the vicar was Revd Walter H Horne.

33. St John the Baptist, Orwell Road. The vicar was Revd Arthur Stantial, the curate Revd Sidney Huntley.

34. Sailors: the term refers to enlisted men in contrast to officers.

35. Hythe School of Musketry, Kent. Founded in 1853, it retained its old title even when muskets were replaced by rifles in the British Army. It was renamed the Small Arms School in 1919.

am off as they do physical drill then on from 11–12.15. In the afternoon 2–3.15. Then we march down the Town to F Coy for a lecture at 3.45–4. I am to lecture on Tuesday.

Much love

from very loving

Philip

MC 643/4/3

8. "The White Horse" 3. Loyal North Lancs Regt: Old Felixstowe

Thursday
Feb 12th

Dear Father

The reason why I did not get the letter on Sunday was because it was addressed "The Postern".[36] It was there all night but I did not go there after I got up till 3pm so did not see it till I went back there. It's as well really not to address letters to the Postern as I often do not go there till late afternoon once I am up.

The draft went out early on Tuesday morning and was taken out by Andrews[37] so de Blaby & I are still here. Nichol and Strong[38] went to Hythe yesterday & I expect Gardner will return to-day or to-morrow.[39] Your letter & Mothers came yesterday, and the photos & the letter from Gobagger[40] today. Please thank <you both> Mother so much for the photos, I think they are very good, I don't expect I shall use nearly all the dozen and will return any I don't use in case any one asks you for one. I am having a fleece lining made for my mackintosh, it is to be ready on Saturday. I am afraid I shall have to order another pair of boots from Pond[41] as my servant went & put my good pair too near the fire to dry & spoilt the leather; they are all right for work here but would not last long abroad. I have not ordered

---

36. 'his new sleeping quarters' added by Philip's mother. The Postern was a large house in Marcus Road, Felixstowe.

37. 'a very nice boy (Cambridge) & quite one of P's best friends there' added by Philip's mother.

38. '(P's Oriel friend)' added by Philip's mother.

39. 'They go to Hythe for gunnery instruction. I hope P. may be sent before he goes to France.' added by Philip's mother.

40. Philip's aunt Julia Burges: see Introduction and Appendix 3.

41. James Pond, Castle Meadow, Norwich, boot and shoe manufacturer.

the loaded stick yet as I have not got the address Have you the Land &
Water[42] in which it was?[43] I was on telephone duty last night and got on
quite well. The War Office asked for another draft & more officers last night
but at present we have no men trained enough though we are about 2000
strong. Very likely a big draft & several officers go in 3 or 4 weeks I should
think. I took Strong out to the Banks on Sunday, we had a very nice time,
which finished with a ride back in drenching rain against the wind. I went
to a very jolly tea party on Tuesday. Miss Robinson,[44] the girl I mentioned
before as having met at the Adjutants asked me. There were 4 other girls
there & 4 subalterns. The last two days have been beautifully mild. I am
enjoying life thoroughly & though threatened with a coughy cold hope to
keep it in check with all sorts of pills.
Much love

From very loving

Philip

MC 643/4/4

9.   3 Loyal North Lancs Regt. Old Felixstowe.

Sunday Feb.15th

Dearest Mother & Father

The chief change this week has been the abolition of night telephone duty!
I was the last to do it, on Thursday now instead of each night there being
4 subalterns up, one on telephone, one doing 'dip' one being orderly officer
and the other doing B Coy sentries corresponding to our 'dip', there is now
only one up, all the duties being done by the orderly officer. The duties are
not not done but are all done by one. The orderly officer has to spend the

---

42. *Country Gentleman and Land and Water*: a magazine for country people.

43. 'Officers are arming themselves with this weapon, for use in a hand to hand struggle!
They slash right & left with it, & use revolver in other-hand.' added by Philip's mother.

44. See letter 5. The two Miss Robinsons were Phyllis (24 in 1915) and Moira (20). Their
mother, formerly Alice Frank Blackburne Robinson, widow, married Richard Earle Welby
in London in 1899, and is the Mrs Welby of Philip's letters. Welby was a professional
soldier, described in the 1911 census as 'Captain – Militia retired'. The family were then
living in East Coker, Somerset. On the outbreak of war, he became a captain in the 3rd
Suffolk regiment and he and his family must have moved to the Felixstowe area. An 'R
Welby, Suffolk Regiment', listed on the Felixstowe and Walton Residents' War Memorial,
but not on the Felixstowe War memorial, may be a relative: he is not traceable on the
Commonwealth War Graves Commission site.

night in the room in the house next the telephone ie where Father & I had tea with Capt & Mrs Torbett, it's quite a nice room & there is a fire. I was orderly officer last night & yesterday. Of course you get a lot more work to do at night but you don't get so many nights as you combine all in one. You have to do the guards & B Coy & A Coy sentries twice each night! & superintend the usual telephone reports being sent in 3 times a night. It was a boisterously windy night last night but I got on all right. I have been in bed all this morning and am writing this at 2pm just before I go to the Band. My fleece lining was finished last night. I <u>am</u> pleased with it. Its <u>so</u> light and so nice & warm. It's the best fleece I could get and I am tremendously pleased with it. I will write to Pond myself & get some more boots. I had a nasty throat & cough for a day or two but the throat is alright now & the cough is going. I am fighting it with all sorts of pills! I did enjoy your letter to-day I've had letters both from Aunts Connie & Emmie this week end. I have been wearing Aunt Evelyn's socks this week, they are the best & warmest I've ever worn. Poor Andrews went off in a great hurry, he was told at 3pm on Monday & went at 5.30 am Tuesday. He was wonderfully cheery – The regt: is only 500 strong in France now & is at the base again. I go about with de Blaby now and Gardner is back now. Today is a curious day, it's going to <u>pour</u> with rain soon. Yes I <u>do</u> like the photos. I will send the Banks one. There was an officers' rugger match v the Bedfords yesterday I was going to play but cried off owing to being orderly officer & my cold. Salhouse is certainly "coming along" – Father must not get a coldy cough it would never do. Time seems to fly along here.

Much love

Your very loving

Philip

MC 643/4/5

10.   Feb: 19th

3rd Loyal North Lancs Regt Old Felixstowe
Wednesday

My dear Father

I did enjoy your letter which came this morning. The bottle of cough mixture came on Monday & I've nearly finished it now, it seems very good stuff at any rate my cough is hardly noticeable now. I expect you soon had to take the full dose when Mother found you were taking "dose, five years and under… one tea spoonful!" I am writing this at 3 pm in my room at Postern. It is one of Felixstowe's very worst days, a <u>tremendous</u> gale blowing, you can literally hardly walk against it and there's driving rain too. However with my lined 'mack' and waterproof hatcover! I find I am very weather proof. It's so changeable, (the weather I mean not the hatcover!) yesterday was a beautiful spring like day. There seem to be only six of us doing orderly officer now, so my turn for duty has come round again tomorrow. Well I only hope the spring like day & night come round again. We are sending out another draft in a day or two. This time 60 men are going. They are all ready & the War Office wired this morning to say they were to hold themselves in readiness. Officers names to follow later. We do not know who will go. I should think I shall just <u>not</u> go this time. Still one knows now it can't be so long before I do go. De Blaby & I have decided we will go together on a nice warm sunshiny day with a calm sea; those are our conditions for going which we think of sending to the War Office! On a blustering day we greet each other at breakfast and decide that unless the weather clears we can't go <u>this</u> day! On Sunday I sent for some loaded sticks on approval, I will choose one & let you know which I have. Thank you <u>so</u> much! I <u>do</u> think you have reason to be proud of the Egg Collection. You did start a splendid work. Tell Mother I am writing about the 'Land & Water' boot. I have arranged another football match for Saturday this time v the 3rd Norfolks. I will tell you all about it in Sunday's letter.

Much love to all

Your very loving

Philip[45]

MC 643/4/6

11. 3rd Loyal North Lanc Regt. Old Felixstowe

Feb 21

Dearest Mother & Father

We had a splendid game of football yesterday against the 3rd Norfolks. I could not get together a side composed entirely of officers so we had 5 officers & 6 sergeants. They had 4 officers and 7 men of other ranks. We

---

45. 'This is his last letter & daily I've been fearing a wire, but so far so good – None has came so hope they'll send him to Hythe 1st to learn gun practice – & then that he <u>may</u> go with the big draught.' added by Philip's mother.

played on the Town ground though not on the best one, there are 3 grounds there one a boy's ground. We had to play on that the 2nd half as the others were lent to other regts. However at ½ time nobody was playing on ground no 2 so we moved on to that which was full size. We got on much better then. It was 1–0 for us at ½ time and we eventually won 3–0. Only their goalkeeper saved them from a worse defeat as at one time we fairly peppered the goal with shots.

We had a sergeant playing centre forward who was supposed to be the best centre forward in Aldershot when he was with our 1st Bn. there. He scored all three goals, 2 straight from my centres, I was playing outside left & got on quite well.

Today is a perfectly glorious day, warm & springlike, de Blaby & I walked down to St. Johns this morning where we joined forces with Gardner. After Church we walked back along the front. On Thursday one of the two Curwen brothers went out to France by himself. Our draft of 60 men is going out on Tuesday morning I believe, but is being taken out by a subaltern from the 3rd Suffolks there!! So there are still the other Curwen & de Blaby and <u>perhaps</u> Nichol (though he probably won't go as he's only 17 yet) before me. I like the photo of our home very much but have no earthly idea who Miss Little is.[46] Poor Betsy[47] – she really mustn't get frightened like that. <u>I</u> don't think the Germans will ever get here now! I don't think there is <u>any</u> chance of my going to Hythe. Only so many (very few one or two) officers are allowed each Battalion for machine guns. All do not do the course. I generally sleep most of my time on duty now. When you come in after your 2nd round you can doze in front of the fire till 7.30. The General[48] gave us a practice alarm at manning the trenches yesterday morning at 7 am. I was woken at exactly 7 and was up here in Old Felixstowe with all my clothes on before 7.10, closely followed by my Company at the double. On Friday morning as I was watching the company drill the <u>General</u> wandered past & came up to me & asked me several questions about the Coy which I answered to his satisfaction (i.e. no. of men on parade, no of men in Coy., what all were doing on parade & off, average length of service of a certain squad etc). Much love

Your very loving Philip.

MC 643/4/7

---

46. Not otherwise identified.

47. Perhaps Philip's aunt Elizabeth; otherwise some unidentified family acquaintance.

48. Major-General H. T. Jones-Vaughan, the 'colonel' of the loyal North Lancashire Regiment between December 1909 and April 1916.

12. "On duty" Old Felixstowe

Thursday Feb. 25. 1 a.m.

My dear Father

As you see I am writing this in the early hours of Thursday. It is my turn
for orderly officer again and I have just come in after my first visiting
round. It is a beautiful moonlight night and it is freezing <u>hard</u>! However
it is a splendid night to go round on, as you can see where you are. I have
to write on this paper as I did not bring any proper writing paper here.
Your letter came alright this morning and I will return Col. C's[49] with
this. I heard from Mrs C. the other day. Please thank Ruth for her letter
wh. I enjoyed very much. I have arranged a great footer match for this
Saturday. Our officers & sergeants XI v E Coy XI. Now E have a really
good side, they are far & away the best Coy. side, they have scored 34
goals to 3 in their last 4 matches against the best of the other Coys. they
could find. They have several 'pros'! So we want to beat them but I shall
be tremendously pleased if we do. You see I am throwing all my energy
in games into the soccer so find no time for hockey though a few men &
an officer or two go down each week & join some club in Felixstowe to
play I believe. My time for going out seems to have been put off for a bit
again, as they sent Suffolks with our draft. Of course we are very short
of officers here at present as many are on sick leave while the Suffolks
had plenty to spare. I imagine we shall be able to send a big draft in 2
or 3 weeks though whether I shall go before it, after it or with is one of
the great unanswerable questions! I don't think this battalion will ever
go out as a whole, not at any rate while Germany has any fleet left, no
S.R.[50] battalion on coast defence will; besides if they sent out the draft
supplying battalions where are the drafts going to come from? Strong &
Nichol will be back from Hythe this weekend which will be nice. You
have a very hard time there, 10 hours work a day. I think this is a very
intelligent letter written as it is at this time, don't you? I had some OXO[51]

49. Lt-Colonel Stephen Charles, a neighbour of the Hewetsons at Wroxham House. He
had been in the Lancashire Fusiliers. Charles shared with the Hewetsons an interest in the
Society for the Propagation of the Gospel, becoming chairman of the Norwich diocesan
committee in 1925.

50. Special Reserve: as well as being a training battalion, 3 Bn was also part of the
Harwich fortress defences in case of invasion.

51. Extract of beef: the name was first used in 1900, becoming much more popular after
1910 when it was first produced in cube form. Regarded as a good form of instant nutrition,
Oxo was included in troops' emergency rations packs during the war.

& biscuits when I came in & must have a snooze now before I set out again.

Much love to all your very loving Philip.

13.   Thursday

My dear Father

I am afraid my letter is rather late this week, and won't get to you till Saturday I was orderly officer on Tuesday it was a pouring wet day, so I didn't mind having to sit in all day. The first time round the Sentries was 'orrible, blowy and rainy, however next time round at 3.30 am it was a lovely morning. I got some good sleep in between time in a deck chair, rolled up in a blanket. I felt quite fit in the morning but slept from 9–12. In the afternoon I had some good mixed tennis at the Masons. Miss Mason & Miss Robinson & 2 of us. I am playing <u>much</u> better this year, really fairly well. Then today I went out to the Banks, and had a <u>jolly</u> time, and some splendid tennis.

Tomorrow I have an invitation from Miss Robinson to make up a four on the Felixstowe Club Courts, which I am greatly looking forward to. Three tennis parties in 3 days! Not so bad? Nothing more about me going out yet except that I am next to go de Blaby & Livesey (an Old Carthusian & Cambridge man, v. nice) have both had their names sent in too I believe, so I may go with others when I go. The mo bike[52] punctured today but otherwise is in splendid order…
I am tremendously fit

Very much love Your v loving

Philip.

14.   Sunday [?7 *Mar.*]

Dearest Mother & Father

I am writing this at 7.15 pm so I am hurrying rather to catch the post, I have had a very busy day. Yesterday I had a splendid time, some Beagles

---

52. Philip has bought a motor cycle, letter 23 revealing it to be a 'Sun', a British motorcycle first produced in 1911: a new model would have cost about £30 in 1915.

met about 3 miles from here & some of us arranged to go. Four of us taxied out to the Hall where the meet was in footer things with our great coats on which we left in Capel Hall.[53] We were unluckily ½ hour late but came up with the hounds at 3pm. The "field" consisted of about 12 to 15 N. Lancs officers & 6 or 7 girls (all of whom I knew). However when we had been running a bit 5 of us subalterns were soon right ahead with the "pack" and the masters. We ran till 5 pm without a halt, over ploughed fields, dykes, hedges, golflinks, everywhere! Great fun. I jumped into the middle of one dyke, quite by mistake I assure you. It rained at the end, and we finished by the station covered with mud & scratches & wet through but supremely happy. We did not "kill"! This morning I was roused by an orderly at 8.29 am to attend a meeting at 8.30 am without fail in the huts, to discuss programme for recruits for this week, there were the officers of the 4 recruits companies & their Serg: Majors. Meeting lasted till 9.30 when I got some breakfast and then went to finish my toilet! Not a very good beginning to a Sunday. I went to Church in Parish Ch: here at 11 & stopped to H.C.[54] after. In the afternoon I decided to go out to Capel Hall & fetch my great coat wh: I had left there yesterday. It was a very windy day but I biked out & brought it back returning very hot about 4.15. De Blaby & I have met some very nice people here, the Moores,[55] in the Recreation Room, there is a rippingly pretty & jolly daughter, (unfortunately she's engaged) but still she's splendid. Well on Wednesday we are going to sing to the men & she is going to accompany us; so we went & called on Mrs Moore on Friday & were asked to tea today, from which function I've just returned. I'm keeping very fit. I don't know details of my Hythe trip yet. The War Office wrote to say they had not yet been told if I was fit for Service abroad after my leave yesterday; and I've just heard I am to go to Harwich tomorrow to have a Medical Board!! I don't know that it means anything, probably not. I don't know whether Hythe stops me going abroad; but I should not think I shall be wanted yet.

Will let you know Hythe details later

Much love

from Philip.

MC 643/11/8

---

53. A large house in Trimley St Martin: its occupier was Mr Alexander Keith, described in the 1911 census as 'gentleman farmer'.

54. Holy Communion.

55. Major Edward St Francis Moore and his wife Caroline, of The Ferns, Beach Road, Felixstowe. They had two daughters, Anita (born c.1890) and Mary (born c.1892).

15.   3rd Loyal North Lancashire Regt: Old Felixstowe

My dear Father

I think I have got what will be very good news for you this letter. Capt. Loch told me this morning that I had been selected to go to Hythe on March 15 for a course in Range Finding. The course is only a six days one but at any rate I suppose I am bound to be this side of the channel for another 3 weeks at least now! It will be an interesting course I think and of course I shall enjoy the change at Hythe. I believe they work you very hard there but I shall probably be able to get into see Gobagger in the evenings sometimes. Last night an order came through for the second Curwen[56]to go to the front, so now there is only de Blaby to go before me however I suppose while I am at Hythe I shall be skipped over. I have been having a simply <u>splendid</u> week so far. I have suddenly been taken with a craze for learning to ride. I went out yesterday from 3–4.15 with Nichol & Scott two other subalterns and had a grand ride. Of course I bumped about terribly, but enjoyed myself thoroughly. Trotting is very hard to me at present as I can't get the rhythm. However I managed a gallop (!) better. We went down over the old golf links, lovely turfy country right down by the sea and fairly careered about. After the ride Nichol & I went & called on the Miss Robinsons where we had a nice tea & enjoyed ourselves thoroughly.

This afternoon I have been riding again. I got on better today and hope if I ride continually for a week or 10 days to feel at home on a horse. It's grand exercise, but my word it does bump you & shakes your inside upside down!! The horses have lots of spirit in them & I am not learning <u>gradually</u>! gallops & all! None of the three horses will be left behind if one starts off & we <u>do</u> go. In the middle of a gallop this afternoon my animal put his head down & let out with both his hind legs (nice for a novice) my hat went flying but I stayed on & continued the gallop willy nilly as there was no pulling her in with her stable mate flying ahead! It's <u>great</u> fun! I hope to go out tomorrow too if I can borrow a horse again. I rode Colonel Cowper-Essex's[57] yesterday, a <u>huge</u> beast.

This afternoon I was greeted very warmly (and did the same to him) by a corporal who used to be in A Company and went out with the 500 draft in Dec. He was a very nice chap & used to play in the Coy: football team I got together. He stopped 5 machine gun bullets and still has 3 in him. However he's very cheery and has lots of interesting things to tell. We were to have

---

56. 'Twins with such a nice Mother!' added by Philip's mother.
57. 'in command' added by Philip's mother.

had a hockey match on Wednesday (yesterday) v the 10th Norfolks but they had to scratch at the last moment. I often get into the Priory[58] Recreation Room here now & am going in this evening to listen to the band, and talk to the ladies who sell.

Much love to all

Your very loving

Philip.

MC 643/4/10

16.   3rd L.N.Lanc. Regt: Old Felixstowe

Thursday [*11 Mar.*][59]

My dear Father

Regarding my course at Hythe I had the following notice sent me from the Adjutant. "You are selected for a Range-Takers course at Hythe commencing on Monday 15th instant" – so I suppose the latest I can get there is Sunday night. I am going to see the Colonel tomorrow & get leave to leave here on Saturday. I will send you a card tomorrow to say whether I go all the way there on Saturday or not. I think it will be best to break the journey in London. Monday of course is rather an awkward day to start a course. At any rate I hope not to be here on Sunday so it will be best to send my letter to *c/o* Gobagger. I am going to see if Bleistein can get leave & stay the night with him & get over to Aunt Emmie or some relation on Sunday. If he can't I shall stay with a relation if they can have me. Bleistein wrote to me & asked if I couldn't get off for a weekend some time.

I had a splendid time last night. De Blaby & I went into the Recreation Room at 7.15 and met our fair accompanist. Then we muchly trembling or pretending to started our concert to a room <u>packed</u> with Tommies. We each sang about 3 songs & got some of the men to sing too. Everything went <u>swimmingly</u>, & we did not finish till 8.30! Being then ½ hour late for mess – Miss Moore said we'd better come & have some cold supper <if> with them; so as Mr. Moore had come up too we went back with them and had a jolly scramble supper of whatever they could find, we were there till 10.15 and had a grand time. We then came back here & for safety's sake apologised to the

---

58. A large house in Felixstowe High Road, its name deriving ultimately from the medieval Benedictine priory in the town.

59. Envelope postmarked Felixstowe 11 Mar. 1915.

Colonel for missing Mess, he did not mind at all, though he probably would have if we hadn't reported ourselves as we came in.

My Medical Board on Monday[60] only lasted a minute! Apparently after sick leave you should have a board to return you to duty, this I never had; & the War Office wanted to know if I was still "sick" as I had not been officially returned to duty tho' I have been doing duty for 8 weeks now. I have the loaded stick here now, it's price is 12/6. Yes my electric torch is getting ready for another refill now. I will pay the Blackwell[61] Bill by <check> cheque if you send it. I am orderly officer today. It's a <u>pitch</u> black night, so I shall probably walk into several obstacles on my way round. There is another draft of 100 men going soon. It's no good speculating who goes with it for nobody knows.
Much love

Your very loving Philip.

MC 643/4/9

17.   3. L. N. Lanc: Regt. Old Felixstowe

March 21

Dearest Father

I <u>was</u> pleased to get a Sunday letter this morning! & one from Ruth too! Thank you so much for the new inside for the torch. I am afraid I have not written home for a long time now, but I expect Mother has told you most of the news now. I got on allright in the exam yesterday, we all passed. We were asked a good many questions and had to explain things but it was not very difficult. I managed to catch the 11 o'clock train up to town, and five of us travelled up together. We got up to town at 2.20 and I got a train down to Purley at 3.8. I was with Uncle L'E. for tea from 4–5.30 and caught a 5.40 up to town. He seemed very pleased to see me. My train from Liverpool St. left at 7.45 so I got a meal there before I started. I was in Postern once more by 10.30. I thoroughly enjoyed my time at Hythe, it was very nice being able to get over to Folkestone and see so much of Mother & the two Aunts. It was a very interesting course, though at present I have <u>no</u> idea as to what difference having taken it will make to me. Unless by some means or other (what means I don't know) I can get an instrument here there's no chance of my starting an instruction class. I shall ask about that to-morrow. At any

---

60. 8 March.
61. Specialist and technical bookshop in Oxford, founded in 1879.

rate it will probably take a long time to get an instrument & I shall go back to ordinary Coy: work again for a time. Meanwhile while I have been away Capt. Hill who was my Coy: Commander in E Coy: has gone out and a 2nd Lieut: junior to me is at present temporarily looking after E Coy: so I want if <u>possible</u> to get the command of E Coy: over 300 men! That I shall have to ask about tomorrow too. Capt. Greenhill and Lieut Diver have both gone out too. This morning Nichol [,] de Blaby & I walked down to St. Johns. It's a <u>glorious</u> springlike day. I found two invitations to tea this afternoon one from the Banks & the other from the Moores so I am going to bike out to the Banks. In 3 weeks time there is to be a <u>big</u> match Felixstowe Garrison v The Corinthians.[62] There is to be a "gate" and they're expecting 4000 spectators. There is huge excitement, practice matches are being played and a Selection Committee formed. I shall be on the Committee but of course shall not play.

Much love to you all yr very loving Philip.

MC 643/4/11

18.   Old Felixstowe

Tuesday [?23 Mar.]

My dear Ruth

You soon settle down to the ordinary routine here again and I am orderly officer to-day. At present I have been put back in A Coy:, my old Coy: under Capt. Loch in which I started here. I would rather have stopped in E; of course Strong is in A but so is that terrible fellow Morris, still he is expecting to go to the front in a day or two. I am rather amused to see how you all like lacrosse now you've had a go at it, do you remember how the thought of it jolly nearly gave you a relapse when you were mumpy! I hope you beat West Runton this time. I thought when we motored through there during my sick leave the school looked empty. You see I am quite an expert in Girls Schools now after my visit to Hythe. I expect Mother has told you what new experiences I went through at Bayham House,[63] <u>most</u> interesting I can assure you. They included a dance with me as the only man, a concert, a singing lesson and 2 suppers. The dance was splendid and as I had remembered not to go in hobnailed boots and as I had such an abundance

---

62. An amateur football club of enormous reputation and quality: in the 1880s its members made up most of the England national team.
63. The school in Folkestone run by Philip's aunts.

of beauty to choose my partners from everything went swimmingly. The singing lesson too was very amusing, I was sitting not quite at the front and not quite at the side facing them. I agreed very strongly with Aunt Helen once when she told them they weren't opening their mouths, enough, after that I made them smile several times and was then removed! We had a selection committee yesterday to pick a regimental XI to play against the Bedfords[64] on Saturday. This is a trial match to help in the selection of the Felixstowe Garrison XI v the Corinthians on April 10. I am to play outside left in the Regimental XI and shall be captain. One other officer is playing, inside right.

The garrison XI will be picked from all the regiments here. I went over to the Banks on Sunday, and had a nice tea party. It's a horrible job being orderly officer, hanging about here all day and sitting up all night, still I daresay I shall survive. Mother will like to know that the shop at Folkestone has never sent my boots yet; I am writing to Gobagger to ask her to stir them up!

Love from

Philip.

MC 643/11/20

19.   3rd L. N. Lanc: Regt: Old Felixstowe

28.3.15

Dearest Mother & Father

I ought really to have been orderly officer to-day but Morris was inoculated on Thursday and was orderly officer on Friday so I had to do his duty. So you see I am not on to-day. We have been having some extraordinary weather, freezing every night & sometimes snowing; then during the day, bright sunshine but out of the sun <u>biting</u> wind & cold. So the waist coat which arrived yesterday is very welcome! It <u>is</u> nice, splendidly made. I put it on at once and have worn it ever since. The waders too will be useful if I go out. And the mittens very useful! Thank you so much for them all. On Thursday we had a battalion Trial game of football in order to choose a regimental XI for yesterday. We started at 4.30 and only played ½ an hour each way, it was very cold and windy so we did not have a very good game, however the

---

64. The 3rd (Reserve) and 4th (Special Reserve) battalions of the Bedfordshire Regiment were among the many other battalions in Felixstowe in 1915.

'Probables' just beat the possibles 3–2. Yesterday we played a match v the 3rd
Bedfords. It was a trial match in view of the Corinthian match. We played
on the Town ground and there was a huge crowd watching. We had a very
good team on paper but somehow we did not get very well together. It was
a very good & exciting game to watch I'm told, and we just lost by the odd
goal in three. I was playing outside left but unfortunately they starved me.
I think if you come down it would be best to come the week end of April
10 you will then see the Corinthian match. There is a big Brigade field day
tomorrow starting at 2.30 am. (terrible time to get up) Think of breakfast
at 6.30. I shall be in command of the Company as Morris is orderly officer
today and Strong tomorrow. When we went out on Friday in a route
march I went in my full Tommies kit for the first time. I did not load up
everything full, but still it was good practice carrying things though I did
not find them very heavy.
My new boots came alright and are very nice. I do not think I am in any
need of provisions though I am sure the Mess would appreciate a home
made cake. I walked down as usual to St. Johns with Nichol[,] de Blaby and
Strong, the Vicar preached on the Mystery of the Sacrament. As far as I can
make out he is a Roman Catholic!! He said some funny things.[65]
A telegram has just come through and Morris is to go out to the front. Good
Friday will be a 'Sunday' for everybody here.
Much love

your very loving

Philip.

MC 643/4/12

*Philip spent some time in April/May 1915 with his parents at Salhouse while he
recovering from measles.*

20.   Monday [*3 May*]

Dearest all

Here's a line to tell you all about my journey. You know the officer we saw
in the next carriage to mine at the station, well when we had been going
about 5 minutes he came in and greeted me very warmly and asked me if I
remembered him. I didn't. He was an old railway companion of mine about
3 years ago! yet he remembered me! He travelled up with me from Liverpool

---

65. The concept of the sacraments as being 'mysteries' is a common form of language
within the Roman Catholic church and High Church elements within the Anglican church.

St to Sheringham after my last O.T.C. Camp when at Repton. He was at Uppingham then & he & family spent August at Sheringham. He too had had measles & was returning to Colchester so we travelled together to Ipswich. We had to change at Norwich which I did not know – tho' he did. At Ipswich I got some hot tea & 2 sandwiches & then ate the home sandwiches in the train. On arriving here owing to the two biggish bags & oil I took a taxi to the White Horse & booked the bike & fetched it up to-day. I came to the Mess where I found most of the officers who all seemed very surprised to see me. They seemed to think I'd had Pneumonic [*sic*] or something dreadful. We are all still living at Postern. It & all in it had been isolated for about a week when Carr got it but are all about now. Carr is back again too. Loch, Torbett, Henderson, Faulkner, Forbes are all on a months sick leave for various reasons. I am still in A Coy. This place is a bit slow and 'orrible at present after the lovely time I had at home. I am to have a board soon. Scott who took out "my" draft has come back. My bed was terrible in comparison to civilization but I shall get used to it soon.

Much love

Your very loving

Philip
Parade at 7 am each day!!

MC 643/11/17

21.   The Loyal North Lancashire Regt, Felixstowe

Sunday May 9

Dearest All,

I have managed to get one day's good play at tennis. Hugh & I had 2½ good sets on Friday. I had a very energetic day. To begin with it was boiling hot and we had a field day. We started at 8.30 am and marched 5 or 6 miles. Then we started operations which lasted about 2 hours & as I wore full equipment, pack & all and our company did a good deal of running about it was hot work. By the time we had collected and marched home it was 2.45 and we <u>were</u> hungry. After a short rest after lunch I played tennis with H.S. from 4.30 – 6. He won the first set 6–3. Then I got 6–4 and was 4–2 when we had to stop at 6. I dashed back to Postern and had a bath & change & was at the White House at 6.30 for the weekly Officer's Conference. We play at a house quite close to Postern. H.S. knows the people & they have a nice court. We were really playing quite well after the 1st set. Then at 7.30 I went to dinner with a man in the 10th Norfolks whom I met when I was at Hythe. Yesterday & to-day have been sun shiny days but tremendously windy which spoilt yesterday for tennis & today for motor biking. I went to St Johns with de Blaby this morning. The curate took the service as the vicar (so he told us) heard last night at 10.30 that his son had been killed in action on Thursday.[66] I am so sorry about Ruth! What bad luck – in her exam term too – but still it's a good thing what Miss Wise says.[67] What a pair we are, first one then t'other. I am at present very fit and very sunburnt, my nose & cheeks especially, they will peel tho' I keep them greased. The bike is still satisfactory. The carburettor gets bunged up occasionally & has to be cleaned out but she goes very well on the whole. Capt Torbett is back once again though I haven't seen him yet. I have not been Ord: Off. yet but shall probably get my turn when my 2 weeks Home Duty end on Tuesday. Much love

Your very loving Philip.

MC 643/4/13

22. Thursday [*13 May*]

My dear Father

At last the weather has changed, I've seldom seen such a day. It's simply drenching, and has done so all day, coming down in torrents and blowing a hurricane off the sea all the time. It's bad luck that it chose to day to do this for H.S. and I were going over to the Banks for tennis. We were going to bike over, take our tennis things and change there.

We got some more good tennis on Tuesday, a single, at the same house. Your racquet is splendid! I enjoy the work in the Company now and on these glorious days it's quite fun marching out 5 or 6 miles doing a scheme and then marching back. You do have an appetite when you get in about 2 pm. Things seem exciting and rather serious in the war don't they? Germany is unspeakable. That enquiry into outrages published today caused huge indignation here as I suppose everywhere. All say she must be absolutely

---

66. Frank Stantial, a second lieutenant in the 3rd Battalion, Suffolk Regiment, was killed in action at Ypres on 4 April 1915: he was 26 years old. His name is on the Felixstowe war memorial.

67. Miss Wise, the headmistress of Norwich Girls' High School. Ruth has presumably caught measles.

swept away.[68] We send another draft in a day or two. I do hope Ruth is better and look forward to her recovery here.

Very much love to all your Philip

The weekly Officers' Conference is in 10 minutes so I must stop.

MC 643/11/23

23.   The Loyal North Lancashire Regt Felixstowe

Sunday May 16

Dearest All

I expect when you open your papers tomorrow morning you will see that our 1st Battalion has indeed been in action in deadly earnest once again.[69] We have lost 11 officers in the last few days. Seven of our own and four others attached to us out there from other regiments. Gardner and another 2 Lt: (a man promoted from the 1st Bn: where he was a Sergt. Major) went out yesterday morning and Barker who has been out once and been home wounded is going out again in a few days with this draft, he is the Hamilton's[70] friend you know and joined just before I did. I must confess that I asked to be allowed to go out too, everybody feels when all these fine men get knocked over that they must go out & as it were avenge them. But I was told my time was not to come for at least a week. Also that the Battalion will now probably be out of action for a month or so now, as someone says there are only 400 men left, but still so far no one has any absolutely reliable news. This is I suppose what other regiments have been going through all these weeks that we have been resting, so we have been very fortunate to be out of it so long. I really expected to go out with this draft and bought myself a very cunning periscope, so I feel very ready. However of course they may not hurry to send officers out if the Bn: goes out of action for a time. I am indeed pleased I got the "Sun" now, it is very useful and always gives one something to do. I had a new plug put in the other day and now she is running better than ever. I had another run into Ipswich yesterday. We went to the Hippodrome and when we came out there was a <u>huge</u> crowd in the

68. The Bryce Report into German brutality against the civilian population of invaded Belgium was published on 12 May 1915: its conclusion was that atrocities, including massacres and looting, had indeed occurred.

69. At Aubers Ridge, the battle taking place on 7–9 May 1915.

70. Not otherwise identified.

main street engaged in breaking the windows of a German butcher's shop.[71] It would of course be nice to have you here at Whitsuntide but I'm thinking that if I go out in 10 days or 2 weeks time you'd just miss me and a second visit to see me off would hardly be worth it. Would it be better to wait to decide till I can tell you if I expect to go this weekend.

If so come. If I do not go for a fortnights or 10 days come then?! It's a lovely Sunday and I shall probably go over to the Banks as it was wet on Thursday. De Blaby & I went to St John's this morning It seems funny being here for another week as I was quite sure to go. Who'll win? Julian[72] or I? Has Julian gone yet I wonder. I'm keeping very fit, and enjoying life, But as I expect you realise longing to get out. The longer one waits the warmer the weather and the less trouble over clothes, thank goodness. I'm not wearing the socks that I'm taking out with me. Well very likely I shall see you soon. Very much love

Your very loving

Philip.

MC 643/4/14 and MC 643/11/28

24.   Thursday [?*20 May*]

My dear Father

The tennis things arrived quite safely, though I have not managed to get a game yet. For one thing the courts are not so plentiful as I imagined they were on my first return and also after being out from 8.30 am to perhaps 1.30 or even 2.30 as on Tuesday I do not feel extra keen on a game generally when the weather is so hot. It is really extraordinarily hot! Some subs have already bathed in the sea but I have not. The cakes which Mother sent to-day look really ripping and we are going to have them for tea to-day, I expect I shall have as hearty messages of appreciation to send as were sent for the marmalade. They <u>did</u> like the marmalade. The Colonel himself said he had never liked marmalade so much for many years; and he could not stop his

---

71. There were anti-German riots in several British cities at this time. They were sparked by the sinking by a German submarine of the liner *Lusitania* 18 kilometres off the Irish coast on 7 May: 1,198 people were drowned, including almost 100 children. The British made propaganda out of the tragedy, citing it as an example of Hunnish atrocity. However, she does appear to have been carrying munitions: before she sailed, the Germans issued public warnings that they regarded her as a legitimate target.

72. Tyndale-Biscoe.

breakfast once he started on the marma:! We are having quite an energetic time these hot days; generally marching out 5 or 6 miles, doing a 'scheme' which necessitates a good deal of running about, then marching back. you use a change of clothing per day practically. Did Mother definitely order my khaki aertexes, as I am quite ready for them, and any more thin vests or pants that I have. The day for winter clothing seems at present to have quite passed away my eyes do not trouble me now & I am very fit and <u>longing</u> for my chance to come again. <u>I</u> seem to get keener on going out each day! though those who've been there tell me it's a silly thing to do!!

Much love Your very loving Philip.

MC 643/11/19

25.   The Loyal North Lancashire Regt Felixstowe

Thursday [*27 May*][73]

My dear Father

I enjoyed your ripping long letter this morning – and Ruth's yesterday; but she should not have got beaten after leading 5–1! I certainly am having a good time. Monday was a half holiday but Carr took my afternoon duty so I played tennis all afternoon. I had six real good sets. I did my night duty that night, it was a lovely fine moonlight night and I got some good sleep in between times so rather enjoyed it than otherwise. On Tuesday I took Carr's afternoon orderly officer. Yesterday we had a great day in the field. We started at 9 and marched out about 8 miles. We then did an outpost scheme, and after having lunch out which was good fun on a <u>glorious</u> hot day in a wood (where you saw us that day when you motored back). We started back about 2.30 & got back here about 4.30. After a bath, a change and some tea I was playing tennis by 5.30 and had 3 good sets with a sub: Wood, & a Mrs & Miss Allen[74], the latter of whom W. who's about 32 is v keen on! Today I'm off to the Banks for Tennis. The refleshlets Mother sent me are splendid on a march; so are the thin aertex shirts. I am tremendously fit. I have 'o' more about going out yet. It would as you say be splendid if you were more of a mechanic to go out & drive an ambulance or something? You <u>could</u> go as a chaplain you know, and you'd be splendid!! Suppose you could go

---

73. 'Last before going to Front May 27th 1915' added by Philip's mother.

74. Later letters show that Mrs Allen had two daughters: she was the husband of Colonel Allen, who was in France 1915, back in Felixstowe 1916. Colonel Allen is not otherwise identified; he was not in the LNLR.

as a chaplain to a big hospital town or to a 'Base' not stay in England nor go right in the trenches?? Still if you did go it <u>would</u> be a big upheaval? and you're doing such good work where you are. But it's interesting to think about.

Much love

Your very loving

Philip.

MC 643/4/15

26.   The Base.[75] Friday afternoon.[?*4 June*]

Here's your first letter from Overseas you will have got my p.c. describing 1st part of journey. We embarked at 5 pm, started at 6. It was quite calm but very foggy when we got out when it rolled a little but I was alright. The officers (9) had a good dinner on board, & it was interesting after watching our escort. I turned in about 9 on the floor of a little cabin, one other there. I slept fairly well with my head on my luggage & wearing my "woolly", fleece lining & "mac", I was quite warm but the floor was a bit hard. We drew up along the quay at Havre in the very small hours of the morning & I came up on deck to see the 1st lights of France & then turned in again till 5.30 when I got some hot water & shaved & got a sort of a wash. Good breakfast on board about 6.30.

    Disembark 7.30. Hang about till 8.30. Then push off to march 5 miles to our Camp. <u>Very</u> hot & dusty but v cheery. Intensely interesting, get my 1st sight of French troops, transport Wagons. (Continued at 9.20 pm in Mess ante room). Uncle Henry[76] rode up this afternoon & I have just come back from an afternoon in Havre with him. He looks very fit. I had tea with him in his headquarters (a hotel). Then we wandered round & did some shopping (I brought a looking glass for shaving etc, a collapsible bucket & had my watch glass mended, it had broken coming across. All this in French if you please.) After shopping he gave me a splendid dinner, in a restaurant, a farewell one, as until just now we expected to go up to the Front tomorrow (Sat:) We had amongst other things asparagus, strawberries & champagne. Awfully good of him. As the trains are v few between he sent me back in a taxi. I got a lift into Havre in a Ford driven by a YMCA lady. When I got

---

75. First place of encampment in France before heading to the front line: Philip's was at Harfleur, five miles outside [Le] Havre.

76. See Appendix 3.

back here I found in tonight's orders that our draft was to be inspected at 8 am tomorrow (Sat:) & go for a 2 hours route march after. So apparently we are not to go up yet but shall do very soon. Perhaps Sunday. I have got a respirator, an identity disc, field dressing <u>and</u> a Tommies tunic.

One thing I remember is I never paid my servant at Felixstowe, I left a 10/- P.O. on my table wh: is for him I wonder if he got it. The first person who greeted me here was Marriott of Repton who lives at Cromer; he is in the 3rd Northamptons. The men are in tents, officers in huts. Nice hut mess & anteroom. A good many officers here.

Very much love

Philip.

MC 643/5/2

27.   [*Bethune ?7 June*]

My very dear family

I don't quite know where to begin. I hope you got my p.c. of Rouen sent off Sunday.[77] I'm writing on Monday evening. We travelled all yesterday. Left the Camp at Harfleur at 10am. <u>Boiling</u> hot. I was in charge of draft with 2 other subs attached to us. One from S. Lancs: & 1 from Manchesters. Marched 4 or 5 miles to Montvilliers where troop train was being made up for front. Got there 11.30. Walked about, & officers went & got some cooling drinks at little inn outside. Men embarked 7 in carriage, Officers 4. We in 1st class carriage. Comfy. Got Havre 2.30. Shunting left 3. These trains never go much more than 11–15 miles an hour, keep stopping. People get out & walk along. Very funny. All along the journey all the French men, women & children come to doors & windows & cheer & wave, sometimes "Vive L'angleterre," we & the Tommies lean out & vigorously reply. The country is lovely. We lunched in the train. I had some cold tongue, bread wh: I had bought & biscuits etc. Thoroughly enjoyed journey. Got to Rouen at 6pm. Where we had 2 hours & I sent off my p.c. Such a lovely place. I went into a Patisserie shop (now then Ruth!) & had some iced lemonade & strawberries. Started off again at 8. A <u>huge</u> troop train, 3 engines, but <u>so</u> slowly. Our men were splendid. So cheery, singing & waving etc all the time. I again had a nice messy picknicky meal. Soon after this we turned in & I slept v. fairly with intervals till 6.30 about. Soon after the train had one of its many halts, this time near a little stream. Out we hopped. I filled my canvas bucket

---

77. 6 June.

(bought at Havre) & had a wash. Train began to move as I was drying but just emptied bucket etc & walked along & hopped in. Managed a shave & then another meal, same things only this time called breakfast! We were told we should arrive at our destination (Béthune) before 11 am. Country gets a bit more interesting. Some French troops about. But <u>no</u> signs of war. Life goes on as usual they say up to within 1½ miles of trenches.

We arrived here, the destination at 11.30 Monday & were met by the adjutant. The battalion is resting, has been since Friday but does not know for how long. We are 7 miles from the trenches, & the guns are rumbling hard all the time. The Germans shell this place occasionally they say, & I've just been seeing some of the holes! We are in luxurious billets. Scattered about by companies. I have a lovely room, 4 post bed, sheets, beautiful furniture. It is the room the Prince of Wales[78] slept in for 40 days when here!!! What about that!! B & C Coys mess together next door, also a big house. This is a biggish place, typically French all paved streets. Lots of troops. But civilian life goes on as usual. This is a <u>choice</u> billet. & we're v lucky to be here! All sorts of food, potted meats, & tongues. Cakes & delicacies are much appreciated, as all contribute & its necessary or rather usual to take a good store when you're going in trenches.

I found your letters waiting for me here. They did not come to the base. I <u>was</u> pleased to get the electric torch. I thought I'd left it behind. Also please send me some scissors mine broke. I'm writing this at 8. We are just going to have dinner. I found Gardner, Barker, Livings & Diver here from Felixstowe, that's all. All very pleased to see me I never heard the 3 cheers given for me. I found a letter from Gobagger here too. We probably shant go into the trenches for 2 or 3 days. All is so far v. interesting. It is curious to hear the guns go boom boom – – – all the time & to think I'm really at the front. A Major Brown just arrived commands my Coy & there are 2 other subs in it v nice. Now don't worry about me. You know I'm very happy & very Trusting.

dearest dearest love

to you all

your v loving Philip.

MC 643/5/3

---

78. Prince Edward (1894–1972), Prince of Wales, later (uncrowned) King Edward VIII, later Duke of Windsor. In the war, he travelled the battle areas in a Daimler to give moral support to the troops.

28.   North Lancs Regt.

2nd Brigade 1st Division British Expeditionary Force
France
Tuesday 4 p.m. [?*8 June*]

My very dear all I know I only wrote yesterday but I know you'll be interested in to-days news. I'm afraid its rather changed my view of the pleasantness of this place. Last night those horrible Germans thought fit to shell this place and between 12 & 3.45 they sent from 50–100 shells(!!!) into it! I was very tired & slept soundly at first until at 3.15 I was awoken by a huge sort of whistling swi- – – – – sh coming straight at me in a crescendo followed immediately by a <u>huge</u> report & bang then falling masonry!! You may think you can imagine my feelings but you cant. I lay in bed & didn't know what to do; as a matter of fact this one fell about 100 yds away in a house. You hear them coming with a huge whistle & don't know where they're going till they burst. Nobody pretends not to be frightened inside!! very much so you feel so power<ful>less! Then followed a dreadful 10 minutes (for me at any rate as it was my baptism of fire.) What it will be like to be bombarded by 100's of shells I <u>don't</u> know – – – they sent over about 6 or 7 more all <u>fairly</u> close. Till suddenly there was a huge report and this house shook and <u>all</u> the windows in front including mine smashed!! Then we jumped out of bed the Major (comdg: my Coy) his servants & I took refuge downstairs. They stopped the shelling for a bit then. About 3.50 we went out into the road (a little narrow 10<–11> yrds wide cobbled road) houses each side & found that the shell had blown up the front door of the house <u>next door</u> & smashed all the windows round. They sent some more over but into another part of the town. No casualties so far as is known. At 5 am we went to bed again as things seemed quiet, Praying for no more. They stopped & I managed to get to sleep till 7 am. Some more to-night??

It may sound exciting but I guarantee it isn't!! While it lasts its terrifying. Of course as soon as it's over its just like a bad dream & you're <u>absolutely</u> yourself again. At least that's my experience. This morning was too hot for words; simply melting. Please send my aertex shirts. We all live in shirt sleeves. No tunics. Adjutants Parade the whole Bn. was from 10–12 then from 12–45 our Coy: went to some swimming baths & bathed. I went in too, oh it was lovely. From 2–3 a tremendous thunder storm cleared the air. Then since then I've been helping pay out the Coy. Lots of refreshlets & cooling sucks please – The guns are thundering away in the near distance, 6 or 7 miles.

I am very well & settling down splendidly
Very much love

from Philip

Please send larger writing block.

MC 643/5/4

29. Thursday June 10, 7 pm

1st L.N. Lanc Regt.
1st Division B.E.F. France

My very dear Father & Mother How I enjoy your letters. We get letters once a day and you should see the eagerness with which they are awaited. Most or should I say all the officers get a good budget each time & we all say we've never had so many letters. I've just got yours written on Tuesday so I expect by now you will have got my p.c. & other 2 letters. I suppose I ought not really to have put in where we are so I'm sure you'll leave that out in sending round letters, the idea isn't so much that it matters where we are but from knowing that any one can tell (1) where our Brigade is (2) Where our Division is; two very important items. Well we are still here and have had no more bombardments since Monday. It is a very pleasant Life. We have a B & C Companies mess there. There are 9 of us, a very jolly crew. The major who commands my Coy is a very nice man indeed, Irish.[79] I should think 40–45. He was in S.A. war. Was out here in the Warwick Regt in Nov & Dec. then became adjutant of our 10th Bn. then a Staff officer out here managing Transport. Then he joined here the same day as I did. So you see he's had some experience. Then there's a Capt. Etches a dear old boy commanding C. Coy. who's been out here 5 or 6 months. He knows & thinks no end of Uncle Cecil whom he vigorously quoted as an ideal missionary last night. He was at Worcester, Oxford. After that come 7 subalterns. One is a promoted Sgt. Maj: from 1st Bn: who of course has been out before & since at Felixstowe. All the others except me are attached. Three of them have had 3 days in the trenches but as you see we are all fairly new arrivals. We get on very well together. We don't work very hard on parades as we are resting & the weather is so hot. Each morning at 7 the Coy, goes for ½ an hours "run or walk" in shirt sleeves. We take it in turns to get up & we have to be careful to go due West away from the trenches. Then the morning parade is from 9.30 to about 12.15. After that you are generally pretty glad of a good

---

79. Major Monteagle-Browne: see Appendix 2.

wash down before lunch. In the afternoon there is generally nothing much, an inspection of billets perhaps or paying out etc, Other things we have been told to do are inspection of feet, rifles, respirators, ammunition etc. There are one or two rather nice patisserie shops wh you can drop into in the afternoon for ices or tea – The evening soon goes with writing letters. Dinner is generally about 7, a jolly meal, then you're quite ready for bed.

Of course at present B & C Coys. mess together, but in the trenches we mess separately. I am to be Mess President of B Coy. and to-day I've been having a most amusing time airing my French. I've been buying a frying pan, tea pot, stew pot (for potatoes etc) enamel plates, mugs, knives, forks, spoons, some sardines, potted meat & tinned fruit, but only 1 tin of each of the eatables they are so dear. Each Coy apparently takes a mess box into the trenches with food & crockery in for its Officers Mess. Magazines will be very useful. Punch, Bystander, Sketch, Tatler, Strand etc any of those. We share all food & such things among the Coy officers. Each contributes. I have had letters from Gobagger, Aunt Helen, Nellie Banks & Julie as well as the home letters. Could you ask aunt R: if she wld: send magazines or extra eating dainties, instead of baccy as I really don't use the 'bacco. The troops we relieve in the trenches went in today so we may go in 4 days, But we don't know. I think I must stop now.

Very much love to all. Your very loving

Philip.

MC 643/5/5

30. Sunday June 13 1915, 5.30 pm

1st Bn. Loyal North Lanc. Regt.
1st Division B.E.F. France

My very dear all. I expect you are wondering where I am this Sunday. as a matter of fact we are still here in these billets, I don't think I have written home for 2 days, but I have written a letter or two each day to somebody. We have had no more shells and so I have had splendid undisturbed nights. The Punch & Bystander have arrived, they were most welcome, thank you so much. We all rush at those things. We are really very well off for the daily papers. We get them mostly 24 hours late, we get all the papers such as a Times, Mail, Mirror at breakfast. Of course they are 24 hours late but when you've had them like that for a few days of course you don't realise that & it seems just as if they are the day's papers provided you don't look at the date. Each day here is much the same as another, I gave you the programme last letter, we do the same programme each day. Today however being Sunday was different naturally. There was Church Parade in a square in the Town at 10.10am. I was rather looking forward to it. However I have been selected to be Bomb & Throwing Officer for my Coy. There is one from each Coy. We four had to parade at Orderly Room at 9 am this morning. When we got there we were shown a farm on a map and told to be there by 10 am. It was about 3 miles walk, when we got there we found about 25 officers & some N.C.O.s. It was a lovely morning, however the country was not very interesting dusty roads, cornfields, & no hedges you know, lots of transport & little parties of French & English soldiers about. We were instructed by an R.E. officer. It's rather interesting though I can't describe all the apparatus to you. The bombs themselves weigh perhaps a pound, & may be made of cast iron or merely of jam tins filled with explosives or shrapnel.[80] They explode when the fuse goes off, which is 5 seconds after you set it going so you have to get rid of it quickly. You throw them by hand about 30 yds; when they make a big explosion. We were learning this morning how to fit in the fuse, and throw the bomb. By the time we had finished it was 12 and by the time we were back here it was 12.45

7 pm. Continued. I was suddenly called off to Orderly Room for further instructions re bombing. We 4 officers are the Battalion Bombers & have got to take 80 men (20 per Coy) & practise & train them and ourselves tomorrow. Parade 8.15 am. It'll be an interesting job & comforting to feel <we> when in the trenches we have these dangerous weapons of defense & offense ready on our persons to use against the enemy! After lunch today I got a welcome budget of letters, Father's, one from aunt Mary & splendid long one from Gobagger, who wanted to know how long it took to come, so will you tell her. I wrote to her yesterday so will not be writing to her again perhaps before you do. Please thank her so much for the tinned apricots she sent & say her offer of fresh fruit would be most welcome, specially when we are in the trenches. Which I expect we shall be some time this week. My letters seem to take longer to get home than yours to come here. How we love our letters. After reading my letters I walked out into the country with Gardner & lay down in an orchard. Nice places are however very

---

80. 'Bombs' or grenades played an important role in trench warfare – a properly lobbed grenade could kill more men than a rifle. 'Jam tins' were a very primitive form, simply a tin packed with guncotton and shrapnel: they had to be ignited by a 'striker' worn on the arm. They resembled the tin in which a soldier was given his jam ration – and these tins might be used as improvised grenades in an emergency. The Mills bomb was introduced in May 1915. It had its own fuse, ignited when removing a pin, and was the direct ancestor of the grenades familiar from films of the Second World War and later conflicts.

hard to find, I have as you see had no Church Services today but haven't forgotten it's Sunday & shall get some little reading out of my Prayer Book. One "Tommy" whose letter I was censoring today said after mentioning Church Parade – "so you see we don't forget our duty to God as well as to our King & Country when we are out of the trenches resting" – Rather nice I thought. I like censoring their letters, There's a great contrast in them –

Now some tips to Father on the motorbike 1. Always turn off the oil a little time before you stop, otherwise all the oil in the pipe goes on into the carburettor and bungs it up. 2. Have the oil regulator at 1 to 1½ round about 20 miles per hour; and increase it in proportion to pace. 3. I was doing 60 to 70 miles per gallon quite! I expect it will be very useful to you. I enjoyed Bany's letter & P.J.s.[81] I am keeping tremendously fit. I am not wearing a Tommies' tunic but my own without the braid on the sleeves but with the star on shoulders.[82] Now I must stop.

With dearest love your v loving Philip.

MC 643/5/6

31.   address of near relative in France:-

Lieut Col: Hewetson R.A.M.
No 6 Stationey [*sic*] Hospital
Havre [83]
1.L.N.L., B.E.F., France
Thursday June 17 3 pm

Dearest all. Here is a new series of letters which must be headed "In the Trenches" – for here I am. We are not yet in the actual front line but shall be when you get this. We are about 300 yds behind the actual firing line and are connected with it by communication trenches[84]. We left our billets yesterday at 11.30 am, and marched for 3 hrs. It was boiling hot. As we got about 1 to 1½ miles away we went very carefully with intervals between platoons of 100 yds to avoid shellfire. As we got to within a mile about houses became heaps of bricks and all was ruin & desolation. Our own

---

81. PJ is Powys-Jones [see Introduction]; 'Bany' is not identifiable.

82. Philip's dress may reflect the common view that an officer identifiable by his uniform was liable to be targeted by enemy snipers.

83. Philip apparently wrote this address on his notepaper, then decided to use the paper for his letter home

84. On 16 June the battalion went into local reserve lines to relieve the Scots Guards – 'B' Coy moved into dug outs at 'Glasgow Road'.

guns were all about tho' you couldn't see them and they kept going off with terrific reports right on top of you as it seemed. French peasants were living in their tumble down villages up to within 1½ to 2 miles. At last we filed into communication trenches. They are about 2 ft wide & 7 to 8 feet deep so unless a lucky shell drops right into one you are quite safe. The trenches our men are in are about 5 or 6 feet deep, they are made in 2 levels, one to walk along and a platform about 1 ft high & 1 ft broad to stand on to fire. They are about 3 ft wide. Thus you fire over a parapet not through a loophole.[85]

6.   Drawing by Philip from letter 31

Of course we are 3 to 4 hundred yds behind the fire trenches but it's as well not to show your head over the parapet as stray bullets fly over sometimes & there are snipers about. Still unless they deliberately shell us we are in <u>fairly</u> safe quarters. Of course if they do that in these reserve trenches we can go to ground in our "dug outs" – mine in wh: 2 of us sleep is a very nice one. About 8 ft long by 3 ft. 6" high with a roof of logs & 2 ft 6" of sand bags. I am writing in it now as some German shells are just starting flying about. The floor is covered with straw – I don't have any meals here but only sleep. About 10 yds further up the trench there is a bigger dug out of 2 rooms. One for sleeping is about twice as large as mine – the other we have our meals in & you can just stand in it. It will just & only just fit the 5 of us. We have a little table 3ft by 1ft & 4 old chairs, and a rickety old writing desk. Some old family & wedding groups also rescued from the <u>ruined</u> village <u>just</u> behind us are on the mud walls. It is a jolly life so far as we've had a quiet time today. Nothing to do except wander round occasionally & look after your men, & set them little jobs improving the trenches. Last night there was a <u>tremendous</u> bombardment going on. Such roars & crashes. Both sides plugging in for all they were worth / ½ hour later / You'd like to see me here in my dug out, with my waterproof sheet spread out on the floor. I've just been to my platoon to put off a rifle inspection as a few German shrapnel have been over here, nothing to worry about, but as well to keep

85. Philip has sketched a rough drawing of it.

under cover, however a battery of ours just behind is giving them a good dusting now. Yest we got no food between 8 am & 6 pm but were eventually none the worse for it. I sat up with another subaltern visiting, sentries etc till 12.30. Then I turned in till 2 am. Then we "stood to arms" from 2–3.30 then I slept from 4–7, but do not feel tired today. It's a wonderful feeling at night. Sometimes it's quite like a Brocks firework display with these flares going up & lighting up the country like great rockets or Roman candles. Then another time a rifle bullet goes p-------ing over yr head, a stray one & quite safe as you're probably deep down in a trench. Then a shell or two goes screaming by <but> & if its one from our guns you mentally speed it on its way. Another sight you're always seeing is aeroplanes high up in sky, with little white puffs of clouds keeping appearing all round & under them. They are too high for the inexperienced to tell whether they're friend or foe but the gunners on each side know & are shelling them! I keep very fit. Now with dearest love I must stop your v loving Philip

MC 643/5/7

32.   Friday 18.6.15 [*FSP*]

Lovely weather

Splendid budget of letters & parcels last night, your parcel splendid. And a ripping big cake & letter from A. Emm so good of her. I'll try & write to her. We are still here in these reserve trenches but go up to the firing line tomorrow. By the time you get this we shall be getting back to billets, any illus: or weekly papers (the weeks Daily Mirror can be got bound) would be more than welcome for my men. As we are at present it's a jolly existence we are sort of picknicking rabbits so long as they don't shell us. They did a little this morning but we went to ground. I am still very fit. No more news since yesterday. P.

MC 643/5/8

33.   Sunday June 20 3 pm

1. Loyal North Lanc. Regt. B.E.F. France

Dearest Mother Father & Ruth, I'm afraid you are probably being anxious about me and thinking of me as in the firing line! So all of us thought we should be whereas instead we are all back in our old billets in Bethune!! None of us dreamt of such a thing on Friday. But yesterday morning when we were all getting ready to move up into the firing line, a message came to say "Relieving Orders Cancelled" – War is a funny thing or rather perhaps I shld say the ways of the army – the soldier never knows his movements for certain an hour ahead let alone a day – and as for a week well of course it would be more than absurd to even guess what we might be doing. Soon after that order came another came to say that instead of relieving the troops in the front line we were ourselves to be relieved & to march back to B. at 12.30 for one night & to be ready to move off today at an hour's notice – no reasons given of course! The whole 1st Division was relieved (censor please). There was much speculation as to where & when we were going. One idea is that the whole 1st Division is to have a good rest; it has of course been right "in" things <the> and had a very bad time for months. If that happens I shall be an old soldier out here before I've spent a day in the firing trenches, but I hope that wont be so! As tho' the Division as a whole may need a rest I certainly don't! Another idea and the most likely one is that we are taking over some more of the French line – They have done tremendously well the last week you know & gained a lot. It was wonderful to hear their guns away on our right, they never stop. A continuous rumble. We may keep up a huge bombardment for some hours but whenever our guns stop away in the distance you hear the French, day & night. Well neither of those ideas have been realised yet & we are still here. Now at 2 hours notice instead of one. So we may & probably shall be here another night, but you never know. It seems like it however, as last night when we marched in here we were told we could not have our valises but we have just been given them so it looks as if we're going to stop here for a day or two. That's why I am writing on this big paper, it was in my valise, & I was able to get it & other comforts which were imposs. in the trenches from the valise.

Well in case we were being relieved for a long rest I determined to get into the firing line before we left. So I walked up there with the Major. As the crow flies it was only about 300 yrds from our trenches, but going along all the zig zag communication trenches you walk quite a mile. You never go straight for more than 5 to 6 yards. They are as I said from 6–8 ft deep about 2 feet wide never more & like this[86] and so on ad infinitum. Where we got to the Germans were 70 yards away. In this part of the line we are about 500 yds further West than we were in December, so if people in England think a rush is possible, well tell them that the opposing forces have sat opposite each other in this sector in exactly the same places since January in fact only 20 yards from each other. Nothing but High Explosive will turn either out.

---

86. Philip has drawn a rough sketch of the trenches.

Still in this part too we must remember we are the very apex of a salient & it is hardly the part of the salient to advance. In our reserve trenches we might be somewhere where the X is.

During the 3 days I had in these trenches we were shelled each day but nothing serious. No casualties in my Coy, though D Coy had a few. I collected several pieces of shell which fell near our dug out but left them in a little pile there as I expect it's very easy to get them whenever you go into the trenches – I had a new experience on Friday afternoon: The Germans were shelling a place about 600 yards in the * left* front of our trenches with big Jack Johnsons[87]. They put well over thirty there in the afternoon. I'd seen pictures as you have of these things bursting but never could have imagined it. Great clouds of black smoke 2 or 3 times as high & big as a house rise up with a huge roaring explosion. Most fascinating to watch. Several times they must have hit a house or what was one once for the smoke was all reddish. I believe there was a bridge there that they were shelling – another very wonderful sight & one that the oldest soldier is never tired of watching though its a daily occurrence is the aeroplanes. They really are marvellous. You see sometimes as many as 6 in the air at once, its exciting speculating whether they're German or Allies. Which ever they are as soon as they get within range of the enemies guns you see little white clouds (as it seems) suddenly appearing all round, under & sometimes if they are low above them. It is shrapnel bursting & has a very pretty effect. If they get directly above you you go to cover as the pieces come hurtling down. It is wonderful how they escape, yet on they go flying above the enemies positions; and you hold your breath if <one> a shell goes very near him, and breath again as with wonderful skill he rights himself & goes on, altering his altitude to put off the next aim. Knowing all the time that if they are hit it's a quick dive to earth & a sudden death. You can imagine it's thrilling.

Well yesterday we left the trenches at 3 pm & arrived back here about 5.30. It was great to be in a bed with sheets once more & to be able to wash without wondering whether a shell or a bullet was coming your way! I must say I thoroughly enjoyed my 3 days "dans les trencheés" but of course the infernal machines of war are apt to upset your equilibrium occasionally.[88] My word I <u>did</u> sleep! I think pyjamas would be useful on such occasions.

87. Nickname for heavy enemy shells: it came from the name of Jack Johnson (1878–1946) the world champion heavyweight boxer (1908–15).

88. According to the Regimental Diary, the battalion were in the reserve trenches from 16 June to 19 June, then returning to the Bethune area. Their work included improvement and upkeep of the trenches.

Can you send a pair? This morning there was no chance of Church, for one thing we were expecting to move any minute & for another I knew of no. C of E Service if it had been possible. However I read Epis. Gosp & Psalms so didn't do badly. Your parcels arrived in the trenches. Thank you so much for the things. I've also had a lovely cake from Mrs Turner[89] & a parcel from Mrs Bleistein,[90] its very good of them both. Writing this long letter has brought me to tea time so must stop now
with dear love your very loving Philip

Keeping well, never better

your Thursday letter came today

Some cheap cigarettes for my men wld be most welcome; also Weekly Mirrors or something. They have 'o' to read ever – Relations might like to help. Can you send 2 mouth organs![91]

MC 643/5/9

34.   Wednesday [FSP][?23 June]

Afraid have not written since Sunday. Still in billets, all going well. Getting a good deal of extra work to do with my bombers. Been out 4–7 & 5–8 the last 2 evenings. Interesting letter from Ruth today. No idea when we leave this place. Weather still very hot. Writing this just before turning in to bed so hope it catches post.

Best love

P.

MC 643/5/10

---

89. A Suffolk acquaintance: later letters show she has daughters called Margery and Sylvia. Probably Blanche Turner the wife of George Denn Turner, farmer, of Newbourne Hall near Woodbridge: their daughters, Margery and Mary Sylvia, would have been respectively 25 and 22 in 1916.

90. The mother of Philip's friend at Oxford University.

91. Placed at head of letter.

35.   Friday 25th June

1st L.N.L. Regt. B.E.F. France [92]

My very dearest all It certainly requires the pen of a very ready writer to do justice to the history of the last two days; perhaps those most full of incident & certainly the most novel of my life. We are certainly living a very soldiers life, thanking God each night if we find a roof over our head & a meal ready, if not quite prepared to sleep under the stars & eat bully beef. However, I'd better try & describe these doings or you'll be looking at the end of the letter before you've read this. After my hurried p.c. to you on Wednesday evening I was woken at 6.30 am next morning to say we were "to move at 9.30 am". That was nice & definite wasn't it. That's all we knew except rumours when we "moved" – It was a boiling hot day. However the march was not so interesting so I'll skip it –

<u>Continued Saturday</u> – The march lasted from 9.30 – 12.30 it was very dusty but we got along alright we arrived at our destination wondering where we were going to live & how to feed. I may as well tell you we "moved" about 6 miles further West, not to the trenches this time, we are in for a rest for a week or two perhaps more. We found ourselves in a village about twice (?) -* or less* – the size of Wroxham very very French – funny little houses, all along a straggling long street, with the usual French dirty street. We turned the men (our Coy) through a funny sort of barn & through a little Cottage garden into a field. There they lay until their dinner arrived at about 1.15. It had been cooking on the march<ing> on the "cookers" – The officers as soon as they saw the men well started on their food were taken by a Tommy who had come on in front as a billeting orderly to their "billets"! Oh the billets, I wish you could have seen them. Our mess room was the kitchen of a bigger cottage than the rest. Fairly clean – you walked straight on to it through a door made in 2 halves like a stable door. On the ground floor was another little room in which the family consisting of a very respectable peasant woman & 4 or 5 little children took up their abode. Our servants brought up our Mess box off the transport & by 2.30 we were sitting down to a good meal of tongue potted meat & tinned. That's where goods from home come in useful when you have no time to cook. Immediately after dinner we dashed off to see about the men. You should have seen us after the march, boots, puttees, coats etc, quite whitish with dust & our faces none too clean. We hadn't had good billets allotted to the men, dirty tumble down sheds or barns,

---

92. 'Lapuquey' added in a later hand.

and we had an amusing time poking round trying to find more room airing our best French and asking for "place pour soldats" the good people then launch into a rapid flow of French and you have to wave your hands & mutter "perdu" & "plus lentement", unless you're brave enough to say "Oui" or "Non" & then you never know what you're letting yourself in for. However after a time we got our men some sort of place, each subaltern of course is responsible for the comfort etc of his own platoon. My men were in two rotten sheds, but I went to a place next door & after <u>some</u> parleying managed to buy them some straw. After settling them in we officers got to our billets I shared one with another sub in the Coy., Newman. We <u>did</u> have a queer place, we were in an "Estaminet" – one of the many little beer houses. Every other house nearly is an Estaminet, not like our Eng: <u>pubs</u>; but merely a place where you can drop in & sit down & have some of the horrible French beer or the red wine etc. No drunkenness like in our pubs as the French don't drink like that they just drop in for something to cool them, & their beer & wine is not intoxicating unless drunk by the barrel. Well this place was a detached sort of cottage, the front parlour was a bar; a red bricked floor & some Kitcheny chairs, a little counter in one corner for selling drinks and a <u>huge</u> basket of washing all ready for ironing, an untidy little peasant girl of 16 selling the wine, another & more untidy little girl of 14 ironing the miscellaneous garments, a dirty little child of 8 & the fond fat mother sitting in the doorway. A little room out of this was the place where "shaving done by young lady" was performed; the young lady being the eldest daughter. Out of this led some rickety stairs straight up in to what I suppose the family considered a very fine room, it really was more like a large wooden platform, a great clumsy yellow wooden bedstead occupied most of it and round the walls hung the family's (afore mentioned) Sunday go-to-meeting garments. Out of this led two other rooms, small. One for me, one for the <rest of the> family![93] I won the toss for choice of rooms with Newman so chose the inner one, as the family didn't all have to pass through it to get to their room! Though very crude the place was clean, and the beds too. Mattresses were stuffed with straw & were 2 to 3 feet thick(!) As a precautionary measure I dosed both beds heavily with Keatings.[94] The linen was clean but wonderful stuff, so thick still I slept well. To give you an idea of the troops that moved that day, they passed through that village without stopped from 10 am–7 pm!! a whole

---

93. Philip has drawn a rough sketch of the set-up.

94. A very popular insect powder, advertised as getting rid of 'fleas, bugs, beetles, cockroaches and moths'.

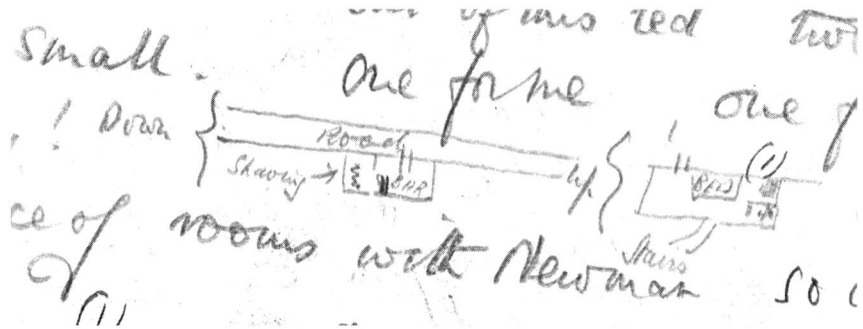

7.   Drawing by Philip from letter 35

division, a truly wonderful sight, I sat on the window sill & watched them. Infantry, & all the transport for each battalion, R.F.A.; ASC: RE, horses mules, waggons, motor lorries, guns, men, right up to the Chaplains <u>never</u> stopping for <u>9 hours</u>. I've never seen so many troops or imagined so many, & then I suppose I only saw ½ the Division & think of all the Divisions. Well I shall be writing tomorrow to tell you the rest. Suffice to say we (B & C Coys) were only allowed 1 day in that place as the billets were not good enough. A & D Coys stayed where they were. But we have to move at 3.30 pm yesterday afternoon in <a> pouring thundering lightning weather. The latter two stopped while we marched but not the rain. We have come further west to the next village about 2½ more miles in <u>pouring</u> rain. We arrived soaked & again went thro' the billeting question, we are now settled in a very straggly place of as far as I've yet seen about 1500 people. I am very well & apparently we're here for a Divisional rest of a week or so. Another draft came from Felixstowe yesterday, 200 of those Manchesters, brought by a sub – Livesey. Must stop now
very cheery & happy

your very loving Philip

Please tell Louisa[95] how sorry I was to hear her sad news. Still she'll be proud of him – Pro Patria.

MC 643/5/11

---

95. Louisa Mathew, a long term live-in servant at Salhouse, born in 1881: the reference is probably to a fiancé rather than a family member. Pro Patria means 'for [the] country, an abbreviation of 'Dulce et decorum est pro patria mori', 'It is sweet and right to die for one's country', a phase used with increasing irony by war poets such as Wilfred Owen.

36.[96]

your account of the trip to Lowestoft. None of us are "bored" out here now, only feeling a bit excited – The Capt. Newman you mention is this Newman. He is Commanding D. Coy. Look out for my Lieut. Gazette – I think it ought to have appeared, but have not seen Times lately. I should not send any parcels for a few days as we may not get them. I now feel very pleased about the opportunities I made use of last Sunday and you know I trust in God in everything. I will write whenever I can.
Now with dearest love
Your very loving

Philip

Field Marshal French has just been thro' here in a car.[97]

MC 643/11/30

37. [*26 June 1915, FSP*]

To cancel news in letter re rest. Off to trenches tomorrow. Just heard. P
26.6.15

MC 643/5/12

38. [*28 June, FSP*]

Monday. In the fire trenches.
5.15 pm.

Arrived here last night. Marched from 10 AM – 7 pm! Scramble lunch in pouring thunderstorm at 1.30. No food between then & 10 am this morning. Sleep 3 hours. Flourishing on it. *Boots & legs* Covered in mud. Trenches all clay-chalk, & after heavy rain filthy. No washing or shaving! I'm a splendid sight & shall be worse still in a day or so. 250 yds from Germans. Safe trenches. Quiet so far. Few shrapnel at a working party under men just now so we've stopped till dark. Got your letter & parcel of pyjamas & clothes just before leaving for the trenches. Looking forward to Harrods parcels[98]. Weather being unsettled. Keeping very fit. Too dirty for long letter. Much love. P.

MC 643/5/13

---

96. Part only, undated.

97. Sir John French (1852–1925), Commander-in-Chief of the British Expeditionary Force from the outbreak of war to December 1915.

98. The well-known London store, which sent parcels to officers at the Front.

39.   29 June [*FSP*]

Tuesday 10 15pm

All well. Here for 5 days. 2 gone. Weather bad. Working hard night & day – shelled heavily this afternoon but Laus Deo[99] no casualties from it. Keeping fit, dirty & smiling! P.

MC 643/5/14

40.   Wednesday 5.40pm. [*30 June, FSP*]

Still alright. Trenches dreadful. Liquid mud & water up to ankles & in many places above boots. Covered in clay & chalky soil – in fact filthy. Can't write letter, working 20 hours out of 24. Been shelled since 1 pm! Shall be very glad to get out, & rest again. Everybody cheery as poss but not having too easy a time.

Much love P.

MC 643/5/15

41.   L.N.L. Regt. B.E.F.

1.7.15

Dearest Ruth

This letter shall go to you. You will have got my p.c.'s written each day, telling you meagre details. I don't think I shall have time for much more now. But I am writing in Gardner's dug out, away on the left of our portion of trench, & just behind the second line of fire trenches ie about 50 yards from fire trench. It is in a quarry, dug into the side nearest the enemy, rather comfy for I'm sitting on a chair writing at a little table. We've had a quiet day today so far 6pm though our guns are just starting their "evening hymn of hate" & I'm afraid the Germans will start theirs in reply soon. I had two fairly narrow escapes yesterday from shells, but though 4 out the many pitched within 5 yards of me I was covered with showers of the earth thrown up & nothing worse. As soon as you hear them coming at you you fall flat or crouch down & – – – wait! after the roar of the explosion & falling earth is over you just say "Thank God" & go on! When you hear them coming you gradually can tell whether they are going right over & beyond you or stopping near you. In the former case of course there's no need to crouch. I am a dreadful sight. I have*

---

99. 'Praise God' (Latin).

not* washed even my little finger since Sunday!! nor yet shaved. My boots &
puttees are caked in solid mud & wet through. My trousers, jacket & cap
also all my equipment are patched all over with mud! I got two <u>very</u> welcome
letters from Mother written on Sunday & Monday today, & one from Father
yesterday, no parcel yet. Unfortunately my dug out candle fell over last night
& set fire to my "pack" – burning that, my towel, airpillow, 1 pr socks &
some of my holdall before it was put out. All the other things were saved; but
can you replace these please? I believe we are being relieved tomorrow, & I
can tell you nobody will be sorry. We have been doing a tremendous amount
of digging & averaging 4 hours sleep in 24! Still I have "stuck it" very well.
It's wonderful what <a man> *the men* can do. The Tommies are wonderful.
Cigarettes w'd be most welcome for them. I have 50 men under me.
Dearest love to all, I am very cheery

from Philip.

MC 643/5/16

42. Friday 7.25 pm. [*2 July, FSP*]

Here we are safe in a farm in billets about 3 miles from the trenches. We had a
quiet finish; but are all v tired & happy to be out. We are probably here 5 days
then – – -? A letter from you & Father today, & such a welcome parcel with
face cream, socks, towel etc. also a splendid one from Mrs Turner with cigs for
the men & cakes choc & sardines. I'm longing for a wash & a bed. I expect
you got a pc each day from me in the trenches I'll always try & do that so
please send me more. Shld <u>love</u> some shampoo powder as suggested much love

P.

MC 643/5/17

43. 1.L.N.L. Regt B.E.F. France

Saturday July 3

Dearest Mother what lovely parcels you do send, thank you ever so much for
them all. The last one has just arrived with the calves jelly, peppermints etc;
a splendid one. I have now got quite a name in the Coy for my parcels, you
see Measham[100] send regularly. I'm writing to them tonight & I've had 2
from Mrs Turner & odd ones from Aunt Em etc; I'm writing now lying out
in a little field behind the farm where we are billeted, it's pretty country &

---

100. Philip's relatives. See Introduction and Appendix 3.

we're in a French village with the usual cobbled dirty roads but we're on the outskirts & the country is very nice. I could imagine I was in Eng: in peace time only for the war noises. You see we are only about 2½ miles from the trenches so some of our guns are all round us. They are so dug in & hidden that you can't see them. Some however must be very close here as they keep going off with huge reports –

We are not "resting" here though we shall have a fairly slack time. Having done our time in the firing line we are now "in reserve" close up; ready to move at ½ an hours notice. You see there are roughly 4 stages. 1) in the firing line. 2) in support, ie in the trenches about 100 yds behind firing line 3) in reserve. 4) resting – When in the trench three Coys in a battalion are generally no 1 and 1 Coy is no 2. If we are lucky we shall get no 4 after our 5 days here as no 3. Oh the joy last night of a bed & a wash. I slept from 10.30 – 8.30, we did not have breakfast till 9.30 & the men have spent the day cleaning up. We averaged 4 hours sleep (broken) in the 24 in the trenches. The remainder spent walking in & out up & down the narrow trench ankle deep in mud & water. But really though very unpleasant we were always cheery & slopped through it, & I can say I enjoyed my 5 days; I got some thorough experience of being under shell fire in them & have got 4 beautiful chunks of shells as mementoes of the three that burst near me on Wednesday evening. I collected 3 or 4 handfuls of bits but kept these as the best. A trench is a wonderfully safe place under shellfire, it is so deep & narrow. Though we probably had 100's of shells at us those days none pitched in the trench though some hit the parapet & a shell unless it's shrapnel is <fairly> very local in effect. I lost one poor man in my platoon sniped through the head looking over the parapet, his second day in the trenches, from the last draft. As you know that was my first sight of a man "killed in action" but I'm glad to say I took it quite naturally. I am going to write to his people. I am very glad to hear Harold has a commission, he has got in a branch of the service which will suit him I think.[101] Your letter written Thursday came today. Your picture of me is fairly accurate though we were more often wearing waistcoats & great coats than shirt sleeves this time in. I used to try to imagine the trenches & fighting area before I came out but you can't! Seeing it is the only thing <u>and</u> hearing it. I should like some< Eno &> fruit salts. And Bp Ton last bottle broke.
More tomorrow

Dearest love from Philip

---

101. Philip's cousin Harold Tyndale-Biscoe, in the Royal Flying Corps. He was Julian's brother.

I am very well and cheery

One feels after coming out of the trenches one has a lot to be Thankful for.

44. 1.L.N.L. Regt. B.E.F. France. Sunday [*4 July*]

Dearest All Nothing has happened since I wrote yesterday, but I can't miss my Sunday letter when it's possible to write. I got your letter written on Thursday today. You know you mustn't think we are having a very bad time, those five days were certainly a hard time and made one wonder how our men ever "stuck it" in the winter, but we all came through all right & are none the worse for it. It's a great experience. Marching back from the trenches for 2 miles or so you keep seeing old disused trenches, broken rusty barbed wire, and shell holes. And you try & imagine these places as the scene of some of the titanic winter struggles. Sometimes you see a little wooden Cross, and nearly every other house in the little French village we passed thro' is raised right to the ground or has 3 sides or ½ a roof. Yet you see the inhabitants still in those that have not been hit. Today the heat is absolutely oppressive but we are hoping the day will end in a thunder storm. The great objection to France now is the Flies, oh they are dreadful!! Specially as we live in a not too clean farmhouse.

The parcels you send me are splendid, & outnumber everybody else's in the Mess! The one today was v useful, cigs, tobacco, hair powder & papers & socks. I was v. interested in the papers we had not seen one the 5 days we were in the trenches. Do you realise that Lt J. G. Smyth V.C. is my Repton friend, you'll find his photo in my drawer, I used to know him <u>well</u>, he was in the Priory.[102]

We had a nice Church Parade in the open under the trees this morning; only our Bn; all the Ch. of E. men and officers, voluntary tho' most came. It was my first service since leaving Eng. & I did enjoy it, it was good to hear those men just come out from 5 days in the trenches, some after near escapes, singing the hymns & following the Prayers etc. The chaplain gave a good short helpful address of about 5 minutes. Very well still..

Dearest love, your loving

Philip.

---

102. Notice of Smyth's award appeared in the *London Gazette* on 29 June 1915. The Priory was one of the 'houses' within Repton school.

45.   July 6 Tuesday [*FSP*]

Still in the same place. Weather extraordinarily hot. Having a slack time each day but work from 9 pm to small hours of the morning each night. Then we have breakfast about 10 am no idea <u>of</u> where, when or how we shall move or what do next. Keeping very fit Much love P.

MC 643/5/20

46.   1ˢᵗ L.N. Lanc Regt B.E.F. France

Thursday July 8

My very dear All you will I know be wondering where I am now and what doing. We moved from the village, which we went to, after the trenches, yesterday. We have not however gone further away but have moved up to another village about 1 mile from the firing line if that. I call it a village but parts of it are a very sad sight, it is continually shelled and here you see "war." To such an extent is it knocked about that many of the troops here live in dug outs. My Coy: does for one, & I too sleep in a dug tho' the B Coy officers have their meals in a cottage just the other side of the road which has so far escaped a direct hit on it. (Just had an interval for tea, very nice too. Sardines in tomato sauce, marmalade cake & some cherries just come to Newman. A very good tea, and I made the most of it as I've got to parade at 6.30, and then march to the trenches & dig from 7–10 and then return to my evening meal. While we were in the other village we still worked. For we paraded at 8.30 each evening. Then marched for about 1½ hours "Somewhere in N. France" towards the firing line. We then dug roughly from 10–1 am got back about 2.30 am Had some tea & cake or biscuits then into bed till 8.30 am & jolly ready for it too. A tremendous lot of digging is going on now, you may read the signs in the Papers, the Kaiser's again after "Calais" or will be soon so they say.[103] We continue the work we started from there from here now, it's better as it's a shorter walk. As I said they have a habit of shelling this place and they greeted us at tea time yesterday by doing it. It got hot in this little part of the world so we retired into a cellar below the house till it was over & were quite safe. We are next a farm, built in a square with a courtyard in the middle as all Fr farms. This they hit 4 times and when we came out into the road it was covered with bricks & tiles and

---

103. Kaiser Wilhelm II (1859–1941), Emperor of Germany 1888–1918. Although German attacks were expected in the summer of 1915, they did not in fact materialise.

debris of all sorts. The only casualties 2 hens & 2 pigeons! Father's & Ruth's letters yesterday & Mother's lovely long Tuesday one today. Well done Ruth at tennis! I heard from K.A.W.[104] & Hugh too yesterday we do enjoy letters. Parcels seem hung up at present. No Harrods or A & N yet.[105] I can still say I am very fit, though the extreme heat makes one slack & a bit liverish sometimes. On the whole splendid tho! Could do with some Bp Tons. Dearest love

P.

MC 643/5/21

47. Friday 6.30 pm [*9 July, FSP*]

Still flourishing. If nothing happens to stop it I shall have a full night's sleep tonight, the 2nd in 13 days, so am looking forward to it. No digging tonight. Another letter from you today & an airpillow fr H.S.[106] I can get pack here. A splendid parcel from Gobagger. It has taken exactly 14 days so parcels take longer. Uncle Fred has sent papers for the men. Not shelled us again yet. Concussion of our own guns close to breaks our windows unless they are kept open. Getting lively now. Alright so long as the compliment's not returned. Weather cooler. Very fit & cheery. Much love

P.

MC 643/5/22

48. 1st L.N.L. Regt B.E.F. France

Sunday July 11

My very dear all, here's another Sunday letter. As you say in your Thursday letter which came to-day you expected us to move on Wednesday & as you now know we did. We are now hoping for another on Tuesday, this time back West for a week or 10 days rest. This we shall be quite ready for as we shall have had a hard 15 days work, though only 5 days were spent in the trenches the other 10 have been spent quite close up, always liable to be heavily shelled at any time and also digging hard! This new German offensive that everybody is talking about is certainly making us

---

104. Not otherwise identified.

105. The Army and Navy Stores: a major London department store, which, like Harrods, sent out parcels.

106. Hugh Strong.

work. As the ground here is hard chalk after you get down a foot or two you can imagine it takes some hard digging. When you dig at night it's very interesting, lots of our guns are just behind us and keep going off with huge reports, first you see the flash, then you hear the huge cracking report of the gun, and this is the most interesting if it's a dark night & you are quick at looking up you can see the white hot shells as they pass over your head! You then hear them whistling away in the distance, then next you see their flash as they burst and some seconds after you hear the explosion. It all requires practice of course, and I'm not by any means an adept at it yet, but you get to be able to tell the burst of the shell from the report of the gun, whether when shells pass over head to some far target, they are your own going or theirs arriving; whether when you hear a German shell coming towards you it is going to pitch short, whether it is aimed at you or whether it is going to pass harmlessly over your head and hit some poor village behind – To be able to do this naturally saves a tremendous amount of unnecessary speculation & ducking behind cover. It's very fascinating in the trenches, you hear these big "coalboxes" etc come whistling at you, you wonder where it's coming, however some of the men know at once it will pass over, & the Tommies take no notice of them though they may be pitching <only> 30–100 yards away only. A big shell always gives you plenty of time to flop down or dive into a handy dug out as you hear them coming 2 or 3 seconds before they burst. That's why shrapnel is so deadly, it gives you no warning, you just hear swish bang, swish bang as they burst. You call them "Pip-Squeaks" or "Yes-Nos" – . Where we are digging now is about 1000 yards behind the firing line. It is the scene of the furious fighting between the French & Germans in January. Here the French drove the Germans back.[107] Through the new trench we are making runs the old German trench at right angles to our new one. The broken barbed wire entanglements are still up in front, and though much overgrown in places the Germ: trench is still 5 or 6 feet deep. In many places it has been blown in, I suppose by the bombardment it must have had before being captured. The dug outs have mostly fallen in but you can see where they are & some are still in fair repair. The German loop holes can still be looked through though all you see is a hay crop. The country is rolling pastureland, a few clumps of trees away behind us and some pit heads. In the near distance are

---

107. The Germans attacked the Allied front line near Givenchy on 25 January 1915: after fierce fighting by the French, the advance was stopped, the Germans driven back and lost trenches recovered.

some villages, all more or less knocked about by shelling, one especially received its death knell a few days ago & is now little more than a collection of ruined houses, I was looking at it through glasses to-day. It is a mere scrap heap of bricks. Nearer to us a few yards away, in fact just behind the old German line are some bricks with what was once a roof on them which were once a French peasants home. The ground all round is made up of graves, little wooden crosses or little mounds, one poor Bosch only <u>just</u> under the soil, all signs of "War" – It is very interesting wandering round looking for souvenirs, however there is not much to be found now as the ground has probably had many an eager eye scanning since January. Lying about everywhere are old bottles, remains of stoves, pots & pans, cartridge clips, etc. I found an old waterproof, an old rotting blue French tunic, a German pack, but all too weather spoilt to do more than turn them over with my stick These relics are not of course in the open country but in & near to the trenches.

The papers & the Powers-that-be out here are evidently expecting a big German offensive here soon. We are told so. Well if they come we are ready for them. It is what the men have been waiting for for months. Let them make their big effort we shall cause them many more casualties if they attack than if we attack. When they do however they will – it will be neck or nothing – here's the explanation of our practically working day & night digging for 10 days. Don't worry about the "pack" – as H.S. says I didn't want that replacing, I had the regulation Tommies pack on my back & can get that replaced here. Father's letter written Thursday came today too. I had a ripping box of fresh fruit from Measham yesterday & sent a p.c. in acknowledgement. Yes I noticed Gardner seconded I think it is quite time I was too, I want my second star! I've been gazetted 11 months now you know! Today being Sunday has made no difference to our daily routine. Digging Parade 8.15 am march up there, dig 9am–12.45. Back here 1.30 Lunch. Then the mens letters to be censored. Then read our own letters. Tea. Writing now 6pm. Tonight we dig from 9 pm–12 – I shall be extraordinarily pleased when Hugh comes out, I shall like an old friend here, though the subs. out here are quite a nice lot. Of course Gardner & Livesey are both here, & it's nice when I meet them. Newman is best of the others. You made a good shot with number two in your letter. It was a bulls eye. Today's not been so hot, but cool & inclined to rain. It's extraordinary how easy it is to entirely forget what day of the week it is here. The Bps Tons & Eno came yesterday. Orders just come no digging tonight – Cheery Oh!! It shows you never know ½ an hour ahead what you'll be doing next. Well very dear love to you all. These 5 weeks have already taught me much of the "Power of Prayer" & the need for it. It makes us all "think" out here. Dear love

your very loving Philip.

49.   Tuesday afternoon [*13 July, FSP*]

Just going to move 5 miles back. Hope we stay there a few days at least. Splendid parcel from Harrod's yesterday, also another from Folkestone. We've had breakfast 6.30 the last 2 days & dug yesterday 8–2 pm and today 8–12. Very close weather. Two things I want 1) a pair of "stocking puttees" v. useful at night in trenches as they are made like a stocking & can be taken on & off quickly. 2) a "holdall" for my washing requisites. Greatly looking forward to getting out of my clothes for a good night's sleep again, will write fuller when we've moved. We had a good selection of parcels yest so have several dainties about. I hope Sunday's letter did not get delayed, it was a bit late. This place has been shelled the last 2 days but we were out of it at the time – Still keeping fit.

Much love P.

50.   1 L.N.L. B.E.F. France [*19 July*][108]

Sunday

Dearest all, not much news as we are still here in our coal mining village & have no idea now when or where we shall move. One thing I want you to send by return if possible. All the subalterns have got to get them. That is my 2 books on military matters one called "Infantry Training" & the other "Field Service Pocket Book", they shld be with my Felixstowe things, quite small about 3 inches square. This morning we had breakfast at 8.30 & an officers meeting at 9.30. Church Parade was to be at 11. All the Coys: paraded ready to march there & we started & then found we did not know where the Service was! or some muddle, so we had to be 'about turned' & marched back so there was no Ch: Parade today. Last night our M.O. (doctor) got up a good concert out of doors. The performers being drawn from the N. Lancs and another battalion also in billets here. The latter had a regimental band out here so with some good songs too the

---

108. Dated by postmark.

Concert was quite a success About 12.30 this morning 3 of us subalterns in this Coy went into a cottage garden here & bought 2 good plates full of "framboises" (raspberries) wh: we picked ourselves & had for lunch, very good too. You must not worry about me being tired, because I am not! In the trenches you get used to snatching spells of ½ hour or more & you soon get used to it. Naturally one is sleepy at times but nothing to <u>worry</u> about. When we're out in billets we really have a very easy & jolly life as we are doing now. You can go up to the top of the coal pit here & get a view for miles all round, & can see a lot thro' glasses. It's very interesting. I shall be v pleased if Hugh comes out. The other B Coy officers well we get on alright but I'd like Hugh out here too. Keeping well-er than ever now. Very dear love to all

Philip.

MC 643/5/25

51. 1. L.N.L. Regt. B.E.F. France

Tuesday July 20

Dearest all we have moved once more, and are now in a village in billets nearer the firing line[109]. We moved by night yesterday and marched from 9–11. This owing to the road on which we finished our march being able to be seen by the Germans. The place here is badly knocked about & can easily be seen by the Germans from their observation posts or balloons so we have to be careful how we walk about by day. At least the men are not allowed out in groups & are supposed to stay in their billets during day time. We are again going to do a lot of digging here. The billets are I think the worst we have been in so far. Three of us in a little room above a sort of estaminet & shop combined kept by a woman whose husband has been a prisoner since September. We found two iron bed-steads with straw mattresses on them. One had two so we decided to put one on the floor for one of us & the other two would have the 2 beds. We tossed for the three positions, the floor & the 2 beds. One bed was much better *than* the other. I was very fortunate & won the toss so got the best bed, with my valise & air pillow I was really much better off than at first seemed possible so were we all. I can't answer yr: last letter as letters can't come up till after dark here.

---

109. On 19 July the Loyal North Lancashires were relieved by 1ˢᵗ King's Liverpool (6ᵗʰ Brigade) and withdrew to billets in the Verquin-Bethune area.

The birthday cake has come & is much appreciated by all. Another parcel came yesterday, potted meat etc but badly smashed! On Sunday evening the mine manager in whose house we were billeted invited us all to dinner & gave us a splendid feed with some wine & cigars. It was nice sitting down at a table cloth etc again & being waited on. In case of bombardment here there are good cellars & trenches. The Church here has no roof & only ½ a tower. Many houses knocked about too. Very well still

Dearest love – Philip.

MC 643/5/26

52.   1ˢᵗ L.N.L. Regt. B.E.F. France

July 23 1915

My very dear all I am afraid I have not written since Tuesday. There was not much news on Wednesday but yesterday I meant to write but had unexpectedly to go up with a digging party and did not get back in time to write. In this letter I am enclosing some pics of the village about ½ an hours march from here where we go & dig. There is not one house standing. There was some of the fiercest fighting of the war there last October when the French drove out the Germans by street fighting which lasted 5 weeks![110] It is a town of the dead, not a living civilian anywhere, just as if there had been a colossal earthquake. Houses with no roofs & no walls – everything overgrown. Rusty twisted unrecognisable pieces of furniture, wagons, farm machines etc. Telegraph poles broken in half with twisted wires all round them. Shell holes in the road. It has been shelled continually since October & there is now nothing much left to shell except piles of bricks & tumble down walls. The stocking puttees arrived yesterday, thank you so much they will be most welcome & useful. Some currants arrived too but the tin was dented <it> in and the currants had become juice & "juiced" everything. I had one of the official p.c.s from Julian on which he had left uncrossed out "I am sick & hope to be discharged soon" – He had also left other words uncrossed out wh: made no sense so I don't know whether he is ill or whether he was trying to make a poor joke!? I had just written to him so my letter & this curious p.c. of his may have crossed. I got the pudding recipes alright & we are now waiting till we can get flour wh we can't in this poor little village. We have got our mess

---

110. The initial German advance was halted and eventually thrust back in October 1914 – the amount of France occupied by the Germans was reduced from 7.5% to 4% before stalemate and trench warfare set in.

in a little cottage owned by an old couple of 85 & 83 respectively. Dear old people who have just settled down here as a last home bought *out* of their savings. It was I hear very pathetic to see them yesterday, when the place was being heavily shelled for a short time, sitting together down in their cellar. I was not here as I was away with digging party but watched the shells bursting through my glasses. They knocked the houses about a good deal and one unfortunately hit the barn in wh: half my platoon were, it killed one & wounded 4. Another shell killed my servant.[111] I am so sorry about it, such a nice young chap who left Felixstowe with me 7 weeks ago yesterday. I have written to their people & sent back a few little belongings such as letters found in their pockets. We buried one in the little Churchyard here. My servant died on the way to hospital.

An amusing side to the shelling however is that you may see Mgor Browne's[112] name in the casualty list, a tiny piece hit him in the finger & he only had to put a piece of sticking plaster on it but he has gone in as "wounded".

I am as well as anything, flourishing & cheery!! Very pleased that the Sergeant who I last had under me at F : & left behind there has just come out & is under me here! I heard from Mrs Banks yest: she sent a small parcel & I had some cakes (2) from Mrs Turner, v. g. of them. We shall be going tonight in the trenches again on Sunday for 4 or 5 days. But this Coy: will not be <u>right</u> up in the firing line. So don't worry. I am well & cheery, & what more can you want?

Very dear love, your very loving

Philip.

MC 643/5/27

53. 1.L.N.L. Regt B.E.F. France

Sunday July 25 1915

My very dear Mother, Father & Ruth, I am writing this immediately after lunch, it is now 2 pm & I expect you are at S. School while F has a well earned rest in the study before going on to Salhouse. We are going up into the trenches to night, starting from here at half past eight. I thought

---

111. The men in question are probably Private Samuel Williams and Private Robert Barclay, of 1 Bn, both killed in action on 22 June: Williams was buried in Fouquieres churchyard.

112. See Appendix 2.

I should be able to have a nice slack Sunday all to myself but one officer per Coy: has got to be up in the trenches wh: we are going into by 5 pm to take over trench stores, that means the permanent ammunition, bombs etc. I am to go wh: means leaving here about 4 and then waiting about up there till the Bn: arrives about 9.30. I shall invite myself to a meal with the regt: there already. I also believe Gardner is already up there somewhere with his machine guns so I shall try & find him & have a chat so time may not pass so heavily after all. But it is a horrible nuisance having to go up there at that hour, hours before the Bn: even starts. A most welcome parcel arrived from home last night with <u>books</u> in, "Quinneys"[113] & a magazine <u>and</u> a "space", the paper was broken & something had fallen out, was it my two infantry books, I thought it probably was – still it won't matter much. I can always say they started but were not passed by the Censor or something like that, & I don't suppose we shall ever want them so very badly tho' we *were* ordered to get them – some of the usual & unnecessary "red tape" <u>I</u> consider – I did enjoy Ruth's last letter, I rolled with joy & laughed like anything over her description of poor Miss de P: – of course I was very sorry for her, but was awfully amused at the idea of R. being asked what she'd done to Miss de P[114]. I understand that most of the work in these trenches will be digging by night, so we shall be able I hope very much in this Coy: at any rate to spend a good deal of the day sleeping or reading & writing specially as we are not right in the Firing Line so if that is so you can imagine how I shall <u>love</u> a good book. A man has just come in with the 2 Infantry Bks & a ripping pencil, most useful, they were found at the bottom of the mail bag! So they broke out this end of their journey. I wonder how F[115] is getting on with the mo-bike. I look forward to when I again spin along on it. I played in my footer match yesterday evening. It was very hot especially in puttees & nailed boots etc. Still we had a good game & just lost 1–2. You often found yourself in long grass or corn. Still the Tommies loved it. Then it was my turn to go digging at night. So I was up there from 9–1 am, superintending the party from this Coy. I was back & in bed by 2 am. This morning another party went digging & this afternoon another. Tonight we move. So Sunday is just the same as other days. I was glad of a quiet morning this morning. I am still v, well & cheery. Do you realise when you get this I shall have been out nearly 2 months.

---

113. Probably the comic play by Horace Annesley Vachell, first published in 1913.
114. Miss de Putron, Ruth's games mistress at Norwich High School for Girls.
115. 'ather' added by Philip's mother.

Very dear love

your very loving

Philip

We are in trenches till Saturday I believe.

54.   1 L.N.L. Regt B.F.F. France [*30 July*]¹¹⁶

Friday 4.15pm

My dear Ruth I had a splendid post to-day & after the parcel that came I feel like taking back a few of the things I said yesterday about parcels being delayed & lost, but I won't because tho' this one came quickly I do know how v. many never come at all both for the men & the officers. The one that came today had the peas & chicken in it, a <u>great</u> success. We had some of the peas with tongue for lunch & are going to have the rest with the chicken for dinner tonight – shan't we have had a day in the food way!! Both are beautifully fresh & I <u>am</u> looking forward to some home chicken. I also got Mother's letter & yours, I always enjoy yr news. We've had a very slack day today not nearly as strenuous as the time table ones quoted yesterday. Last night I personally was not out with a digging party & got to bed from 11–2 and again from 4–8, so got some good sleep. Before going to bed at 11 I was doing some very interesting work eg. marking out the lines of the new trench with tape ready for digging out in front of our present firing line. Quite exciting work too, out in the open, but beyond an occasional sniper everything was quiet & of course even snipers cannot shoot accurately at night. It's all guess work. So we were really very safe, if we had been seen we could always have flopped down in the long grass. Both sides dig at night & neither bothers about the other, as if they do it means stopping all their own work to do it. This morning after breakfast I inspected my platoon's rifles etc. Then there was 'o' to do but laze. The Germans must have decided that we must sleep too much so they shelled us. But no damage was done as all fell outside the trench. It's a lovely day again, but nowadays it's very cold at nights. Two months out today! I've enjoyed reading papers, mags & lazing today.

Much love from Philip.

---

116. Dated by postmark.

55.   1. L. N. Lanc. Regt. B.E.F. France

July 31 1915

My very dear Mother & Father The last two parcels which have arrived have been too splendid for words. Thank you ever so much for them. The one contained the chicken & peas & those ripping peppermint "cracklets" – we had the chicken & peas for dinner at night, & the home grown products <u>were</u> just [*sic*] appreciated. The next parcel that came arrived to-day, the sweet & fruit one, in splendid condition, calling forth tremendous shrieks of delight as you can imagine when it was opened in this dugout. I'm afraid that when the renowned chicken rissoles arrive they'll cause a stampede!! I also got Mother's letter this morning written on Tuesday, & calculated to get here on Friday but posts are generally a day later in the trenches. I certainly am very pleased to have my old sergeant from Felixstowe, oh yes, when you meet old friends out here you always shake hands whether they are N C Os or men. Sgt. Trimmer is in another Coy. & I never see him. I had a tremendous piece of good fortune today. Phillips has come out from Felixstowe, he has been at the base for 10 days & came up to join us in the trenches last night. He has come to this Coy, this morning and is to command B Coy. Isn't that splendid! I am awfully pleased. I could not manage a letter yesterday as I turned into my dugout and slept all the afternoon. Which I expect will please you very much. During that time there was a terrific <bombard> (no) thunderstorm & torrents of rain for about ½ an hour. When I woke up about 5.15, the trenches were once more liquid mud & water, & all the wood for fires wet through, everything was sopping wet. However we slopped about as we did in the other trenches. The servants got us some tea somehow by 5.45. When the trenches are like that they are dreadfully uncomfortable & you are caked in mud very soon, or rather everything you touch is muddy, however it is wonderful what a lot of amusement you get out of your discomfort <u>and</u> (very much so) other peoples. When we were walking down the trenches in the evening going down to digging it was really killing to see Newman floundering & slopping about in front of me, so nearly & so often nearly sitting down in a puddle, & I expect I presented the same appearance to my follower. We dug from 9–1.30 am. And I got to bed at 4 as usual & slept like a log till 8.30. Going to bed with ½ the trenches on your boots is not a practise I should recommend & so I am going to ask you to send my "gum-boots" out, and also as the mornings & nights are so cold now please send my brown "woolly" with long sleeves. It is nice & long in the body. I always wear a body belt in the trenches and this last time I've always put on a thin vest but next time in I shall put on a thick one. Of course you only need an aertex shirt by day but the nights <u>are</u> cold. I have thick vests out here I think, if not I'll let you know to morrow. It would be better to send out the woolly by itself as the boots might be delayed. Also I'm quite ready for some cigarettes when you send some. We leave the trenches tonight & you can think of me for a few days sleeping in pyjamas & a bed, and having a real thorough wash. The first for 12 days! Today has been a lovely summer day after yesterday's wet & we are all drying. Still fit as anything. It's really a splendid open air life.

Very much love

Your very loving

Philip.

MC 643/5/30

---

56. 1st. L.N.L. Regt B.E.F. France

August 1 1915

My very dear all Here's another Sunday letter, not written from the trenches this time. We moved out last night as I said we were going to in yesterday's letter. We did not leave the trenches till nearly 11 pm. And then had a 3 hour march by night. It was really a lovely night & quite fine. Of course it's a bit of a hard finish for some of the men to 6 days in the trenches to march that distance with feet & boots not improved by the sloppy conditions which we had the last 2 days in. However the Coy really got along well, specially my platoon (I think). We brought up the rear of the Coy, & I marched alongside the leading "four" – For the last 1½ hours I hardly stopped whistling once, I kept on starting tunes, & some of the cheery souls in front joined in, & so we kept up quite a swinging step. Of course there are always some men who decide before we've started even that it's a dreadful long march & so sulk & "grouse" all the time. But it would do you good to see the cheery ones, trudging along, muddy & tired <u>perhaps</u>, but singing, whistling, & cracking jokes the whole time! We are back once more in billets with <u>beds & sheets</u> for the first time for 12 days, <u>and</u> in pyjamas once more! I have been in the town[117] twice before. It is where I joined the Battalion two months ago tomorrow. I slept till 9.30 this morning & then got up & had a perfectly splendid toilet.

I am sharing a room with Phillips. It is in a sort of artisans little cottage. A row of little houses in one road – in one I sleep & the downstairs room

---

117. Bethune.

of another is the Coy. Mess. The owners of my house put a tub full of water in their "parlour" downstairs so I had a ripping bath. There is a voluntary C. of E. Service some where here this evening wh: I shall try & get to. Two such <u>splendid</u> long letters from you today. I am wondering if a letter (written to Ruth for her birthday I think) ever arrived? For in <it> your last letters you keep wondering if I don't want more cigarettes for myself – and today Father doesn't seem sure if the 1250 he sent ever came? Now in<the> some letta [*sic*] I'm sure I both asked for some more for myself & also said how <u>very</u> much the men appreciated the 1250 and send their thanks to the giver. I thought I had put this in the letter to Ruth. I am glad you have got 2 goods maps of the war. The one you got first is really very good and ought to last you for the present. You really mustn't be so extravagant & go buying anything bigger yet. I was amused at M's bit about Bp. Tons I <u>do</u> take them sometimes though when I feel I want them. What <u>I am</u> enjoying is "Quinneys" – and the magazines too. Aunt Helen sent 2 6d novels today. It's V. interesting you mentioning about the photographs – Because we 4 subs. of B. Coy have been 'taken' – at that village where we stopped in the mine manager's house and the scoundrel of a man has never sent them to us – but we are on his tracks! You ask about washing – well the usual procedure is to have your bath <u>in</u> your basin or rather near your basin. You manage to wash all over but that's the only receptacle for water you have. You really get quite an adept at that sort of thing. A "toilet" in the trenches is really quite a work of art too! I gather from your letter that Julian is quite well, his p.c. therefore strikes me as being peculiarly asinine. Officers do not send p.c. about saying they are ill when they are not "for a joke"!! In night work in the trench a servant always gets us tea or cocoa when we finish. It's a lovely August day so hot. I'm writing in shirt sleeves, & can't imagine how I wanted warm things yesterday; the weather however is always cold in the early morning. I must stop now – with very dear love

your very loving

Philip.

MC 643/5/31

57.   Monday [*2 Aug.*]

Dearest mother & father

Just a hurried line – post time. Here's a bad photo I'm afraid of B. Coy Subs. Cut off our legs & we look better. Another letter from Mother today. Busy today. Had a ripping ride on horseback this afternoon, out about 3 miles &

back to watch some bombing practice; all by myself. Got on well, though caught in a violent thunderstorm – otherwise lovely day. Gooseberries just come. In better condition than last currants, but inclined to squishy squash. So nice to have "home" fruit but I <u>really</u> don't think fresh <u>garden</u> fruit is worth the postage. Its always so risky sending it & if it spoils it invariably spoils the rest of the parcel. There are other things more valuable to us which we can't buy here. Fruit we can! Letter from Vera[118] today awfully jolly of her, & a parcel from Mrs Bleistein!

Dear love P.

MC 643/5/32

58. 1ˢᵗ L.N. Lanc. Regt, B.E.F. France

3.viii.15

My dear Father I think I ought to be patriotic! What I mean to say is I've now got £70 in the Bank! and I want you to get me some "War Loan" – I don't know how it's done but I am going to enclose a cheque for £15 payable to you & will you please do the rest? I sound awfully rich don't I so I think I cannot very well not help the Loan.[119] No more news since yesterday. Thunderstormy all day. I'm not stiff after my ride! The gooseberries we had after dinner last night & they were very good. Another letter from Mother to-day & a parcel from Gobagger.
Much love to all

your very loving

Philip.

MC 643/5/33

59. Thursday

My very dear all Just another short note. Mother's letter written on Sheringham beach came today, it's not so difficult to picture you all there. Tonight the officers of B. Coy are entertaining the officers of the D Coy & Major Monteagle–Browne now commanding the Batt while the C.O. is on leave for dinner tonight. This is the menu, not bad for active Service.

---

118. Vera Ward daughter of Edward and Zilla Ward of Salhouse Hall, thus a near neighbour of Philip and his family: she was about 24 in 1915. Letter 110 mentions an unidentified 'Vera's He', presumably her boyfriend/fiance.

119. War loans (debt securities) were issued by the Government to finance the war. The first was issued in November 1914. Philip is referring to the second, issued in June 1915.

<u>Hors d'oeuvre</u> (olives, salted herring, Tomatoes & hard boiled egg)
<u>Consommé</u>
<u>Fish</u> (cold fried plaice. Potato Salad)
<u>Roast Beef</u> Potatoes Vegetables
<u>Tinned Pheasant</u> & slice ham. Green Salad
<u>Patisseries</u>
<u>Cheese</u> (2 sorts)
<u>Fruit</u> Melon & Greengages
<u>Coffee</u>
Liqueur
French wines to drink or Beer. There what do you think of that! all in the little back room of an artisan's little house. We were entertained by D the last time we were here 4 weeks ago so it's our turn now. Our time is up here tomorrow & we go back to the trenches tomorrow where or for how long I don't know. We've had a good time here, & I've enjoyed the good night's rests, I expect my "woolly" will be coming? Had a short route march this morning & this afternoon have been shopping for this evening. Weather is much more like August now hot – very well – dear love

your very loving Philip.

MC 643/5/34

60.   Somewhere in France

August 7 1915

My very dear all Here I am once more – In the Trenches – this time up in the firing line.[120] However it's a fairly good place as we are about three hundred yards from the enemy trenches. We got here at 7 last night. I remembered this time to put some good chocolate in my pocket for which I and the others were extremely thankful, as the Mess Box did not arrive till the small hours of the morning.

The regiment we relieved went up high in my estimation as the officers who occupied this dugout left some wine & beer behind so I was able to have some choc, & wine before I turned in about 9.30 – I slept till just after 2 when I got up & have been round & about ever since. It's now 2.45 p.m. At 4 am this morning the servants got us some cocoa & we had some bread,

---

120. According to the Regimental Diary, the battalion left billets and marched by platoon through Beuvry to Annequin and relieved the 1st Black Watch. 'B' Company was assigned the left (north) section of the front line. As Philip notes, the German trenches were about 300 yards away.

butter & potted meat, most welcome. They are very nice dry trenches, cut in sandy soil rather than chalk & so much better. I enjoyed the days rest we had very much & the brown woolly arrived just in time & the cigarettes, tobacco & cocoatina – thank you so much. I'm afraid I must miss thanking relations & friends personally for all the parcels! Mrs Bleistein sent another last week. I share a dug out with Phillips. There are 2 rooms in it. Both about 8ft by 5. One the Mess the other the bedroom. We sleep one above the other, like in a ship's berths. I'm just going to turn in for a snooze now. Very well & cheery. Very dear love

Your very loving Philip.

MC 643/5/35

61. Monday

My very dear all. I am back in billets once more, we only had 48 hours in the trenches this time, & left last night at 7pm. We've come back to the village where we were after those 5 bad days in, but not into the same billets, but into better ones. The Mess is a nice big room in what was a biggish bakery, we've got the ex-front parlour. Not much furniture but what there is is good & the room is clean & about as big as our dining room, quite a luxury! a nice round table in the middle, 5 cane chairs, 1 easy one, a side board; & big looking glass over the mantelpiece & on it a clock wh: doesn't go. I've got a room next door, in quite a nice house. The room is bare, bare walls & floor a bed in one corner & 2 chairs, one with no bottom – <u>But</u> there is electric light. The room is clean but rather too near a Courtyard wh: savours rather too much of the farm! now occupied by some French transport horses. We had a fairly quiet time in the trenches, snipers very busy, & also some trench mortars hurled at us, but all rather to our left & no damage done by them.

The weather was good & the trenches comfortable, being made up with a lot of sandbags, wh: always keep them in better condition. I went out with Goldie & 12 men from 11–12 on Saturday night to cut the grass in front of our barbed wire but we were seen & had to get back into the trench after about an hours' work.[121] The chicken & peas arrived & were excellent, thank you so much. Only don't put ham in it's inclined to turn. The gum boots came too & I enjoyed all the extras. also a parcel of lem: crystals

---

121. The Regimental Diary notes that a group of men were immediately sent out to cut the grass in front of the wire. This was to avoid the risk of German attackers reaching the British front line without being spotted.

today, most useful. I enjoyed F's letter today & was very amused to see my letters in print.[122] "Stand to" & its time however are "contraband" goods, not be mentioned. You were asking how to use the map you had. Well you count the figures along the bottom then up. This X is 2. 4.[123]

Very well

Dear love

Philip.

MC 643/5/36

62. 1. L.N.L. Regt.

B.E.F. France

9. VIII. 15 Monday 7 pm (Post missed to-day)

My dear Ruth. A letter from Father came this afternoon wh: said you were going to Folkestone on Monday so I presume you've gone today! I didn't expect to be here now, this time we were only in the trenches for 48 hours so are back in the billets some time before I thought we should be. We left the trenches at 7 pm last night & got here just before 9. We were about 250–350 yards from the German trenches, the distance varied a little. You could see their trenches quite well through a periscope. A periscope is absolutely invaluable. It is however quite safe to look over the parapet for a few seconds provided you don't look over in the same place twice running – That's the whole secret of looking over safely. No sniper can hit a man if he only pops up for a few secs in an unexpected place. It's when some one looks over several times in the same place that the sniper can wait for him.[124] It's very difficult in most places to see the enemy trenches & for

---

122. Parts of Philip's letters had been published by his parents in the Wroxham and Salhouse church magazine, August 1915.

123. Philip has drawn a small chart.

124. The sniping is described in the Regimental Diary:: 'A continuous bombing duel day and night and very sharp sniping on the part of the enemy is our daily round. We have two batteries who open fire when ordered in retaliation to the enemy's shelling which is not heavy.... We also make use of a large number of rifle grenades, by this means and with the aid of several trench mortars the enemy is kept under, but he has by far the upper hand in sniping. This is entirely due to our lack of real bullet-proof iron loop holes with shutters. Those now in the trenches are not bullet-proof and give no security to man firing through them hence the German picked shots can watch the whole of our line with absolute security and whenever a head, hand or periscope shows above our parapet it is fired on at once. And in most cases hit!'[16 August 1915]

them to see ours, for the parapet is only about 2 feet above the ground &
with long grass or corn perhaps in between it's very difficult to see or be
seen. I've not seen a German yet, it's certainly a curious war[125]. A lot of the
rifle shooting is done on pure chance. You aim occasional shots all day &
night at the enemy trenches & they at ours. You hear the shots hitting the
parapet or whistling overhead but it doesn't mean they see anything to shoot
at but merely that the firer hopes that some shot of his may hit an incautious
sentry. However in the trenches now there's no need to look over as there
are periscopes.[126] The Germans opposite us were very lively at night & used
to keep up a continuous pot-shooting at our trenches. During the day they
were quieter. On Saturday night I was very pleased to find no shooting
going on as I had to go with a small party of men to cut the grass in front
of our barbed wire. However when we'd been there about ½ hour they seem
to suspect we were there. They sent up several flares in our direction & had
some pot shots wh: all went overhead. When they do this you just lie flat
as a pancake face downwards on the ground & you can't be seen. You work
on hands & knees. However a bit later they seemed to make up their minds
we really were out & the shooting became more "personal", so as it was not
worth while losing a man for the sake of some grass I brought my party in;
all safe & sound. We really had quite a nice time those 2 days. They did
not shell the part of the line held by this Coy. Three of my platoon however
had a wonderful escape. The Germans during the 2 days sent over a good
many "trench mortars", big high explosives bombs fired from a little sort
of cannon! However most of them fell 50–150 yds on our left. However on
Sat. morning they'd been coming a bit nearer. A sergeant of mine & 2 of
my men were together in a bay of the trench (ie a stretch of trench between
2 traverses)[127] when they suddenly saw something land on the sandbag

---

125. The parapet was a mound of earth at the front of the trench: a similar mound at
the back of the trench was called a parados. It was a mistake for these to be too high, as
the Regimental Diary noted on 8 August: 'The parados on these trenches are very high and
consequently dangerous in that they just catch a 'pip-squeak' which would otherwise pass
over the whole trench and explode outside. We had three men wounded by a shell bursting
on impact with the parados.' As a result, the men levelled them down to below the parapet
at the front side of the trench: the Germans saw them carry out this work and two of the
men were hit by snipers.
126. According to the Regimental Diary, the Germans put up an old sheet above their
trenches with the words 'God Bless Our Emperor. Wauschau lost for you'. The Lancashires
riddled the sheet with bullet holes in reply. The western front was not the only area of
battle: the Germans were also involved in fighting the Russians on the Eastern Front – they
captured Warsaw on 5 August 1915.
127. Philip has drawn a small sketch of this.

8.   Drawing by Philip from letter 62

parapet. Realising what it was, the Sgt said "Come on it's not gone off yet" they managed to get about 10 feet along the trench & lay flat when off it went & blew in the whole of the front of the trench & ½ filled it up! None were touched. It's extraordinary that it did not explode instantaneously. Those 2 or 3 secs saved them. Such things however do not disturb "Tommy" & I soon had them building up the damage. An hour or so afterwards there was no sign of anything. We are now back in the village where we went after those 5 wet days in the trenches. Our men are in the same billets but thank goodness we have left that smelly & fly pestered Mess in the farm & have a better one. Please give my love to Gobagger & any other relations at Folkestone. & also send this letter home as I have not written quite so fully on these special pieces of news. Have a good time at Folkestone

Much love from

Philip[128]

MC 643/5/37

---

128. In envelope addressed to: Miss R Hewetson c/o Miss J S Burges, Bayham House, Coolinge Lane, W. Folkestone, England

63. Wednesday

Aug 11
1ˢᵗ L.N.L. Regt B.E.F. France

My very dear Mother & Father, I've just been having my usual afternoon snooze. It's now 4.30 & I am starting this before tea sitting at the window in my own billet. I was woken up just now by several reports, wh: sounded to me like shells bursting, in my sleepy state I thought they were aeroplane shells, so went out to see & found I was right. Some daring German aviator had managed to fly right over our lines & had got as far back as this village. Our guns were shelling him hard & he had to beat a retreat. They were shooting v. well but could not hit him.

Today our Coy went digging v. early to avoid the heat. They started from here at 6 am. & then dug from 7–11 & back by 12. However today I am Bn. Orderly officer so have to stay here. I've had a nice slack day & did not get up till 8 am. We're getting our summer weather now & it's very hot. It's really a glorious evening now, not a cloud in the sky. Blazing sun with just a nice breeze. I can always snooze no matter how much I slept the night before! & always take an opportunity of doing so. – Oh! what palpitations. The aforementioned "nice breeze" has just caught up this letter & whirled it out of the window but with a mighty lunge I caught it! For a second I had a vision of sitting down & writing it all again

5.30 Yes thank you. Very nice tea. French bread, ration jam & butter & homey cake – Phillips has presented 2 tablecloths & 12 napkins to the Mess wh: improve things & being Mess Pres had to buy them. I got yr letter enclosing the M.F.O.'s letter from Southampton. I'm furious with him & am going to show the letter to the Adjutant & C.O. That a man shld be able to have a "cushy" job like that at home & then make ridiculous mistakes – well to put it bluntly what this Mess thinks of him could not be put in a letter! I thought you'd be surprised at our dinner – of course that's only a very "once in a way" splash!! The good madame helped but our soldier cook did most & a very pretty Mademoiselle, a refugee from La Bassée & a niece of Madame's laid the table for us & folded the serviettes. Don't trouble about my mack. It's lasting <u>well</u>. Yes please adapt the lining into a "British warm" sort of garment. With collar <u>&</u> pockets, nice big fleecy ones then when I get leave wh. <u>ought</u> to be before the winter months I could bring it back with me & my big coat. At present I'm alright though. I liked your Hymn Prayer. Waterproof leggings don't want <u>yet</u>. I'm glad I look the youngest in the photo. I am – I'm sorry I couldn't get a message to yr "Mothers" in time. Phillips is roaring with laughter over "Quinneys" you may be sure I take care of myself in danger zones – I enclose the letter I got from my servant's wife I hear his photo & my letter to his wife were in the Manchester papers. Perhaps this will get to you on Aug 14 – well many happy returns of it.

Very dear love Your very loving Philip.

MC 643/5/38

64.   1ˢᵗ L.N. Lanc. Regt B.E.F. France

Sunday August 15

My very dear Mother & Father Thank you so much for the loving letters for my birthday. Most of the parcels you mention have not come yet, though I got a splendid box of fruit from you & one from Measham & also another box of things from Measham I think. I certainly had an extraordinary birthday. I spent the day superintending all the companies of the battalion in Bombing practice; this took up my time from 10 am – 6pm so I had a full day. A service was arranged for 9.15 am this morning and I arranged to go with Newman & was looking forward to it very much at the beginning of my new year. However it turned out a drenching morning, it did not rain it came down in more than bucket loads & everything is streaming, roads & all, it has now turned into an ordinary wet day so you can see an open air service was quite impossible. I <u>was</u> annoyed but shall make the best of it <u>myself</u>. This is our last day in billets as we leave at 3.30 this afternoon for the trenches.[129] They are not so nice as ones we've been in before I believe & we shall only be in 3 days, so when you get this I ought to be coming out once more. I may not be able to get letters written but will always send a p.c. We've really had a good rest this time. Billets are always a change. I'm writing this at 10.30 am and we've got a parade in ½ an hour to see the men have got everything before they go into the trenches. My gum boots will be useful if its going to rain like this much.

---

129. The battalion moved from Sailly Labourse at 3.45 pm on 15 August, marching by way of Annequin Fosses, the Railway and Lewis Alley and Maison Rouge Alley to a point described in the Regimental Diary as Z2. The diary notes: 'this sub-section has a bad reputation and our front line runs to within 20 to 30 yds from the enemy's trenches in places. The line is very irregular and in front the whole ground is cut up by numerous craters the eastern edges of which are occupied by the Germans.... We have a large assortment of trench mortars, bombs, rifle grenades, spring guns s etc all of which we use continuously and with great effect against the enemy. The actual trenches are good but in places the parapets are thin on the top owing to sand bags being put up without proper authority or arrangement.'

As Father says it _is_ unfortunate how few services we get here.

Three months is the regulation time here before leave, but as six of us came in 1 week & only 2 are allowed away at a time, it'll be nearer 4 months before I get away as I was about the last of the six. Still it's something to look forward to! Sun's out now but the damage is done.

Very dear love Your very loving Philip.

_MC 643/5/39_

65.   Thursday Aug 19

My very dear Mother & Father Thank you both so ever so much for the lovely parcels which you keep sending me. I'm sure no other officer has such dear parents who keep him so well up in all the Home news as your ripping letters do. I just devour them. And I have got quite a name in the battalion for my parcels. Today I got a splendid box of grape nuts, quaker oats, figs, fruit, cream etc, and last night I was greeted when I got out of the trenches by another(!) chicken, peas and cake!!! Then today too came the cigars (oh thank you _so_ much) & the books from Ruth, most welcome, I will be writing to her. I am looking forward to a read & a smoke soon – now from that last sentence you will have gathered that I am no longer in the trenches. No – we came out yesterday evening as I said we should, we actually began to file away from that firing line at 7pm and got here about 9.45 I think. Jolly tired & caked in mud! However everything vanished from my mind of that sort when I saw my bedroom – It is the nicest room I've been in since that first beauty I had when I first came out; and it is practically as good as that. It is in a dear little house owned by 2 maiden artisan women. Quite superior and rather like Mrs Farman's style!![130] It is a room about the size of the one Ruth had before she went to the spare room, or a bit smaller. There is a _real good_ bed in it, not the usual _very_ coarse sheets on a loose straw mattress & pillow you generally get in the billets but real nice stuff. There is a carpet on the floor, a washstand & glass, with all the necessaries on it right down to a tooth glass & slop pail (very unusual all these luxuries in France), a cane chair, & a better soft bottomed one. A marble topped cupboard near my bed, a chest of drawers & another little table! There!! What do you think of that – The window looks out on the cobble road, but (also unusual) between the house & the road there's a little garden about 30 feet by 12 packed with shrubs, &

---

130. There were several people of this name in Salhouse: the most likely is Elizabeth Farman, a widow who ran the greengrocer's shop: at the age of 76, her furnishings would no doubt seem antiquated to Philip.

some creepers up the house. The window faces South & as this village is on a bit of a hill you get a good view. I have evidently found favour in the eyes of the good lady as this morning she presented me with 5 pears & now this afternoon she conducted me into the best parlour, quite a nice little room, quiet & cool, & told me to write in here she wldn't let me write upstairs as I was going to. There is an arm chair (!), a thing I've not touched or seen certainly not sat in for nearly 11 weeks, waiting for me, my books, my cigar soon, so you see I've struck a good patch this time! Well I think I deserve it after the last trenches. I should not choose them to spend a pleasant time in if I were looking for such a place. You see 30–50 yards is not far & you're on the go most of the time. Add to which the weather was <u>abominable</u> and the trenches <u>filthy</u>.[131] These particular trenches (I'll tell you now we're <u>out</u> of them again) have a bad name but we were in when things were quieter than usual tho' as I said in my last p.c. it was the liveliest 3 days I've had so far. The Germans are afraid to shell us too much as the lines are so close that a bad shot might quite easily hit their own front line, however we got some shells at us. Our gunners are apparently surer of their skill for they shell the German front line & sometimes it seems as if our shells are going to hit us from behind. What both sides trouble each most with are trench mortars. The best of these is that you can see them <u>coming</u> – looking like a black oblong sausage about 2 feet long & 5 or 6 inches in diameter they are fired at a range varying from one to three 100 hundred[132] (not in extracts of letters I think) and go up to a height of 50–100 feet in order to get them to fall into the trench. They make a noise bigger than a big shell when they burst & shake everything for a long way round. They are most tremendously highly explosive. It is most exciting dodging them when you see them coming. As you don't hear them coming thro' the air, but only hear a slight report when their gun fires it's a case of "Keeping your eyes skinned" as they say out here. However they damage nobody unless they fall right in the trench and this they never did. They blew in our parapet often though – Their chief effect is "moral<e>" – The other things we trouble each other with are rifle grenades

---

131. Regimental Diary, 18 August: 'After a quiet night we opened the day by an offensive with bombs, rifle grenades and trench mortars on the enemy's lines at 4 am. After half an hour this met with an answer. This answer was finally silenced at 5.00 am by a continual artillery fire from the 30th Battery and some lighter shells from the 114th. The rest of the morning was quiet'. The weather was also a problem: "B' trenches muddy and wretched in the evening.... Rain caused several landslides of trench walls owing to their having a sloping rather than a vertical surface and also owing to the haphazard way sandbags have been built up in places.'
132. Not clearly expressed; Philip means that the range is from 100 to 300 yards.

& hand bombs. Both sides exchange these 3 pleasant little articles in varying quantities all day & night, though of course occasionally you get an hour or two's quiet, generally at meal times. Both sides are very much the same you know *in some ways* – both English & German must have breakfast etc & also some rest between 4 & 7 early morning after the strain of the night. One German shouted out <once> one morning, "When do you have breakfast, we have ours at 7!" But that sort of thing is foolish as it calls down a rain of bombs on that part of the trench! As I told you I was responsible as bombing officer for the rifle grenades & bombs which B. Coy sent at the trenches opposite us and I kept my bombers & myself V. busy I can tell you. Well that's enough for the trenches I think – I've had some interesting photos sent me from Julie & "Margy"[133] – I hope Ruth's camera is doing wonders, she ought to know it well by now. Mother & Ruth on Sheringham beach are in one of the photos. I am so sorry I've never written to Aunt Lalla but do you know I never recognised the writing & have been totally at sea as to who was sending them. Please send me Aunt Emmie's address too – you must have had a dreadful wetting in Norwich, and I hope no colds or evil effects followed. I didn't get up till 9 this morning & after a ripping clean up got in clean clothes & had breakfast at 10. Can you sent my "slacks" & brown shoes – we can always wear them in billets & they'll be such a relief – Gardner has just been & had a nice chat, he hopes to be going on leave <whe> tomorrow. We get a clear week in England when we go but I don't know when my turn will be. Now some news – though do not build on it or tell anyone yet. Instead of going back to the <word illegible> trenches after this we may be going right back, 10 or 12 miles west for a months rest! It's long been in the air – but I'll tell you further developments as they arrive.

Very dear love Your very loving Philip

My pencil's getting quite short!!

Hope you'll get this on Sunday?

MC 643/5/40 and 643/11/29

66.   Tuesday [?24 Aug.]

In the Trenches

My very dear Mother & Father I'm managing in spite of what I said to get a letter to you, though I am afraid I missed my p.c. yesterday. We arrived

---

133. Julia Langdale-Smith see Appendix 3; Margery Turner, see note 89.

"here" at about 6 pm on Sunday night & found as we expected that the trenches were all slush & water after the terrific thunderstorms of the day. I am writing this sitting in our dug out waiting for lunch. I am caked in mud; it has rained & thundered most of the 48 hours we have been in so far, though to-day has been better. Again it's a case of no washing or shaving. The trenches are in worse condition than they were those horrible 5 days before. This time however I'm rejoicing in the possession of my gum boots. They are solidly encased in mud; so are my knees & a few inches above them, solid caked mud. Hands, tunic, hat, mackintosh all mud – These are exciting sort of trenches, the Germans trenches are only thirty-five yards away, in one place they are as close as 15 to 20, while in another they are as far away as 70 or 80. But on the average they are thirty-five. You have to talk in very low voices as of course if you gave any special order or talked about the situation in your ordinary voice they might very easily hear. The other night we heard them shouting at us, and last night they were whistling, there is a dog in their trenches which you can hear bark at times. They have put a board up on their trenches with some writing on it but we cant quite make out what it is. Of course there is no looking over in trenches like these, all observing is done through periscopes. Their snipers are very good shots at these, and that nice one I brought out (the concertina thing) got a bullet through the top of the glass yesterday when Goldie was using it. I have a spare but wld like another. <Two of> 3 letters, 1 From Father & 2 from Mother have just come, one written on my birthday. The cigars have not come yet but I <u>shall</u> enjoy them when they do – only the fruit parcel so far. As I'm bombing officer I have lots of work to do. I am responsible for all the "Late" wh: comes from our Coy. I fire rifle grenades & bombs from a sort of big spring catapult gun each day. It's quite interesting. When we came in 2 days [*ago*] I was the only one who knew how to work either now I have taught several NCOs & we reply at once if they send things over us, with more than they send. We go out to morrow night back to the village where we were in the coal mine. My boots are all right I've just had them resoled.

Muddy but well & cheery

Very dear love Your very loving Philip[134]

MC 643/5/41

---

134. 'This came after the next one! Evidently delayed': endorsement by Phillip's mother on the envelope.

67. Thursday 26.VIII.15

My very dear Mother & Father

The enclosed was handed to me yesterday, so you see I am now a Temporary Lieutenant. It is a sort of Field promotion, only the 3rd Bn (to which I belong) can recommend me for a full Lieutenant but I am now a Temporary Lieut. in the 1st Battn. and shall remain so until I get my full promotion from the 3rd Batt. You need not put in the Tempy though in addresses I think. It is really I suppose a good thing to have been recommended for promotion by the 1st Batt out here without waiting my turn to come through the Felixstowe authorities. At any rate I am pleased.[135]

We left our last billets on Tuesday at 5.30 p.m., as I told you in that hurried letter just before we left. We got "here" just about 9.[136] Phillips had been out all day & got back just before we started. As he had ridden a long way he wanted to <rid> walk for a change so I rode part of the way.

The men are in the same billets as before but thank goodness we have changed. No billets here are much to be desired but we have "bettered ourselves" somehow. Our mess in an empty cottage on the edge on the village. Two fair-sized rooms downstairs are all it possesses, a loft <u>and</u> a cellar (most necessary here). The servants have a nice stove for cooking in one room. In the other there is a table, 4 chairs & a bed with 2 mattresses on it. Phillips sleeps on the bed in his sleeping bag, & I sleep in mine on the floor, not at all a bad bed though you have to sleep ½ dressed. Yesterday was a day of lazing (<u>perfect</u> weather). A sudden message came at 6.30 pm for a digging party from B. Coy so I went off with this at 7 and got back at 1 am. As we came back we heard shells going over & thought they might be going to this village when we got here we found a shell dropping in every 2 to 3 minutes. So we sat on the outskirts till the Huns had presumably gone to bed & then marched on. They had sent over about 30 shells but did no damage. They sent 2 big ones in this morning too but did no damage. There are 6 or 7 officers for leave before me yet which means if they send 2 at a time another 4 weeks only. So I might (my own guess) get leave the end of Sept.

I'm longing for that week!!

I <u>am</u> so pleased you are both going to get away for a bit of a change. I thought I had mentioned Ivor's candlesticks!? Please tell him they are <u>most</u>

---

135. Philip was appointed temporary captain on 20 August [*London Gazette*, 1 October 1915]

136. On 24 August, the battalion moved from Verquin into their old billets at Noyelles.

useful in dugouts & billets & have already seen quite a lot of the war. Our servants generally manage to get a meal for us after these tramps changing billets; we get a bit tired but not "done" or anywhere near it, and a good sleep soon puts you right. We'll discuss all about winter clothes when I come home. Three letters today, your two & Ruths' such an interesting & amusing one from her! My long lost letter must have been delayed by the post, I am quite innocent! I did not throw many bombs personally but fired the rifle grenades & superintended the bombing catapult & the posts.
I must stop now

With dear love Your very loving Philip.

MC 643/5/42

68.   Friday [28 Aug., FSP]¹³⁷

Ripping parcels last night, slacks & shoes <u>and</u> the books, thank you so much, they <u>are</u> welcome & even more so the anti-bite mixture; it came at a most opportune time "enuf said" – weather is boiling. but we are all flourishing. Capt. Torbett & 2 other officers arrive from F. today but no sign of H.S., de B etc.¹³⁸ Can't understand it, have heard nothing, do <u>hope</u> they're coming here. Very well, enjoying the weather, Much love P.

MC 643/5/43

69.   Sunday 29.VIII.15 ¹³⁹

My very dear Mother & Father

I have never been able to appreciate what the feelings of the tramp with no roof to his head are so well as I have the last 24 hours. I'll tell you our misadventures. The Bn moved into trenches yesterday but this Coy. was to move up to the village of wh: I sent you those p.c.s with the name scratched out¹⁴⁰ where all the fierce fighting in October. We were not to go into trenches but to stay out & go up & dig at night. We arrived here at 7.30

137. Dated by postmark.

138. Strong and de Blaby.

139. In envelope addressed to Salhouse Vicarage, changed by Philip to c/o Mrs Townend, Swepstone Rectory, Ashby de la Zouch, where Philip's parents were staying with friends.

140. Vermelles. The Regimental Diary notes the great difficulty of obtaining billets in Vermelles owing to the large number of troops in the area.

last night expecting to find some cellars for us, for they are the only things left to live in here. However there were no billets. We took the men straight up to dig & got back about half past twelve By continual wandering round Phillips managed to find a house, almost untouched in wh we squashed 90 men, the rest fitted in somewhere. The accommodation we got was lent us by the gunners. We had to turn out at 7.30 in the morning and took the men into a field behind the village where they had breakfast & lay till 12.30 by which time we had managed to find isolated cellars to fit small parties of men & got them all in. There is a good large cellar under what was once a brewery here (I think you've got a p.c. of it) wh is now used as a reading room & place of shelter for troops during the day. It's about 200 feet long! One end is all collapsed, but we've got a corner & made a room with some canvas walls & here we are at present. We shan't be here so long I hope. We go digging tonight. I've been getting some sleep wh I wanted this afternoon. Very well in spite of our homeless state of a few hours ago.

Much love yr loving Philip.

MC 643/5/44

70.   In the Trenches Tuesday Aug 31. 1915 [141]

My very dear Mother & Father

I am wondering very much whether you have gone to Measham[142] at any rate I will send this there as I did my last, written on Sunday. I am also very pleased you have got Ruth back & am wondering whether she is keeping house at home or if she's gone with you, at any rate if I've time I'll send her a separate letter. But in case I can't please give my best congratulations, I think its <u>so</u> splendid & am awfully pleased with her.[143] Her letters to me are splendid & lots of pieces make me roar with laughter – Tell her I agree with what she said in her letter very heartily, tell her she'd better do more than she said she would. Well as you see we're in trenches again, & I for one am very pleased – I'd much rather be there than in that place of cellars – we came in about 5 pm last night. The Coy. is not in the firing line but in support. As a matter of fact I am further back still in a "Keep", a veritable maze of trenches.

---

141. In envelope addressed to: Rev W Hewetson c/o Mrs Townend [etc as note 139]. Note on back of envelope: 'We have read it but not Measham. Just come Thursday 5 pm. Mary'.

142. See Introduction.

143. This relates to Ruth's success in her exams at school in the summer term 1915: Senior Oxford, Class II according to the school magazine.

I am here with ½ the Coy under my charge, while Phillips, Goldie & Helm are further up with the other ½. I go up to them for meals, about 10 minutes up the trenches. We go out digging at night. Goldie went out last night & I go tonight. So last night with the exception of an hour for stand to I slept solidly in a nice dug out, beautifully warm. I must have had quite 8 hours sleep. Being so far back, & having most of the men digging there was no need for me to be on duty. This morning I was busy; one thing I had to do was draw a plan of my maze-like Keep for the C.O. This took me nearly 2 hours, doing it all to scale. This afternoon I've just done a most ripping toilet, shaved & had a most comforting wash. It's now 4.30 pm so I shall be walking up to tea soon. I <u>have</u> been enjoying "the Unnamed" by Le Q.[144] Two letters from you to-day written on Friday & Saturday and a parcel. Thank you <u>so</u> much, <u>cigarettes</u>, matches, lemonade, shortbread, Quaker oats etc – <u>Splendid</u>! On Sunday chicken, peas, grape nuts & pudding – Unfortunately you could smell the first two <u>yards</u> away!! The pudding we were to have had last night but we were hustled up here. If I can find a pot for boiling we must have it brought. Otherwise I hope it will keep a day or two. We go back for a 3 weeks rest on Thursday. At present 2 officers are going on leave on Wednesday and 2 Saturday – if they keep that up I should get <u>home</u> on the 16th Sept!!! But you never know if they will increase the numbers that go during the rest or whether they'll decrease them. Still the longed for day shld not be far off!! I heard from Hugo today. He & Bratton[145] have gone to our 4th Batt(T) out here & are v. disappointed I think.

<u>So am I!</u>

Very dear love Your very living Philip

<u>Very</u> well thank you!

MC 643/5/45

71.   Saturday Sept 4

My own dear "Fam'ly" I am afraid you won't have had a letter from me for several days, as I said on my p.c. I wonder when that will arrive, the same post as this I should think. I almost forget where my last news ended. I believe it was our 2nd day in the trenches (Tuesday). Well that night it was my turn to be in charge of the digging party. we started out at 8.30, we had

---

144. *The Unnamed – a romance of modern Italy*, by William le Queux (1864–1927), first published in 1902.

145. They both arrived in France on 21 August, and joined the 4th Battalion.

to go up to the front line & then out by an underground sap. It may sound exciting but really it was most dreadfully uncomfortable, it was about 3 feet wide and varied in height from 3ft to 5' 6", so you were always doubled up, it ran out for about 60 yards when it ended in a slope & you came out into the open. Then another 30 yards or so & you came to the trench we were digging. As it was, the 2nd night they had dug at it it was already some 3ft deep & there was therefore a certain amount of cover when we got there. The Germans were about 150 yards away on our right & 300 straight to our front. They used to fire at us with rifles & machine guns & when I was there sent 4 shells quite close, one about 15 yards away but they only worried us the 1st hour of the four & did no damage. You see the diggers were well under cover. They obviously go to bed about 10 pm as after that things were much quieter!! I got about 2 hours sleep before stand to but afterwards I slept till 11 am! The next 24 hours I was rather badly troubled with diarrhoea (now you're not to worry) I got some pills from the Doctor & as I was only in the Keep I took things v. quietly (for instance I did not stand to on Thursday) I dieted(!) I had some real good bread & milk & didn't eat meat & by the time we were relieved on Thursday I was <u>alright</u>! It poured with rain as it always does apparently when we are in. I am quite well now, & you can rest assured of that as I have told I was not well those days. It was a bit rotten at the time as it makes you feel very low & the weather was bad; I don't mind having a bit of a talk on my ailment as it's well now. At any rate as I was back in the Keep I got away at 3.30 pm some 3 hours before the rest of the Battalion. We had a 3 hours march, & I had 2 platoons, some 80 men to conduct. We went in small parties of about 15 men within 100 yards between each party. Even so going through the much shelled village of the p.c.s I sent you we were nearly caught. One small field gun shell got nearest. We had just got thro' the village & were on a track when it came whistling over & hit the track <u>plumb</u> in the middle just 10 yards in front of me! They sent me no more but for safety I took the men across the fields & we were alright. The other officers roared with laughter at the story as I told it the next morning!! The great thing is to take these things as jokes & laugh at your temporary discomfort afterwards. Well I arrived & found there was a bed for Phillips but we <3> subs were to sleep on the floor. However my 3 hours start of the Batt: stood me in good stead & I bustled round & found 3 beds; including my old one in the "Miss Farman's house" – we were only there one night but enough time to get a change & a wash, both needed. We left there 1.30 yesterday & marched 4 hours in <u>pouring</u> rain. I had my mack on & it stood it well. We are now quite 15 miles from the firing line the furthest I have been for 13 weeks, I don't know how long we're here for 3 days or 3 weeks!! Nobody does, but it's probably the former. Lovely homemade cake today & letters from Lowestoft. No more news about leave yet – very dear love

Your very loving Philip

More news if any tomorrow
Quite well now.

MC 643/5/46

72.   'France' Sunday Sept 5

My very dear Ruth. This shall be addressed to you. We are still back here in our village 15 miles behind. But it's been a busy day and I didn't think we should be here this evening. This morning we got the order to be ready to move anytime after 1pm. So all was hurry & business, we had lots to do, fitting new boots & socks for the men, just after the order to move came another order came to say "move cancelled" so we are still here. However I believe we move tomorrow. Rumour which is very often right out here says we are going up in motor buses to a village some five miles behind the line, I don't think we are going into trenches so don't worry, any of you! This morning I had a chance of my first H Communion since I've been out here. There was no Church Parade this morning as the move was expected; but an early Service was announced for 8 am in the Chateau here, a really lovely place & grounds, so I arranged to go with Newman. When the whole congregation had assembled it consisted of 6 L.N.L. officers, the Brig General of the 3rd Brig, & a Staff Capt: no men turned up. It was a nice little service. The last few days we've had buckets of rain, but now it's a beautiful evening. I hope you've done well for the 9th & got my message (never mind expense); give them all my love & good wishes as I'm not there; as we are moving tomorrow I shall not be able to write so I am enclosing a little letter for you to give them on the morning of the 9th. Lots of congraggers[146] on the 2nd – I think it splendid.[147] We are just going to have the homemade cake for tea. I've had a bit of a laze this afternoon. Shall have lots to tell you when I come home on leave

Your very loving Philip

MC 643/5/47

---

146. Slang for congratulations. 'Congratters' is more common but 'congraggers' is recognised as an alternative in Eric Partridge, *Dictionary of Slang and Unconventional English* (1937).

147. See note 143.

73.   Somewhere in France

Sunday Sept 5 1915

My own very dear Mother & Father

Just a little letter for Ruth to give you on the morning of the 9th just full of loving thoughts and congratulations on your "Silver Wedding Day". Such a day, I do just wish I was there to greet you both in person, but this letter must do it for me. May Ruth and I be able to greet the very best of Mothers and Fathers on very many more Sept 9th's. That's what I say.

Now all the news has been put in Ruth's letter so I must close with very many more fond thoughts & wishes & congratulations. I shall indeed be thinking of you all, as I did early this morning.

Your very loving

Philip.

MC 643/5/48

74.   1st L.N.L. Regt B.E.F. France

Sept 7 1915

My very dear Mother & Father

Well, the motor bus ride I spoke of on Sunday never came off so apparently we are to stop here; nobody seems to know for how long. But I daresay it will be a week or so. Meanwhile the "Rest" so called seems to mean a good deal of work. It is a rest from trench warfare, but the time is occupied in hard training. All the sort of things we used to do at Felixstowe and what the regular soldier does in his peace training. Each morning at 7 the men are taken for ½ an hours "walk and run" by one of the subalterns in the Coy, we each take it in turn. Then morning parade 9–12 and afternoon parade 2–4 In F: <some> the afternoon hours used to be rather nominal but they are not here. Still as long as we have the glorious weather we've had today I don't mind how much work we do. We are billeted in a pretty little village on a hill. There is a plateau behind us from wh: you get a really <u>magnificent</u> view. The country just round here is really very pretty, wooded, & a great contrast to the country up at the "front." At the top of this plateau is the home of some of the Flying Corps, and here are some 20 or 30 aeroplanes. They are arriving & departing all day for the front.

The 2 parcels arrived safely, the one from L. & the other from Buzzard.[148] I have not opened yet but am looking forward to eating your health in it on Thursday. At present we are ½ way through Cook's splendid cake. There are still 5 in front of me for leave, but if only they could go my turn wld soon be here. Such things are far above control by each Batt. they are a matter for the Division; which allows so many (0.1.2 or 3) officers away from each regt. at a time! Much love yr Very loving

Philip.

MC 643/5/49

75. "In France"

Friday 17.IX.15

My very dear Mother & Father

Here we are still in this village – for how long I can't say & if I did know I couldn't say. Still the same glorious weather, still the same parades, you come in very dusty, hot & thirsty, but very bronzed, fit, and hungry. I think we are all enjoying the place, I am at any rate. Here is a cutting that the regimental quartermaster sergeant showed me to-day. He had sent it to the Morning News & Leader & I cut this out. Unofficially "mentioned in dispatches" you see! Isn't it amazing – keep it, I'm awfully pleased with it. Thank you so much for the parcel wh: came to-day with your letter. I really think the most <u>useful</u> thing was the hand kerchief, that brings my total up to 3 now, it was 2! <u>Please</u> send some more. I have also heard from Bleistein, Uncle Henry & Gobagger lately & Measham are most kind with their regular supply of tongue & sardines. Though the hand kerchief gave me excessive joy to behold the cigars ran it a very good second. You ask me about tobacco, well I don't smoke <much> a pipe out here at all now; but some more cigarettes would be most welcome. The band I mentioned in my letter to Ruth was very good 2 nights ago. We go & sit out on the stone sort of balcony or "façade" of the "Chateau" (a lovely place in beautiful grounds) where the Batt's Head-Qrtrs are & listen. Last night all the officers dined there with the Colonel. Tonight there is a Battn concert there. The men all come & sit round on the grass or on benches & we sit up on the balcony & the evening passes very pleasantly. Time soon passes with parades all day &

---

148. Philip habitually refers to place names rather than personal names: the parcels have been posted by friends or family members in Lowestoft and Leighton Buzzard.

games etc in the evenings. It is 15 weeks since I landed in France today! I am as fit as can be & feel ready for anything!
With much love

Your very loving

Philip.

MC 643/5/50

76.   In France

Sunday 19.IX.15

My very dear Mother & Father you'll be pleased to hear I expect that we are still where we have been for the next sixteen days – still I cannot guarantee being here next Sunday, I should think we shall move this week but you never know. We continue to have a most enjoyable time, mingled with lots of work. On Friday we had a really first class concert it lasted from 8pm to well after 11! The Divisional band played and some of our men & some of the R.A.M.C. who have a large advanced Hospital here contributed, among them the Matron. There were some <u>real</u> good items, songs (serious & comic) recitations, etc. The whole Battalion must have been sitting round on the grass in front of the château and half the civilian inhabitants I should think too! The band played by the light of acetylene lamps & candles & the whole evening was <u>most</u> enjoyable. Yesterday evening B Coy. played A Coy at football, starting at 5.30 pm. It was an excellent game, very warm work, which ended in a draw of 3 all; by the close of the game 6.40 pm you could not see the ball, it soon gets dark now. I enjoyed the game thoroughly. We seem to be having our summer weather now, it is certainly the best spell we've had this year. Today has been a glorious day, not a sign of a single cloud in the sky all day. We had Church Parade at 11.30. About 20 minute walk to a sheltered field on the side of the hill. We joined with the King's Liverpool Regt & formed a great big semicircle with the band & chaplain in the middle. We had a splendid service, the chaplain was a Major (Rev.) Blackburn the Divisional chaplain. I have never heard such a preacher. He was splendid, everybody says so. He took his ideas from the Passage wh: mentions "the cloud of witnesses", he spoke beautifully & <u>touched</u> men & officers. A real fighting sermon and a "Trumpet Call". It must & will have great effect on all who heard it. We followed it up with "Fight the good fight" – afterwards he asked as many as would to stay to H.C.; which he held in a corner of the field, very nicely, he had a portable H.C. table! Quite 70 men & officers stayed I should think, I was one – I wish I could tell you why all this appealed to us but I can't – now. A letter from Mother & one from R. today enclosing Bp of M. v nice of him[149]. How imposing my letters look, well you've certainly been discreet, I certainly didn't know I was to spring to such fame, never been fitter or cheerier!! Very dear love

Your v loving Philip.

MC 643/5/51

On 24 September the Battalion moved forward from Males-les Mines to battle positions on the front. The following day, the British attacked in the action now known as the Battle of Loos. Philip was hit early in the day and lay out in the open for nine hours before he could be brought in. He was badly wounded in the left arm, and was to lose the use of his fingers for six months. He was sent to a Military Hospital in Chelsea, and moved in October to a convalescent hospital near Winchester.

77. Hursley Park Winchester[150]

Sunday [*17 Oct. 1915*]

My very dear Mother & Father

How very strange once more to be writing my Sunday letter in England and in civilian clothes – quite respectably dressed now too! I made a great advance yesterday, I got my wounded arm into a coat sleeve! It goes in alright now that I have not got a "fomentation" with all its attendant cotton wool swathing the arm. Of course it has to be 'eased' in as I have not got the arm straight yet, but once it is on it is quite comfortable & I've got a black sling which goes outside the coat & really I look quite respectable! You'd see a change in me too. My 10 days here so far have done wonders & I am looking & feeling practically my old self again. I am getting rid of that silent mood I got & am more lively now too. The wound is getting on splendidly, of course it was a huge hole so when I say it is healing it doesn't mean that

---

149. Edmund Knox (1847–1937), Bishop of Manchester 1903–1921. He was Philip's godfather, no doubt having become acquainted with the Hewetsons when he was Archdeacon of Birmingham (1894–1903). The letter, dated 13 September 1915, survives in the Hewetson family archive at the Norfolk Record Office; Knox congratulates Philip on his promotion and expresses his hope for a scheme of national service, which he distinguishes from conscription [NRO, MC 643/38].

150. Hursley Park had been bought by George Cooper (1856–1940), a Scottish lawyer and his wealthy American wife Mary in 1902. Sir George (as he became in 1906) donated five million pounds to the war effort, while Mary turned two floors of the house into a hospital for officers.

the hole is going yet but it's gradually closing together in the arm – thus.[151]
But it is now quite clean & healthy. I am being massaged. I get a good deal
of pain in the arm & hand, but that has got to be. It varies. Last night I
had a fairly good night, the night before rotten. My fingers even have made
an advance. The little finger always been normal, that is the only one not
affected on the hand. The one next goes about ½ way. The other two & the
thumb you remember were the bad ones. Well the thumb I can't even get a
hair's breadth out the straight, but the others have made some progress!! The
first finger joint will just move now. The middle finger goes just a fraction
more. Isn't it splendidly encouraging. It seems to show the nerve can't be
actually <u>cut</u>. When I got Father's p.c. about the clothes I wired to Chelsea
and asked them to forward them here so I hope they will come. Mother's
letter about Chelsea <rath> pleased me for I really am settled here now &
making such splendid progress & they are all so kind (staff) that I feel I
want to stay a bit longer till we see how I get on. The 2 collars & pin were
most welcome. Yesterday afternoon 3 of us went for a drive in the "Ford"
(one of Sir G.C.'s[152] cars) wh: I enjoyed v. much. This morning I went to
Church; the first service in an English Ch: for nearly 5 months!! This letter
came from Aunt R. to you. I am writing this after tea in the billiard room.
very cosy. I thought I might (if Dr. allows) <appl> get <a> weekend leave
this week & meet you in town? It is a recognised thing here if anybody
wants & Dr. allows! Much love yr v. loving Philip

Please send my camera[153]

MC 643/6/1

78. Hursley Park Winchester

Tuesday

My very dear Mother

Only a short note! I've got leave from Friday to Monday, so shall see you &
Ruth then – I hope Ruth can get off on Friday, if not write & I could come
Sat. to Tuesday. But if we go to a Sat. Matinee it's <fa> better to arrive in
town on Friday isn't it. It <u>will</u> be splendid. I've got tons of money, <an> so
<u>I</u> am going to give you both a splendid time out of my earnings! Now then
– I <u>shall</u> love it. We'll talk over everything then. Unless I hear otherwise I'll

---

151. Philip has made a sketch of his wound.
152. Sir George Cooper.
153. Added at head of letter.

arrive Waterloo 1.45 Friday. Shall we meet or I go 26 Cumberland Terrace. Is it SW ??[154]

I am looking forward to seeing you and you will see a change in me Much love

Your very loving Philip

I never saw about my captaincy going! Have you the cutting.[155]

MC 643/6/2

79.   Lady Cooper's Hospital Hursley Park Winchester

Wednesday [*3 Nov. 1915*]

My very dear Father

I expect you saw in yesterday's Gazette that I was to be Lieut: in the 3rd Batt; so that's alright, no temporary about it this time! Wood & Nichol (both still at F.[156]) Wharton (killed on the 25th) Fairbairn (transferred to Flying Corps) & Gilliland (prisoner since Dec:) were also promoted.[157] I got a big batch of all your letters written just before & after you knew I was wounded forwarded to me yesterday, and tho' they were nearly 5 weeks old I much enjoyed reading them. I also got this magnificent long letter from Gardner wh: I think you will like to wade through. It is intensely interesting & gives one a very great idea of the 25[th][158]. He writes on the first & last page of each sheet & then goes inside. Please keep the letter for me. I wrote to Mrs Cator yesterday about massage so ought to get an answer soon.[159] I shall wait to ask the Dr about a move till I can show him her letter. My weekend had no ill effects, and I had a good journey getting tea on the train. Can you send me Uncle John's address as I should like to go & see them on the way home. Also before I go to town can Mother send my evening clothes in case I go to an evening theatre with the Bleisteins;

---

154. The Tyndale-Biscoe London home. SW refers to the London postal district: in fact Cumberland Terrace, on the east side of Regent's Park, is in NW.

155. The *London Gazette* of 22 October 1915 announced the relinquishment of the temporary captaincy, dated 26 September 1915 (the day after the Battle of Loos).

156. Felixstowe.

157. The announcement was in the supplement to the *London Gazette* of 1 November 1915.

158. 25 September, the Battle of Loos where Philip had been wounded.

159. Mrs Margaret Cator ran a Red Cross Hospital at her home at Woodbastwick Hall, Norfolk, not far from Salhouse.

just my short dinner jacket, the trousers, waistcoat (black) shirt, 1 collar, & links & studs, also my spats!

I am awfully pleased as I manage to play billiards now, tho' the faulty rest I make with my left hand makes my scoring somewhat erratic!! We've had 2 lovely days since I've been back and we went for a ripping drive yesterday afternoon. How splendid for you to have the Ford[160] once again I hope it's not going to give much trouble. We shall have to start looking round for what motor bike & sidecar you <u>are</u> going to get if you are going to –

With much love

Your very loving

Philip.

MC 643/6/3

80.   Hursley Park Winchester

Friday

My very dear Father

Just a line to tell you how splendidly I am going on. The wound is now clean! You can hardly realise what a wonderful quick recovery that is. Of course it was dreadfully septic, but by draining it, fomenting it & bathing it it has now become clean and the bruises & swelling are going fast. To-day for the first time I had a dry dressing on it, a great advance. The nurse says by next Wednes: or Thursday the flesh ought to have grown & closed up the hole & then the skin will start to grow over it. I have started massage for the arm & hand & the fingers already show more life & signs of movements, though small at present. I want to stay here <u>till</u> the <u>wound</u> has healed as they all know it so well now; I have a <u>very</u> good nurse & it is a great thing to be tended by someone who really knows & takes an interest in the wound. In myself too I am much better & feel quite different. Now when the wound has healed I <u>may</u> be able to get a Medical Board & if I can arrange to get massage as an outpatient in a military hospital might not have to stay <u>in</u> hospital. On the other hand if I can't arrange that I should have to get the Transfer & go to a hospital merely for massage, as by then my wound

---

160. Ford motor car, also referred to in letter 184. Cars were not common before the First World War, with about 132,000 families in Britain owning one: as the rector of a scattered country parish, William Hewetson would have found a car or motor cycle an advantage.

would require no attention. I thought if it is impossible to get massage as an outpatient in Norwich, I might stay with some Uncle or Aunt in town & go to a London Hospital. If that were so I could easily <help towards> pay something to help feed me as I have £96 in the bank. These are all ideas but I thought I'd put them in to show why I want to stop here for another week or 10 days & then perhaps do without the transfer – but I must ask the Doctor when he thinks I shall be fit for a Board. It's a pity to stay in Hosp: if you can be an outpatient. Much love

to all your very loving

Philip

MC 643/6/4

Philip went back to Salhouse to recuperate, returning to Felixstowe in April 1916.

81.   The Orwell Hotel, Felixstowe

April 25th 1916[161]

My very dear Mother & Father

Just a line to let you know where I am for tonight. The journey soon passed. I got some tea at Ipswich & came on by the 5.20. I took a taxi to the Orderly Room with all my baggage where I was warmly greeted by Sgt Howe who telephoned to Henderson who was at his house. I taxied back to the White Horse *Headqrts:* where I saw Col. Cowper Essex in a chair; him I saluted & he was very nice and said they were very muddly & upset etc, up all last night, enquired tenderly about me & all of you!

Then I turned round & saw Nichol *joined when I did, but only 17 then so not yet out* & while chatting with him. Henderson *the Adjutant* came in & was very nice & said I'd better come here for the night & go see him at 9.30 tomorrow. I'll write more fully about it all tomorrow. I then came here. Then took my bike to be mended. Bought a stick & came back for dinner wh: I've just had. Nothing done last night here only lots of alarms & scares! However I've got a bed for <u>tonight</u>.
Very dear love

from Philip

Just going to post this.

MC 643/7/1

---

161. 'The day he left us again' added by Philip's mother.

82.   26.4.16

My very dear Ruth

A letter for you this time! Well I'm in the Huts! In a few days apparently
we are going to hand over the School House, Laurel Farm, Golf Club etc to
a garrison Batt: so there was no chance of going there. At present I am the
senior officer who lives and eats in the huts. There are several senior officers
who command Coys in the huts but they are all married & live out. Loch
is away on sick leave & one of the Curwen bros, who is here is in hospital.
The others are all 2 Lieuts joined since I left. Of course it's too early to talk
of what they're like yet but there seem several likely ones among them. I
am in F. Coy which is the Expeditionary Force Coy: ie. consists entirely of
men back from the front and as far as I can gather its work is all medical
inspections!! It is commanded by a Lieut Reed (6 days senior to me), who
lost an eye on the Aisne and is on light duty still attending hospital here.
He has a South African medal ribbon on so I gather is somewhat over 30.
My little room is about 15ft for 8 & I shall be fairly comfortable there I
hope. I got a cheap chest of drawers. I have an <u>excellent</u> servant. I have been
greeted by several men back from the front & otherwise & met one of my
old platoon. I enjoy these meetings. Stone & Gemmel (1st & 2nd Lieuts) both
out with me are here wh is nice. Today I've really done nothing much, no
parades. As far as I can see nobody is overworked here. Letters they tell me
are liable to be censored now so I can't tell you things I would like to. It is
not worth the risk I'm afraid. Will have lots to tell Father when he comes.
Don't send Bob[162] or gramoph yet. Enjoyed Mother's & Mollie's letters
today.

Much love from your ever loving brother Philip Hewetson

Please send my fountain pen[163]

MC 643/7/2

83.   Sunday [*?30 Apr.*]

Dearest all

The first week back here has passed well and it feels just as if I had been
back weeks. One soon settles down & enjoys the new old-life. We have
now in charge of A Coy: a second Lieutenant from our 1st Bn: who was

---

162. Philip's dog.
163. Added at head of letter.

invalided home months ago & who joined here 6 weeks ago. There is all
the difference between him & Loch. Of course Loch was very nice as a
man but he's nearly always sick and even when here he was rather sloppy
& allowed the Coy: to get very slack. He was such a worrier. Well our new
O.C. is very keen and it adds a new interest to the work and has made
me much keener. The subalterns in the Coy: each have their own special
platoon to look after and I am enjoying the work more. I expect you have
got my letter & telegram for tennis things now. I wired not because there
was such an extra special hurry but because I missed the post with my letter
on Friday & so knew you would not be able to post the parcel till Monday.
There is a lot of tennis going on among the officers of the battalion and
I ought to be able to get a game most days if I like. I went into Harwich
on Tuesday morning & told them about my eyes & they gave me 2 weeks
Home Duty. My bike was very useful in getting me down to the Pier &
back a good 3½ miles each way. My eyes troubled me at the beginning
of the week but are <u>much</u> better now. I am very sun burnt. I've quite got
used to my little bed & blankets & am very comfortable so do not want
mattress or sheets. We finish afternoon parades at 4. Then with tea, some
motor biking, a walk, (which I often do so, it's very lovely along the coast
in the evening now), some tennis & changing for dinner time soon goes.
After dinner I spend a short time reading the evening papers & then off to
bed. I'm up at or soon after 6. each morning for parade at seven. I wake
quite easily. On Thursday evening I went to dinner at Laurel Farm, one of
our outposts with Gardner & Bratton. After dinner we had some music
& I did not leave till 11. Soon after I got back the Zeppelin came over
here, though I neither saw nor heard it. It dropped two bombs in Harwich
harbour which were heard here. The next afternoon as I expect you saw
there was a Taube off Lowestoft.[164] All the aeroplanes here were very active.
That evening we heard 4 zeppelins were coming straight for us(!) however
apparently they sheered off. Of course they do not come for nothing, they
are scouting & probably learn a lot about the defences. If they lose their
way they drop bombs and by reading our papers next day they see exactly
where they were and how they went wrong; cute, eh? (as Aunt Emmie
would say!) Yesterday Hugh and I planned a little recreation so we got
leave from the Colonel to go into Ipswich, you can only go on Saturdays
& Sundays now. We left here at 3.30, then we found a splendid little tea
place in "Switch". After tea we saw some good pictures in a Cinema, then

---

164. German aeroplane, designed in 1910, the first mass-produced military plane in
Germany. The name means 'Dove' (derived from the shape of the wings).

after a little walk in Ipswich we had dinner & went on afterwards to the Theatre. Where we saw the "Quaker Girl"[165], which Ruth & I once saw at Norwich, there were several new songs in it and it was a very good company so we enjoyed ourselves thoroughly. We motor biked both ways. My bike is going splendidly. It runs best with the spark retarded. This afternoon we're starting at the Band & probably biking out to the Banks for tea. I went to St. John's this morning.

Much love

Your very loving

Philip

I enjoyed the letters & photos. 2nd lot of photos are very good.
The black spots are caused by air bubbles on the plate I think. I should advise Ruth never to fix or wash plates one on top of the other.

MC 643/11/18

84.   Sunday [?7 *May*]

My very dear Mother & Father

Here is the start of the Sunday letters again. Mother's arrived by this mornings post quite correctly. O how I enjoyed it, and am looking forward to the C.F.N. this evening[166]. Of course everything is so very different from home that I cannot say that I have settled down nor that I am any means pleased with life at Felixstowe in general as it is now. Though as I tell myself I have not been back here a week yet, and am really in a stage of eliminating those who are quite impossible and still looking for those who will be possible as friends. You know how we've often deplored some of the latter day officers, their manners & their conversation etc well we seem to have some specimens in this Mess of that type and they do make me boil!! I am however keeping my eyes very wide open, specially watching 2 or 3 who seem much more likely to fit in with me. They are much quieter & I hope will be the sort I want when I get to know them. Keep the impossible specimens away and there are a few who seem to be able to show good points but this other crowd very much incline to join the rotters when together. Now you see!

---

165. Popular musical comedy, book by James T Tanner, first performed in London in 1913.
166. 'The Church Fam[ily] Newspaper' added by Philip's mother.

In F. Coy, we have 400 men or over & I've found several old friends, all who were out with me greet me warmly & I them. I've met several of my old platoon, & picked up scraps of news from them; amongst others, they say a fair number of the Batt: <u>did</u> manage to get through the wire but not enough to do any good. I had a <u>long</u> talk with Col. C-Essex yesterday, for nearly ½ hour, he was v interested in everything. In spite of having 400 men in the Coy: it is the exception to have more than 20 or 30 men on parade & generally there are none! To begin all the employed men, off: servants, cooks, mess waiters etc. 100 or so in number belong to us. Also all the sergeant instructors. Then we supply men for all the fatigues & the numbers for parade soon dwindles to 0. So you see after breakfast I may often find myself with practically <u>nothing</u> to do! So <u>please</u> tell Bob to hurry up & get well, he'd be a great companion here as you'll see. I've seen a good deal of Nichol. There <were> was a big garrison cross country race yesterday & I helped him check at one of the points then went to tea at the Felix with him. You know that barrier you had to pass always at Walton just outside here, well now there is a guard on there night & day, and no one may come in by day without a pass or go out by night without one. However just at present <u>no-one</u> may leave the garrison at all, so can't pass that barrier, ie. I cannot go even to the Banks! Isn't it annoying! Some scare I suppose. They had one before & it lasted 4 weeks! We might be in a besieged city. You can go out about 2 miles anywhere, that's all –.

Whenever there's a Zep. scare we all have to get up & dress & remain so till they've left the country again. A <u>most</u> annoying practice specially if they are in Scotland or some distant land! Light Duty does not excuse me from <light> orderly officer apparently, at any rate it's not very hard work & something to do is better than nothing. *I'm Ord Off tomorrow.* Nichol was to have come to Church with me this morning but did not turn up so I went alone & enjoyed it. We feed quite well in the Mess don't send a cake, I shouldn't like to see some of my Messmates eating one of your lovely cakes! Well I've cleared off some of the grumbles and feel better, and probably I shall soon begin to feel more settled.

Weather is lovely so is the sea.

Dearest love your very loving Philip

It is, I think, so nice to be able to think of Aunt Emmie with no more suffering.[167]

MC 643/7/3

---

167. Aunt Emily died in Croydon on 27 April 1916, aged 58.

85.   Wednesday

My dear Ruth

Here's some photos I expect you'll like. I think they're rather good & hope
they will find favour in your sight. Keep them as I had 2 prints made of
them. I am quite beginning to drop into the old life again now, and have
actually been on parade from 9.30–12.30 and 2–3.30 today so I've been quite
busy. I am also settling down much more among my companions & am
finding some friends, chiefly from the Postern crowd though. I fill up the
days pretty well and do not find them drag so much now. We are still shut
up here & allowed to go nowhere so we cannot get far afield. I am thinking
of calling on the Masons today or tomorrow. I manage to make myself
quite comfortable on my camp bed; and there is a long table of packing
cases & boards so with my chest of drawers I am fairly well set up. My
servant polishes my buttons till they nearly dazzle me & my boots & belt
are beautiful! We've got a conscientious objector here who has hunger struck
now for 6 days, Goodness knows what will eventually happen to him.[168]
How's Bob? I hope he is recovering!

Much love to all from Philip

Did you see Sidney Peake "wounded"[169]

MC 643/7/5

86.   Sunday

My dearest Mother & Father

Bob arrived quite safely by the 3 train yesterday. I met him at the station
& he was just delighted to see me! as of course I was to see him. He
looked splendid I thought. I took him for a walk round the town & then
brought him up here & showed him his new quarters, he seems to have

---

168. Conscription had just been introduced. The first 'conscientious objectors' were
forced into the army, ordered over to France and threatened with being shot. Later in the
war, they were treated with more leniency, being offered alternatives such as the Royal Army
Medical Corps or the Non Combatant Corps (whose members wore uniforms and drilled
but did not carry guns). A small number of people who refused to wear uniform were sent
to labour camps, cutting trees etc. Those who refused to accept any of these alternatives
were the ones who faced imprisonment – and the very harsh prison conditions of the early
twentieth century.

169. Sidney was a son of Rev Vincent Peake, vicar of nearby Hoveton: he survived the
war. His sister Marjory is mentioned in letter 129.

quite settled into them. My servant knocked 2 packing cases together &
they really make quite a nice kennel. He is lying on the floor in my room
while I write this. He <u>will</u> be a nice companion. This morning I've been
to Church parade. Nowadays one officer per Coy: has to attend & there
is a Captain in charge of the whole parade. We assemble on the Battalion
Parade Ground at 9.45 and march to Church headed by the Band; about
350 men and 7 officers this morning. Mr Horne[170] took the Service and I
expect gave us something the same as you give at the Wroxham soldiers
service. It was quite a nice service. The Band plays everything, hymns,
Venite etc, & all the men's voices make a splendid noise – after service we
form up & march back to the Hutments with the Band. I was going for
a walk with Bob after this but it has started to drench with rain so I am
writing instead. I called on the Masons on Friday with a 2nd Lieut, Garrod
by name. He lives at Woodbridge & his people know them. I knew his
brother who joined when I did here but was killed in May. I like him & go
about chiefly with him, he's 19 & was a[t] Marlborough. Our call however
only consisted in ringing the doorbell & going away again for the Masons
were out. However luckily when I met Bob yesterday I found Mr & Miss
Mason coming off the same train, they were very pleased to see me and
Garrod & I are both going in to supper tonight which will be very nice.
Then I am going to tea with Reed my Coy. Commander you'll remember.
He is married & has a little girl of 9. He is an older man with 17 years of
service! he was given a commission on the Aisne, tho' you'd never know
he'd risen from the ranks, as he's extremely nice.

I am continuing this after lunch, it is still absolutely drenching so it is nice
to have Bob & some letters to write with a prospect of both tea & supper out
to follow – up till yesterday I have been the senior officer dining in this mess
& have always had to take the head of the table. However yesterday a major
arrived from the Golf Club which we are giving up so I am relieved. So far
he has done nothing but talk about food & drink & grumble thoroughly at
both as provided in the Mess! So he's not started very high on the ladder of
my estimation! He doesn't <u>seem</u> to have any other topic of conversation in
him. I hope it is not like this tomorrow if Father bikes down, anyhow I'm
afraid the roads <would> will be dreadful. I have not found a room yet but
am going round tomorrow morning. One of the majors here went off last
week to Ireland to hold Courtmartials on the rebels, we all rather envy him
& hope he piles on the sentences.[171] We are having to sleep in our clothes all

170. See note 32.
171. The Irish rebellion of 1916: on Easter Monday an attempted rising was defeated

these nights – they don't tell us why! it seems a contrast to those of us who've slept in pyjamas less than a mile from the front line trenches! However I take my boots off & substitute stocking puttees for ordinary ones, take off my tunic & collar & don't do badly. I expect I shall be able to give Father lots of news when he comes. I'm settling down much more now. I heard from Gardner yesterday & he <u>hopes</u> to be sent back here on May 18. But you never can tell. It would be splendid if he were.

Lots of love Your loving

Philip.

MC 643/7/6

87.   Wednesday

My very dear Father

It certainly was impossible weather, both on Monday & Tuesday & I thought you'd hardly come. I've much enjoyed both Ruth's and Mother's letters. Bob is a <u>great</u> favourite with everybody, they all admire him & think *him* a real good boy. More especially tho' do they love his ways. On Monday Nichol & Stone went off to France at very short notice. Nichol wild with joy at his long hoped for chance. Stone going out for the 3rd time! We have 8 more officers waiting to go to "the East"[172] – now that Nichol has gone I am going to try and move up to Postern if I can get leave. There is room for me there & tho' I should still mess here my friends are there. Please send me some more pyjamas I find I only bought one pair. I have been sleeping in them just lately as the weather has been so bad. Also please send the book I kept the list of letters I wrote & received in. It has the number of the War Office letter in it by which I claim for massage! Today I've sent in another claim for a wound gratuity which I hope'll be successful. We had a very nice time on Sunday evening, they're very nice people & were very pleased to see me back & hear about things. It was very nice & homely, <u>we</u> did all the clearing away & waiting at supper! I

---

by the British army. In the subsequent trials several of the leaders were sentenced to death, and many others received prison sentences. Philip's Anglo-Irish ancestry on his mother's side may account for his lack of sympathy for the 'rebels'.

172. The 3rd (Reserve) Battalion provided junior officers for all the battalions of the LNLR, including those fighting further afield than France. The 6th Bn was in Mesopotamia from March 1916, fighting against the Turkish army: four officers were killed or died of wounds after an attack on 5 April, so reinforcements were clearly needed.

<u>shall</u> enjoy the books M. sent today v much, Many are greatly appreciating the 1ˢᵗ 7 Divisions[173] which I lend them, It is a <u>great</u> book. Has "Johnny" N[174] finished "With the Guns"??[175] as I have promised it one or two here, so could you ask him & send it on. I'm quite enjoying life here again now. Lots of love to all

your ever loving Philip.

MC 643/7/7

88.   Felixstowe

May 14 1916

My very dear Mother & Ruth

I expect Father will be here by the time you get this. I wrote him a p.c. last night & most stupidly forgot to post it so I am afraid he won't get it before he starts so I shall wire to him early tomorrow morning. I hope he will have a fine day, it looks rather threatening at present. I was most pleasantly excited to get a letter from the War Office this morning to say "Sir, I am commanded by the Army Council to acknowledge the receipt of your letter of the 10 inst. on the subject of a wound gratuity which shall receive attention" – So I am now very hopeful at any rate it is a step farther than my last application went. I <u>do</u> hope they send me a nice fat cheque!! I got your letter last night this week. I haven't read the C.F.N. yet but will look out for what you mention. The last few days I have been revelling in "Gen. John Regan"[176] it is a splendid book, & one has lots of chances of reading. I had another Sub sharing my room for 2 nights, but he started for E. Africa[177] yesterday, so I am alone again. I have not troubled <my> to apply for a change to Postern as my room is quite comfortable now that I am alone. I think I should rather like the gramophone! It would be specially nice on

---

173. Ernest W. Hamilton, *The First Seven Divisions: being a detailed account of the fighting from Mons to Ypres*, (first ed. 1916): an immensely popular book, in its 21ˢᵗ edition by 1918.

174. Not otherwise identified.

175. *F.O.O.* [Forward Observation Officer, a pen-name of Major Cecil John Charles Street], published in 1916.

176. A novel by George A Birmingham [pen-name of James Owen Hannay (1865–1950)], published in 1913.

177. See note 172. The 2ⁿᵈ Bn LNLR had been in India when the war broke out and was sent to British East Africa, where a war was fought against the troops of German East Africa. The battalion was in East Africa until October 1917.

wet days & lonely times, though I am afraid you'd miss it! It poured with rain all yesterday morning though it cleared up later. I was Orderly Officer so had to stay in all day. However time did not drag very much, and I got somebody to answer for me for an hour & ½ in the evening, while I went to a meeting at the Felix. There are to be some big garrison sports on Whit Monday here & the Colonel, the adjutant & Cramer Roberts between them decided to ask me to be the N. Lanc: representative on the Committee so I am! & that's where I went last night. This morning 5 of us went to Church at Mr Horne's Church in Old Felixstowe, quite a crowd of us! My arm seems just about the same & still hurts me in heat or cold. It must be getting nearly time for my Board again but I shall <be> not be passed fit yet. Bob gets lots of meat etc from cook & servants & doesn't at all appreciate biscuits now. I'm sorry about it but can't help it. He's great fun.
I like that photo of Julian

Lots of love yr every loving

Philip.

MC 643/7/8

89.   21.5.16

My very dear Mother & Father

These last few days have been simply gloriously hot days and I have found lots to do. I find my arm does not mind tennis, provided I do not do too much in the way of running about etc. So I have played the last 4 days. I played 3 times on the town courts & I was one of a mens four each time. I seem to be in quite good form! and play with a Capt. Harrison & a sub named Aldred, who are both quite good. Then yesterday I had a lovely afternoon. I motorbiked over to the Banks' for tennis & had a splendid [*time*] they were v. pleased to see me. There were 2 Bedford subs there both very nice & good tennis players. Also a Miss Havell whom I knew last year, an awful stick, quite young 21 or so but absolutely Mid Victorian, & 2 girls from Ipswich whose sisters I met there at tennis last year once. We had some splendid tennis & I did not leave till 7pm. My Board on Thursday took me off light duty & put me on Home Service for a month. There doesn't seem to be any difference between the two, except that Home Service is a step nearer to "Fit" than light duty! I may of course get more H.S. next Board. I am being kept very busy with these sports, and am practically doing everything in organising battalion sports for tomorrow Tuesday & Wednesday. I am at the head of a committee of all the Coy. Sgt. Majors and an officer from each Coy, but none of them are very full of ideas, they more or less agree when I suggest. However we are well on our way now, I've got all the entries in & officials appointed. At present I'm busy arranging all the heats while tomorrow afternoon we mark out the ground – lots of work! Henderson told me on Wednesday that he would want me to command a Coy soon as I should be very useful to him training men as I had been to the front, much more so he said than some of these old "dug-out" majors! He also said I would be a Captain soon, as there ought to no difficulty about my promotion as I had been Tempy Capt once. It may however take 6 or 8 weeks as certain papers have to be signed by the 1ˢᵗ Batt. This all naturally pleased me v much. More so as he told me he wanted me to go to the station next day & meet Col. Sanderson & conduct him to the Mess. This I did, & got a splendid welcome from him, he was home on 10 days leave, & was very pleased to see me again.

How <u>splendidly</u> you packed the gramophone! It arrived yesterday quite safely & I fetched it up in a taxi. I shall love having it to play. This morning I went to Church at St Johns. Afterwards I met Mrs Welby.[178] You met her this time last year, you remember I used to play tennis with them. I thought she'd left F'stowe, however she has been here all this time so I am going to tea there this afternoon. I have decided I think not to move to Postern but stay here now. I heard from Gardner this morning, he was given 3 <u>more</u> weeks(!) last Thursday –

Much love

Your v loving

Philip.

MC 643/7/9

90.   My dear Ruth (the Cute'Un)

I am at present Acting Assistant Adjutant! When I went Orderly Room on Sunday evening I took over Curwen's job from him. I get to Orderly Room each morning between 9.15 & 9.30 and am generally there till 12 or 12.30, though it varies of course I can go as soon as I have finished whatever paper there are to be signed. Then I go up there again about 2 or 2–15 and stay till 4, and I have about ½ an hour to an hour's work in the evening. I thought at first I should not be able to find time for tennis but I generally manage some between 4.30 and 6.30. On Tuesday I played with Mrs Welby and yesterday

---

178. See note 44.

I went to the Masons. Today we have got a good men's four arranged but it is blowing so hard I don't know if it'll be worth it. You know that photo on a p.c. of the 4 B. Coy & subalterns in France I've got, well will you send me one as Gemmel is v. anxious to have one! I have still got Bob with me and am keeping him chained up more, he went away from Monday Midday to Tuesday 9 a.m., & I gave have [*sic*] a terrific thrashing when he came back & he's been all right since. There's a really splendid Coy: of a sort of Pierrot at the Cinema theatre here this week, and they are getting <u>crowded</u> houses. About 16 of us went all together last night. I got a letter from Mother this morning I suppose she's home now.

Much love from

Philip.

MC 643/11/2

91.   F'lixstowe

Sunday 28.5.16

My very dear Mother & Father

I'll write a joint letter & then it can be forwarded. Its as hot as ever, glorious weather, I am in my thinnest summer clothes every day, several people have started bathing but I have not done so yet; I am writing this immediately after lunch. This morning I went off to the old Felixstowe Church but was the only L.N.L. officer there. After Church I saw the two Miss Masons who asked me in to supper this evening so I am going there at 8. I was to have gone to tennis at the Banks yesterday but got a p.c. putting it off, however I got some excellent sets here. I played with Harrison a Capt who now commands F, Coy a nephew of Colonel H. against Cramer Roberts and Tripp a brother of the D.S.O.[179] man we had seven sets and though we were beaten every time it was always 7–5 or 6–4, we had some real good tennis and I am pleased to say my arm allows me to play. On Thursday evening I went out to dinner with Captain & Mrs Loch who have a small house now. The other guest was Col: Harrison, so I was in splendid company and felt quite honoured! as I told you, I believe, I have been "acting-resident-assistant-adjutant" to Curwen while Henderson has been away.

---

179. Distinguished Service Order, instituted 1886, awarded for meritorious or distinguished service: for officers only, generally given to those above the rank of Captain. In the first years of the war it could be given to staff officers, but from January 1917 was restricted to those serving under fire.

Well Curwen goes away tomorrow and Henderson came back last night. I have been summoned to Orderly Room for 6.30 tonight so I expect I shall be taking over Curwens job while he's away it will mean a lot of office work while it lasts I am afraid. However it's nice to be chosen for the job, as it is a more or less responsible one! "My" Battalion sports went off quite successfully. Preliminary heats on Monday & Thursday & the Finals on Wednesday, with the Band playing & the C.O. giving the prizes. It meant lots of organization & I pleased with the result. The letter from Woburn got here on Sat: night I do not think such men as Clifford[180] <u>should</u> be found clerkly jobs, let them learn to <u>fight</u>! Bob gets fed by everybody and strays a good deal I <u>may</u> have to send him home again.

Much love your loving Philip[181]

MC 643/7/10

92.   Sunday June 4

My very dear Mother & Father

Today is just an absolute change from the lovely weather we have been having, it's blowing cold hurricanes & trying to rain! The rain started yesterday afternoon, however I managed to get some tennis in. I was playing at the Havells some people I used to know last year & as their court dries very quickly we got some good sets. This afternoon I must go and call on the Lochs, you know how I hate calling but as I haven't been since I went to dinner there I must go & pay a duty call I s'pose! It wasn't our Nichol you saw as "killed", he is Lieut E. F. Nichol, this was Tempy Sec. Lieut E. J. Nich<u>olls</u>! he was in the 10th Batt. I believe. I have quite enjoyed my week of assistant adjutancy it didn't keep me so tied as I feared it might. Curwen returns on Wednesday so I've 3 more days of it. Did you see in the paper yesterday that Phillips now a tempy Major was given the Military Cross;[182] also Jack Marriott from Cromer who is in the Northamptons. Bob is a bit better behaved now but is off on a wander somewhere now, I shall have to beat the wandering trick out of him. We knew nothing about the

---

180. Clifford Gilbert, full name John Clifford Milson Gilbert, born c.1878, solicitor, lived at Cringleford, Norfolk 1911, by 1916 resident at the Manor House, Wroxham.

181. 'Miss Wise gave R her letter at school, which she put straight with her run. I shall write tomorrow.' added by Philip's father.

182. Created in December 1914 for commissioned officers of rank of Captain or below and for Warrant officers. Awarded for gallantry during active operations against the enemy.

Naval Battle[183] until the evening telegrams on Friday. It does not seem so bad now as the first telegrams made out. It certainly gives one to think! & makes you realise this war is not a "walk over" for us – Do you realise that is was exactly a year ago today that I got on a train at Havre to go up to the Front! Isn't it extraordinary, a whole year! and the war still seems about the same – well it's getting near calling time, so I must stop,

your very loving

Philip.

MC 643/7/11

93.   June 8th Thursday

My dear Father

We've had a great excitement here this week. I could not tell you about it on Sunday though we knew it was going to happen & had been practising for it hard. It was the occasion of the visit of the King[184] and a Royal Review.[185] You saw no doubt in the papers that he was out of London on Tuesday morning but that the sad & awful news of Ld Kitchener's death[186]

---

183. The Battle of Jutland, the only direct confrontation between the British and German High Seas Fleets was fought on 31 May 1916. The result was indecisive: the British lost three battle cruisers, three armoured cruisers and eight destroyers, while the Germans lost one battleship, one battle cruiser, four light cruisers and five destroyers. British casualties were the greater, with 6,097 officers and men killed to the Germans' 2,545.

184. George Frederick Ernest Albert (1865–1936), George V, King of the United Kingdom and the British Dominions and Emperor of India from 6 May 1910 until his death.

185. *The Times* for 7 June 1916 includes this court circular: 'June 6: The King attended by Captain B. Godfrey-Faussett, R.N., Lieut-Colonel Clive Wigram and Major R. H. Seymour, inspected troops in the Eastern Command today'.

186. Herbert Kitchener (1859–1916), victorious at the Battle of Ombdurman 1890, Chief of Staff in Second Boer War 1900–2; Commander-in-Chief of the Army in India 1902–9; Secretary of state for War from 1914. Field Marshal Lord Kitchener left Scapa Flow on the *Hampshire* on 5 June 1916, bound for Russia: within two hours the ship struck a mine and Kitchener and most of the crew were drowned. Interestingly, cousin Julian had a different view of Kitchener's death: 'It is curious how everyone in England seems to feel the loss of Lord Kitchener. It has not had the slightest effect on the troops out here [at the Front]. We had all felt that his work was really over before the news of his death came along. We regarded him as more of a political figurehead and representative of the Army to Foreign Powers. I think people in England were apt to idolize him a bit, and did not realize that practically all the work and responsibility was being borne by others at the time of his death'. (Tyndale-Biscoe *op. cit.* p. 8)

was conveyed to him, well he was here, and though it was the first news he got on arriving here about 11 he carried on with the <usual> programme though he looked very tired & worried, the reason we did not know till afterwards. There were a tremendous number of troops, from both sides of the river, <u>battalions</u> of them. We were all drawn up on the golf Links facing the saluting base. The King rode on to the ground at 12.15 between rows of cheering civilians kept back by the lines of unarmed soldiers. He rode his lovely black charger out into the centre – all the officers were drawn up in front with drawn swords and as he came on the thousands of men with fixed bayonets presented arms, we gave the royal salute and the massed band of 300 to 400 men played "God Save the King" – Then led by the general we roared out 3 lusty cheers! After that he rode down the lines and I could have stroked his horse as he passed me he was so close. Then after some manoeuvring we all marched past him by Companies, I was on the right of our Coy, so got another splendid view. When we were all drawn up again various Colonels & staff officers were presented to him. Then pursued by 3 more hearty cheers he rode back to the station & we dispersed. It was a most interesting morning. They took a cinema film of it all <but> which can be seen here now but unfortunately with our usual luck the Lancs are not on it!

Kitchener's death must have been a dreadful blow to him as it is to everybody. What <u>seems</u> so wrong is that apparently there was no escort of destroyers with the cruiser. I finished my time as Assistant Adjutant last night as Curwen is back again. On Monday Lindsell who is at present Acting Adjutant to the 1st Batt, spent a day of his leave down here. He went out after the 25th. Then yesterday Phillips also home on leave came down for a few hours. Barker wounded in March and just out of hospital has also been here for 2 or 3 days seeing his brother, so we've had quite a reunion, & I've naturally <u>greatly</u> enjoyed seeing them all. Tomorrow – Goldie a cousin of the Goldie killed on the 25th[187] is coming down. He has been out since October 1914!! and has 2 or 3 weeks leave, so is spending a night here. Aren't we reuniting, specially if Gardner comes back at last soon! I'm very busy with the sports so must stop now.

With much love

Your loving

Philip.

MC 643/7/12

---

187. The Battle of Loos, where Philip was wounded.

94. Whit Sunday June 11th 1916

My very dear Mother & Father

Oh! we are having dreadful weather, thunderstorms & <u>torrents</u> of rain every day this week, & it's threatening all day to-day – however we get some fine intervals, but it has effectively stopped all tennis this last week & now we are only <u>hoping</u> it'll be fine tomorrow. It will be a grand Fete day if only it is fine – I enclose a programme so that you can see the size of the sports, & there are stalls & sideshows & bands & baby competitions (!) & tea etc! It is all in aid of the Suffolk Red Cross. All the ladies of Felixstowe are doing the teas & I seem to be in for more than one tea if I go to the different tables I've promised! Oh it's doing its usual drench again now :- Last night I found out by Orders that I was detailed to march the Roman Cath: party to their Church at 8.45 am this morning & as I had to get in breakfast too I could not go to an early service. I got them down there by 9. am and as I didn't see any point in going in too I came back here & went down there again in ¾ hour's time to march them back. Then I went up to Old Felixstowe Church at 11, there were 8 of our officers there & 4 of us stayed afterwards. Mr Horne gave us a very nice service. This afternoon if only it will keep decently fine I am going to bicycle out to the Banks for tea. I was delighted last night to hear that Gardner is coming back at last to-morrow!

I've got mixed tennis fours arranged for Tuesday & Wednesday so am doing well! My valise is being repaired. I should think a Khaki blanket would be <u>most</u> useful. I believe I have a Board at the end of this week or beginning of next and should <u>think</u> they would give me another month H.S., but it is absolutely no good speculating as I can't tell at all really. I should not go to those rooms Father had – one of our married officers is living there! also I think they're very expensive – But I ought to be able to get home before you need bother about room here – much love you very loving

Philip.

MC 643/7/13

95. Felixstowe

Wednesday

My very dear Father

Our great Fête day on Monday was dreadful! It simply drenched with rain all day, it was very sad, everybody was wet through & cold & shivery! In the centre of the ground were all the sports and round the edge all sorts of marquees(?), some big ones for tea, & others with different stalls in them, then there was a baby show & all sorts of side shows, Aunt Sallies etc etc, including a Pierrot entertainment given by the Navy. In spite of the weather they cleared £300 for the Red Cross! If it had been fine they expected to double that. I am afraid after a certain time I quite gave up watching the sports, & adjourned to the tea tent where tea was being served by the ladies of F: In spite of the rain I managed to have quite a good time. Last night Gardner turned up & is now sharing this room with me which is very nice. Yesterday was another blustering wet cold day, impossible for tennis, however I dropped in to tea with the Welbys with whom I was to have played if fine. I am hoping very much it will keep fine today for my other mixed tennis four. For owing to this continual bad weather *all the* a certain number of F. residents who've got tennis parties today have arranged if it is wet to have a room at Felix & have a small dance. As neither Tripp or I who are both playing can dance you can imagine we want it to keep fine. We are playing at 4 pm, and it is nearly 3 now, it's fine but very threatening. Major Torbett came back here last night too, he has had heart trouble I believe. We now have 4 Majors here!

Much love your very loving Philip

No news about my Board yet.

MC 643/11/15

96. The Hutments, Sunday June 18

My very dear Mother & Father

The weather seems to have changed again at last, which is splendid. We did have 10 horrible cold wet days didn't we! my arm does not like that sort of thing & used to go ice cold & ache a good deal at times. It really seems very much the same to me tho' I suppose it is always gradually improving. There is a <u>little</u> more muscle in the thumb I think but it is still quite wasted. I have a Board again tomorrow & I should think I am sure for another month Home Service. Well it did just stay fine on Wednesday & we got our tennis. It was very windy but we got some jolly games. We were all the guests of Colonel (home from France) & Mrs Allen,[188] they have 2 rather pretty daughters, one of whose birthdays it was. I knew them last year & they live here. There were 5 officers in all & 4 girls so we kept 2 courts going all the time. I was very pleased it did turn out a tennis and not a dancing day. If

---

188. See above, note 74.

we had had to try dancing we should have gone in slacks & brown shoes, that is quite alright & the recognised kit for it now!

Wasn't it splendid Uncle Henry being in Dispatches, it is very ridiculous though that no-one is ever recommended from the N.Lancs. I had a long letter from Gobagger yesterday & one from Hugo which seems to have crossed a long one I wrote to him. Yesterday I took Garrod out to the Banks' for tennis & we had a very jolly time. Tomorrow I am playing with Miss Robinson. I was also asked to the Masons but had to refuse. However on the top of it all I find I am Orderly Officer. You see I am getting quite a lot of society here now! I'm getting to know quite a lot of people now, & generally meet some one I know when I go down the Town, or at the Felix or Tennis Courts. Best of luck to Ruth in the exam on Tuesday. It's very nice having Gardner here we seem to agree well. He & Tripp & I went to Old F. Church this morning

very dear love your v loving

Philip.

MC 643/7/14

97.   Tuesday

I had my Board yesterday & was given another month's H Service so that's alright! I got my tennis in yesterday in spite of being Orderly Officer. Please send my "sword frog" – we've all got to wear them now. It's a leather thing to fasten on my belt & is hanging on the back door leading in to the Bathroom I think, it's like this[189] a leather slab with 2 straps on it! It's lovely weather again & I'm playing lots of tennis.
Letter from R[190] this morning

Love Philip.

MC 643/7/15

98.   Sunday June 25

My very dear Mother & Father

Felixstowe is really getting quite jolly nowadays. Lots of tennis & people to know. The weather has been rather against tennis again lately though. On

---

189. Small picture drawn.
190. Ruth

Wednesday we sent off 3 more officers to France, among them was Tripp which was rather a pity from my point of view, as we were playing a lot of tennis together & as we knew the same people we often got asked out together. We had got a tennis & tea party arranged for the day before he went out but as that fell through we went to tea there instead. There is not a great deal of hard works to be done in our Coy each day. As usual not many men are for parade, generally between 20 & 30, it means 2 or 3 hours parade a day, generally less which doesn't sound too strenuous does it! Henderson said something to me again last week about giving me a Coy soon but there isn't one for me at present. Bratton who<m> you will remember went to the 4th Batt: with Hugo came back here on Tuesday for light duty, he seems very fit & plays tennis, he says he's quite alright. Gardner is not – he soon gets very 'done', heart pumps away too fast, & he gets out of breath very easily.

7pm. I am just going to finish this & then take it down to the post. This afternoon G & I went & called on Mrs Henderson whom we found in – she is young, pretty & jolly. They have a little girl of 2 and a baby of 5 weeks! After that we strolled on down to the Felix & listened to the band which plays there every Sunday afternoon. This morning I took F. Coy to Church Parade. We had an open air service, formed up in a square. Unfortunately the Band are all on leave so 3 of us subs had to lead the singing! It was rather – well —"!!!" I have not asked for a weekend yet as if I wait a bit longer I might get more. I haven't started bathing yet. Last week I decided again to send Bob home but I find he's still here! What a nuisance Harry[191] going – I like the idea of the Curate man, I hadn't heard. I think Mother's speech splendid.

Much love your v loving Philip.

MC 643/7/16

99.   Old Felixstowe

Sunday July 2?[192]

My very dear Mother & Father

Everybody here is of course full of last nights and this mornings news of the Great British offensive![193] Excitement here is local as last night the War Office

---

191. Philip Henry ('Harry') Bulmer was curate at Salhouse with Wroxham from 1912 to 1915 when he moved to Walthamstow. Presumably there was a plan for a replacement curate, but one was not in fact appointed.

192. The question mark is Philip's: his dating is correct.

193. The first day of the Battle of the Somme, 1 July 1916, is the day that comes to

wired for 13 officers, trained or untrained it didn't matter! from this battalion alone – The Adjutant has had to send in the names today, but nobody knows yet who is going or when. Apparently the 1st Batt: has been losing again. But I am very anxious about Hugh & de Blaby. For of course the 4th is exactly where the offensive is & I had a letter from Hugo 2 weeks ago hinting hints. It may be all very grand, but as Gardner, Gemmel & I who are the only ones here who've been through a big offensive say, the real thing is very different from anything anyone who has not been there can imagine. Still I think we've all got our blood up again (in a way)! Yesterday I had been asked over to tennis at Ipswich by some people whom I met at the Banks. I had met some of the daughters there. However as bad luck would have it I found myself detailed for Batt Duty at 2 pm. This lasted till 4.15, but I thought it worth going over so on my mo: bike I was there by 5 pm. They are a jolly, big family, the Maynes[194]. He is Chief Police Commissioner or something like that, they've got a ripping big house & garden. I took Elkington over with me & we had some goodish tennis & then raced back just in time for dinner. I should like to have seen our tennis court & garden on Saturday certainly, it must have been a splendid sight with all its fair & beauteous "attributes" – ![195] This week a girl friend of Gardner's & her brother have motored down here from town. The brother is a Naval Division man from Antwerp & is interned in Holland, but is on 3 months leave on parole. They have a ripping car which they use for driving wounded about. I've been out in it today with them and am going to tea with them this afternoon. When I came in last night, I found Bob's head & neck covered in blood, he must have had a huge fight, nothing much was wrong though, all the bleeding came from one torn ear chiefly; he is looking cleaner now after some scrubbing. I went down & watched the dancing last night but did not start on my career as a dancer, as you must dine there if you dance & I hadn't.

Much love your v loving Philip.

MC 643/7/17

---

people's minds when they think of the First World War, thousands of men mown down by withering machine gun fire as they went over the top and tried to cross No Man's Land to reach the German front line. It was the bloodiest day in the history of the British Army, 20,000 men being killed and many more wounded, missing or taken prisoner. It was only the first day in a battle that went on until November.

194. Jasper G Mayne was Chief Constable, East Suffolk police. His wife's name was Cecily and they had six children, including daughters Clare (21 in 1915) and Dorothy (19 in that year), the two of most interest to Philip. Their eldest son was James, born in 1893. They lived at Tumbricane, Belstead Road, Ipswich.

195. This refers to the Norwich Girls' High School tennis tournament, held at the Hewetson's home.

100.   Old Felixstowe

Sunday July 9

My very dear Mother & Father

We've had two ripping Summer days yesterday & today & I've had a splendid time. Yesterday afternoon I went out to Trimley for tennis with the Banks. They are awfully nice & had two of the Mayne girls over from Ipswich, (as I had hoped!). I was there from 3.30–7 and we had some splendid sets. I did not go to the Felix in the evening, it was too hot, instead I took Bob for a walk along the sea front. The dancing never goes on after 10.30 pm. It's not allowed to. We are all having to be vaccinated now if we haven't been done during the last 4 years. I had to be done this morning & am hoping it won't have any evil effects on me. I was done on the right arm as I didn't want to be done on the wounded one. After being "done" I went along to Old Felixstowe Church with Barker. This afternoon I had a splendid time. The Curwen bros: have got a Ford. However they are selling it tomorrow as its too expensive to keep up, so they planned a last days ride. There were 4 of us, they two, Gemmel and I. We started after lunch and went through Ipswich to Stowmarket then back to Ipswich, out towards Woodbridge & so home. I am interested to hear about the Scotch Colonel. The Engineers attached to the 1st Division were the Lowland R.E. so ask him if he belongs to them. We <u>often</u> took working parties to work under them. Three more names have been added now to the 13 asked for last week; and 4 of them are now under orders for E. Africa, but the others are all still here – waiting – . I heard from P.J.[196] yesterday from Rhodesia, a letter written on June 10. We are all keenly interested in the offensive. News is very good when we hear of "Pushes" "on both fronts[197]. I think "Fritz" must be getting very flustered now. With dear love

your very loving Philip.

MC 643/7/18

---

196. Lionel Powys Jones.

197. The Russian army attacked in both the centre and north parts of the Eastern Front in July. The attacks resulted in little gain of territory and much loss of life: however, they forced the Germans to transfer to the east seven divisions that would otherwise have been used as a response to the British attack on the Somme.

101.   Wednesday

My very dear Father

We've had a big clearance of officers to-day. This morning we sent off seven subalterns to France. They were only warned early this morning to have to be on board tomorrow at 9 am so have had no time for any leave. The four warned for E. Africa have not actually gone yet. I decided not to play tennis on Monday as I had been vaccinated on Sunday, but I need not have troubled as a tremendous thunderstorm put tennis out of the question for everybody. I have had no evil effects from vaccination yet though the two places on my arm are very inclined to be irritating, which I believe shows it has "taken". Yesterday I spent the day being Orderly Officer so shall be glad of a good night in bed tonight. Today has turned in a <u>horrible</u> day; though that is nothing new. Its raining hard and a gale is blowing too! All Companies are of course short of officers now & will be still shorter soon. We are losing 2 from F. Coy wh: brings us down to 3. Though I believe the battalion will have several more gazetted to it soon. We have heard no more about own gold braid stripe yet, since it appeared in the paper, nor have I seen any braid![198] I suppose it will arrive <u>some</u> time! Personally I do not think it was necessary at all. What was wanted was a badge for <u>discharged</u> men. The present system is <u>grossly</u> unfair, as men like Gardner & Gemmel, both badly gassed, which is worse than a wound, cannot wear it!!
Much love

Your very loving Philip.

MC 643/11/16

102.   Old Felixstowe

Sunday 16.7.16

My very dear Mother & Father

The usual old thing rain, rain, rain, however I had a simply topping day yesterday. It was really a glorious day and as my vaccination continues to take in a mildish way I had to find something other than tennis to do. Four

---

198. Wound stripes were first authorised under an Army Order of 6 July 1916: the stripe was two inches long, of gold braid and worn on the left sleeve of the jacket (one stripe was worn for each wound, so people might have several). Other people clearly shared the concerns expressed by Philip: an Instruction of 3 November 1916 stated that officers and men wounded by gas *were* entitled to the distinction.

of us planned a river trip, we went down to Bawdsey Ferry[199] and hired a sailing boat, a ripping fast 4 ton yacht like they race on the Broads with. It was a good day for sailing as there was a strongish breeze. Too stiff for us to sail the boat in so the old "salt" came with us. The river is about 3 times as broad as our river at Wroxham. We sailed up the river for about 1½ hours to a place where we had tea, and then came back down stream with the wind behind us in ½ an hour. We all enjoyed ourselves thoroughly. But the day was not over yet!!

On Friday night Henderson (the adjt: you know) rang me up to know if I danced so as I had *had* one lesson I thought I would *not* say no; however I said I was dreadfully bad which he assured me was not the point at all, which was he said "did I like it?" I boldly said yes. Then came the explanation of all this. They had got a daughter of Cramer-Roberts staying with them & wanted me to come & dine with them on Saturday night & go with them and dance at the Felix afterwards, so as you can very likely guess I accepted. We had dinner at Henderson's house at 7.45. There were 5 of us, Cramer Roberts & daughter, Mrs Henderson, Henderson & self. They had somehow arranged that we should dance there without dining there first. We all went down there in a taxi after dinner. Miss Cramer Roberts has still got her hair down & is about 17 I should think. She is a most awfully jolly girl, not very particularly pretty, but full of fun and a very good dancer. She has lots to say for herself, she is the younger of his two daughters. I was rather anxious about my dancing but got on really quite well I think, I danced 3 or 4 with Miss C-R, and 4 with other partners! So I have launched out! My two arms did not trouble me at all. My vaccination marks have come up into nasty looking things but do not trouble me much. The arm just round them is a little swollen & I have to be careful of it. Thank you so much for the ripping box of peppermint crisps, I think they are making the vaccination disappear already. My other arm seems to me to keep very much the same, though I have not noticed it getting cold so often lately it is still very soft & I get the same pain in it. It will be interesting to know what my Board say. I should think if they give me another month I might wait a bit for leave & then get 5 or 6 days. I hardly think I could get that long now if I am given another month. But I'll let you know by Wed or Thurs I am not sure when my Board will be yet. Isn't the news splendid, though the casualty lists are dreadful. It'll be great if the cavalry have really got at them at last.[200]

---

199. Bawdsey, a Suffolk village on the River Deben, connected to Felixstowe by a vehicle and passenger ferry; between 1894 and 1931 it was a steam-drawn chain ferry.
200. On 14 July, the cavalry were used in the second phase of the Battle of the Somme: acting as a mobile exploitation force, they charged and cleared enemy outposts between

Much love

Your very loving

Philip.

MC 643/7/19

103.   26 July 1916[201]

My very dear Ruth

This is not an official document but I thought I'd just put the Orderly Room stamp on it! I am writing this in my "office"! There does not seem to be such a great deal of work to do here nowadays though I have to sit & wait for it all the same. I made a pilgrimage down the town this morning & chose a really <a> rather "dinky" little regimental Brooch for you which I hope you'll get tomorrow. It really is rather s'nice I think! & when I saw it I simply had to buy it I hope it won't stick into your throat. I had quite a good journey back I changed at Norwich where 2 subalterns of the 3rd Norfolks also going back here got in with me & we had quite an interesting journey. At Ipswich I found Garrod & Palmer who had been to Woodbridge for the day & here I was met at the station by Gardner & Sandie. I've got a palatial room at the White Horse as big as yours or Mother's nearly. Properly furnished, big double bed, chairs, table, 2(!) chests of drawers, washand stand etc! The Mess is however rather quiet & restrained after the Huts, too many Colonels about, but I'm not there much and go round to Huts or Postern after Mess generally. I had some <thing> topping tennis at the Masons & was playing pretty well for me, they had all brand new balls & I fairly smote them. I am playing again to-day but do not have too much time as I cannot leave till I have opened the afternoon post which doesn't come in till nearly 4.30 pm. I hope your Monday show went off swimmingly, with much love to all

your v loving Philip.

Lieut. & Asst Adjt 3RD Bn Loyal N Lancashire Regt[202]

MC 643/7/20

High and Delville Woods, then holding the line until they were relieved. Popular myth has it that they were mown down by machine gun fire but in fact the two cavalry regiments involved lost only eight killed.

201. The date has been printed with the official battalion stamp.

202. These words not hand written but stamped with an official stamp.

104.   August 3 1916

My very dear Father

The weather is <u>simply</u> stewing, oh it's hot, but its very nice really though uniform's hot. The trouble is these beastly Zepps are always getting us up in the night nowadays. It was interesting to hear they were so near you on Monday. We had a great night here last night. We got a splendid view twice as the search-lights found them & they showed as plain as anything. They had a nasty time as all the guns strafed them from all round, it was quite a battle!! shells and bombs bursting, though not so very near here, but tremendously exciting.

When I was home on leave I brought a cheque for £3. 15. 0 for June field allowance with me which I intended to send to Cox.[203] This I never did as far as I can remember, but I can't find the cheque anywhere now, so wonder if I left it at home. Can you search? My hand does not like this heat at all! So it is a good thing I'm in England at present. I still continue to have lots of tennis and have been doing rather well lately. Do you see J. N. Richardson in to-days Casualty List wounded? I'm keeping my eyes open for rooms. Much love

Your v loving

Philip.

MC 643/7/21

105.   August 6

My very dear Mother & Father

We are enjoying another simply glorious day and in a short time Gardner & I are going to bike over to the Banks' for tea, as I haven't seen them for some time. Then Gemmel has his people down here & I am going to supper with them tonight. He has been passed fit again (too soon!) and is expecting to go out again any day now. We are sending 6 more subs to France in a day or so. My work keeps me busy but I manage to fit in other things too, but my Saturday & Sunday slacker days are very welcome. I was playing tennis all yesterday afternoon with the Gemmels & Robinsons who had a joint party. Then I dined at the Felix with Mrs Welby, the 2

---

203. Cox and Co., Philip's bankers; founded in 1758 and by the end of the Napoleonic Wars were bankers for practically the whole army. Amalgamated with King's and both taken over by Lloyd's in 1923.

daughters & a Suffolk major before the dance. There I did my duty right nobly as I danced 10 dances out of a possible total of 11, a thing I should have thought absolutely impossible a few weeks ago! I seem to be a passable dancer nowadays, at any rate courage goes a long way & does a lot, & I boldly butt in & ask for dances. I hear rooms are <u>very</u> hard to get as Felixstowe is simply chock full of people but I am going to have a huge hunt tomorrow. Henderson is going away from the 14th to the 20th about I believe and I am to be left as adjutant of the battalion!!! So I shall be very busy if that is so I am wondering if you had better come at the end of that week or the beginning of the next? Still I will let you know later. It will be jolly having you all here for a time and very nice if Amie[204] comes for a few days. I went to Church again with Barker this morning. I am keeping very well and enjoying life thoroughly much love

your very loving

Philip.

MC 643/7/22

106.   August 13

My very dear Mother & Father

I had just been wondering if I should get my Sunday letter tomorrow or vice versa or what would happen and now I am to have two! That <u>is</u> splendid of you. How ripping it will be to see you all Wednesday, I went down there yesterday & found out you had wired to take them. They are really in a lovely position & I am sure you will like them. I hope she's a good cook etc! I shall of course be very busy all day this next week, but shall be able to see you tea time & in the evenings. It doesn't really matter how often I dine out. Last week end I dined out <Friday> Sat, Sunday, Monday & Tuesday! I am afraid I shan't get any tennis this week before Saturday which is <u>very</u> sad. It is really a very responsible job being left as Adjutant of the whole battalion, and I shall have lots to remember & think of but Henderson is leaving me very minute instructions, so I ought to be alright. I don't believe I ever told you that my official appointment as Ass. Adjt: came through from the War Office 2 or 3 days ago so I am bound to be kept here for some little time at any rate now! I invested in a bathing costume this last week but haven't used it yet. There is <u>lots</u> of bathing here now which Ruth will enjoy, also boats & fishing! I think you will all find lots of interest as we are really rather an

204. Amie Evershed: see Introduction.

interesting place, lots of war time interests, while the many visitors here now give it a peace time touch occasionally. I've had some ripping tennis the last 3 days & just at <u>present</u> I am playing better than I have ever before I think which certainly makes me enjoy it more than ever. I've got a new thin tunic now, it was only ready on Friday so is very new at present – but very nice! I found the lost cheque in my bag! I had looked there but missed it somehow. It's nice to think I shan't spend this birthday trying to blow myself up with bombs!! With very dear love for tomorrow.

Au Revoir till Wednesday

Your very loving Philip.

MC 643/7/23

107.   Sunday [*20 Aug.*]

My very dear Mother & Father

I am afraid this will not get to you tomorrow that is to say Monday as I am writing rather late in the evening. Oh what glorious weather this is at last, we are enjoying of it! Lots of sunburning & stewing and lots of tennis. My new job keeps me in a good deal but I cut it short as possible. I am there from roughly 9 to 12, sometimes 12.30. Then I go back between 2 and 3.30 & stop till nearly 4.30 then there is about ½ an hours work in the evening between 7 and 8 sometime. There is no work on Sat: afternoon, but I always have to fit in the evening ½ hour, for evening passes and postal work. On Sunday I just appear for ½ an hour or so in the morning & again in the evening for posts. Of course I am not necessarily working all the time. I have a nice airy room. I still continue to be very "gay." I had some splendid tennis with Mrs Welby & Miss Robinson yesterday afternoon, we started off with a 12–10 set! In the evening Barker & I dined at the Felix together, so that we could dance if we felt inclined. It was too hot to do too much so I only danced 3 dances, but enjoyed the evening very much. This morning after ½ an hour in my office I joined Barker at Church. After lunch I snoozed in the White Horse Garden, which is really awfully jolly, before going round to the Masons. Then since supper Bratton & I have been sitting out in the garden again. It is very nice having it to sit out in, & it is a <u>very</u> pretty old world garden with a nice lawn with old fruit trees dotted over it. I am so glad Bob is behaving I don't think he wants t<u>oo</u> much meat; a nice meaty bone occasionally & some scraps or gravy in the evening. This hot weather is sure to make him a bit listless. A 1d or 2d lump of sulphur in his water is a good thing I believe. All the beautiful pillowcases & sheets you sent back

with me are having a rest now as the White Horse supplies its inmates with its own line. You say "at any rate you'll have all your nights now" well I had a chunk out of one of mine last week. I was up from 1.30 a.m. to 4 the night those Zepps started though they were not near us, still it did not affect me at all next day. I had a visitor 2 evenings ago. the Senior chaplain here is a Co-Norfolk Vicar, he is the Vicar of Rudham rather curious?[205] Of course I did not know him but he had heard who I was & came up to see me. I'll start finding some rooms this week –
Much love

your very loving Philip.

MC 643/7/24

Philip's parents and Ruth stayed for three weeks at Felixstowe in late August/ early September, hence a gap in the sequence of letters. They were in Felixstowe for Philip's 23rd birthday on 24 August 1916

108. Sep: 10 1916

My very dear Mother & Father

It seems quite strange to be writing my Sunday letter home again after these 3 weeks. Luckily Thursday's lovely weather lasted for the next two days and I have managed to get some really splendid tennis in. on Friday we had a good men's four and yesterday there were 4 of us & also Miss Mason and Miss Robinson (not the sulky one!) so we had a good mixed four going and the odd two of us always joined up with the 2 goodish men I know in the Norfolks who were on the courts. You know I <u>did</u> mean to remember Sept 9th[206] and then I never did so now I am sending many loving wishes for many more Sept 9ths! Yesterday evening we gave the Felix dance a rest, all the four of us. However a party of 5 of us, Grove, Goldie, Leonard, Loch & self went to the Cinema after dinner and then looked in at the Felix just after 10 but it was rather empty. We met Maynard who was hit in the head on the 25th there, he is now on permanent Home Service & attached to the Suffolk Depot in Bury. This morning I joined Bratton & his mother (Mrs Wintle) who arrived down here again yesterday at the Church up here. I have started Locke's "Septimus"[207] but have not read v much of it yet. I enjoyed your lovely long letter this morning, I have taken no further steps

---

205. Revd Hugh John Dukinfield Astley, vicar of East and West Rudham, Norfolk, from 1896.
206. The Hewetsons' wedding anniversary.
207. William J Locke (1863–1930) *Septimus* (1st edn 1909).

about the Army yet, things seem to slide at present! I am so glad Bob has been behaving so well, of course he <u>would</u> the dear dog – Ugh – Dix[208], he's squashed at any rate. I wish the p'lice would have a raid and snaffle that young Teddie boy!![209] Hooray – Sun is coming out, it's been cloudy all day so far. We've got a good four (mens). I should love to see Ruth with her hair up, she ought to be photographed – It was extraordinary how the N. Lanc. officers did not go to the Felix yesterday! Why? Absence of the Misses Hewetson & Leonard!![210] Much love

Your very loving Philip.

MC 643/7/25

109.   Wednesday

My very dear Father

Work is very slack just at present in the office here so I am writing my letters. I enjoyed yours this morning. What rotten luck getting a puncture, I wonder if you took off the belt to push the bike back, it makes it so much easier, it does not sound as if you did. My word! What absolute cads those cottagers must have been not to lend you anything to prop it up with. They deserved to have some really very nasty rude things said to them! I got some good tennis yesterday at Sir F Wilson's Place – I hadn't been there before.[211] Goldie & Bratton are unfortunately both passed fit for G.S. again and as Gardner's papers applying for a transfer to the Machine Gun Corps have been forwarded it looks as if we shall be losing those 3 excellent fellows soon which will be very sad! Barker & I will then be the only Over Sea's set left. We are having an Over Seas meeting to night, it looks like being the last for some time. Just at present all leave is stopped so I don't look like getting to see Julian this weekend. I think it is while they are doing all these round ups for shirkers. So many wear both officers & mens' uniforms who have no right to it & shelter behind it. However it may come on again any day, & I

---

208. Perhaps Edward Dix (born 1883), son of Salhouse farmer James Dix.

209. This phrase is most commonly associated with the youth culture of the 1950s: those teddy boys were imitating the clothing styles of the original Edwardian 'dandies' to which Philip is referring.

210. Ruth Hewetson and Ada Leonard. Ada was the sister of 2nd Lt Hugh Leonard. Eight years older than Ruth, she was born in Hyderabad in India: the family was one of the many British families in colonial service.

211. Sir Frederick Wilson, Justice of the Peace, lived at High Row in Felixstowe High Street.

hope it won't be long. I had my 1st lesson at Bridge last night, it is really very like Whist. But as you know I was never <u>too</u> keen on that. But I think it is very useful to know Bridge even if you don't play much. But it will be nice on winters evening after mess. I do enjoy those chocolates mother sent & my hand is often going inside the box when I am in my room.

Much love your very

loving Philip.

MC 643/11/14

110.   17.9.1916

My very dear Mother & Father

This letter will miss tonight's post I am afraid as I am writing it rather late. Leave is still all stopped so if Julian is expecting to get out of hospital I shall not hurry for my weekend leave. It would as you say be very nice to get them both down here for a night or two. It is rather amusing to hear what you say about Major Wakley! They say "poor man" do they?! Well I don't think you'd find anybody who knew Wakley who wouldn't say "<u>poor</u> <u>poor</u> girl" I don't know him personally but I've often been told that you would have to go a really very long way to find anybody with a good word for him. I don't know where he is now, not here at any rate. We are to lose Bratton & Goldie in the near future, they are to go to Mesopotamia.[212] Goldie is delighted Bratton's opinions are divided, there are several points both for & against the Garden of Eden! Chiefly against I think. Still there are <u>good</u> points for it which it is as well to remember if you have <u>got</u> to go there. They have no orders yet & of course it may be weeks yet before they go – we hope so. We had some good tennis yesterday, Miss Mason, Bratton, Goldie & I, it was a lovely day for it. In the evening Goldie, Grove & I had a nice little dinner at the Felix & then had a very <nice> amusing time watching & criticising the dancers, we didn't take part ourselves. This morning after Church up here, a nice Harvest Festival Service with our Band playing the hymns, I went down & had lunch with Bratton and his people. Then we all went on & had some tennis at the Blunts[213] where you remember I went to tea one Sunday you were here. The Somme films are coming here the 2nd week in

---

212. See note 172. Mesopotamia was an unhealthy place in which to serve, Wylly writing 'many small reinforcements had reached the Battalion, both in officers and men, but these scarcely made up for the casualties caused by sickness'. (Wylly, *op. cit.*, p. 246)

213. Not otherwise identified.

October & I expect it will be very hard to get seats.[214] I was <u>very</u> pleased to see that the boy (for he was hardly more) who was my Platoon Sergt: all last Summer was awarded the military medal last week.[215] What's the matter with Vera's "He"[216] is he <u>never</u> going out?? Yes I am sorry about Geo Page & will write.[217] Things seem to be going very well now in France & everywhere don't they? It is most cheering & encouraging.

Much love

Your very loving Philip.

MC 643/7/26

III.   Thursday *21 Sept 1916*

My very dear Father

I expect you saw in the Gazette[218] today that I was made "Captain"! Isn't it splendid – and dated back to May 2 too, I am overcome by my wealth, both present & future! I knew last night, as a letter came to the C.O. from the War Office to say those promotions would appear in the Gazette at an early date and then it went & appeared the next day! I've been having lots of congratulations & everybody seems fearfully pleased. I haven't got my Captain's stars on yet but expect I shall blaze out in all glory tomorrow, muchly blushing & feeling very conspicuous! "Captain and Assistant Adjutant" looks very well doesn't it? I now get 18/- a day!! Certainly we <u>are</u> paid handsomely! Nothing much has happened this week, it's getting really too cold for tennis though I played yesterday. Yesterday morning I went out on the route march as Acting Adjutant as Henderson said it would be a good change for me, & I shall try & go each Wednesday if poss: Col Harrison was in Command & we rode along at the head of the battalion. We <rode> went about 11 miles, but I

---

214. The documentary film of *The Battle of the Somme*, made by official cinematographers Geoffrey Malins and John McDowell. It was released on 10 August 1916, a month after the events it depicts, and generally released on 21 August. Its realistic portrayal of the battle made it immensely popular: twenty million people saw the film in the first six weeks of its release.

215. The Military Medal was instituted 25 March 1916, an equivalent for other ranks to the Military Cross for officers. For the award to Sgt. John Balderson of the LNLR see *London Gazette* 1 Sept. 1916.

216. See note 118.

217. George Page, son of George and Charlotte Page of Salhouse, in the Norfolk Regiment, killed in action in France on 4 September 1916: he was nineteen years old. Buried at Corbie. He had left school by the time he was fourteen to work as a hawker's assistant.

218. *London Gazette* 21 September 1916.

dismounted & walked about 6 of them, I thoroughly enjoyed the exercise. This Thursday last year we <we> actually started at 8pm for the trenches from which we attacked, we spent today in a brick yard. What a change this year. How splendid this offensive is, we do seem to be doing <u>splendidly</u>.[219] Much love

Your very loving
Philip.

MC 643/7/27

112. Sunday Sept 24

My very dear Mother & Father

Well now I am walking about rigged up as a proper "Captain", 3 stars & two rings round my coat sleeve & feeling very conspicuous & very pleased with myself! The "and to remain seconded" applies to Fairbairn, as he is seconded into the Flying Corps. It has nothing to do with us. The Zeppelin season has unfortunately started again though they did not trouble us last night. We are delighted to hear that this time two have been brought down near London! A few more & they'll stop coming altogether I should think. Henderson took the first watch last night and as the raid finished early soon after 3 am. I didn't have to sit up so long as I usually do. The tennis season is rapidly finishing but I got some real good tennis yesterday, & met a Mrs Chambers(?) whose husband was succeeded at Coastguard & Coast watching work by Commander W. Hewetson! She knew the name at once & asked if I was any relation to him. Company football matches are in full swing now which looks like winter starting but I shall stick to tennis as long as possible. My claim for money for renewing my lost kit has come back as I must have a certificate stating that the clothes were destroyed & why!! A ridiculous & preposterous thing to ask for – but can you tell me what was the number of the hospital I was in in Versailles, as I am going to write to them. They will probably have moved 30 or 40 times since then & the letter will probably never reach them still it's worth trying. What is Julian's address at Surbiton I must write & get him down here. Just fancy tomorrow being Sept 25 1916. Who ever would have thought it possible that I would be

---

219. The continuation of the Battle of Somme. The British conducted a successful attack in the Flers/High Wood area on 15 September: the battle was notable for the first-ever use of the tank as a weapon.

in England a year! Bratton & Goldie have had their orders for Mesopot cancelled & are now likely to go to the 9th Suffolks in France!! Isn't that unmentionable! We are also likely to lose Gardner very soon now as he'll be off to Grantham.[220] I had one most amusing telegram of congratulation from Ascot! "Congratulations old sport love from Flossie & the twins!" a clever joke by Jove![221] It's a glorious day today & I'm having a lazy afternoon sitting writing letters & reading in the garden.
Much love

Your very loving Philip.

MC 643/7/28

113.   Old Felixstowe

Thursday

My very dear Father

I am afraid my midweekly letter is rather late this week. I got your letter this morning. Things seem to go along very much the same here & I am feeling very settled in as it were, and I am quite content to stay here for the summer though at times I have violent moods of deciding I will be passed fit again. My hand seems to improve very slowly & one only wonders how long a Board will go on deciding it is bad enough to keep me at home I do wish the summer would hurry up & come, we shall be having autumn soon!! we play tennis most days but they are not really tennis days. On Tuesday I went to the Masons with Garrod & we had 5 or 6 quite good sets. Yesterday I was playing a men's four on the Club Courts. In the evening I went out to dinner with Mrs Welby & her 2 daughters the Miss Robinsons whom you met when you came down to see me off to France. After dinner I was [*made to*] have a dancing lesson! This was great fun, specially as a very jolly major in the Suffolks came in after dinner. I got on awfully well (or so they said). Now they are telling me I shall have to dance at the weekly dance at the Felix but I am not at all sure I am brave enough for that yet! We keep on bustling men off to various theatres of war a draft or two most weeks! I am enclosing the 6 prints Ruth asked for of herself & also some others which will interest you. Please keep the latter or return them as I haven't any duplicates

---

220. The Machine Gun Training Centre was set up in 1915, located at Belton Park and Harrowby, Grantham, Lincolnshire.

221. Perhaps referring to the cross-dressing incident described in the Introduction.

I must stop now

with much love Your v loving

Philip.

MC 643/7/29

114. 27.9.16

My very dearest Father

I have enjoyed yours & Ruth's letters yesterday & to-day. Have you I wonder remembered the no: of my hospital because it may take some time to trace them & longer to get to the reply back! We lost Goldie & Bratton yesterday, they've gone off to France. Goldie only arrived back from leave at 1 pm & had to be at Folkestone by 10 am this morning. Poor old Bratton only got here at 7.40 p.m. I met him at the station with all his things for the front which I had packed for him & sent him back to London by the 8 o'clock train. A horrible rush for him & a rotten way of going off. His mother came today & fetched away the rest of his things, he'd got home at midnight & had to leave by the 8.30 am train this morning. The orders only came thro' for them on Tuesday morning or we could have recalled them earlier you must have missed Faulknor, Wharton & Wood's names in the "In Memoriam", they were in on Monday.[222] The L.N.L. have done well again today. 1 V.C., 2 DSOs and 3(?) M.C.s.[223] They are in the 10th & 7th Bns I believe. How splendid about Dix, that letter was a master stroke! I went out again on the route march today, riding, we went about 10 miles, right round over the marches, I walked some of the way & as it was a beautiful morning enjoyed it all thoroughly. We are getting swarms of officers back from the front now from our 7, 8, 9 & 10th Bns. They all come here now. I am playing what I expect will be my last game of tennis on Saturday. Much love your v. loving

Philip.

MC 643/7/30

---

222. Captain Robert Sylvester John Faulknor, aged 27, Lieutenant H G Wood and second Lieutenant Frank Wharton, aged 25, were all killed in action at Loos on 25 September 1915, the battle in which Philip was wounded. The battalion lost seventeen officers and 489 men – very nearly half its strength – on the one day.

223. Lt Thomas Orde Lawder Wilkinson of the 7th Battalion won the Victoria Cross for 'conspicuous bravery in manning a machine gun during an attack, and attempting to bring in a wounded man.' The award was posthumous: Wilkinson was shot through the heart and died instantly.

115.   1.10.16

My very dear Mother & Father

I don't like this winter time a bit, at this time yesterday I was playing tennis and now to-day it is quite dark! I had a letter from Hugo on Friday, he has been wounded and writes from no: 8 General Hospital France. He hasn't been in the casualty list yet, he was hit just below the hip bone and the wound is very dirty so they aren't letting him across to England yet. It sounds fairly severe but nothing too bad I hope and I am <u>delighted</u> he is out of it at all at last, I shall get leave & go & see him as soon as he lands in an English hospital. How splendid about Julian's military X! I should think he jolly well does deserve it we always heard how splendidly he was doing[224]. I did enjoy the splendid long Sunday letter <this> morning and have already read the Labour pamphlet. I got to my office at 10 this morning but found an unusual amount to do for a Sunday morning and was at work solidly till 12! so couldn't get to Church. However I generally manage to read something when I don't get there & did today. I finished the tennis season definitely by some tennis at the Blunts yesterday. In the evening I dined out with Dr & Mrs Havell & Miss H at the Felix and their son who is home on 7 days leave from France, Miss Blunt completed the party. Afterwards we danced. There were <u>very</u> few people there, only 10 or 12 couples which was rather nice. This afternoon Leonard & I went for a ride over the marshes. Leonard on his Machine Gun horse & I on Henderson's. I have got my leggings now & when they have got nicely coloured shall look very smart!! I have got a ripping pair of glasses in place of my lost ones. I claimed for them on a different form. Goldie & Bratton have gone to our 10th Batt. I think. I have heard no more as to when Henderson goes. I see a good deal of Leonard now & like him v much. His Mother has been ill & had an operation but is getting on well now. I read Lloyd Geo's speech with great appreciation & interest, a fine straight talk![225] I went to dinner with the Hornes on Wednesday with Barker & found them very nice indeed. I got

---

224. Julian was awarded the Military Cross for bravery on the Western Front, the citation in the *London Gazette* 20 October 1916, reading: 'For conspicuous gallantry as FOO [Forward Observation Officer] in action. Mended wires under heavy shell fire and signalled with a flag under machine gun fire till severely wounded by a splinter of a shell. Even then he carried on, but his lung being pierced he found himself unable to talk.'

225. David Lloyd George (1863–1945), Liberal Party politician, Chancellor of the Exchequer 1908–15, Minister of Munitions in Asquith's coalition government from May 1915. He had spoken with American reporters about the need to engage fully in the war: see *The Times* 29 September 1916. In December 1916 he became Prime Minister.

several congrats: on my 3rd star yesterday & last night! Well I am just off to my evening work. Much love

Your very loving Philip.

MC 643/7/31

116. 4.10.16

My very dear Ruth

Your letter and Father's both arrived this morning so I had a nice budget to read at breakfast. We seem to have dropped right into winter now, and it has rained & blown every day this week. However my little office isn't half bad on such days with a fire in it, and is really quite cosy in the evenings with the red curtains drawn. We heard nothing of the raid on Sunday night, though as you say I was in my arm chair in the White Horse between 2 and 4.30 am. We have lost poor old Gardner now, he got a wire on Monday morning to report at Grantham by 4pm that day which of course quite impossible, however he left that afternoon & broke the journey in London. I wrote a long letter to Julian this week to try & arrange a meeting and a spree in London sometime. I have no idea where he is so sent it to Godalming[226] and am hoping it will eventually reach him sometime before Xmas! How curious you not being made Captain of the Britons[227], I think they must want lessons on the correct thing to do & how & when to do it. Tell father I haven't actually invested any money yet but have got the particulars about it all ready. I started making my room a bit more comfortable yesterday now that it is winter. I got a few pictures & rearranged things a bit and it is much improved. I had lent my gramophone to Gardner lately but have it back now he's gone & shall much enjoy it again. Did you see Gemmel has at last got his 2nd star? it was in today's Gazette, quite time too! yes I rather fancy myself in my leggings! they are gradually getting a lovely dark shiny colour. Must stop now

Much love from Philip.

MC 643/7/32

---

226. Julian's Aunt Ethel and cousins, including 'Mollie' Biscoe, lived at Pinehurst, Godalming, Surrey.
227. Ruth's 'house' at Norwich Girls' High School.

117.   Oct: 8. 1916

My very dear Father

I think this should be a letter all to yourself as I am writing on your birthday. Do you remember it was just this day <two> a year ago when you came down to Hursley, and saw me in all that queer kit getting out of the motor ambulance! I did enjoy Mother's news this morning, It is interesting to see C. Gilbert[228] has donned khaki at last. I suppose he's been to a Cadet Corps[229] for 4 months? Otherwise how on earth has he got a commission. Mrs Horne told me this morning that Hugo is still pretty bad, and only eats milk and grapes. Poor old chap, I hope he soon gets well enough to come over to England. It must be 3 to 4 weeks since he was hit now. It is a lovely day today tho' chilly. Barker & I went to Church this morning. This afternoon we are going for a ride and then to tea with the Hornes. I wrote to Julian last week and heard back from him yesterday. I wanted to arrange a meeting with him and he has written to say he is at Cumberland Terrace next Saturday being Oct 14: his 21st birthday, they are gathering a concourse of friends & relations there and he wants me to be there. I have already got leave from Henderson for the weekend so I shall have a spree in town. Henderson is going to be away from Tuesday to Thursday and I am going to act as Adjutant while he is away. So I am going to send my name in for a nice good leave! I will send you further details of my plans when I know them. I do not at all know when H: is going, and as I am getting on much better with him now I shall be rather sorry when he does! Gardner will probably be at Grantham for 2 months and then go out in the Machine Gun Corps. However Harrison is on a weeks leave and so I am acting <President> Mess President here now in the White Horse! Barker & I keep very much together now & get on very well we have a lot in common I think. This is a great time for making friends, though you never know how long you'll have them and the old Repton & Oriel friends seem quite out of touch chiefly I think because no one knows <u>where</u> anybody is! I shall be reading that book Mother sent me this evening. I don't at all understand what that Gazette of Grove means! an alteration in date of 1 day.[230] Much love

---

228. See note 180.

229. An Officer Cadet Battalion. In 1916 a new system for the training of officers was introduced: a temporary commission could be granted after a training course of 4½ months. The entrant must have either served in the ranks or have been with an Officers' Training Corps. Later letters show that several of Philip's officer friends trained these Cadet Battalions, especially after having been wounded at the Front.

230. The *London Gazette* 3 October 1916 stated that Grove's promotion from temporary

Your v. loving Philip.

118. Thursday

My very dear Mother

I'm afraid my mid-week letter will be a weekend letter this week. Henderson has been away since Tuesday and it has kept me very busy. In fact both yesterday & today I hardly glanced at the paper even till 7.30 pm. However he is coming back tonight & will be at duty again tomorrow morning. I am feeling awfully excited about this week end. I leave here 3 p.m. Friday and have leave till Monday night!! I am being met by Julian & we shall go to some theatre together. I shall be stopping at 26 Cum: Terrace, if there is room. At any rate that is to be my Headquarters, they are expecting quite a party on Saturday I believe. Aunt Blanche seems to be temporarily in possession of 26 C.T. I shall <u>greatly</u> enjoy the change from my office work, and seeing everybody whoever "they" are going to be! Phillips, now a tempy: Lieut Colonel(!) came down here for the inside of the day today. The 1st Batt: are resting at present & he is home on a well earned leave. The Batt: has been through all the Somme fighting and has done simply <u>splendidly</u> but has suffered cruelly. It was very nice seeing him again & he was looking extraordinary fit. I had a good long talk with him & he told me all about my old platoon. He tells me poor old Jim Gemmel is suffering from a sort of loss of memory.[231] I hope to see him on Saturday, he's in hospital in London. Much love

Your very loving

Philip.

119. 22.10.16

My very dear Mother & Father

It is just about 3 pm. and I have been having a very interesting hour or so enjoying some of the those papers you sent me. I was also reading that book

---

Lt to Captain was with effect from 2 April 1916, substituted for the notification in the *Gazette* of 1 April 1916.

231. Gemmell was wounded at Flers at the end of September.

"The Sacrament"[232] & enjoyed it thoroughly. Winter really seems to have descended on us again & I can quite see Felixstowe has not forgotten how to be cold, and I shall be glad of my thick underclothes any time now. At present I find I can manage with either a thick vest <u>or</u> a woolly waistcoat, the time hasn't quite come for both "simultaneous like" but is not far off. My little office is quite warm with a nice fire and in the evening with the red curtains drawn it really is quite cosy. Officers often drop in to see me & my fire off parade in the morning. An extraordinarily nice new 2nd Lieut: joined here on Wednesday. He is aged 40, & was in the Public School Batt: with whom he did 6 months in France as a Company Sergt major. He soon found out who I was when he heard my name. His name is C. T. S. Smith & he was a master at the Grammar School at Thame!! and remembers Father well! wasn't that splendid. He is down at the Signalling School Landguard now but I hope to see some more of him. Another interesting piece of news, only I've forgotten to tell you before – some 2 or 3 weeks I was on my bike down the town when I was stopped by a Lance Corporal in the Essex Regt. It was Debbitch(?) I don't know how you spell it! He was off to France in a few days & seemed very pleased just to see me. It was nice just being able to say goodbye & I was another bit of Salhouse for him when he thought he'd left it quite behind! Mrs Horne told me this morning that she'd heard Hugo was in Eastbourne, but Cox promised to let me know as soon as he landed & I've not heard yet so I am wondering. Poor lad, he must be having a rotten time to take so long getting across. I had a long & shakyly written letter from Jim Gemmel 2 days ago. He is out of hospital but is in a rotten state, all nerves, he was buried by a shell, temporarily lost use of both legs, arms, speech & memory. All are to some extent recovered now but one wonders how far he will ever recover from a shock like that.

We have about 60 officers here now & one can hardly keep pace with their names even. They've nearly all been out & come from all our New Army Battalions. Henderson seems to think he may go at the end of November or early Dec:. I shall be very sorry when he does go personally. I shall never forget Julian's escapade, I've told several of it here & they "!!"[233] Did you see the award of his Mil. X. in the paper yesterday, splendid! also to "Whiskers" (J N Richardson). Also to Waterworth (3rd Batt: 1st LNL) and Leake 1st Batt. No – Mollie soon went last weekend – Aunt Bl: hadn't asked them for the night and they came up in the morning & caught an after tea

---

232. Probably *The Sacrament* by 'An Officer' [L. L.], first published in 1916.

233. Presumably the time when he attended a family party dressed as a woman: see Introduction.

train back. I find a good deal of time for reading now & have got myself 1 or 2 more books lately. My old hand still tries to imitate ice on these chillsome days & aches a little but nothing to speak of – I generally fit in a brisk walk during the day & evenings easily pass, as some of us congregate in Postern where there is a piano & up here with a gramophone & with a cosy fire etc – we're not be pitied.

Very much love your very loving

Philip

I wrote to Cox last week & told them I wanted a £50 6% Exchequer Bond!

MC 643/7/35

120.   Thursday

My very dear Father

My midweek letter will be rather late this week again, but I have been very busy this week and somehow letter writing times slip by. On Tuesday Henderson was away all day so I was kept pretty busy. Yesterday I had a court martial case in the morning, and when my afternoon work was done I had to go down to the Brigade office for an Adjutants' Conference at 5.30 which lasted till 7. and then when we got back I had my usual evening's work to do. Henderson is not at all "fit" at present & has got to take things easy, so I am getting more work to do. He has not got to do any night work for instance so I am hoping very much no Zepps come near us as I shall have no relief! This morning all the adjutants & C.O.'s rode around the country with the Brigade Major. I rode the General's horse which the Brig: Major lent me, and we were out from 9.15–12.30, so I daresay I shall be pretty stiff tomorrow. I felt a tremendous swell(!) riding along to the rendezvous with the Brig: Major. I went down to the Brig. Headqurs on my mo-bike & we rode the 3 or 4 miles to the rendezvous together. You did have rotten luck with your motor bike, mine has been doing all sorts of rotten things lately & I know what it feels like – however mine is in great form just at present. I use it very little but it comes in very useful at times. I hope to get some football this weekend, so can you send my things, blue shorts & Repton footer stockings & garters(!) if there are any about. I always forget the latter. Salhouse seems to have suffered in casualties lately; Ruth told me the names.[234] We expect to be out all day tomorrow on a field day. I shall

---

234. Of the nineteen names on the Salhouse war memorial, no less than four are known

be acting adjt: as Henderson will not come out, we are going to take our dinners with us so I hope it is fine & warm. Much love Your very loving

Philip.

121.   29.10.16

My very dear Mother & Father

This is rotten paper for my fountain pen its so rough & it always misfires on it so I have to use an ordinary one. My busy week continued on Friday as we were out from 10 to 3. It was a very blowy, rainy day and there was no horse available for me so I walked which was really better as it was warmer. We took up a line of defence & there we sat. I was acting Adjt: to the Batt: and when operations finished the Colonel took me back in his car which he had had brought out to him. We had Batt: Hd. Qrs. in a nice thick hedge so were fairly sheltered. I was pretty hungry & cold when we got back but after an hour's work in my office I was carried off to tea by Plant, probably a new name to you, we've nearly always missed each other when I've been out he's been here & vice versa. He's 3rd Batt: 1st Lieut, he originally enlisted as a gentleman ranker at the beginning of the war in our 1st Batt: & went out just after the "Retreat". He's about 29 & married & they're very nice & jollily homey. I've been to tea there again this afternoon. Yesterday afternoon I watched the Regiment XI beat the Suffolks 8–2, last Saturday they beat Stowmarket munition makers 8–0. They are a really very good team, & we have some class players among them. My footer things arrived but were not needed after all this week! Then Barker & I went to tea at the Masons & afterwards Miss Mason & we went on to the Wilsons & played Badminton, my first initiation into the game. The Masons are unfortunately leaving here this week for the 4 winter months! they always do apparently, they go just the other side of Ipswich where they have a house. I hope to go over on my mo-bike sometimes & see them. Miss Mason has had a course of motor driving & hopes to get a job as chauffeur at the War Office soon. I do always enjoy my Sunday letters and also the printed letters in them, I generally sit down to them after lunch. I really do not know about Folkestone! you see I only had leave 3 weeks ago next

---

to have been killed in action in the single month of September 1916: George Catchpole and Edward Fox were in the Norfolk Regiment, Frederick Clarke in the Canadian Infantry and Archie Grimes in the Coldstream Guards.

week!! Of course there's no harm in asking for more but I don't want to be always "leave-grabbing". I'd love it if I could get there. And if I go Ruth must, Gobagger is paying her fare one way & I the other! I wish mother could come too! But question is shall I get there! I don't quite know what is the matter with Henderson, he gets very bad neuralgia & I don't think he has ever really got over the effects of his dysentery. Mrs Henderson is going on Wednesday I believe but is coming back again, they seem very uncertain in their movements. I shall enjoy that book of R.L.S. I expect[235]. We've sent 6 more officers off to-today, 4 quite unknown qualities, having arrived & gone again v. quickly. Shipp has gone, he's been here 18 months & thought he'd never get out, owing to having very bad eyes & throat but they've passed him at last. He was a topping chap. Well I must stop now, with very dear love your v loving

Philip.

MC 643/7/36

122. 5.11.16

My very dear Mother & Father

I've <u>never</u> known such hurricanes of wind, it is blowing as if it would like to blow everything down, it's quite impossible sort of weather. Yesterday however was better and the Football team were playing at Stowmarket so I got the Doctor to take two of us over there in his car. We only saw about ½ the match but it was a nice afternoon's trip. It is 23 or 24 miles each way. Coming back it was rather amusing as we only had one very faint light in front and couldn't see at all, however we crawled back alright. I met Mrs Henderson after Church this morning and she has asked me to tea this afternoon. I rather think she is going tomorrow as he is moving into Leonard's room in the White Horse. Col. Harrison is leaving us temporarily to-morrow too. He has been trying to get some command of a battalion and is to go over to Harwich to be attached to another Batt: there sort of "on approval", a mad idea! as he'll only be holding the same sort of position there as he held here for 27 months! I am to be Mess President while he is away. I think I must send you some socks to mend this week as mine are mostly in holes! Yes do give those old thick khaki shirts away.

---

235. Robert Louis Stevenson (1850–94): Ruth was studying him at school. Best known for his novels, Stevenson also wrote essays and travel books: of the latter, *An Inland Voyage* (1878), describing a canoe tour in Belgium and France, might be considered especially appropriate for Philip on the Western Front.

Barker is away on leave this weekend. I think Folkestone would have been rather far for a short leave & also <u>too</u> close to my last. As it is I shall be able to get another leave home in 3 or 4 weeks perhaps! I wonder if Julian's leave has been extended, and when & if he is likely to go to Salhouse? I've had interesting letters from Gardner, Bratton & Goldie lately. G: has apparently been rather <u>too</u> busy for his liking repelling Hun attacks on the Somme, & attacking & capturing Huns in turn. I much want to see Ruth as a "young lidy". Oh dear I've gone & dipped my pen in the red ink! A Rev. E.A Burroughs (Hertford Coll) is coming here on Tuesday to speak on the "The Wider issues of the War" in connection with the Mission.[236] It is for officers of the L.N.L. & is in Mrs Cobbold's[237] house with Col. Cowper-Essex presiding; tea & meeting. He's going to all the Regts here I believe. I'll tell you about it next letter, when I've been.

Much love your very loving

Philip.

MC 643/7/37

123. Thursday

9.11.16

My very dear Father

I generally seem to write my "midweek" letter on Thursday nowadays. We are rejoicing to-day in some glorious weather after those horrible rainy hurricanes. Yesterday I was prosecuting on a Court Martial at the Pier. After waiting there all morning I found my case would not come on till the afternoon so came back here to lunch & went down afterwards on my motor bike. When I got there the back wheel was absolutely flat, & as it is 4 miles away I was wondering what to do. Luckily my case was over at 3pm & there was a train at 3.17 so I got a Sergeant to put it into the carriage

---

236. Revd. Edward Arthur Burroughs (1882–1934), fellow and classical lecturer at Hertford College, Oxford, from 1905, and leading evangelical clergyman, later Bishop of Ripon. He wrote a series of letters to the Times in 1915 urging spiritual renewal in the country: these were published as *The Eternal Goal* (1915), and he wrote *The Valley of Decision* (1916) on the same theme. In 1916, the Church of England held a National Mission of Repentance and Hope.

237. Mrs Cicely Cobbold, lived at The Lodge, Felixstowe. Her husband, Philip Wyndham Cobbold, of Cobbold's Brewery, Ipswich, and a local Justice of the Peace, was serving in the 4th Suffolk (Territorial) Regiment.

with him so that the Railway wouldn't refuse to take it with petrol in it & brought it up to the Town Station, & so solved my difficulties. We are sending three more officers out today but none you know. On Tuesday we had our meeting at the Cobbolds'. About 25 to 30 officers were [*there*], we had a stand up tea first & then went into another room & Mr Burroughs spoke for nearly an hour. He said the reason Germany went to war was owing to her doctrine that "Might is Right," ie, the State is the highest authority there is, which when applied to individuals comes to mean "Do wrong if it benefits you." We realised the wrong in this doctrine, but was there anything in our national life to show that we meant much further. If we realised there was a Higher Authority than the State it was Conscience which is God, did we live up to it! He talked about the difficulties that would come after the war, and said there was only one way to meet them. The danger was if we did not bother about the things the war would bring no good. He enlarged greatly on Sir D Beatty's message to England[238], "So long as England sleeps the war will last, but when she comes with a prayer on her lips then we may begin to look for the end." He also quoted & enlarged on two letters from officers at the front which you've probably seen, one said "If I were not a better man after what I've been through, it would not be fair to God" – another said something like "I think England has a lot to learn from this war & God is waiting till she has learnt it" He spoke of all this in connection with the National Mission, he was intensely interesting & practical. The Colonel was in the chair & made two very nice little speeches before & after. After he (Burroughs) gave out some Nat: Miss: pamphlets.

I am kept pretty busy now with my work & the P.M.C work. I am glad Bob is such a companion. I got Ruth's letter by the same post as yours. I enjoyed them both greatly.

Much love Your v loving

Philip.

MC 643/7/38

---

238. David Beatty, first Earl Beatty (1871–1936), headed battle cruiser squadron, 1913–16, commander-in-chief of the Grand Fleet, 1916–19, First Sea Lord, 1919–27. His message was in the form of an open letter to the Society for the Promotion of Christian Knowledge, published in the press in January 1916: 'England remains to come out of the stupor of self-satisfaction and complacency into which her flourishing condition steeped her. Until stirred out of this condition and a religious revival occurs, just so long will the war continue.'

124.   12.11.16

My very dear Mother & Father

A simply glorious Sunday, sun shining & no wind, just a ripping day! Yesterday was too so Barker & I thought we would motor bike into Ipswich. My back tyre was soft when I started but I blew it up and hoped it would last. We got about 6 miles when bump- bump – down it went, flat as a pancake. Luckily there were 2 solitary cottages near & at one of them we managed to borrow some rubber solution which neither of us had got with us. We found it was an old patch leaking & as we could not get it off we stuck another one over it as a temporary measure & hoped! Off we went again & got about 3 more miles when down it went again. This time we had no rubber solution & were miles from anywhere as you know places on that road can be. Well I was just contemplating pushing it the 3½ miles into Ipswich!! when up came one of Tollemache's beer drays.[239] We hailed the driver & told him of my misfortune, & he was quite willing to take it into Ipswich with him. So we rearranged the beer barrels & hoisted up the bike, & I was just preparing to climb up too & drive & rumble along with him too! when along came a motor going to Felixstowe, luckily we knew the people in it (a Mrs Liddell[240] with whom we are going to supper tonight) & stopped the car & asked her to befriend <us> me. So I drove back here in her car & my bike went on to Ipswich Station with the beer barrels, I have got the people at the station here to wire for it so hope to see it some day soon. All's well that ends well & Barker & I both had tea at the Liddell's. Though I can't help feeling I missed a very amusing & novel ride into the capital of Suffolk on a beer barrel!! In the evening I had to see a draft off & then as it was 8.15 & too late for dinner here B & I went & had dinner at the Grand Hotel, where we danced you know. In the evening we had a great surprise as Nichol turned up! He got tired of waiting for an overdue Board so came back here, but he can't stop & must go back & wait for his Board. He seems very fit. Livings too rejoined yesterday, He's been out since a month before I did, he's been wounded 4 or 5 times & has the M.C. At the beginning of the war he was a Sergeant in the 1st. He's an excellent fellow. This afternoon B & I are going to see the Hornes. I will send you

---

239. Tollemache, a Suffolk brewery based at Upper Brook Street Ipswich.

240. Mrs Helen Liddell and her husband Edward lived at Martello Place, Golf Road, Felixstowe: he had private means. Their children were Edward (15 in 1916), Harry (14), Richard (13) and Helen (11).

my socks. I <u>am</u> so glad everybody is so nice now. Do remember me to all the "speshuls" like Mrs Farman, Page, Ainsworthy![241]

Much love Your very loving

Philip[242]

MC 643/7/39

125. Nov 15. 1916

My very dear Ruth

How can I write to you if I do not know where "Mrs Tippett"(?) lives? Where does she! at any rate this must go home as I doubt if, even I addressed it to Miss R Hewetson. Editress.[243] c/o Mrs Tippett, Norwich, it would reach you. How-somever they will read it at home first so 't'will serve a double purpose. I got your letter & Father's both together this morning. Nothing much happens here. I had a very interesting Sunday. Roly Barker & I went to the Hornes for tea & quite enjoyed it there. It is better there than it used to be as they have got rather a nice young prettyish governess, which relieves the rather monotony of only Hornes. Before that we watched the Regt footer XI beat the Suffolks 8–0! In the evening we went to supper with Mrs Liddell. She is very nice & lives opposite the Hendersons. There are three boys & a girl in the family ranging from about 16 to 8 years old. The boys are away at school & the girl aged about 10 or 11 is at home with Mrs L: They have a ripping house & we had a very nice evening, and didn't leave till just on 11 p.m. My mo-bike returned from Ipswich quite safely & now with a new outer tube on the back-wheel is feeling very fit. I think you ought to drop on Bob if he digs too much, he'll be such a nuisance & soon it would be impossible to stop him. It is a <u>bad</u> habit for him to get into I think, as he'll do too much damage; also if he digs when there is nothing in the way of rats there it'll stop him ever being much good as a ratter. Father

241. There is no Ainsworthy in the Salhouse census for 1911 or the 1916 trade directory: the reference is probably to Alfred Ainsworth, a local land steward who lived at The Wood, Salhouse. See note 130 for Farman, note 217 for Page family.

242. 'To Ruth – I wonder how yr bad week (?) has gone on. I trust you've taken care. Father had a spill yesterday & has a knee! Amis has to motor him to Frettenham. It's not water but a bad graze, doctor etc etc.' added by Philip's mother before sending the letter on to Ruth, who was staying in Norwich, see letter 125.

243. Referring to Ruth's work as editress of the school magazine *Parvum in Multo*: she edited the Autumn 1916 issue.

says Aunt Bl: mentions me going out again in a letter to Mother. Of course I am a fixture here at present but I probably said to Julian that I didn't know for how long I should have this job & that though I had no great longing for shells & bullets again yet I did not (& <u>do not</u>) feel I can <u>shelter behind</u> a Home Service job for <u>too</u> many months. "Compree?" We have been having glorious weather lately tho' cold again to-day. I get very cosy in my room with a fire & a book.

Much love to all from your v loving Philip.

MC 643/7/40

126.   Wednesday

My very dear Father

My letter this midweek will be a bit earlier than usual. I wrote to Gobagger to-day and told her I could not manage to get off this weekend as I only had leave less than 3 weeks ago. I wish her "do" as she calls it had been a few weeks later as I should have enjoyed it very much. Things here seem to go on very much the same day after day, nothing much happening. I go & sit in my office and am kept fairly busy. When I am not working I read up military law & books on different military subjects, so as to get as much military knowledge into my head as possible. My motor bike got another fit of the sulks this week, and I could not find out what was wrong. However the Shop soon put it right by cleaning out the carburettor and putting the points of the plug closer together, and it is now in good order again. It does not like wet weather, and that is about the only sort we get here now, that and <u>hurricanes</u> of wind. Mother told me my winter shirts needed patching but I think it would be <getter> better to get new ones altogether perhaps. At present the ones I have here seem quite alright. Our mess here has been very small this week, only the 2 Colonels, the Doctor, Leonard & myself. Three others are on leave & one on a course. I always have to sit at the head of the table now. The senior captain in the mess always does, the Doctor is really but he won't so I do! I wonder if the "Pulham pig"[244] which 'Clifford'[245] is guarding is the one that comes down here occasionally for a sail, a most ludicrous thing! They say it comes from the Norwich direction. Much love

---

244. British airships, flying out of their base at Pulham, Norfolk.
245. See note 180.

Your very loving Philip.

MC 643/11/27

127. 19.11.16

My very dear Mother & Father

I did so enjoy the Sunday letter this morning as of course I always do, and was so sorry to hear about the mo-bike accident, it must have been a horrible shaking up, & I'm so glad the knee has no water on it and that it was all no worse than it was. Oh those socks! I really did mean to send them nearly everyday & then somehow I never did but I'm making fresh resolutions. I am very sorry to hear about the Clarkes' loss & will write to him.[246] We have lost one of the very best "boy" officers again, for he was nothing more only just 20, young Cyril Tripp who went out from here in July. I saw a very great deal of him after I came back until he went out & had been writing to him regularly since; he was a topping chap, one of the best you could find anywhere in every way. His brother the D S O was killed with the 1st you know about 2 or 3 months ago.

This place is getting colder and colder, everyday now it blows great hurricanes of freezing wind! We did not actually get snow here yesterday tho' it tried to in the morning however it turned into rain. Oh how it blows! I have all my thickest things on, including body belt the last few days; and do not think I want my leather & fur waistcoats at present, not as most of my time is spent indoors, if I had to be on parade it would be different. I often hold quite a little reception in my office during the morning, as several officers finding parade rather cold imagine they have "business"(!) at Orderly Room. Once there the "business" is generally found to be my fire!! A new order has come out that we must wear boots with 'slacks' now in public places instead of shoes. So as I was in Ipswich yesterday I got another pair as my pair at present are too heavy for off-times. I am very interested in Ruth's idea of going on Canteen work in France.[247] I think it's a splendid idea, I'm sure she'd love it and it would be a great experience & I should think jolly interesting. Miss Mason went for 3 months last winter. I often do think a very great deal about the whole question of my keeping this Asst: Adjt: job. Specially on such occasions as when my friends go out for a 2nd time, take when Jim Gemmel went out for a 2nd time before he was fit, and when I hear of these topping good fellows getting killed. At present I am full of an idea

---

246. Lance Corporal Frederick Clarke: see note 234.
247. The first mention in Philip's letters of Ruth's thoughts on her role in the war.

which I should like to talk over with you. But this is it in a nutshell, when I go out again I should like to go with the "Tanks"![248] I believe they are <u>the</u> coming thing. There is an officer here who has friends in them & he has told me several things about them & is getting me all necessary information The great points about them seem to be that you are in a very combatant branch of the army with a certainty of doing a lot of damage to Germans in general. You have no trench life! The <u>only</u> thing that can damage them is a <u>direct</u> hit from a <u>big</u> shell, a very rare possibility at the pace they <u>will</u> be able to go!! Leonard wants to go into them with me, only at present we are keeping it quiet. It would mean a month or two more in England probably training in them, after I give up my Asst Adjt job wh: I don't intend to do for another 2 months, making 6 months of A. Adjt. But of course these are only ideas at present. But I am full of this one, bursting with it; there would be a great chance of doing well too.

I am going to have a lazy evening over my fire tonight with a book. I have written to Hugo twice since he has been back in England but he hasn't answered. Mrs Horne tells me she's heard he is still pretty bad and I am afraid he must be. He is not even sitting up in bed yet & it must be nearly 3 months ago since he was hit?! My hand goes icy in this weather & aches a bit. I asked the Dr about it & he said it would be at least a year yet before it was <u>normal</u> again! I am so glad Bob is such a dear! only he mustn't upset mo-bikes.

Very dear love

Your very loving

Philip.

MC 643/7/41

128. 22.XI.16

My very dear Father

I have been very interested in the photos of "Tanks" which have been appearing in the Daily Mirror & Daily Mail of yesterday and to-day. Have you seen them? You ought to. I have heard no further news about them yet & of course am not really sure that it <u>is</u> possible to get into them, but am just waiting to hear! Leonard asked me to ask Mother from Mrs Milthorpe

---

248. The Tank was a new weapon of war, designed to break the defensive grip of the machine gun. It was a British invention, and was first used in battle on 15 September 1916: see note 219.

if you would send her back the book she lent when here. Leonard forgot to tell me for some time & now I forgot for some time until today but I've remembered at last! Henderson is going away on a fortnight's sick leave tomorrow and D R Curwen is going to act for him which pleases me very much as I should not have wanted to do the work for so long also it is impossible for one man to get the work done nowadays. I heard from Hugo this week, he is still pretty bad & expects to be on his back for some longish time yet. We've been rejoicing in two beautiful warm sunshiney days, a splendid change, though the evenings are chilly. I really did remember to send off the socks this week, they went off on Tuesday, I hope they arrived alright. They are starting Tea dances at the Felix this Saturday instead of evening as in the summer. But I am not going this week at any rate, I am not very keen on it. I hope your knee is better now, it is splendid having such a helper in Mr Hicks.[249]
I heard from Uncle Joseph this week
much love

Your very loving

Philip.

MC 643/7/42

129.   26.XI.16 [250]

My very dear Mother & Father

It is a simply glorious day, really quite warm sun shining brightly, it makes such a difference. I did so enjoy your extra long letter this morning, it was full of news. I have got a pair of those beautiful new socks on, thank you ever so for them, they are splendid thick ones. I really did send you all that had holes in them, they weren't by any means all hole-y. How splendid about Uncle Henry, he <u>has</u> done well! I have had a letter from Gardner about 'Tanks' as I wrote to him about – He says that the usual way of getting into them is through the Mach: Gun Corps, you go to that like he has then

---

249. William Hewetson was being helped by a younger clergyman, Revd Henry Hicks, ordained in 1908: Hicks became rector of Saxlingham Thorpe, Norfolk, in 1918.
250. 'Isn't this good news? I wonder does he mean <u>this</u> weekend? If you have a chance of 2 Shakespeare plays I will pay half a ticket as well as Miss de P's. If she is not paying for you & you can go to 2, I will pay <u>one</u>. Go and try to get a plum coloured warm tie, or silk one (about 10/-) if you can & have it on appro for me to see. You must look nice! What <u>about yr photo</u>? Where are Philip's letters which I have sent on to you?' added to the letter by Philip's mother before forwarding it to Ruth. Miss de P is Ruth's teacher Miss de Putron.

transfer to the Heavy Mach: Guns: I do not exactly want to do that, it wld: mean going to Grantham & transferring altogether. However I believe it may be possible to go straight to where they are, wh: is in Norfolk[251], but I don't quite know how one does that so I am very undecided still. It is very interesting to hear all about the Miss: Hall. I'm sure I shall enjoy that Naval Book you sent me. Henderson practically said that if leave was managed at Xmas this year as it was last, that is to say all officers and men get leave in 3 periods of 5 days, that I was to go for the Xmas period so it looks as if I shall get home for the third Xmas! It would be nice if you came for a week in January? I might get a weekend next week but am not at all sure. It all depends if there is much to do. I reckon I must have signed my name nearly 300 times on various documents yesterday morning! I have got 2 conscientious objectors for trial by Court Martial tomorrow! On Friday night I had the White Horse all to myself to sleep in, the Colonel was on leave. Col Harrison is still at Harwich. Henderson is on sick leave & the Doctor is living out with his family! I can't imagine Marjory Peake[252] being engaged she seems so young but I suppose she isn't! I am going to supper with Mrs Liddell again tonight Things go on just the same here each day. Much love

Your very loving Philip.

MC 643/7/43

130.   Thursday [*30 Nov.*]

My very dear Father

This is only a short letter as the post is going I have applied for leave from 2 pm Saturday till 10 pm Monday, so I hope it will be approved. Trains I see are bad from Ipswich, unless I catch the 2.6 or 2.18 which means leaving here 12–34 there is nothing till 4.45 from Ipswich which means leaving here 2.40. I <u>may</u> be able to catch the 12.34 but as I have 3 prisoners for trial by Court Martial in the morning, it is doubtful. Howsomever I'll wire you on Saturday morning as to which train I'm coming by. It will be a splendid little peep! Short, but I am <u>greatly</u> looking forward to it – I had great doubts as to whether I should be able to get away but think all's right now. Much love yr loving Philip.

MC 643/11/13

---

251. Tanks were developed in the open Breckland country around Thetford in Norfolk and north Suffolk.
252. See note 169. Marjory would have been 19 or 20 years old.

131.   7.12.16

My very dear Father

Nothing has happened since I got here, so this will be just like a p.c in an envelope. I got dinner on the train coming from Norwich to Ipswich & came on direct here I got here about 9.15. They'd had a lovely day here, no snow. I was on a Court Martial this morning & one case alone of mine took 2½ hours, Luckily it was the only one I had. I found my pipe here when I got back my servant had never packed it. Nichol is in this mess again now. Henderson comes back tomorrow. I am getting some more information about "Tanks", I hear it may be possible to get into them without going to Grantham, wh: would be well worth re-considering – much love

Your loving

Philip.

MC 643/7/44

132.   10.12.16

My very dear Mother & Father

It is one of those raw, damp, very cold days! Ugh! Yesterday as with you it rained hard. I had 2 cases for trial by Court Martial in the morning, but the president & members were hopeless & knew practically nothing about their job which made things drag out very much. Eventually we did not finish till 3.30 pm. however as it was so wet in the afternoon I did not mind. In the evening I had to see a draft off by the 8 train & it had cleared by then. Afterwards, Leonard, Barker, Parker & I went on & had dinner at the Grand. Henderson came back on Friday night but to me seemed no better than when he went away. This proved to be so as yesterday evening he collapsed with flu & a temperature & today has been taken to the Cliff Hosp: This is bad luck on Curwen whom I found suffering from a chill in bed when I came back. However he is up again now & has got to carry on as Adjutant. This morning I went to Church on my lonesome, but it was very cold & empty! This afternoon Leonard & I made a great resolution to go & pay a call! an act of great bravery as you know. So we went to the Blunts whom I haven't seen for a long time. Miss B. is back again, & there was quite a tea party there, we eventually stayed quite a long time 4–5.45 and are only just back. I am going to supper with the Liddells tonight. No more news about tanks yet; though I hope to get some rather definite information in a day or so. There is 1st Batt: pre war Capt: come here today who is Adjt:

of a new Tanks Corps now being formed. He is looking for officers I believe, & I want to get some information from him tomorrow.

I am keeping very well. Much love

Your v loving Philip.

MC 643/7/45

133.[253]   Sunday 17.12.16

My very dear Mother & Father

Expect me on Wednesday! I don't know what time. Leave is being granted in 4 periods of 5 days, 10% officers & men away at a time, they are Dec 16–21, then 21st to 26th, 26th to 31st and Jan: 1st–6th. Six officers go at a time, and as the Xmas period includes a Saturday, Sunday & Xmasday it is the best period for me to go as I shall miss least work here then. No travelling can be done between 22nd and 25th inclusive, so the Xmas period has to begin on the 21st and end on the 26th. The order about Xmas leave only came in yesterday morning and as that was already the 16th there was a lot of work getting the 10% of men off, making & signing something between 150 and 200 extra passes & warrants! This week has been very busy & Curwen & I have been <u>hard</u> at it. I was on a Court Martial & other work till 12.15 yesterday then had ½ an hour with the dentist. My tooth does not trouble a bit, he is killing the nerve, lots had died during the week & he scooped it all out put some more stuff in to kill some more. I go again tomorrow. Then after a hurried lunch I worked from 1.30–2.30. I turned the Orderly Officer on to sign all the passes. At the Playhouse there was a Matinee Performance of "Eliza Comes to Stay"[254] – got up in aid of Prisoners of War. This was the 2nd performance, the first being on Wednesday, the two realised £90!! It was <u>awfully</u> well done, excellent acting! The place was packed, as the papers would say "All Felixstowe was there" – I went with Barker. Afterwards he & I, Plant & Mrs Plant, Mrs Liddell & her small daughter went on to tea at the Felix, which for a change was full as ever it used to be, and watched the afternoon dance. I didn't dance as I had nailed boots on & had to go early. There were quite a lot of people there. At 7.30 I had to see a draft off and then as it was too late for mess by 8.30, <I &> Mrs Plant had asked me to dinner, so I went round there at 8.30 & spent the evening with them; so really I had a very nice

---

253. The first page of the letter has been crossed through by Philip.

254. A farce by Henry Vernon Esmond [Harry Esmond Jack] (1869–1922), first published in 1913.

Saturday. The poor old Colonel went to London yesterday & came in for a London fog, his train was 2 hours late getting back & he did not arrive at the Mess till 12.45 a.m! Capt. Henderson is still in Hosp: & is to have a months leave! Poor Curwen! Mrs H. is here & I met her yesterday. I do not think I need any tonics or <food> *flu* medicines, I have no intention of catching anything & still have my stone cold bath each morning. The pyjamas you got are excellent and beautifully warm! The pants too are warm, though I confess I like feeling my knees bare, but perhaps you could alter them? I think warm short ones are v. hard to get. I hope to have my breeches ready by Wednesday so I shall have them to come home in. Today is a simply glorious day, frosty and sunshiney. Barker & I are going to tea with the Padré, he has got his orders to go to France & will soon be leaving us. I will wire you or drop you a line when I arrive on Wednesday.

Much love

your very loving

Philip

P.P.S 7.30 pm
Please note black edged writing order!
    There has been a muddle over our Xmas leave.
    The order reads "10% of troops will be given leave during Xmas period, this 10% will be spread over period Dec 15–Jan 7"
    We read it to mean a succession of 10% going away in 4 periods, this would have of course meant 40% away. So now none of us can go except the lucky 10% who got away yesterday. It is bad luck but the order was worded very ambiguously.
    We've sent our 10% & now nobody else can go. Our 10% was 6 officers, these should have been spread over the period, instead of which we'd hoped to have 4 lots of 6. We were too ambitious & have fallen!!!

All wrong no leave see P.P.S![255]

MC 643/7/46

134.   Saturday Dec 23

My very dear Mother & Father & Ruth

I do hope this will arrive on Xmas morning to bring you lots of love and best Christmas wishes! How strange to be writing you a Xmas letter. I am hoping

---

255. Inserted at head of letter.

too that my parcels will arrive in time, I posted them yesterday morning. Mother, please if the gloves do not fit, they can be changed. I wasn't at all sure what size to get. I like the wrist part and thought they would be nice and warm. The gauntlets on Father's gloves ought to be just right for cold weather & motoring. And I hope I have acted according to 'hints' and directions in the music case! A lovely <u>pile</u> of parcels arrived from you all yesterday, but I have been very good so far and not opened them, tho' its very tempting. You see they are all in my room, and not hidden away in a hamper under Father's watchful eye! However I mean to keep them for Xmas day. I greatly enjoyed the "Parvum in Multo" & comments thereon![256] I have heard from Measham & Gobagger so far. I hope the Germans leave us alone and do not worry us with any sort of raids this year. I never managed to get anything for Louisa but am sending her a Regimental Xmas card. I can't tell you any plans for Xmas day yet as I don't know what we shall be doing. In the evening I am going to dinner with Capt: Harrison and his wife. I shall be thinking of you all all through the day beginning at 8 o'clock. The Messroom looks very nice & is all decorated with holly etc. I expect we shall have a very jolly time and so must you. With lots of love and a <u>very very Happy</u> Xmas.

P.S On Boxing Day evening there is a Dance & I shall be there.

Your very loving

Philip.

MC 643/7/47

135.   28.12.16

My very dear family

I must just send you a short letter what lovely presents, thank you all ever so much, I had <u>Such</u> a crowd of parcels with them all. The flask <u>is</u> a beauty, I do <u>just</u> like it, a lovely present; also the record cases, records and other things. Ruth's photo is awfully sweet, and I am greatly looking forward to reading "Bullets & Billets".[257] Xmas day here was very wet but I had a really splendid day. At 8 o'clock early Service all of us practically from this Mess turned up, seven of us in, I went with Leonard. About 35 were there. Then I went again at 11, this time joining with Mrs Liddell & Plant & Leonard.

---

256. See note 243.

257. Probably the recently-published book of that name by Bruce Bairnsfather, although there was an earlier book of the same name (sub-titled 'the adventures of a trooper'), by Hugh St Leger (published in 1902).

After Ch: we walked round to Mrs Liddell's house. Then at 1.45 we had our Xmas lunch, turkey & plum pudding etc. We were late as the Colonel had to go round all the men's dinners first. In the afternoon we had a real Xmas tea party at the Liddells, 15 of us, great fun! Mrs L & her 4 children, Grove & his missus, Plant & Mrs P:, Barker, Leonard, Curwen & self & others, we had great fun, crackers & games till 6, uproarious mirth. Then a little work at Orderly Room. Then 7.30 dinner with Capt & Mrs Harrison, not a bad day?! Now in dreadful hurry, off to Orderly Room, then must change, then to Felix for dinner & dance, party of 6 of us.

Much love

your v loving

Philip.

MC 643/7/48

136. Felixstowe

Thursday [?*4 Jan. 1917*]

My dear Ruth

"Voici une lettre pour vous" as the best French scholars would all undoubtedly exclaim! I got your letter & Mother's on Tuesday evening just as I was starting down to what they call the "Oil Tanks guard". There are a lot of sentries all round the Felixstowe docks etc: and each regt here takes it in turn week about to supply officers who are on duty there for 24 hours & are in charge of the sentries there. You live in the Pier Hotel & mess with the A.S.C. it is quite a decent job, you have to visit the sentries 3 times by night which I did at 9, 11 and 4 & twice by day, you sleep in your clothes. I went down there on my motor bike, and took my washing things in my haversack. The 13 officers have not gone yet, and nobody knows yet when they will. I had thought of mo biking home on Sunday for the day but see Father is away all day so will put it off. I might apply for some leave next week but don't know that I shall get more than 48 hours. I am glad the curate gardener is a success, make him play tennis with you after he "done" the garden. Father tells me Mr Hanks[258] is going to be vicar of Eastbourne I think F. should get some place like that!! We seem to have struck some summer weather at last, a'tany rate it's close enough. I am very loth to start dancing in public on Saturday but feel I ought

---

258. G M Hanks became vicar of Eastbourne All Saints in 1916, having formerly been rector of Whitechapel St Mary: he was presumably a family friend.

to as some people took the trouble to give me a lesson! I wasn't bad either so they said. Every Thursday after tea now we sit in trenches for an hour or two "for practice" so that the silly old general can see us there. Its most annoying

Much love from

Philip.

MC 643/11/9

137. Arundel Hotel, Victoria Embankment, London WC.[259] [?15 Mar.]

Thursday

My very dear Mother & Father

You will have got my wire – Well here I am as you see in London! Roly[260] has come up with me to see me off. There are 17 of us going, including Reggie Weber which is splendid. As Roly is going to India this is a little farewell "bust" for us three together. I am going down to Folkestone this evening & am going to wire to Gobagger to put me up. Then I have to report at 10 a.m, I do not know when we cross not necessarily at once but sometime tomorrow. It is splendid going with Reggie. A huge box of my belongings will arrive carriage forward, but let me know how much it is, as it is a heavy box also the borrowed bag. How about the C.A.?[261] I am beautifully ready & have everything, & am quite fit, so there's no need for any worry about me at all! I won't forget to write as soon as I land in France. It will be nice seeing G. & she'll tell you all about me. I had a splendid off & Roly, Reggie & G S Curwen & I had a little farewell dinner on Tuesday night – Roly goes to India Office on 21st so will soon be off.

Now ever so much love, I sent the news to Ruth.

My address for a few days after landing will be Capt – – – L.N.L. 25. I.B.D. B.E.F. France but do not send anything very important there as it might not be forwarded

Your very loving

Philip.

MC 643/11/3

---

259. Written on headed notepaper.

260. Roly Barker: see Appendix 2.

261. Church Army: Philip's father came to France with this organisation, supplying refreshments to troops behind the front line.

Philip embarked from Folkestone for Boulogne on 16 March 1917. He joined his battalion (the 9ᵗʰ Loyal North Lancashires) on 21 March, assuming the duties of Acting Adjutant and taking over command of 'C' Coy. on the following day. The Division of which Philip's battalion was a part was in reserve on the 21 March, moving to the Wulverghem sector of the front a week later. It remained there (apart from a spell in reserve between 30 April and 11 May) and was there for the Battle of Messines in June.

138.   Friday 16.3.17

My very dear Mother

Just a line to let you know I am safely across the Channel. The boat sailed at – and we were across between 1 & 2[262]. Some little time was taken up in getting our baggage & booking it. We have to report again at 6pm and then go up to the Base. It is interesting being here again I enjoyed my visit to Gobagger. It has been lovely & everything has worked smoothly. It is ripping having Reggie with me.[263]

Much love Your v loving

Philip.

MC 643/8/3

139.   At the Base[264]

Sunday 18.3.17

My very dear Mother & Father

You can tell by the appearance of this letter that I am still in the land of civilization. I am of course still at the Base; in the village which is about 20 minutes walk from the part of the camp I am in there is a <u>ripping</u> club where I am writing. It is a French house rippingly fitted up. Downstairs a very nice tea room where you get a really excellent tea, scones, cakes etc, a very pretty room, (you can also get dinner here). Upstairs are 3 sitting reading & writing rooms, very prettily decorated, with beautiful arm chairs, sofas, etc. It is a great boon. I suppose it is run anonymously by some good person; so you see we have somewhere to go while we are here. Well now

---

262. A very short word, presumably the time of sailing has physically been cut out. The letter is endorsed 'passed by the field censor': it was the base censor who made this excision.
263. Reginald Weber.
264. On notepaper headed 'Officers' Club'.

I will go on with the story from where I finished my short letter on Friday my evening Our train as I told you was to go at 6.30 but as is usual with troop trains on this side it did not do so. It did eventually start about 8.15 and then proceeded to beat all records by taking 3½ hours to do the short journey of 20 miles up to the base. We were rather cold & short of temper as you may imagine when we arrived. We trudged up to the 25th I.B.D. in the dark and after a good deal of search found a resting place. We were given 4 blankets each & tumbled in the dark into our tents, 4 in each. We had no kit brought up that night but made ourselves comfortable with the blankets on the floor. The next morning we sorted out and Reggie & I now share a tent and as I have managed to get hold of a camp bed for myself, with my sleeping bag & valise I had a very good night last night & am quite comfortable. There's quite a good Mess with two ante rooms a hut just like at Felixstowe. Officers who have not been out before have to do parades from 8.30–4.30 each day. Subalterns who have been out before take turns at orderly officer; but Captains who have been out before are not troubled with anything much. This morning I had to parade at 8.15 though & march about 400 men to a big Church Parade Service held in a huge hut at 8.45, I enjoyed it. We may not leave the camp till 3.30 pm but can get leave after that till 8.30. I am afraid I am not going to the 1st after all but to the 9th, however I believe there are some very nice fellows there. Reggie is going to the 8th. I do not know how long I shall be here but am very comfortable and we are having good weather which is very nice as we are in tents. I enjoyed seeing Aunt Helen & Gobagger who I expect has already written to you[265]. I had a very jolly day & a half in London too with Roly[266] & Reggie before going down there. The day before I left Felixstowe (Tuesday) Roly & I went across to an afternoon dance at Dovercourt[267] which was great fun. We came back in a naval launch.

Well now I must stop with very much love

Your v loving

Philip

Any news as to when father crosses yet??

MC 643/8/4

---

265. This is the proof that 'Gobagger' is a nickname for Philip's aunt Julia, who was the headmistress at the school in Folkestone where aunt Helen also taught.
266. Roland Barker.
267. Dovercourt, Essex, a seaside resort close to (and now subsumed by) Harwich.

140. Monday [*19 Mar.*][268]

My very dear Mother

This is just a short letter to tell you I go up to the 9th Batt: to-morrow – I have to report to the R.T.O. at 6.50 am! The train may take hours to get to wherever we go. Shipp[269] who went to the 9th 5 months ago & has been sick at Menton has just arrived here to-day & tells me it is a <u>very</u> nice Batt, nice Colonel. I shall be the Senior (& perhaps only) Captain there; there is a Major and 2nd in command, and <u>several</u> officers from Felixstowe I know (about 10!)[270]. So you see I am quite happy about it all. I got your lovely long letter last night.
now lots of love

Your very loving

Philip.

MC 643/8/5

141. Thursday 22.3.17

In the Field

My very dear Mother & Father

Here I am again "somewhere in France" – I am now with our 9th Battn: We left the Base on Tuesday – we had to be at the station at 6.50 but as usual the train did not leave for hours; as a matter of fact it left at 10 am. Crowds of us there were – Reggie & I & 2 other N Lancs. got a carriage together; same old story as 2 years ago, a crawling train, people kept getting out & walking along beside it to get warm & exercise. We had quite a good time, lots of food!!

It was most interesting seeing what a nice little place we went to some years ago. We finished our journey at 7pm and Reggie & I stayed the night in a town. I caught a train at 6.50 next morning & came on to the next village where I proceeded to try & find the Battn. I <u>eventually</u> found they were marching nearer the line after some weeks rest & would march in that morning. I found them at midday, & joined them at lunch when they had settled into their billets. The C.O has made me Adjutant! Rather nice isn't

---

268. Postmarked 21 Mar.
269. Lieutenant H J Shipp, later wounded at Messines.
270. Wylly names the colonel as Lieut-Col H M Craigie-Halkett (who had assumed command in December 1916), and the major as S J Jervis.

it? They only had a 2Lt doing it – That means another 5/- a day! & not so much discomfort you know! We can only just hear the guns from here. The officers seem very nice. The C.O. belongs to the Highland Light Infantry & really is (as far as I can see) a <u>topping</u> fellow; a nice young major 2nd in com: who has been out 2 years, a youngish chaplain, the doctor & two 2 Lieuts: (one my ass-adjt:) from the HQ mess & I think I shall get on well, though all are new at present. There are about 10 officers I knew at F. Now another excellent thing – The Staff Captain is young Jack Marriott of Repton & Cromer, I am having dinner with him tonight at Bgde Head Q. tonight. The general impression I have got so far is that the Bgde & Batts: are a big sort of family, an excellent Brigadier – so altogether tho' I've only been here 1 day, I am looking forward to things.[271]

now with much love yr very

loving Philip.

MC 643/8/6

142.   Sunday 25.3.17

My very dear Mother & Father

Your letters are all coming on to me from I.B.D. <word illegible> alright, which is good as very often letters are not forwarded. How splendid about the Charles[272], I wonder if Father will have left by the time this reaches you.[273] Since last writing we have moved again but are still some way from the line. The Battn: is in a Hut camp. But we have got a nice Mess in a house & I have got a bed in a farm. Now I hope this won't worry you but I am very annoyed with myself & am in disgrace with myself! I have most unfortunately got a slight chill on the stomach & was <u>inclined</u> to be faint yesterday so the C.O. packed me off to bed after tea yesterday & the Doctor is keeping me there today & has arranged with farmer's wife to give me milk & eggs. I am as you may easily imagine <u>most</u> annoyed with myself for going sick as soon as I join my new battn: but I comfort myself that I really cannot help it & remind myself it is alright as we are not in the trenches & also that by staying in today I really might to be well tomorrow,

---

271. There had been a reshuffling of battalions and brigades at the start of 1916, with the 9th Battalion Loyal North Lancs being transferred into the 7th Division.

272. See note 49.

273. Philip's father travelled to France to offer his services: he eventually undertook work in a Church Army Hut.

so please do not worry. I am very comfortable & not <u>ill</u> only a bit shivery, sicky & diorrhoeaish [*sic*] resulting in a general feeling of not being up to much which will undoubtedly soon pass off. I just tell you all this for you to know, for by the time you get this I shall be alright again, sure as anything – So far according to your letters none of mine have arrived yet but you ought to have got some by now – I had a very nice dinner at Brigade H.Q on Thursday night as Marriott's guest. All the other Adjts: were there. This Brigade & Battn: seem quite a family, everybody knows everybody, the Brigadier was calling everybody nicknames as the C.O. does here. Our mess is a most jolly affair, and the padre aged about 30 & looking about 20 is awfully nice. I am very warm & comfortable in my Jaeger[274] sleeping bag, valise etc on a nice soft mattress on a bed. I shall enjoy my work as Adjutant of the Bn: & of course this means I shall not have all that trench duty & also get more comfortable quarters always which is all very nice as well as 5/- a day extra. Though we are in France we don't know any more about the German retreat than is in the papers so could not tell you much even if wanted![275] I saw a big C.A. hut at the base but have not seen any nearer up <u>yet</u>. There is a big YMCA hut close up here.[276] The good farm lady has just brought me a hot brick wrapped in newspaper for a hot bottle so that is keeping my poor inside warm! So really I do not see how I can help being well tomorrow. Father had better try for the same Division as I went to, I.B.D. Reggie is fairly close to us here & I am going to ride over & see him one day; we shall probably be out of the line some little time yet but one never knows. The Doctor has just sent me some papers down so I am being well looked after. It is bitterly cold weather, you know, freezing hard & blowing, occasionally snowing too. I think a larger writing pad would be useful; also some fountain pen ink in one of those bottles. I've just had 2 visitors. This brick is warming me up splendidly. Very dear love
I got Ruth's letter

Your loving

Philip.

MC 643/8/7

---

274. Clothes retailer, founded in 1884, named from Dr Gustav Jaeger who promoted the benefits of clothing made from animal fibres.

275. In March 1917 the Germans pulled back to a shorter and more rational front line, known to them as the 'Siegfried' Line and to the British as the 'Hindenburg' Line.

276. Both organisations ran huts behind the front line, supplying food and entertainment for the troops: as Christian organisations, both were keen to keep soldiers away from the temptations of alcohol and loose women that the towns behind the lines might offer.

143.   27.3.17

My very dear Mother & Father

I expect you are wondering how I am again well I am quite alright now I took it easy for 2 days, & though feeling decidedly squeamish once or twice I am now quite perky again. We have moved <u>again</u>. So since I have been with the Battn: I have not been given long to get used to one place. Nearer the line this time but in a most palatial billet. A huge house accommodating all the HQ Mess, 7 officers also Orderly Room. Beautiful sort of marble entrance hall, lovely big broad stairs, & each in a nice room, beds & carpets & all complete. A nice sitting & dining room with soft chairs & a fire a carpet on the floor really absolutely civilized except of course most of the windows have lost their glass & are boarded up as a result of a disagreement with the Hun! Best of all though there is a Bath Room! where you can have a hot bath which I am greatly looking forward to. Also we have a piano in the dining room. It snowed hard yesterday, then it freezes in the night thaws & rains in the mornings so the roads are in a dreadful state tho' I suppose they must be getting better now. The last letters I got from you were on Saturday so I have not yet heard from you after you've heard from me. There is another officer joining us today & I am hoping very much it will be Shipp whom I left at the Base. I am now going to change into slacks for dinner, it is worth it as I sleep in the same house as I feed in. I wonder whether Father has crossed yet. Very dear love

Your very loving Philip.

MC 643/8/8

144.   B.E.F. Friday 30.3.17

My very dear Ruth

I think this had better be a letter all to yourself! Just think I have been in France 2 weeks exactly today so time soon flies along. I have now been getting letters from you & you know where I am. Letters are taking some time as one I got from Mother today was written on the 24th so they are taking about a week you see. We are still in our palatial quarters, and I had a lovely hot bath last night in a full length bath. Tell Mother we can buy <u>everything</u> out here now so she mustn't send too much in a parcel. Big Exped: Force Canteens follow everywhere & here there are lots of shops. In fact yesterday I brought some new collars at

Burberry's[277] agents and this lovely writing pad. We live very well & <u>at</u> <u>present</u> are very comfortable. I am enjoying my work as Adjutant. Shipp whom I knew so well at F is here now & he & I had a good dinner together in <u>the</u> Restaurant here last night, it seemed so extraordinary being as close to the front as Wroxham Bridge is to us & yet having a beautiful dinner! in a restaurant.[278] This morning I rode around the country with the C.O. Shipp & I are going over to see Reggie & Goldie either tomorrow or Sunday. They are quite close & we shall ride over. We have a piano in the Mess (dining room) & sing rousing choruses in the evening. Must stop now.

very dear love your very loving

Philip.

MC 643/8/9

145. Monday 2.4.17

My very dear Mother & Father

Your letters are arriving very punctually and you time them awfully well. The one you wrote on Wednesday morning got here on Sunday and today I have got one written on Friday so they do not always take so long you see. Yesterday too I got a parcel which was a great interest *& excitement*. We much enjoyed the after dinner mallows and are looking forward to the cakes for tea. How well you did it up. You have apparently just got my letter about my old "tummy" – well it took just about the week to put itself really right again but now I am feeling very fit. We are having extraordinary weather, this morning when we woke up there was snow on the ground & all the puddles etc were frozen, there has been a biting wind all day too. We are very thankful for our comfortable billets where we still are. As long as we stay here I have a really very easy time. We have breakfast about 8.30 – then I go to Orderly Room & see if there is anything to be done – During the morning the C.O generally takes me a walk round where the Coys are or a ride to Brigade. Sometimes he does this in the morning sometimes in the afternoon. We have Orderly Room at 5.30pm. each day & from then till dinner at 7.30 is my busiest time as I am getting out orders & doing office work. Yesterday we had a Church Parade service at 10. Three Battns were massed together in a big building. In the afternoon Shipp & I rode over

---

277. Fashionable London outfitters, their all-weather coats much used by officers in the trenches.
278. The distance from Salhouse Rectory to Wroxham Bridge is just over a mile.

to see the 8th Batt. I of course as Adjt have a horse of my own & Shipp borrowed one of the Coys. The roads are nearly all horrid cobbles & very bad for riding. Sometimes you get a strip along the side where you can trot. We got over there for tea. They are nearer the trenches & we found the roads very bad. It was awfully nice seeing Reggie again even after 10 days. We also saw Robert Goldie whom of course you remember from Tennis days last Summer. We had a tremendous talk over old times. It is very different seeing people you have something in common with. However nice new acquaintances are you want something to start on! Our Colonel's name is H. M. Craigie-Halkett – I wonder if the Charles know the name? I am the 3rd senior officer in the Batt, only the C.O & Major being senior to me. Father mustn't get impatient at army dilatoriness!! It is always so. Still it is a horrible nuisance being all ready to go for so long – . We mess extraordinarily well. We always have porridge and scrambled, or poached eggs & bacon to start the day with. We also always have a pudding for lunch. The cook can make pastry, dumplings of all sort etc. Dinner too is an excellent meal – In fact if you drop in to a meal you'd never think we were at the war! Canteens etc are brought to a high pitch out here now. Now – yes please – I really should like a nice book occasionally. I have a good deal of time for reading & always enjoy a nice book! Goldie was most impressed by my "luck" – a job in England all the winter & now this Adjtcy:! He couldn't swallow it at all – very dear love your loving

Philip.

MC 643/8/10

146.   Good Friday 6.4.17

My very dear Mother & Father

I am afraid you will not have had a letter from me for some days but I expect you will have gathered that "o" much has happened – Well we left our sumptuous billet this morning & did yet another move. This time a little further back. We were marching from 11 to 2. The march finished in pouring rain & we were very ready for lunch. We are all in farm houses & very scattered & after lunch it took me 2½ hours to go round all the billets. Then came orderly room & some work & I shall be quite ready for dinner. It has been a novel sort of Good Friday & I have often thought how this week last year was the last "extended" week of my long leave. A year ago & here I am only just out here again. I have got a room in the same cottage as my orderly room wh: is convenient! Such a lovely parcel from you 2 days ago, the ginger & ink one, thank you ever so. I like these writing pads too. We shall still be here when you get this I expect & are quite safe here. This will have to be your Easter letter tho' I am afraid it will get to you late. It will be nice to be in Billets & the Padré is arranging Early Service. He tried to get a Service to-day but as we were moving it was impossible. I am settling down well & fit as a fiddle now. I wonder if Father has any news?? It will nice for you all having Uncle L'E there. Please give him my love

Lots of love your v loving Philip.

MC 643/8/11

147.   Easter Day [*8 Apr.*] 1917

My very dear Family

If you get a letter from me in ink you will not go thinking I am very uncomfortable I am sure. As a matter of fact I am writing this in the little front room of this cottage which is my orderly room & a type writer is clicking away and the other 2 clerks are busy writing. We are having perfectly wonderful weather just yesterday & to-day, lovely sunshiny days without a cloud in the sky. We had a big Church parade this morning, and afterwards a Celebration of H.C. in a barn, there were about 15 officers and 80 or 90 men there. I got your letters to-day, but on Friday & Saturday we had no post at all. We are quite out in the country, all living in scattered farms, in this weather, it is really a very jolly life. I am enjoying my work too as Adjutant very much. I have all the detailing to do of everything that is done! parades, working parties etc etc. Though of course not nearly so much actual office work as in England! I have to publish Battn. Orders every evening. I am now as fit as anything again. I am sending home a sacking of surplus kit which may arrive sometime in the next few weeks. I do wonder about Father. And Ruth I s'pose is home now, so that's alright. Very dear love your very loving Philip.

MC 643/8/12

148.   Wednesday [*12 Apr.*][279]

My very dear Mother & Father & Ruth,

There is the whole lot of you! I have not written since Sunday because I had told you we should still be in our land of farm houses. So we are & it

---

279. Dated by postmark.

is now a land of snow! The whole place is white with it lying thick, it has been very cold all this week, and I am glad we are not in the trenches. I was interested in your talk with Col. Charles[280] but he was <u>not</u> right I consider. I have had several letters from Felixstowe & hear that Roly has measles! & also varicosele & is to be operated on so his trip to India is off at present. I hope the war will be over before he need go now! Isn't the news grand! <word illegible> we could hear the guns away in the distance faintly but could tell it was something tremendous; Everybody is feeling jubilant. I am keeping well as anything now, it is extraordinary sort of feeling to come out this time of year & drop straight into a hard winter spell. I cannot tell you much news as we do nothing more than what we might be doing in England, just parades. I generally ride round & see Coys at work, & at other times work in my office myself. I do wonder about Father & feel he must be gone by now. I heard from Gobagger today. I am enjoying my work & the responsibility & all the arranging. I have to keep my thinking parts well wound up – Lots of love Philip.

MC 643/8/13

149.   In the field 14.4.17

My very dear fam'ly I never know now how many of you to write to! I do wonder if Father has arrived in France yet! It is I believe some few days since I have written. We are still out of the trenches, but we have had another move since last I wrote. As the Colonel and the Major had both gone on in advance I was in charge of the Battalion & marched them along here. We are in a very nice Hutment camp not so far behind the line. We have a very comfortable H.Q Mess where I am now writing. I have a little hut all to myself just across the way, about 10 feet – there's a camp bed in it, a trestle table & a shelf or two. I sleep in my valise. All the men are in Huts & we are very comfortable also I have a hut for my clerks & a little office all to myself which is really very convenient. The bad weather seems to have gone at present & we have had fine weather for two <nights> days tho' none too warm in the mornings, specially at 7am this morning when I was out.

This afternoon I walked round with the Colonel, we finished up at our transport lines where we had tea – we got horses & on the way met our 8th Bn: on the way back after coming out of the trenches! I was just able to get

---

280. See note 49. Born in 1858, Colonel Charles was more than thirty years senior to Philip, who may have found his views on the army out of date. Such officers were often referred to as 'old dug outs' by the younger generation.

a few minutes talk with Reggie & a wave to Goldie & one or two others. Also a wave from a boy who was in my platoon in the 1ˢᵗ Bn & has since been W: F[281] and come out here again – I was most awfully pleased to meet them all.

I got Ruth's letter written on Easter day on Thursday & another enclosing Julian's yesterday. I am keeping well as anything now & am very busy but as I have said before greatly enjoying my work. On Thursday Shipp & I walked into a village about a mile from our scattered farms & went to a sort of tea & dinner rooms for officers in quite a nice French house – we had a very nice tea <u>and</u> there was a gramophone there and I found a "Theodore & Co" record there so we played it & got quite excited.[282] The night before we had dinner there. In our camp here there is a "Cinema" with a change of programme twice weekly! Isn't it an extraordinary war. Baths, Cinemas, YMCA Huts etc all are quite close up!! I am still enjoying the ginger! and you will like to know the <ginger was> biscuits were much appreciated by all.

Very dear love from your very loving

Philip.

MC 643/8/14

150.   Tuesday [*17 Apr.*][283]

My very dear Family I cannot help talking about it, I know I really shouldn't, and it does not I suppose show much brain but I must just say what awful weather we are having. I am not really as hard up for news as that you know. But just fancy it is the middle of April and I am wearing two waistcoats to-day. Last night there was a hurricane of cold wind & driving rain, to-day has been the same, & sometimes hail and finishing with driving snow! We are very pleased to be in our snug huts still. No letters came on Sat. and Sunday but I had had two yesterday & to-day. Poor Father! still waiting! Well now you realize how the army machine works. Yesterday afternoon I walked up with the Colonel to the trenches; my first time in the trenches for about 20 months! We had about 1½ hours walk to the front line & got some ripping views of all the country behind the Hun trenches from various points. We

---

281. Probably an abbreviation for 'Wounded: Felixstowe'.

282. A popular musical comedy based on a French comedy by Paul Gavault: the English version opened in London on 19 September 1916.

283. Endorsed by Philip's mother: '14 April?' her guess as to the date he wrote the letter. In fact, as it is dated 'Tuesday' it must have been written on 17 April. Postmarked 18 April.

started at 2 and got back about 7 pm. We got a lift in an empty ambulance on the way back which was very welcome. Of course we wear steel helmets now when we go up[284]. I am getting more used to mine but they are rather heavy till you get used to them. I am kept very busy & the days seem to fly by. Your parcel of books arrived the other day. Since I wrote for books I have not opened one! I had such a slack time in our marble halled mansion 10 days ago that I though I would have time for reading but I am beginning to change my mind now! We always get our post about 2 pm and we get the English papers of the day before always. Phillips I hear has been writing to all sorts of high places trying to get me back to the 1st but has failed. He wrote to the Brigadier here (who was in the same Bgde as the 1st) & said he was very sorry he could not get me but he supposed I should prefer an Adjt's job to what he has to offer me ie a Coy: Commander – He also said I was the best platoon commander in the 1st! The Colonel told me this & you may guess I am quite pleased about it; tho' of course he did not mean this to get back to me & I don't want to talk about it. I am keeping well as anything now. I heard from P.J to-day, he is coming to England in 2nd Rhodesian Rgt as a private & will eventually get to France he hopes – he is tremendously excited about it. Well no more news at present. Lots of love your very

loving Philip.

MC 643/8/2

151.   In the field Friday 20.4.17

My very dear Mother & Father

Another move since last I wrote, this time the Battn. has really got into the trenches, so here I am once more. We came in yesterday. It was very easy getting here & the H.Q Mess walked up after the Battn, not like the old days when I had to tramp along with a pack at the head of my platoon. We are very comfortable for tho' we are in the trenches I am not actually in. That is to say we are not living in a dug out but in a farm just behind the line which for some extraordinary reason has not been knocked down! Here I can do my work in a very nice light airy room at a table, what a war! Eight of us sleep together in a sort of sand bagged dugout in the farm, four on each side, 2 above two, on wire mattresses. I haven't got my jaeger

---

284. The first steel helmets were introduced for some front line troops in 1915: they could not withstand a direct hit from a rifle or machine gun bullet, but saved many lives from shrapnel wounds. By early 1916, when the Lancashires received them, a quarter of a million helmets had been issued to the British Army.

sleeping bag here, but of course sleep in my clothes tho' I take my boots off. Of course we are all continually going round the Coys: in the line to visit them. I go round once a day. At night I stay here & attend to anything that is needed. It is splendid as the weather at last seems to have changed, to-day has been a lovely spring day, and now as I am writing this 6pm, it is a lovely evening. It felt quite ordinary wandering round again. I wonder if you realise what a noise goes on this Mess. I'm sure no Mess laughs so long & so often. I am keeping as well & fit as anything. I do wonder about Father. I had a 3 hours tour of the trenches this morning & had lunch with B Coy in their dug out. Lots of love yr ever

loving Philip.

MC 643/8/15

152.   Sunday April 22

My very dear Ruth

Here is a letter all to yourself. One day in the trenches is just like another & tho' I have put Sunday on top I felt quite surprised just now when I signed a 'return' which goes in every Sunday! We are still "in" as you see, but still having glorious weather which makes things very different. I have been quite energetic to day. I got up about 5 am & went up into the front line. It was a lovely morning, beautifully clear & you got a splendid view of the Hun trenches & the country beyond. There are 2 or 3 excellent snipers posts & if you go into those you get a lovely view thro' a little hole in an iron plate.[285] I saw a Hun walk along his trench quite plainly, it was a place where their parapet was low & his whole head showed – He was only about 100 yards away. I got back about 8.30 & was very ready for breakfast. I had had a cup of tea & a biscuit before I went out though! After a little office work I went up again & was in the line from 11 am to 1.30 pm. My orderly goes with me. This afternoon I have been in the farm house. Somebody always has be in of course. Poor Father! he <u>can</u> only wait! At any rate he should be here for the warmer weather now. Tell Mother the Padre's name is M. S. Evers I think he was in India before the war.[286] I heard from Hugh the other day, he was hobbling about still. I expect he enjoyed being where he was. There is a very nice young fellow (23) Cooper[287] just come back off

---

285. A protection against enemy snipers
286. See Appendix 2.
287. Not otherwise identified.

a course, he is Sign. Off & lives at H.Q.[288] I say "young" because Colonels & Majors aged 36–40 may be excellent but they are far from "friends" they may be young for their age but!! Lots of love yr loving Philip.

MC 643/8/16

153.   Monday 23.4.17

My very dear Mother

I do not suppose there will be great deal of news in this because nothing has happened! I have just got your lovely long letter with all the news about Father. I <u>am</u> so interested – how pleased he will be. I do wish I could see him in his khaki. I do just think it is splendid of him. Now that he has really got orders & will be in France by the time you get this it seems more splendid than ever. How we shall be able to talk about all the places we have been to, specially if we are in the same area. It will be splendid if we ever meet. I love hearing about all the things you are doing in the village. I got a splendid post to-day, one from Aunt Ruth & Uncle L'E, and also a long letter from Roly. He is at home now after German measles! We are still enjoying our glorious spring weather, such a change, not a cloud in the sky this evening. From the 30th of April to May 4 *(or 26th to 30th)* I am going to be attached a "Battery", the same kind of artillery as Julian was with. It will be very interesting. You learn as much about the gun as you can in those few days, fire it, & generally have a nice time, living with the gunners, probably seeing lots of Huns from their Observation Posts. All 2nds in commands & Adjutants from our Brigade are going in turn. I still keep as well as anything. Yes I think we do very well out here, and you poor people in England are all being rationed![289] Do not starve too much please. Here I am wasting more space top & bottom but this will just tell you how flourishing I still am. Lots of love

your very loving Philip.

MC 643/8/17

---

288. Signals Officer at Head Quarters.

289. Rationing is generally considered a phenomenon of the Second World War, but it was first introduced during the First World War, originally on a voluntary basis. In February 1917 Colonel Cowper-Essex, now retired and living in the Lake District, wrote to Philip: 'I am living on the Devonport ration, which in my case is mainly porridge, cold mutton and pickled walnuts.'

154. [*24 Apr.*]290

My very dear Ruth

I got your Sunday letter yesterday, ever so many thanks for the cigarettes, they are just what I smoke! I have not had any time to read <u>any</u> book yet but may start one some time. Well we are out of the trenches now and very comfortable in a hut camp. I came out on Wednesday evening, while two Coys stayed in and came out in the small hours of Thursday morning. I have just written Father a letter of welcome, it will be very interesting to hear the sort of work he has to do & how he likes it. The C.O develops a very livery temper at times which is not the best of things to meet as it flies out on anyone & everyone! A party of us are now going to ride over for a jolly afternoon & evening. The Divisional friends are giving an excellent entertainment in – from 5.30–8pm so we are going to ride in, have tea, go & see them & then have dinner in the club there. It'll be a splendid change quite unlike war! I go to my Battery on the night of the 29th, and stay there till May 3. I expect you & Mother will be busy, looking after the hens and the preachers! Don't get mixed & give the preachers hard boiled egg in a saucer for his lunch or anything like that; and be sure you don't take Bob to Church or give the broody hens dog biscuits! I am kept pretty busy, but nothing very newsy happens. I keep fit as anything. Much love from Philip.

MC 643/8/1

155. B.E.F

My very dear Mother

Just a short line to say we are coming out of the trenches to-day. I heard from Father from Uncle John's to-day & he gives me his address. He is at any rate <*word illegible*> going in the right direction which is splendid. The weather has held ever since we came in & we haven't had a drop of rain, however I am greatly looking forward to a change of clothes & a bath! also some pyjamas! you feel you want them all after 7 days in your clothes. Thank you ever so much for the last parcel, I love all those things. Gobagger sent me 2 books too so I am well stocked. My attachment to the Gunners will be from the 30th to the 4th however address all letters as usual. I shall have them sent to me each day. Father says he is not used to taking salutes in his uniform yet! This is an extraordinary place for all sorts of people to &

---

290. Dated by postmark.

from the trenches dropping in <yet> & we keep a sort of open house, with people in to all meals!

I am going back to our hut camp about tea time. The Doctor says do you know the people at Cranwich Rectory, near Mundford, Norfolk.[291] There are two very pretty daughters there, so I am very interested. Lots of love your very loving

Philip.

MC 643/8/18

156.   30.4.17

My very dear Mother I have not been successful in finding our any more about Father's whereabouts yet, and as I have not heard from him again I cannot do much. We are enjoying the most glorious real summer weather now! It is really hot. Well we are now in our much scattered farm house billets again where we were for Easter then it was all snow. Now it is very different & the billets seem quite different too. I do not believe I have told you about my trip to see the Divn: Pierrots. Four of us rode in & had tea at a nice place "Pour officiers" – Then as the "show" started at 6pm we walked along. It was in a lovely big hall, the saving bank of peace time. The first half of the programme was a Pierrot show, really excellent. The place was simply packed with officers & men. The second half was a short play, really well acted, quite first class, it was all most enjoyable. Afterwards we all went to dinner at the Officers' Club & then rode back to camp about 5 miles, it was a lovely spring evening & we all were in great form. Yesterday most of the men were working but we had a service in the Cinema for all who were not at 9.30 – then 4 of us decided to go for a ride, about 12.30 we got to where the 8th Bn: were & I went in & saw Goldie who is now Ass. Adjt. Reggie is away on a Course but I believe he is rather miserable in the Battn: as his C-O seems to have got a "down" on him – I'm very sorry – I found two Capt's I knew at F. had come out so I went to one of their Coys: & had lunch with them & heard latest F. news.

Odd bit Before Gunnery Course:
It is extraordinary how you meet people out here. I met a fellow who was at Oriel in the officers club on Saturday, a year junior to me but we played footer together a good deal. Can you soon send me out my thin vests! If

---

291. Revd Henry Chichele Hart, rector of Cranwich from 1888. His two daughters, Shirley and Alicia, would have been 28 and 26 years old in 1917.

we have much marching I shall want to be coolly clad if this weather goes on, also my aertex drawers? I wonder if my surplus kit has arrived yet – I should not think so. I expect you are busy, you certainly <u>are</u> doing a good war work, feeding the villagers[292] – We moved here this morning so I have missed my 4 days attachment to the gunners – I got your letter written on 26th to-day. If you could how tanned I am getting already you would soon know how fit I was

very much love

Your very loving Philip[293]

MC 643/8/19

157.   B.E.F

Sunday 6.5.17

My very dear Mother

I have had 2 lovely long letters from you just lately. I enjoyed to-day getting extracts from Father's letters. I have just had 2 scraps from him so far. He does not seem very well off for food, poor Father! We do splendidly! really excellent catering, the mess cart goes every day to the nearest town & gets whatever we want. We always have fresh milk & vegetables. We have started this last week cold lunches with salads! I am sure you would envy us if you saw us & I do hope you do not have to eat too skimpy rations! I think it has changed since last I was out, we feed like anything out here! We are still in our farm house billets and this last week has been glorious & the country is looking much better. Hedges are quite green & so are some of the trees. These little farms have little orchards behind them & if we are here a few more days we should see them well in blossom. We <u>have</u> had lovely weather, I got down to quite summer garments, no vest! so please send me any thin things I have. I have not yet found out where Father is but I have 2 C.A. padres on the track & have written to the H.Q. C.A. BEF to find out. We had a big Brigade parade service this morning. This evening I am going out to dinner with Shipp. It is interesting to hear of Father with a "tin hat" & gas masks!! We have an excellent cook in the mess! I think somebody's liver

---

292. Because of wartime food shortages, the Hewetsons had tuned part of their large garden at Salhouse Rectory into an allotment.

293. The letter has been endorsed by Philip's mother: 'P's latest. Came on Sunday (the 5th) (?the 6th)'

is better in this weather, but I am always on my guard & think I must be learning a good deal of different characters.

I had a long letter from Col. Harrison at F. to-day which was very nice & full of news. Hardly anybody left there now, even those one expected to be there months have gone out! Still you know by the time you get this I shall have been out 2 months! Half the time I was out before! It certainly doesn't seem so. You talk about my letters but I think <u>you</u> are just splendid. I seem to get a letter nearly every day. Thinking it over will you only send my little thin vests, I will get the other things from F. <u>new</u>. I am kept very busy, you don't seem to know yet that I have not been to the gunners after all. I daresay soon I may send home a few thick winter undergarments & my fur waistcoat when I get the summer things. I am just as well as anything.

Lots of love Your very loving

Philip.

MC 643/8/26

158.   9.5.17 Wednesday

My very dear Ruth your turn again now!

Only a short one though as there is not a great deal to say. Still in these nice billets, & still this lovely weather. Those are the chief things. The other thing is I am rapidly assuming that sort of red tan colour that pierrots at the sea always paint up in, only mine doesn't wash off! I think I know pretty well where Father is now, but he is just out of reach I'm afraid, still fairly near. I had another huge long letter from Mother *to-day* I had heard of that Norfolk man & will try to find him. Oh! She says she has decided I shall not want summer clothes yet! Oh please <u>un</u>decide her! I also heard from Mrs Turner! and P.J.[294], he is coming across as a private in the Rhodesian Rgt. I have just bought myself a lovely <u>big</u> new sponge & am awfully pleased with it. Will you order me some more hair stuff & cucum & glycerine for face & send me the bill? I am getting much better at riding & fairly gallop about when the Battn: is training, & even took a few <u>small</u> jumps yesterday. It sounds as if Father only lives on his rations, we make tremendous additions to ours! <u>I hope he will</u>

Much love from Philip.

MC 643/8/20

---

294. Powys Jones. See Appendix 2.

159. Saturday 12-5-17

My very dear Mother, Several changes have happened since I last wrote. We left our nice farm house billets & marched a short way to a hutment camp again. However I had only been there two days when I moved again.

That brings us to this morning & where I am now. I am now attached to the battery which I was to have been attached to two weeks ago. I walked up here this morning & am to stay with them for four days. It is still that lovely hot weather & it will be a change, as I shall not have any special work to do naturally; I am just here to pick up any wrinkles I can & get an idea of the war from an artilleryman's point of view & get a small idea of what an infantryman can expect from the gunners. Of course I am living for these days with five complete strangers but I consider it all a good experience; we live in a farm & are very fairly comfortable. I had a splendid surprise as I went in to hear the Pierrot Show again yesterday & ran into Roly's brother whom I knew at F,[295] & who is with our 7th Bn. The same day Leonard came over to see me from the 7th but unfortunately we missed. However there is quite a possibility of several of us meeting at any time which is splendid. I did enjoy your letter with extracts from Fathers to-day. He is very fairly close up I gather & I am awfully pleased he seems to be settling down more, of course it would all seem very strange at first & it is not exactly a life of comfort! I am sending home another huge bundle of kit – it is no use having all my thick stuff out here now. I am keeping just as fit as possible & getting beautifully brown. In our hut camps we had hot baths just across the road & I had cold showers before breakfast in the morning – lovely!

lots of love your very loving

Philip.

MC 643/8/21

160. Wednesday, 16.5.17

My very dear Mother

I am afraid it is a good long time since I wrote, I have as you know been with the Battery all the time but have come back to the Battn to-day. It has been a very nice 4 days change, and I have enjoyed having nothing particular to do, no responsibility but lots of interest; I learnt a good deal

---

295. Henry Barker. See Appendix 2.

about the guns, and finished up this morning by firing one of them. My target was nearly 4000 yards away & over a hill so I have no idea as to what happened to the shells I let loose. I fired just 4. Quite enough tho'. Of course the gunners did all the "laying"[296] of the gun. I just sat on the little seat & pulled the lever – there is a deafening explosion & a huge sort of flash the first time you do it you wonder what on earth is happening. I was firing at a small wood just behind the German line. I had one or two interesting times.

I spent yesterday afternoon *on* a hill just behind our reserve trenches. From there you can see the line for a long way, both ours & theirs. It was a bit misty though so was not a good afternoon. However thro' my glasses I watched the Hun trenches getting a rotten time. I walked back to the Battn. this morning & am now back at my work, feeling all the better for a small change. For of course I did<u>n't</u> <u>want</u> a change but still 4 days away always freshens you up doesn't it? I got your parcel of wearables & eatables. the former I <am> was very pleased to get & the eatables I just <u>do</u> enjoy – I love that ginger! I got your letter enclosing Fathers & his photo – I <u>do</u> think he looks nice. Khaki does suit him. Shipp said "What a ripping face" – do you remember that was what a Mrs Maudslay once said when she saw the photo I had at Oxford! I think they're awfully good. It is extraordinary how these people go on living close up to the line. In a farm close to where the Battery, really only about 1½ miles from the front line there were people & calves & hens running about! I believe the 1st are near here now! so I may see them, it would be topping if I could, I know so many there. Did you see that Nichol who was wounded the other day has now got the M.C. I am awfully pleased. The lemonade tablets have come too, thank you ever so – I think I know just where he is now, really quite closish up I imagine. You can't imagine how well I am keeping. I can't think how I ever had that "tum" when I first came out, just think March 16! now May 16! Half the time I was out before already gone & only once in the line so far.

Lots of love your very

loving Philip.

MC 643/8/22

---

296. Working out the direction and angle of the gun to fire at a target which is out of sight.

161. Thursday 31.5.17

My very dear Mother

We have left our beautiful little village, the stay there was too good to be long! We had a good long march, a train journey & another march & then got back to our old haunts. However that was Tuesday & I was only there one night. I am not now with the Battn: so letters both to and from me may get somewhat delayed, certainly <u>to me</u>, for they will have to be forwarded.

Next time the Battn: goes into the trenches I shall not be with them, there are 6 officers & some men with me, I am in charge. We are like a 2nd XI! So you are not to worry even tho' you do not hear from me. I shall probably be able to write just the same but at any rate you will know I am not with the Battn: We are now on our way back & away – we marched for 4½ hours yesterday from 3 pm to 7.30pm. When we arrived we found a barn ready for us! However we got a meal of "omelette" in an Estaminet and when our kits arrived were very comfortable in a field. We move on again tomorrow.

I expect I shall not get any news from you for a few days, when they once start forwarding them they will of course continue alright.

I got a letter from Allen Bratton yesterday, they are quite close and I am going over to see them all this afternoon. Reggie & R Goldie will be in the same crowd as we are for the next days, so I am very pleased!

Lots of love your v loving

Philip.

MC 643/8/23

162. Monday June 4th 1917

My very dear Mother & Ruth

There is lots to tell you since I last wrote that hurried note in the field last week. Here we are with a new address, though I think you had better still write to the Bn: as they get forwarded. Our new address is "25th Divn Reinforcement Camp. B.E.F." Of course I have no idea how long I shall be here, it all depends on so many things. We are quite comfortable, 2 in a tent at present. We had a long march here. It <u>was</u> hot. The heat really is terrific! So hot that all the skin has peeled or sort of blistered right off my arms after one very hot day in shirt sleeves last week. We are right out of range of the guns & quite prettily placed in fields. Quite a camp of us. When we

arrived there was no arrangement for a Mess beyond a rough sort of canvas
& wooden hut put up. No crockery or anything. However some produced
a tin mug or so, some plates etc, then some of us made a tour into a nice
big town which is quite close & bought the rest of the crockery. We have
messed with the two other Bns: & now have quite a good mess of 17 going.
They've even raised a piano! There is another mess at the other end of this
hut. I shall be interested to hear what you think of this B team for me! It
will take a lot of anxiety away from you. It is all more experience for me, as
I am getting to know more officers. We are even messing with two Battns
from a different Brigade – Tent life too is very jolly. Washing in a field in the
morning. Playing stump cricket, all sorts of games of catch with tennis balls
in the evening & lying about. Of course we <u>work</u> during the day! The Divn.
Band <u>came</u> & played all yesterday afternoon, & one or two others come &
play too. I am enjoying the rest from my labours (<u>temporarily</u>). Though of
course we shall all want news of our Battns & it may be hard to get quickly.

The afternoon I last wrote I went over & saw the 1ˢᵗ Bn with Goldie.
It was topping seeing them all again, <u>crowds</u> of old friends, both officers,
NCOs & men, none from my days, or not many except in the Transport
but many I had met & knew at F – Allen Bratton of course was the chief
one I wanted to see – Grove was there too – Then yesterday Allen & Grove
came over about 15 miles, luckily they got a car, & met Robert Goldie &
me in this town & had lunch all together – It was <u>great</u>. We did have a talk
– of course we were just <u>the</u> "tennis four" of this time last year. Also it was
Grove's birthday & 2 years ago yesterday I just went out to France! So we
found it quite a "DAY". Reggie Weber is here too but on a course in another
part of the village, however I spent a long time with him yesterday evening
& shall do so others – I hadn't seen about C E Stuart Staffs wounded – That
would be Cyril – I must write.

Ever so much love Your very loving

Philip.

MC 643/8/25

163.   Tuesday June 5 1917

My very dear Father I wonder how you are getting on this in this tremendous
heat! I have not heard from you for some time, but I knew I would not as
I have been moving about so – I expect you got my last written in a field
about a week ago, telling you I was "B" Team – well my address now is "25ᵗʰ
Divn: Reinforcement Camp" but of course I have no idea how long it will

be so as it depends on so many things. We are very comfortable here now, all in tents, quite a number of us as you can judge from the address. We do parades & train during the day but the evenings are lovely, and camp life is really very jolly. I am enjoying my temporary release from my Adjts work too. I went over to see the 1st Battn: last week – I found lots of officers I knew, chiefly from Felixstowe of course, also NCOs & men. Robert Goldie went with me – & of course we were most pleased to see Allen Bratton, & Grove too was there, which curiously just made up our last years tennis four – Then 2 days ago Allen & Grove met R. Goldie & me in a town close to us here & we had lunch together, & a huge talk on old times. Curiously enough it was Grove's birthday & the 2nd anniversary of my first trip out here! I expect you know more news than I do now. For we are right back & out of range of the guns, & do not hear what our Battns are doing. The heat has peeled one layer of skin clean off my forearms!

Lots of love your very loving Philip

I told Grove, Allen & Goldie all about you & they were <u>much</u> interested <u>and</u> impressed.

MC 643/8/24

164. [FSP][297]

I am quite well
I have received your letter dated June 5
Letter follows at first opportunity

Philip.

MC 643/8/27

165. [FSP][298]

I am quite well
Letter follows at first opportunity

Philip

9.6.17

MC 643/8/28

---

297. Postmarked 11 June '17 but written earlier: addressed to Mrs Hewetson.
298. Postmarked 15 June: addressed to Mrs Hewetson.

166.   B.E.F June 12 1917[299]

My dear Mother & Ruth

I have not been able to write to you properly for a whole week tho' I hope you got the two field service p.cs I sent you. However here I am just as well and safe & sound as ever! Of course you have read all about it in the papers! Wasn't it just a splendid success – of course I was expecting to be right out of it back with "B" team as I had tried to hint to you in my last letter. Just ½ an hour after I had sent that letter posted on June 5 I got a sudden order to rejoin my Regiment. I got 10 minutes notice & hurriedly packed & was taken back in a motor, about an hour's ride to the Battn – I found them all bivouacked in a field & busy getting ready for everything. I was very anxious to find out why I had been recalled & wondered if Marsh the assist or 2nd string or "A" team Adjt:(!) was sick & I was to go in after all. But that was not so, & I discovered <&> I been recalled for a very nice job. I was not actually to go over the top in the attack itself but was to be attached the Brigade H.Q on our right and act as "liaison" officer between our Brigade & that one. So after a night in the field with the Battn: I started off up to the trenches <wh> to find this Brigade HQ: it was a deep dug out somewhere up in the trenches. It was a hot walk finding it & I found I was very agile & active in spite of my pack & equipment when it came to dodging a few German shells. I managed to get a good lunch at a Battn. H.Q on the way up which was very welcome. I just walked in & looked hot, thirsty & hungry! Everybody keeps open house these days – tho' some of course are more open than others & I was lucky that day to drop on a hospitable Battn! I eventually reached the Bgde HQ. at about 3pm on the afternoon of the 6th. Of course everybody was very busy & I had not much to do. My work was to keep my own Brigade informed of the progress of this Bgde I was attached to as soon as the attack started. The story of the actual attack of course you've read in the papers! So I wont say much especially as I was not actually in it. However I was in a very interesting position being quite close up & with a Bgde HQ, all the messages kept coming in & I knew the progress of the battle. The noise of course was something terrific!! & when at Zero those mines you've read about went up the whole place simply rocked.

---

299. 'Messines' added at top of letter, probably by Philip's mother. The Battle of Messines began at 3.10 am on 7 June when almost a million tons of explosives in mines beneath the German front line were detonated: the explosion could be heard – and felt –in England. The British were able to exploit this and capture old German defence lines some distance behind the front lines, but it is sometimes argued that the Germans had deliberately withdrawn before the attack.

It was very interesting seeing all the Tanks going up, guns being dashed forward after the advance, German prisoners coming down & some of them carrying our wounded, and all the other things connected with a modern terrific battle. For undoubtedly this is so far one of the biggest "shows" of the war – I stayed at the Bgde HQ. till Saturday afternoon, and then went & joined what was left of the Battn, ie just about half of it, & far less in officers though we had 12 officers wounded we only had 1 killed.[300] They have done most awfully well – really well. They were still in the trenches & I relieved Marsh who had been acting Adjt all through the advance, he went back to the Transport lines & I took his place. He needed the rest. We came out last night after being in <the> a place where once old German trenches had been. In many cases living in German dug outs & the men in a German trench which we had repaired after the havoc our fire had wrought. We were really quite comfortable. The ground is an extraordinary sight, battered & churned to nothing but huge holes – a modern battlefield is really beyond description I think – but still you've seen the Somme pictures & this is supposed to be worse as far as destruction & intense artillery fire goes. Well we came out yesterday & there is lots to be done, cleaning up & reorganising the Battn. Shipp was wounded in the thigh, bad enough for England I think but not _too_ bad I hope – I shall miss him _a great deal_.

Well for 6 days nearly I got no letters & then I got a budget on Sunday, I _was_ pleased, sitting in an old German place those letters were just a _joy_. Father's photo came & I _am_ pleased with it, and I always love your letters. How splendid how you go & talk to all these people. Your other letter was written on Monday the 4th. I am still hoping to meet Father but it cannot be yet. We go into the line again tomorrow but only for _ordinary_ trench life.

I think a home made cake would be very nice!! I am very well & very Thankful for the way I came through the attack tho' not of course right in it. Lots of love
Your very loving

Philip

<Tell> Ruth, I got <her> your last letter in the old German lines too! Tell me exactly your impression of Julie![301]

_MC 643/8/29_

---

300. The officer killed was Captain R D Robinson. Wylly gives the battalion casualties at Messines as: 78 killed, 284 wounded and six missing.
301. Julia Langdale-Smith: see Appendix 3.

167.   Thursday 14-6-17

My very dear Mother & Ruth

After all here we are still in our field, we did not go into the trenches after all which pleased us all very much! A big change took place for me yesterday! I am no longer an Adjutant – The Colonel has taken one of the few officers who came right through the attack & I have changed with him and I now command C.Coy. The change itself I am very pleased with. It will be a great relief to me in the way of worrying work! also now I have done <9> 10 months office work & I have often told you how much more I prefer dealing with men than with paper. I shall greatly enjoy having a Coy: all to myself, and feel I shall be able to put much more life & interest into it than into my old work. Though of course I am <u>very</u> glad to have had the privilege & experience of being Adjt of a Battn out here for 3 months, it will always help me. Of course I shall not be in such close contact with certain natures I did not always fit in with, & these people when seen less often will probably be much more welcome <u>when</u> seen. At present tho B team have rejoined there is only one officer in the Coy: besides myself, and I am very busy getting to know all about my Coy: & reorganising it. I got a splendid long letter from you to-day written on June 9. I have not heard from Father for some little time, perhaps posts up here are a bit disarranged at present. I am sure I feel much younger now I have a Coy, of course there is a <u>lot</u> of responsibility in a Coy: but not the constant worry of an Adjt: Somebody has just said to me "you <u>are</u> looking fit". I was interested about Julie – I am so glad Father is thinking of messing with the officers, I am sure they will be <u>glad</u> to have him & so much better for him

Lots of love your very loving

Philip.

MC 643/8/30

168.   Sunday June 17

My very dear Mother

I got your lovely long letter today which you wrote on June 13 so it has come fairly quickly. The heat is still tremendous. We have had a splendid week's rest in our tents in the field, quite a picnic with all our meals on the ground outside, oh we are <u>brown</u> & <u>hot</u>! Well tonight we go back into the line & I have a new role as Coy commander so I am just wondering how I shall get on! This morning we had a nice Church Parade Service, the first I had been able to attend for some weeks! Afterwards I was able to attend Holy Communion, there were about 12 officers & 60 or so men there. I've had nice long letters from Roly & Reggie yesterday. I'm very busy arranging & packing so this is very short, I am well as anything. If I only send a field p.c the next days it will mean I am very <u>busy</u> not in dangerous work, it is more or less ordinary again now

Lots of love yr very loving

Philip.

MC 643/8/31

169.   [*FSP*][302]

I am quite well
Letter follows at first opportunity

Philip

19.6.17

MC 643/8/32

170.   20.6.17

My very dear Mother I think you would be very interested if you could see me. Sitting in a little hole burrowed out of the side of the trench the hole about 4 feet long 2 feet broad & 3 feet high, I am sitting in it with my feet up against the opposite side of the trench. That is all we get for dugouts in this part of the world! We can do no cooking up here, things are sent up cold, but we do very well, bully beef, cold hard boiled eggs, cold boiled bacon & tin fruit. However we rough it a bit more than usual. It poured with rain early this morning & everything turned to sandy mud, but the sun is out broiling <hot> hot so things are drying so am I! for I <u>got wet</u> through going round the line between 4 am & 7.30 this morning but am now quite dry again – I got a lovely long letter from you yesterday. This is a regular battlefield in appearance, a bit of a change from the old trenches! I am <u>very</u> muddy, bronzed & well. I wear an ordinary Tommy's tunic, old breeches, stocking puttees & Tommy's boots, no tie or collar! Now I am in a Company & not at HQ Mess a cake sometimes <u>would</u> be very welcome but do not send often as I know how expensive post is &

---

302. Addressed to Mrs Hewetson.

we still feed very well. Now when you get this we shall probably just about be out of the line again.

Lots of love

Your v loving

Philip.

MC 643/8/33

171.   Saturday 23-6-17

My very dear Ruth. Quite time you had a letter again I think. Well you will not have heard from me for a few days & then not much news. You will soon see that I have not had much time to write when I tell you that in the last 48 hours I have had just <u>2</u> hours sleep! Not bad! Well we are all very pleased to be out of the line once more we came out this morning after 6 nights in the line & certainly I *had* not more than <twenty> 16 hours sleep in the whole 6 days. We did not have anything hot to eat all this time & during the last 2½ days no washing or shaving, add to which it rained & the trenches & ourselves were <u>covered</u> in mud. However I am as fit as anything & tho' certainly a bit sleepy not really very tired. We were relieved at 2 am this morning & during the relief the Bosche chose to shell us pretty heavily but we only had one man hit, we marched about 2 hours to a field & had some hot tea & then came a ride of about 3 hours in motor lorries here, or rather 2½ miles from here, we had to finish by another little march. We managed to get a meal at about 12 & considering we had not had even 1 <u>wink</u> of sleep & no breakfast & had had a pretty rough night we were very ready. This afternoon I have had a topping bath & change & am feeling quite fresh now.

It seems quite impossible to ever imagine oneself doing this sort of thing before the war – I suppose really we couldn't have – It is just fitness makes it possible. It has been very funny at times seeing ourselves trying to keep awake sometimes you can hardly do so even by walking about certainly not if you sit or lie down at all. The trenches we were in were a bit out of the ordinary & I will tell you all about them some day. We are now right back & hope to be so for at least fortnight's rest so you all need not worry about me – of course one never knows really. I've said that period tho we hope for more & may get less! I had a bit of a misfortune going up to the line as the heel of one of my boots & ½ the sole came nearly off & flapped about. I had to tie them on with string & it was very uncomfortable. However I managed to get a pair of Tommy's boots sent up by the Qr master – In the excitement of the relief & shelling the damaged pair got left behind so can you send out that pair I sent home earlier on. I got a lovely long letter from Mother written on June 1, shall just love a cake, we fed wonderfully well in the line this time all tinned stuff, & we had cold boiled eggs & lots of lovely lettuce sent right up to us which is extraordinary considering where we were – must finish now & go get a good snooze.

Much love from

Philip.

MC 643/8/34

172.   Tuesday 26.6.17

My very dear Mother

Thank you ever so for the lovely cake, we did just enjoy it, also the smokes, u-all-nos[303] and other things, they were <u>most</u> welcome, and the cake jolly good. As I do not mess at HQ now such things will be very acceptable sometimes. You asked in one of your letters if I ever got any fruit from you, but I am afraid the parcel must have gone astray as it never turned up – what a shame – however we can get fruit here at times, in fact *pretty often really & it is not worth sending*. Another letter from you today & one from Father yesterday – I am kept well supplied. The last 2 nights we have been on the trek – On Sunday night we started at 10 pm and got into billets about 4 am. A very comfortable farm house we had a good sleep till about 10 next morning – an easy day & then we set off again at 8 pm last night and marched till 2 am – This time unfortunately it was all in pouring rain & we <u>were</u> wet when we arrived here, however a good night worked wonders & as to-day is beautifully fine & we did not have breakfast till nearly 11 am we are feeling none the worse for it. We are off again to-night & then hope to be out of the line & stay there for some little time so you needn't picture me in the trenches for a time yet – We are <u>miles</u> from them. I am greatly enjoying my Coy work & have 3 subalterns now. I greatly enjoy your "real talks" & am "inwardly digesting" all your hints! I never write to relations now I really have not time so please send messages to Measham, Holton, Folkestone etc when you write[304]. When we move like this we have breakfast at 10.30 about. lunch about 1.30 pm

---

303. A mint sweet, American in origin: patented there in 1905.
304. See Appendix 3 for members of Philip's family at Measham, Holton and Folkestone.

and a tea-dinner about 6pm – I am hoping to be able to see something of Reggie & Robert Goldie while we are back here – but I am afraid I am right out of Father's reach.

Much love your very loving

Philip[305]

MC 643/8/35

173.   Friday

29.6.17
My very dear Mother

Here we are in a topping little village miles & miles behind the line forgetting there is such a thing as a war except that we work 7 hours a day training for our next meeting with "la guerre". However you need not <work> worry about me for 2 weeks at any rate. We had some good long marches to get here – I can't quite remember when I wrote but I believe the last one was while we were still on the move. We went by night which was cool except the one night when we dropped *in* for a downpour of rain, & trudged along for 6 hours in the rain! Now we are quite comfortable. It is a pretty little village, not much in the way of houses, rather rickety white plaster farms & cottages etc all scattered round 2 or 3 really large village greens; lots of trees & hills about, altogether very pretty & a ripping change and "rest" from actual war tho' parades from 6.30–7.15, 9–12.30 and 2–4.30 keep me very busy. I am greatly enjoying my Company & as we are training & building up again there is lots of interest. We are in a place where we can get strawberries! and have had huge plates full for tea in our Company Mess the last two evenings! With real fresh butter & milk from this little farm we do not do badly. I have had several letters from Father lately & a lovely one from Ruth today, otherwise there seems to have been a <u>short</u> stoppage in English letters – I got 2 books from Gobagger yesterday – In case I do not have time to write please thank her for me. Ruth says she thinks the Dugouts must be stuffy. Well where we were last time there were <u>no</u> dug outs, & I should hardly call the smell "stuffy" but you get quite used to these things!! you'd like to see me in the evening in my slacks, thin brown socks & nicely polished shoes, hardly very warlike. Little Mademoiselle

---

305. 'Recd July 10': endorsed by Philip's mother. Most letters were received about six days after being posted: for some reason this one took much longer, and was only received after Philip's next letter.

Marie aged 15 in my farm billet said I was "beaucoup swank" when she saw me!

Lots of love

your very loving

Philip

I want to see the column all about m'self in "Dear Friends"[306]

MC 643/8/36

174.   Tuesday July 3

My very dear Mother

I got your letter dated June 27 yesterday with the Reptonian also letters from Ruth, aunt Ruth & Reggie so I did jolly well – I also got your lovely parcel with that ripping cake in it & the other things, thank you <u>ever so</u>. The day before I got the new boots, I am awfully glad you got them, I really wanted them, & they fit just right, no I shall not want the other pair. I will send you a blank cheque & then you can fill in for those and for Bob's "doctor's fee" & "grocer's bill"! I should think that would be best. We are having a lovely time here but working jolly hard & getting very fit. Just an instance will show you what we do. This morning we started off as a battalion on a route march at 5.30 am; this meant getting up at 4.30 am. We marched till 9 am and then had ¾ hour in a field for breakfast, some hot tea & ham sandwiches, my word we were jolly ready for it too! It was getting very hot by then & got hotter as morning wore on. We then did 2 more hours marching & then turned off into a ripping field full of scabias & other wild flowers & all had a topping bathe in a river there. Everybody went in officers & men! It was great. Then after another hours march we got back just before 2pm very ready for a meal; we did about 15 miles but I'm sure I could have done 15 more easily!! I'm fit as a fiddle! & brown as anything – The old woman in the farm where I am billeted is most awfully good to me. The other night <u>as</u> I was going to bed about 10.30pm I was caught & sat down at a table with them & made to eat some topping custardy tart & drink beautiful French liqueur. They have not got summer time here in the villages so naturally sit up later than us.[307] I had a most enjoyable meal in spite of just having

---

306. 'Recd July 5, written June 29': envelope endorsed by Philip's mother. 'Dear Friends' is not identifiable, probably a local church magazine.

307. British Summer Time was first introduced in 1916, a First World War innovation still with us today.

had dinner. Today just before tea I had a cold tub there & a change into cooler clothes & as I was coming away I was presented with a huge plate of cherries(!) which I had to sit down & eat (nothing lothe I can assure you!) This is a splendid rest from war tho' not from work, tho' of course we don't expect the latter. You may get a letter from <*name deleted*> one of my subs[308] who is in England we'll be here when you get this. Much love

your loving

Philip.

MC 643/8/37

175.   Monday July 9

My very dear Father

Here we are, still back in the peaceful areas & likely to be so for another week or so which is quite to our liking – However as I told you before we are having a pretty strenuous time, absolutely not a minute to ourselves before 4.30 pm and then after tea generally a certain amount of arranging to do for the next day and by the time you've had tea & a change & wash there is not a great deal of the day left! It is a splendid healthy life. Yesterday we changed billets with another Battn in the Brigade just for a change for the men and are now in a nice little country town, 3 miles from the village we've been in – We've got a lovely big room for a mess & share it with the B. Coy officers – which is very nice as a bit of a variation & change. You seem to have got a pretty good idea as to our work – I hope you are not being troubled too much by those enemy shells round you – what is the name of your hut, I've forgotten it! and it may be useful! I've done a good deal of riding lately; this week we shall probably be bivouacking out on the ground we shall be training over and this has meant riding over all the ground & reconnoitring it. On Saturday I was riding 3½ hours & yesterday afternoon 4 hours, pretty hard cross country galloping too a lot of it – I enjoy it greatly and am now feeling at home on a horse. The next thing I want to do is jumping, I can take small ditches now but have not tried anything in the nature of a high jump yet.

Much love your v loving

Philip.

MC 643/8/38

---

308. H H Swift: see letters 177, 178.

176. Monday July 9th

My very dear Mother

I do not think I have written for a long time! I knew however that you knew we were still here training & resting so you would not be worrying as a matter of fact we have really been having rather a strenuous, though of course quite a peaceful, time – we did another good long march & finished up with a glorious bathe in the river. One evening the Divn: band came & played at the Chateau where we had Battn: HQ. and the 4 Coy Commanders went up & had dinner there, it was very jolly. The Chateau was a ripping place with a moat round it & big grounds. After dinner we had some boxing among the officers, rather fun – Yesterday we changed places with one of the other Battns: in the Brigade & are now in a sort of little market town, it has quite a number of good shops etc. However this week we are to go out & do sort of manoeuvres most days so we shall probably be bivouacing out most nights, or performing – I have been riding a good deal yesterday & the day before, real long gallops across country. I am a bit stiff after it today – on Saturday I was riding round 3½ hours and yesterday 4 hours hard riding going round the ground we are going to manoeuvre on – Posts seems to be bad at present as posts are very small & I have had no letter from England for 4 or 5 days! But I expect they'll all come along soon.

Much love your loving

Philip.

MC 643/8/39

177. B.E.F. July 13

My very dear Mother

This is just the day for me to write some letters. Yesterday morning the whole Battn: marched out some miles to do some training & bivouac for two nights in the fields. I was however detailed as a member of a Court Martial, so was to follow them as soon as the Court was over. But one of the witnesses who has to come from some distance has never turned up so we are still waiting for him. Luckily the court is being held in my Coy mess, so here I am! just waiting – We adjourned last night and assembled again this morning, but the witness has not turned up yet, & we assemble again this afternoon, I am therefore having a lazy time & have settled down to write letters. I had a long letter from Hugh to-day he says he has been back at Felixstowe for 2 months now & is very bored with it. He says he is on "light duty" & likely to remain so for "the duration" he thinks he is able to play a little tennis, but cannot get about the court much, yet even like that he says he plays better than many fit people! I enjoyed your letter which came with the 2 magazines, also myself in "Dear Friends" – I am sorry to say I cannot trace the last cake!!! Isn't it a <u>shame</u>! The last parcel I got was the cake with the ginger & black currant lozenges – However it may turn up yet, posts have been <u>very</u> bad lately. The weather has changed from that rainy period we had to the beautifully hot summer days again. Do you realise that I have now been longer with the 9th than I was with the 1st! and in 3 days I shall complete my 4 months exactly this time – I hope soon that I may really get a chance of meeting Father; tho' one cannot tell yet. I told Swift to go & see Gobagger if he had time, he is one of my 3 subs; he had been out 10 months without leave! I have since heard from Gobagger all about his visit. We are having a splendid long time right back in civilization aren't we – and I am keeping as fit as a fiddle – Father's 4 months must be getting near an end now? Hasn't he done over three? How you will love to have him back again. I wonder if he'll want to stay longer?

Much love

Your very loving

Philip.

MC 643/8/40

178.   Wednesday 18.7.17

My very dear Mother Ever so many thanks for the last lovely parcel which came yesterday – The cake would take a 1st prize at any competition I'm sure, it was a record <u>beauty</u>! Also just what I love are those crème de menthes & choc. peppermints. I love things like that as I can go to them & comfort myself with one at any old odd time. We were bivouacing out in field when the parcel came. The cigarettes were most welcome as there was a shortage & I had not been able to get any for some days. We were out bivouacing and training for 2 days & nights. Last night it rained hard & this morning & we all got pretty wet so we came back here to our billets for tonight a 2½ hour march – we start off again to morrow at 6.30 am for 2 more days out in the fields if it is fine. However we are still at present back in our "civilization billets". I am glad you got a letter from Swift after all and that it was interesting. It was especially creditable of him as he spent his leave getting "engaged" so might have been forgiven if he had been a bit forgetful. That is the thing to do on leave now, you should really to be really successful I <u>gather</u> either get engaged or married. However I believe they find time a little short if you've nobody in view before you start, so please get a good "selection" ready for me!! You can tell them my Bank balance is quite good and that I am very steady! Of course they may not want to wait <so> as long as they'll have to wait for me but still it will be a very good test I think.

I got a letter from you to-day written on July 13. When you get this I may be a bit nearer to meeting Father.

I am greatly hopeful about Germany's in<u>ternals</u>.[309] I have not met Reggie & Goldie since before the push & should like to see one of the <u>old</u> lot again. But I am getting on very well with all in the Battn now, and am fit & cheery.

Much love your very loving

Philip.

MC 643/8/41

179.   Tuesday 24.7.17

My very dear Mother

I have not been able to write just lately, there has been no outpost for some days & I do not really know if this will go tonight now. This is due to us being on the move once more. We had a tremendous finish to our "rest" last weekend. On Friday we got up at 5 & marched for 2½ hours, then we had an hours rest & then 3 hours parade before lunch. In the afternoon we were working hard from 2 to 8pm. We bivouacked in the field & on Sat morning we did 4 hours parade. In the afternoon we were out from 2 to 7 on a very energetic scheme & then from 8.30 to 11pm we were marching back to our billets, so we had an energetic 2 days. On Sunday we had a Church parade Service in the morning & various things to arrange before an early move by bus yesterday. It was very dusty & after 4 or 5 hours in them we were just like millers simply covered in dust. I hope to see Father in 2 or 3 days now, won't that be splendid. I am to be in B: team again I hear. Though of course it is not <u>exactly</u> again as I saw a certain amount before. I am still keeping

---

309. After three years of war, there was an expectation in every country that the enemy would suffer internal crisis that would bring their participation in the war to an end – it actually happened only in Russia.

as fit as a fiddle. The weather is hot as anything now, very close. Will write again soon, we move each day much love

Your v loving

Philip.

180.   Thursday 27.7.17

My very dear Father

I wonder very much if you got that hurried note I sent you by D.R.L.S. yesterday. I sent it via our Brigade & Division so I think you should get it. I wonder if you understood it? I am afraid a train journey looks a bit impossible now I am here to see; but you might get a lift to this place. I could easily put you up. I have got a very big job as I am acting Adjutant and Quartermaster to the IInd Corps Advanced Reinforcement Camp so I can do anything for you if you can get to this area; anything you want in the way of billets or rations or anything. A Corps is a pretty big thing so I am & shall be very busy at first, especially as nothing is arranged yet at all. I had so looked forward to seeing you this weekend but at present it seems postponed. You could I believe communicate with me through that HQ you found. They would tell you about me as they detailed me for this job. You might perhaps find too that my Battn: was quite close to you, if so do go & see them. Some of them will be coming to see you if they can find you. More later

Your very loving

Philip.

181.   Thursday 27.7.17

My very dear Mother

I hope you got my last letter written 2 days ago but there was no post that night & we moved early next morning so I do not know if it went or not especially as many & great changes have taken place since then or rather they all happened yesterday.

   We got up at 5am & started marching at 6.30 am to continue our move. A huge thunderstorm came on, & deluging rain so we did not have the best of marches. We got to our billets about 10.30. <u>Then</u> I was hauled out of the ranks by the Major who told me I was to be at the Bgde HQ at 12 to be taken off by car. I knew I was to be in "B" Team this time but this was rather sudden. However I soon found out what my job was to be. I am now Acting as Adjutant <u>and</u> Quartermaster <the> to a <u>Corps</u> Reinforcement Camp. A very big job!!! No camp is yet started but a few of us are here in advance, getting the 100 and 1 things that have got to be done thought out & if possible in some way arranged. A <u>Corps</u> is a big thing you know! I am some little way back again & in very nice billets & very comfortable. I may be here between 2 & 4 weeks but have <u>no</u> idea. At any rate go on sending my letters to the Battn: they will get forwarded. I got quite near Father & then this sudden call away has upset things again which is <u>very</u> annoying but may manage to arrange a meeting.

A lovely parcel came from you just as I was moving away from the Battn, thank you <u>ever so</u>, especially for the cigs, & sweets which I brought along. The cake which looked a <u>beauty</u> I left with my Coy: officers as a parting gift as I could not carry it with me, I wish I could have!!

I got 2 of your letters together 2 nights ago & enjoyed your acct: of the wounded's parties. I was & am <u>very</u> sorry to have to leave my Coy: just now but it had to be – Much love your very

loving Philip.

MC 643/8/43/2

182. 31.7.17

My very dear Mother

This is a bad place for news at present as since I left the Battn: a week ago tomorrow I have had no letters at all! I am hoping they will get forwarded some day soon but I am afraid there are other things going on a good deal more important than our letters to-day so we must wait. I think you might send a letter to the 2nd Corps Advanced Reinforcement Camp just to see if it gets here but as I have no idea now how long this camp will last do not send all here. If you write here do not forget to put my Battn: on as this is a huge place. We heard a <u>terrific</u> bombardment this morning & hear rumours of a great success to start with but no definite news yet, we are much too far away. I live at the Corps Camp HQ, with a Major from another Division as Commandant, myself Adjutant & Quartermaster and a Camp M.O, we are very comfortable, I have quite a comfortable room & we have a nice mess just opposite. Of course as you know I was delighted at getting to a Coy and away from my Adjt's: work so I am not too pleased at being shoved in to this job which combines Adjutant's & Quartermaster's work. I really hoped I had got rid of office work but I am just reminding myself this is only a very temporary camp & I am looking forward to the time I get back to the Battn: & people I know etc! and regular posts! nobody seems to know how long we will be here, so I do not know what to do about this as a permanent address. At present we are only very much at a starting point & receive no letters & have no regular means of dispatching them.

Now I must finish with lots of love

Your very loving Philip.

MC 643/8/44

183.   2.8.17[310]

Here we are both met at last, and enjoying a day together well out of reach of the Hun's attentions

Philip
W Hewetson[311]

MC 643/8/45

184.   Saturday August 4

My very dear Mother

We now have a post here and I have had 2 letters from you this week but that is all since I left the Battn: on the 21st July! So they must all be held up somewhere, I have had no other letters but those 2 of yours! However the last 2 days have made up for lots of missing letters as Father and I have at last met out here – I had sent a special letter by despatch rider to him telling him where I was. That was on the day when I left the Battn and then I got a letter from him saying he would try to get over & see me. I was sitting in the little room which does for an office here when I suddenly heard a voice say "Hullo found him at last" and there was Father looking in thro' the window, it was about 3 pm on Thursday. He had managed to get a lift on a lorry part of the way but had had to walk the last 5 or 6 kilometres, and

---

310. Written on Church Army postcard.

311. Addressed to Miss Burges, Bayham House, Folkestone; forwarded to 335 Kingston Road, Wimbledon; then to Salhouse Vicarage Norwich.

as it was raining he was naturally very muddy and a bit hot & tired. It <u>was</u> nice to see him & he came into the mess & we had lots to talk about. In the evening the Major & M.O. were going out to dinner so Father & I had an evening all to ourselves which was ripping. I got him a nice room and bed in the same house as I am in and he did not leave till yesterday afternoon when we got him a lift in an ambulance car nearly <u>all</u> the way back. We found lots to talk about & Father looked very brown & well and he was <u>full</u> of news & interest all about the hut & men he has met. He seems to have to rough it a good deal but says he thoroughly enjoys it – It <u>was</u> nice meeting, just a bit of 'home' to each of us, quite like a little bit of leave. I am still at this camp and as we have a daily post I think it would be best to address my letters to 2nd Corps Advanced Reinforcement Camp B E F, not forgetting to put on the battalion as before so that if I had left they would know where to forward them. This may mean missing a few days when the camp breaks up but we are sure to be here some little time yet and so it is worth while getting letters direct <u>now</u>. It has rained steadily and heavily for 4 whole days and nights now & the roads even right back here are appalling, I believe right up in the line they are worse than in the winter as the ground is so cut up by shellfire, rain just turns it into impassable waist deep mud. We get very little news here & just have to rely on the papers which we often do not get for 2 or 3 days. However otherwise we are very comfortable now, and the "Camp" is a going concern. I am by no means overworked. Just think of 3 years ago to-day, we were just arriving at Bude,[312] poor old "Ford"-

Much love Your very

loving Philip.

MC 643/8/46

185. Tuesday August 7

My very dear Mother & Ruth

I am afraid my last letter to you sounded very grumpy but if so it really gave quite a wrong impression! Today I am pleased as punch, I've just got some letters forwarded on, one from Ruth written on July 23! that's long enough isn't it – One from you on July 24 and one on August 1st. However now I know you know where I am & what I am doing & you will also have heard about Father's visit here. Well here I am still in this sleepy little village, far

---

312. Bude is on the north coast of Cornwall. The Hewetsons were presumably on a family holiday there on 4 August 1914 – the day that war was declared.

from the battle – and in a general way picking up a good deal of knowledge on a new branch of military work & facing a good deal of experience. It certainly is an experience to be continually living & mixing with strangers and I am finding myself quite different and absolutely able to get on & take my place with them. These letters of yours had been forwarded to the Corps Reinforcement Camp, do not forget we are the 2ⁿᵈ Corps Advanced Reinforcement Camp, it just makes all the difference & now you can send letters etc here straight. I think we may be here a bit longer than I expected owing to the recent bad weather. However I hope very much not too long as I do not want to be away from the Battn: too long! It is rotten here getting no news, not even about the Battn: & I am wanting news about Reggie badly – & all the others. You may rest assured I am getting good nights now & really getting very lazy, we do not have breakfast till "nine-ish" and I have an excellent bed. Now you say you may go to Sheringham![313] Jolly good idea, I really think you ought, I am sure after all the work & worry you've been having a change would be just what you want – & the hens & potatoes can all look after themselves! There now I hope to hear you are going – Leonard was not wounded, he went home sick I think – I am hard at work taking in your programmes for my leave!! It sounds most interesting. Lots of love your

very loving Philip.

MC 643/8/47

186.   Friday 10.8.17

My very dear Mother

Many happy returns of my birthday to you! I should just about think this will arrive on the 14ᵗʰ I should think I will still be here almost certainly, but one never really knows.

I believe my battalion had something to settle with the Bosche early this morning but I do not know anything definite.[314] I had a splendid change yesterday I went away for the day. I went down to the sea with a Major from another Divn. We started in the morning about 9 am & managed to cadge rides on a lorry & in 2 different French motors & soon got there. The Major went to see his brother who has a staff appt. there. We had lunch together did

---

313. Fishing village and tourist spot on the North Norfolk coast on a direct railway line from Salhouse: the air on the coast was considered bracing and so suitable for those recovering from illness.

314. On this day, the 9ᵗʰ Battalion took part in attacking the Westhoek Ridge. Lieutenant H H Swift was among those killed in the attack.

some shopping, & I had a lovely full length bath. We were very lucky coming back as we got hold of a R.A.M.C. Colonel who brought us nearly all the way back. We brought back some lovely fresh fish for dinner – The weather seems to have cleared at last & is lovely today. Your letter came to-day suggesting improvements in my rain protective gear. At present my trench coat is in excellent form, but I think the idea of getting a real good living out of my big coat <u>very</u> good – I am bound to get leave before the winter I think & then may try to get some light sort of oil skin thing. At present boots, clothes, socks etc are all in good form – Letters are coming regularly now

Lots of love

Your very loving Philip.

MC 643/8/48

187.   My very dear Mother

a most tremendous budget to-day! no fewer than 6 letters, 3 from you, 1 from Gobagger 1 from Ruth and 1 from Father; and 2 parcels, a lovely cake from G, please thank her very much for that & her letter and the other parcel had writing paper (most welcome) <u>and</u> the smokes and the books which I shall greatly enjoy reading. Your 3 letters were written on Friday 10th Sunday 12th and the 14th They all got here the same post – to-day – Well I am still at this Camp but I quite thought I should have gone easily by now. I cannot make out why I am still here you see I was left here as the Camp Adjt when our Divnl: "B" teams rejoined again. Of course the Colonel wants me back badly, but I am under orders to stay here until a relief arrives for me," he" has not arrived so I stay here, expecting him to arrive at any time or for a wire to come changing my instructions. So I am rather in an unsettled position. I managed to get over to see the Battn: yesterday, they had come back out of the line close here for a day or so to reorganize.

The C.O hailed me with delight as he thought I had come to stay, they want officers badly, but I had to tell him I had to go back Oh he said your relief has been arranged for & will go to you in 12 hours, well that is nearly 36 hours ago & here I am still! However next time you hear from me I <u>may</u> be back again. I only hope I am given a few hours notice & not packed off at an unearthly hour. I have been pretty busy today, new arrivals – I shall have greatly enjoyed my time here when the time comes to go and be very Thankful for it. My chances of getting over to Father are "nil" at present as in my unsettled condition I cannot leave the village here for any time. The tinned chickens have not turned up yet so I hope somebody has eaten them by now & that they are not wandering about getting more & more 'niffy'. I think there is just a chance I might get some leave in September but one never knows when it will stop, or start or go on, or how many will go etc etc. However we will hope it will do something favourable. I am keeping fit as a fiddle.

Your very loving

Philip.

MC 643/8/49

188. Tuesday <July> August 21

My very dear Ruth

I don't think you have had a letter to yourself in ages – Well no nearer anywhere yet. In fact a little further away if anything. We moved yesterday morning & are now very near where I have been at the A.R.C. In fact today I rode over & had tea with them there in my old mess. We have got a nice billet for the Coy, some in a barn & some in tents. The farm stands in the middle of a ripping great grass field. We are having a great time & have managed to get a football & rig up some goalposts. We had a great game last night, one platoon against the other. The two subs each played for their platoon & I played for one & the Coy Sergt Major for the others. It was hot. They are playing again tonight.

Tomorrow I am getting up Company Sports for them. They are most fearfully keen on the idea & we are going to have all sorts of amusing races, 3-legged, blindfold wheelbarrow etc etc – This Brigade has done most awfully well in the recent fighting & been specially congratulated & today we had the honour of being specially inspected by Sir D. Haig.[315] A most beautiful parcel came to-day from the ARC, it was Mother's with the most luscious sweets in – lots & lots of thanks, I shall just enjoy them. I saw Ostrehan "missing" but cannot find anything out of course as I don't know where his Battn is (Mother asked) – I got Mother's letter forwarded on from the ARC – She wrote on 16th & it got here to-day so that's not bad – I expect we shall still be "in comfort" when you get this

---

315. Sir Douglas Haig (1861–1928); Commander of First Army 1915; succeeded French as Commander-in-chief of the British Expeditionary Force in December 1915, remaining in command until the end of the war.

Much love from

Philip.

MC 643/8/50

189.   Friday August 24

My very dear Mother

Here we are still in this nice farm billet & likely to be here a little time yet, at any rate when you get this. On Wednesday I had rather a nice day. It was very like a trip I had just 2 years ago out here if you remember. Two officers from each Battn in the Brigade went off to see a way of defeating the wily Hun. We had a long motor ride all on the top of an old bus, it took 3 hours & was through very pretty country so I thoroughly enjoyed it – The actual demonstration only lasted a few minutes & after lunch in a nice big town we drove back.

   In the evening we had a great time. We had organised Sports for the Company – The first event was a prize for the best turned out man in the Company. I had asked the Colonel & the Regt Sergt Maj: to come & judge. The C.O was so pleased at my getting up the sports that he sent the Regt: Band up to our field & had told all the other Coys they must have sports too!! The sports were a <u>great</u> success, three legged races, wrestling on each other's backs, wheelbarrow races, races in gas masks etc! The men loved it & we had huge entries, which pleased us all very much as so often they will watch but not join in. The C.O. was awfully pleased & very congratulatory. All the other poss O.C. Coys are being asked why they haven't had sports like C.Coy!! All the men's letters were full of the sports next day. We are having lovely weather & I am greatly enjoying my Company. We are kept very busy. I heard from Roly yesterday, he says he is keeping his leave till I get mine!
I am keeping & looking fitter than ever lots of love

Your very loving

Philip

Here's cheque for Bob etc[316]

MC 643/8/51

---

316. Included in the envelope is a blank cheque made out to Mrs Hewetson and dated 23 August 1917.

190.   Sunday August 26

My very dear Mother

I got your letter written on Tuesday 21ˢᵗ and another on Saturday 18ᵗʰ both together yesterday. I do hope you are quite well & strong again now & had a real good rest in bed. It is splendid that Gobagger & Ruth are both there. I wonder if you are going away for a bit of a change? Don't you think it would be a good thing. Here we are still in our nice farm house billet where we have been all the week. My two subs: are a bit of a change to what I have been used to, through they are very good chaps in their own way.[317] One is a Welshman, who has been out for 15 months in the ranks, quite a young chap – The other has been a grocer in Lancashire, also quite young, rather bumptious with a pencil behind the ear & half a cigarette behind the other, which he smokes in between the courses at meals & reads "Nat Gould's" novels![318] They are both very keen though & not at all bad. We haven't much in common to make our conversation out of but get on very well together & it is really rather amusing! All my special friends in our other Battns: are still alright. I heard from Roly the other day to say he & the two Curwens were dining together to commemorate our 3 years commissions & would be thinking of all of us at the Felix. Father seems to be greatly enjoying his work now that he has got the Canteen to work too. I expect it will just about be September when this reaches you, don't the months fly by. We are very comfortable here & do not seem to be thinking of moving yet. I have been sitting on a Court Martial all day from 10 am to 2.30 pm so did not get back for lunch till 3 pm so I've spent a novel sort of Sunday. Very much

love your very loving

Philip.

MC 643/8/52

---

317. One, presumably the Lancastrian, is R. C. Newth, see letter 202: the Welshman is not otherwise identified.

318. Nat Gould (1857–1919) wrote many novels, most with a horse racing theme: he was the best-selling author in the world at this time. He published about a dozen books in the war years alone, with titles like *The Wizard of the Turf; The Turf Conspiracy; The Rider in Khaki.*

191.   Wednesday August 29

My very dear Mother

This is a just a very short note to tell you that we are still where we have been for the last 10 days. I am writing this about 9.30 pm so this won't be a long letter. We are now stronger in officers in this Coy, for I have got two more subalterns joined me today. I will be able to tell you more about them in a day or two. We are having quite a nice time, although the last few days have been more full of rain than sunshine. I am quite pleased to be still here though. I quite thought I should have had to write & tell you we'd moved before this. I got a letter from you yesterday but there was no post to day so we did not even get the papers. When all these new officers keep arriving it makes me miss the old ones & specially the special friends in the other Battns – They are however a very decent lot but a bit different from the usual & take a bit of "stomaching" at times – We saw an excellent entertainment by Divisional Pierrots tonight.
I am keeping as fit as anything

Very much love

Your very loving Philip.

MC 643/8/53

192.   Monday Sept 3

My very dear Mother

This is just a very short note to tell you we have moved up. I have not been able to write for a few days for we took 2 days coming up. We are not actually in the line now. We are very comfortable in nice dugouts, and not having half a bad time, so you need not worry, At any rate the sooner in the sooner out & the sooner a possible leave. I am as well as anything.

Lots of love Your very

loving Philip.

MC 643/8/54

193.   Tuesday Sept 4

My very dear Mother

Just another very short note. We are still very comfortable, living in dugouts in the ruins. Mine is built up under what was a house a <u>sort</u> of upper storey is still standing above us. We are all Sandbagged in in what I suppose was once a front downstairs room. We have chairs, a table & canvas beds. The servants are in a sort of cellar below us so we live very comfortably as they can cook here. We have our full nights rest but of course sleep in our clothes.

This morning we had one of those reconnoitring trips up to the line that I have described before. It meant getting up at 4 am! The Co. Adjt. and 4 Company Commanders each accompanied by their runner. We were fortunate & had a quick trip each way. I got back about 9.30 am & had a very welcome breakfast at H.Q.

I then came back to my own little house & had a glorious wash & shave in real <u>hot</u> water & am feeling very fresh. It is <u>glorious</u> weather, and as we are not doing anything alarming you need not be disturbed at all about me. I am sure I have never been so fit & well – I am sure you'll think so when you see me –

Very much love your very

Loving Philip.

MC 643/8/55

194.   Thursday Sept 6

My very dear Mother

We have finished our stay in the ruins & go up tonight. So I may only get a p.c. to you or even nothing at all for a few days so don't be wondering what has become of me. I hear from Father that he is going home on the 17th! How pleased you will be. It will be lovely if I can get away soon after that too. Of course <u>nothing</u> has been arranged at all yet but I hope I <u>may</u> get away some time not long after we come out this time. The Bosche gave us a noisy night with gas shells & others 2 days ago but did no damage. I have 2 officers who have not been out before so it means a good deal of extra instructions to them now we are up the line.

Much love your v loving

Philip.

MC 643/8/56

195. Sunday Sept 9

My very dear Mother

Out of the line again!! We were only in from Friday night to Sunday morning, 3 nights & 2 days but it was quite long enough. The part of the line we were in is none too "healthy" and so I am very pleased to get out again. We were brought back in buses to this camp & got here about 5 am, very fairly tired, and after a meal we all turned in and slept till about midday. This camp is quite near to Father's hut, so this afternoon I rode over to see him. He was out when I arrived there about 4.30 pm having tea with some officers somewhere. He came in about 5.15 & was very surprised to see me, as he thought I was still in the line. He had an evening service at 6.30 in the hut & I was there. Oh I can quite see why he wants to come out again. He had a <u>packed</u> hut & such a splendid service, and such a splendid talk he gave us. The singing was absolutely really great – There was an "atmosphere" there and I can tell Father revels in the work and he <u>does</u> look well, much better even I thought than when I saw him before. He says he is going home this Wednesday. I do not know <u>at all</u> when my leave will come, it is all very indefinite. A lovely parcel from you to-day, thank you ever so, cigarettes, U-all-Nos & ginger! I do hope you are <u>much</u> better now.

Much love from very loving

Philip[319]

MC 643/8/57

196. Wednesday Sept 12

My very dear Mother, Father

I expect I can write you a joint letter once again now, I expect you <u>are</u> all 3 talking & exchanging lots of news. I hope the crossing & journey home came off alright to-day. Father will have taken all the latest & most firsthand news of me back. We managed a visit each to each other in the last 2 days so we finished up better in the <twelith> twelfth hour of our front

---

319. Philip's mother added the following note in the margin: 'W was at tea with the officers of the Chinese – One of them had sought him out with a Missionaries officer son. Both English fr. China. The Chinese were doing labour work around him.' The Chinese Labour Corps was made up of almost 100,000 labourers shipped from China to take over labouring tasks and free up soldiers for military duties. About 2,000 of them died, mostly from disease.

stay in France better than we had managed all the other months. However it was only just in time that we met for we have left that district now and we are not at all sorry. Did you see the communique in Monday's paper? that was exactly us, it referred to the lively artillery etc on Sunday night. Well we knew exactly all about it as it was very personal.[320]

We have been 2 days on the trek now, yesterday we travelled in motor buses and to day we had breakfast at 6.0 am and then after about a 5 hour march we arrived "here" – for the night only as we trek off again tomorrow, this time to our destination, where we shall stay & do some hard training for a bit – Do not expect me home on leave just yet. The C.O says he cannot spare me while we are back here training. In a way it is not a bad thing really as there is not a great deal of advantage in going on leave while the Battn is out some way behind the <way> line. I may as well get away while they are in a bit nastier spot! However at present I have no idea of anything – except that I am no:2 on the leave list – and will undoubtedly go on leave "some" day! I did enjoy the cigarettes you sent & am now going to start on Father's. The sweets are excellent. I am enjoying reading E. Dell's "Knave of Diamonds".[321]

Very much love Your loving

Philip.

MC 643/8/58

197.   Saturday Sept 15

My very dear Ruth

We are well settled down once more for a period out of the line again but are working hard. We are in very comfortable billets, in a mining village. All this country is very interesting and has not changed from this time two years ago. We are well back from the line. Mother's letter yesterday with news of Reggie's death came as a bit of a shock to me as I had not heard of it at all.[322] I feel it – as he was quite one of my best friends. Unfortunately though that is just what this hateful war is doing all the time. I hope to go over & see the 8th Bn. in a day or so and find out details. I heard from another source of it today but somehow missed it in the paper myself. I suppose Father has arrived

320. *The Times* of 10 September 1917 refers to German reports of a 'lively artillery duel' near Ypres.
321. Novel by the very popular author Ethel M Dell, first published in 1913.
322. Reggie Weber was killed in action on 5 September 1917: he was 25 years old.

home again now, do not let him come back here again too quickly. Winter out here is very different from summer. He must have done splendid work in his hut – It was absolutely packed the Sunday I went over. I do not know <u>when</u> I am coming, but I do know that it will be very sudden when I do, they never give us any warning, certainly not enough to let people know you're coming – If you do let them know leave is invariably cancelled or something! We must certainly have a <u>short</u> trip to town I think, I shall have a certain amount of shopping to do, ready for the winter months – Fancy 6 months tomorrow since I landed in France this time, so I'm getting on. It will certainly be October before I come now – You <u>do</u> seem to be busy. I do hope Mother is getting better & stronger again, tell here she must take things very easily and at rate she need not imagine me being any where near the line at present.

Much love from Philip.

MC 643/8/59

198. Tuesday 18.9.17

My very dear Mother and Father

At the present moment I am feeling healthily stiff and not a little sore! Quite a peace time feeling, the result of two football matches. On Sunday evening we had a Company trial game and yesterday we played another Coy – We are having an inter Company competition and C. are quite determined to win it. We started well by beating B Coy yesterday after a tremendous tussle, playing extra time on an appallingly rough sort of ploughed field. We now only have to beat A Coy & we'll be champion Coy – my footer muscles are a bit out of practice!

   We are working pretty hard all day, I always enjoy these periods of training, I can get to know the Coy. I always try & know every man in the Coy by name, a not too easy task when they change so very quickly. It is a great time for general smartening up and then off parade getting the men as much sport as possible. There has been no England post for 3 days for me so I suppose I shall get several together. Time fairly flies when we are all so busy. I am as fit and hard as I have ever been. I am getting very tactful & stern (when necessary) in dealing with any one or two impossible subs. However I have managed to get one of them away on a Course for 3 weeks

Much love Your Very

loving Philip.

MC 643/8/60

199.   Monday Sept 24

My very dear Mother & Father

We are still here, we do not get much time to ourselves, as we are at it pretty well all day. In fact very often as to-day, we start again after tea & work all the evening. The poor Coy Commander has no time, for as soon as he has finished parades one day, notes, orders, schemes & programmes of training come pouring in for the next.

I generally start feeling I am really finished & ready for tomorrow about 9.30pm or later! We are having really glorious weather. On days when we have no evening work time is full up with Platoon and Coy football Competitions, and Coy. and Battn Tug of war & Sports etc, also Shooting Competitions, I am scribbling this in between an afternoon and evening parade. I am so glad Mother is getting up & better again now.

The CO. still says he cannot let me go on leave yet as I am a Coy Commander & so others have gone in front of me. My turn will come some day I suppose but I shall have been out about 6½ months when you get this – so I think it's about time I go. I got a letter from Father today which had been to the 7th Battn! They misread his "9". I hope the lumbago is better. Then I had one from Mother yesterday. The last cake I got was 2 weeks ago as we were marching here so I cannot understand if another is lost as you keep asking or if <u>somehow</u> I never mentioned the last. It was a long one and excellent – I am keeping awfully fit – very much love

Your very loving

Philip.

MC 643/8/61

200.   Friday Sept 28

My very dear Mother & Father

I think we are having as hot weather now as we have had all the summer we all enjoy it. We certainly are working as hard as we ever have. This morning as for instance we were up at 5 and on the Range by 6.0 am. Not much time wasted as it is only just light by then.

Ruth's & Father's letters written on the 24th both arrived last night. We had a great day on Wednesday, as we had Divisional sports (enclosed is a souvenir of them so stick onto it). It was a tremendous show, in size & in general effect compare it to the Norwich horse show or something we once went to. Horse jumping etc etc as well as judging of cookers, limbers etc and lots of sports sideshows etc. A most elaborate concern. I don't know in the least when I shall come on leave, but it would not be a bad idea if you sent me a list of trains from Liverpl St – home. It would save me perhaps <u>rushing</u> to catch a train that was not there, or vice versa. Don't think I'm coming at once because I ask for this, it is just a precaution as I've no idea when I shall come! All the Coy: Commanders dined at Bn HQ last night & had a very cheery evening, finishing up with a "sing-song" – Tell Father not to hurry out again, I'm sure the rest will do him good & surely <you> he could take 2 months in between!

Much love Your very loving

Philip.

MC 643/8/62

201.   Sunday Sept 30 1917

My very dear Mother

I got your letter & p.c. written on 25th last night. Doesn't time slip by, 3 years & more now since I <had> just joined at Felixstowe and 2 years since I was wounded. It seems ages ago & yet I can remember it as clearly as if it had been yesterday! Your quoting of the Times about officers after the war was rather interesting but I consider that if they are going to expect men to go back for a 3rd year it just shows they are still living in ante war days.[323] Even if the war were to end tomorrow it would probably be another year before one could go back, & who is going back to start reading under dons after 4 *or more* years! I do not <know> think many. I know that "after the war" (!) I must find something bigger than something bounded by 4 walls; I think <anybody> any young fellow who has commanded men out here, specially perhaps a Coy Commander who takes say 120 men into action, trains & disciplines & is totally responsible for them all in every way could never settle down to office or hum drum life! However that is only <u>my</u> view. But I think Father must have something the same sort of feeling? But I feel everything is much too indefinite to trouble about after the war yet. We are having simply glorious weather, and still working hard. We haven't played

---

323. An article in *The Times* of 17 Sept. 1917 urged that after the war officers be given preference in vacancies in the Civil Services, both in England and the Empire. A follow-up letter, published 20 Sept. 1917, cited the case of a man who had left his University course to enlist, urging 'special provision' for such young men, who would otherwise be disadvantaged by having no degree.

off the Coy footer final yet but one of my platoons has a very good chance of winning the Platoon Competition & is in the semi-final. We are going to have a great try at bringing off the double coup! I am so pleased you are so much better; you must go very easily, it is splendid the Dr has finished his visits. I am as usual as fit as could be & simply full of energy! We are having a splendid long time here aren't we!

Much love your very loving

Philip.

MC 643/8/63

202.   Wednesday Oct 3

My very dear Mother & Father

I got 2 letters yesterday & another to-day so have been kept well up in news, and all possible movements. Mine are still very obscure & it is quite impossible to say in the least degree when I shall get away. I am very short of officers in the Coy, as Newth a very nice fellow whom I was given as 2nd in command & who has been out here some months longer than I have is away at present. My Coy Sergt Major is away too, on special leave; so I am considered the only responsible one left as it were I suppose. Yesterday was a great day for C.Coy as we met & defeated A. Coy in the Coy Footer Final by 2–0, it was a tremendous game & most exciting to watch. Tonight we have had another triumph as one of our platoons has fought its way into the final of the platoon competition so we are pleased with ourselves.

I am very interested in all Father's plannings, he is choosing the right place. Why doesn't he get somewhere near where I was 2 years ago? I hope <u>very</u> much I do not miss him at home, it would be <u>rotten</u>. We are still working hard & all fit as anything.
Much love

Your ever loving

Philip.

MC 643/8/64

203.   6-10-17

My very dear Mother & Father

Immediately after writing my last letter, on Wednesday, we got sudden orders to move, our rest was done. We had a very hurried move next morning. & next day worse still we got orders at 2.0 am to move at 6.0 am! Some hustle. We eventually arrived up in the trenches once again yesterday morning, where we are now.

It is a <u>very</u> quiet part of the line. Now then – I hope to start home on my leave any time about the 12th to 15th! Isn't that splendid – I shall come home absolutely straight out of the trenches I expect. So it won't really be long after you get this when I should be jumping in! I saw my first sumptuous billet & had many old memories brought back to me – It has been raining since we came in here and everything is covered with chalky clay. Well – will see you soon!

Your very loving Philip.

MC 643/8/65

204.   Oct 8 [*FSP*][324]

I have just remembered this is your birthday <u>so</u> many happy returns. I hope you got my letter written 2 days ago telling you we went into the trenches again on the 5th. I have not had a long stay there however as I came out again yesterday, rather <u>seedy</u> with a chill on the tummy. The C.O sent me back to the village where our transport is & I have a nice bed & am staying there all today keeping warm etc, so as to be fit to come on leave on the 13th. I shall not go back to the trenches before I come home. Soon see you now

Much love Philip.

MC 643/8/66

205.   10.10.17 [*FSP*][325]

A letter from you & Father today. I cannot understand why you've had no letters from me for a <u>fortnight</u>! I have written regularly every 2 or 3 days – I am supposed to be coming on leave on 13th but I hear sailings are suspended temporarily so it may be 14th or 15th before I get away now. My chill is better but I am a bit of an old crock at present. However I am having a rest keeping warm etc & have spent most of my days in bed. This is just to warn you I may be a day or 2 late. Much love P.

MC 643/8/67

---

324. Addressed to Rev. W. Hewetson.
325. Addressed to Mrs Hewetson.

206.   My very dear Family

This is to be a race – I am going to give this letter 3 days start home & see who wins. I am due in England on Monday October 15!!
Father <u>must</u> wait for me – I leave here Sunday!
Oh Cheerioh!!

<u>At last</u> Much love

Philip.
11.10.17[326]

MC 643/8/68

Philip returned to England on leave on 15 October 1917. The poor health hinted at in his letters worsened: he was unable to return to France after his leave. He went before a Medical Board at Thetford, Norfolk, on 17 November: he was found to be 'Not fit for General Service', so returned to the reserve battalion at Felixstowe.

207.   Command Depot [*Thetford Army Camp*]

14.11.17.

My very dear Mother

Just a line to tell you any news there is. As I got out of the train at Norwich I was hailed by an officer in the Norfolks, who turned out to be R. F. Popham, you may remember the name as captain of Repton and Oxford Football XI's and one year senior to me only. He had seen me get in at Salhouse. He had another OR with him. They are both stationed at Smallburgh, so we had a short talk on old <u>times</u>. I travelled to Thetford with a very nice young officer, just going out for the 1st time, he of course went on to London. I was to have been examined by a M.O to-day preparatory to my Board, but he never turned up so I shall see him to-morrow; I then expect my Board on Friday or Saturday, which would be splendid. I have managed better at meals so far, you will be glad to hear & was quite talkative! This morning four of us went for a walk together I have been a bit "livery" to-day. I shall try & get a month's home service from the Board I think. I have been reading some more of Sylvia [327]& have nearly finished it now – we had a concert after dinner last night which passed the time quite nicely. I shall be

---

326. '<Nov> Oct 11 & last of the series!': endorsement by Philip's mother.

327. Of several novels entitled *Sylvia*, the most likely is that by Upton Sinclair, published in 1913: its sequel – *Sylvia's Marriage* – came out in the following year.

quite content if I only have 3 or 4 more days here though it is a bit better as you get more at home – Much love

Your v loving

Philip.

MC 643/9/1

208. Felixstowe Tuesday

My very dear Mother

I had my Board yesterday & was passed fit for the wars once more! I really quite expected it. However at present I have been put on the "permanent establishment" here. This is not what I want at all as it means I can be kept here as a Coy: Commander as long as they like. This is really why I have not written till tonight for I was wanting to see the C.O. I have just seen him and asked him about it and he was very nice & says they will not keep me. But they are not going to show me as "available" till Friday Dec 28. (officers are shown each Friday) they really ought to show me this Friday only I am on the "permanent establishment" – you do not receive orders till at least 10 days after you are shown available so I shall not get orders till at least January 7. Now I propose to stay here for Xmas & come home on leave on Dec 26 or 27, for 4 or 5 days! How does that seem to you?? I could perhaps come from Dec 23 or 24 to 28 or 29 but thought perhaps the other would be better. But let me know at once what you think. Is Gobagger with you for both periods, if not I will come the period she is there. Also get Amie[328] for a "chunk"! the 2nd period might be better for her? but I'll wait till I hear from you to decide. I am just as well as can be & playing football tomorrow.

Lots of love Your v. loving

Philip.

MC 643/9/2

Philip's leave was spent at Salhouse, then he returned to Felixstowe

---

328. Amie Evershed, see Introduction.

209.   2.1.18

My very dear Mother

I have been wondering very much how you got on at the dentist to-day – I hope it wasn't too bad – now you mustn't worry about me, my old "tummy" isn't going to trouble me at all. I had lots of that peppermint tincture & a dose from the doctor this morning. I had a good dinner on the train & enjoyed it thoroughly & felt much better after it. I keep on thinking all about my leave, it was just a <u>splendid</u> one. No one has been sent out while I have been away so I am no nearer yet! I am going to supper with Mrs Liddell tonight

Much love Yr v. loving

Philip.

MC 643/9/3

210.   6 Jany 1918

My very dear Mother

I know no more about my stayings or goings now than I did before, of course I am shown available so might get orders anytime. I think I am the only Captain now, one of the others has gone off to a senior officers course & Laurie the other has gone off to a Territorial Batt: at Colchester to go out with them possibly, however he may not go after all & may come back here – meanwhile I am in no particular hurry! I am just as well as anything, nothing to worry about at all, & I am quite enjoying Felixstowe. I much enjoyed your nice long letter this morning. We had a big church Parade all Coy. commanders & 4 subalterns per Coy. afterwards 2 men were decorated by the Brigadier with the Military Medal, one was in my Coy. in the 9th. The chaplain preached us a good sermon, read the King's proclamation[329] & had the special prayers, so we were all there in force, Brigade staff, C.O and all. Yesterday was quite a successful day, the usual dance at the Felix. We went on after dinner till about 11 pm. & I quite enjoyed myself. This afternoon I am having tea with the Loudons. Grove whom you may remember is back here again, he was wounded in the neck

---

329. The King's Proclamation, issued on 7 November 1917, proclaimed Sunday 6 January 1918 as a day of National Prayer. On that day, the Proclamation was read in churches, special prayers said, and a collection made for the Joint War Committee of the British Red Cross Society and the Order of St John.

at Passchaendale[330] with the 1st Battn; he seems & looks very fit. Hugo is on leave at present, his Xmas leave. I was interested to hear about Eric Ward[331] but I don't think he sounds very interesting! I had my pass book from Cox's & find I am rolling in wealth, £225! in hand. I will send your cheque at once but have not got my book in my pocket now. I have started a diary & have done it 4 days so far. I was interested about Father, I think it is a splendid thing that the General has noticed the work & is helping in it, yes send him my great coat. I shall not take it. I have had my first lesson in Bridge I think it is a very good game & very useful to be able to play. I am sure the war will take a turn for the better now & we will soon see a change.

Very much love Your v loving

Philip.

MC 643/9/4

211.   Thursday [*10 Jan. 1918*]

My very dear Ruth

How did the jaunt to town go off & are you an "administrator" in the W.A.A.C.s yet or what? I saw Miss de Putron's[332] name in The Gazette to-day as something in them. We are expecting our consignment here any day now, they are going to be mess waiters & cooks etc. Or perhaps you are contemplating the R.F.C. or V.A.D. which is it? The last two sound much better. There are strong rumours that no more officers are going out for some weeks but nobody can tell; I look like being here a little time longer at any rate but then nothing is certain in this war. Who do you think I had a letter this morning – Sylvia Turner! Really! I can't think why, all I have done to deserve it is to write to thank Mrs T. for the cake. However as I never write to "Margy" I suppose I am being tried with the other; if I do not bite there

---

330. The 3rd Battle of Ypres, or Passchaendale, began 31 July 1917, lasting into November. 1 Bn LNLR was in the front line throughout apart from a break between 13/14 and 19 July.

331. Eric Harding Ward, born c.1889, son of Edward Foote Ward of Salhouse Hall and his wife Bertha. Eric was a lieutenant in the Royal Navy from 1910; 1911 census gives address as HMS Warrior, Plymouth; promoted to lieutenant commander 1918.

332. The former games mistress of Ruth's at Norwich High School: she had left to do war work. Philip's reference is confused: the only Putron reference in the *London Gazette* of 8 January 1918 is to a T/Lt Noel de Putron Roberts; he is also mentioned in the *London Gazette* of 25 Sept. 1917, which records the appointment of Miss de Putron as Deputy Administrator in the Women's Army Auxiliary Corps on 9 July 1917.

what will they do next do you think? perhaps another cake! aren't I horrid – This old place goes on in the same old way, nothing particular or interesting happening. Luckily we didn't have to do a sitting in trenches stunt this week. Yesterday I got a hurried message from Mrs Loudon asking me to go round <u>at once</u>, this was about 5.30. So round I trotted wondering what on earth was the matter – When I got there I found 8 or 10 people there & furniture all pushed away & we passed a very pleasant 1½ hours dancing. It was v. nice as I was feeling a bit bored & thinking the best thing to do was to got to sleep. In the evening Hugo & Alick Plant & I had a little change from the White Horse & dined at the Felix. Bill Plant is coming back on Tuesday. Hugo sends his love to the family, I say he is very lazy & he says his laziness is only equalled by mine – which may (or may not) be true

Much love

Philip.

MC 643/11/4

212.   13.1.18

My very dear Mother

Here is another Sunday letter. I am writing on a small pad as we seem to have run out of the large ones. It is most amusing in the Mess now, we each have a little sort of salt basin with our sugar ration in it.[333] They are all numbered & we use our own ration only. When we have coffee in the ante room after lunch there are all our little sugar bowls on the side. I can manage on mine easily as I do not have sugar in my tea! It is a simply lovely day to-day, not a cloud in the sky, & sun shining I just feel full of "joie de vivre" – of course I have no idea at present as to any further news about my orders. I am hoping all the more now that I get back to the 9th to start with, as Bill Loudon is now acting Adjutant – & that would be splendid for me. I rather like the idea of Father speaking for me to those D.A.C.G.s. It might certainly do some good, though I prefer a sort of temporary to permanent proper red cap staff.

I do not want to leave the regiment altogether. However something I hope will crop up perhaps, though I am quite content to go back to the 9th, in fact I prefer it. I am enjoying my Felixstowe at present and I enjoyed yesterday's dance more than any so far. I danced nearly every one & we went on till

---

333. Sugar was the first product to be rationed in the First World War: rationing began in January 1918 and its effects are mentioned by both Philip and Ruth.

11 pm. I had dinner with the Loudons. I do not think it is really worth while asking for an invitation to the Norwich dance. You see I do not think there is any chance of me getting a leave while I am in this state of "awaiting" – I am interested to hear about Ruth's WRNS & what is said about it. Col: Phillips is coming down here on leave tomorrow & may want me to go back to the 1st but I shall tell him I hope to go to the 9th.

Lots of love your v loving

Philip.

MC 643/9/5

213. Thursday

My very dear Ruth

From your letter this morning it seems as if you think from my wire that I have already got some sort of orders. I meant by "awaiting orders" the period between coming back here off my GS leave and the day I get orders. It is impossible to get away during that time unless for some very special reason; and I hardly can imagine a dance however nice being considered an urgent reason for special leave, can you? Poor new frock – it's a shame you can't use it. I'm awfully interested in your plans, I think the R.F.C. would be very nice or else perhaps an officer ship in the W.A.A.Cs. I wonder when you will go, I see W.R.Ns are not wanted at present, or rather they seem to have more than they want. I wonder if Amie[334] will go with you? I know no more about my movements yet & of course shall not until the very moment they suddenly arrive. We have got thick snow here, as I expect you have too and now it is starting to thaw so there will be a perfectly appalling mess. I am having a fairly busy week as usual. On Tuesday Paton[335] who is in the Norfolks asked me to go round to tea with them so I did – In the evening a crowd of us went to Mrs Liddell's to a sort of party – It was quite fun but somehow seemed a bit slow, that feeling when things do not quite "go" – yesterday I went to the Playhouse in the afternoon where Suffolk officers & local ladies had got up a play "Our Boys" in aid of local hospitals. It was awfully good. Allen Bratton (now M.C.) is coming here this week end on leave –

much love your v. loving

Philip.

MC 643/11/22

---

334. Amie Evershed.
335. J. A. W. Peyton, 2nd Lt 3rd (Reserve) Bn, Norfolk Regiment.

214.   Thursday

My very dear Ruth

What a wonderful long letter! I knew I should put my foot in it somehow over that dance – I always am doing rude things nowadays. But I sent a most beautiful wire to "the Royal" to say we couldn't stay or go there. I never thought of poor Miss Muriel;[336] however "all these little things are sent to try us" as the poet hath it, & the world is still going round I believe so I expect it's alright! Do you know I've got an idea there were all sorts of interesting things in yr: letter but I haven't got it with me now, I've gone & left it somewhere! Look here, I simply <u>can't</u> buy things here, so I'm sending you £1. for Mother's birthday. I'm sure you can something nice, nothing "hen-ny", why not some nice useful thing for when she stops in bed, book rest or special tray? I got a long interesting letter from Father to-day, the first for just over 3 weeks. He seems not have got my letters, or something but I always write twice a week, the last ¾ page is all encouraging me to write to him & I do! I wonder what can have happened. Nobody else gone out, I am not a bit keen on a staff job, I'm much too fit for that sort of thing, and intend to go back to the 9th if I can manage it. The girls who went driving cars from here have all disappeared but I'll try & see what I can find out for you. Don't forget I am a pretty rich brother & if you want some money to learn driving cars etc I can always lend you lots! This weather is topping, absolute spring time. I have got up a hockey XI and am going to play a match against the Suffolks on Saturday which will be good fun.

Much love from Philip.

MC 643/11/6

215.   Thursday

My very dear Ruth

Awfully late with my old epistle this week aren't I! I think your choice of birthday presents for Mother sounds simply splendid, I think I shall always leave the choosing to you in future – oh yes I quite forgot the bill, I did mean to send you the money & I will! We have had two nights of air warnings this week, we heard the old Bosch machine on Monday night & a few guns fired but it didn't last long, on Tuesday they didn't come this way at all; last night they gave us a rest altogether, I was specially glad

---

336. Ruth's school friend Xenia Muriel: see Introduction.

as I should have been on duty. Do you remember those weekly Thursday stunts we always used to have sitting in trenches. We have knocked them off this winter but they started again yesterday, and we sat in our trenches from 1.30 to nearly 5. Very boring as I missed a tea at the Loudons & some drawing room dances. I am known as "Peter" there now which is a good deal better than stiff 'Capt. H.'.[337] Tell Mother I am well set up, I have a splendid canvas kit bag & padlock for it for inside my valise, also a Tommy's cooker[338] & my Camels are on order. However I hope perhaps they may not want me again this week as I am quite content at present. My British warm too is lined now, boots all soled & heeled & socks in good repair! So there – Did you ever order those 6 more photos from Coe?[339] ah – got you there! Please do

Lots of love

Philip.

MC 643/11/10

216.   Sunday 20.1.18

My very dear Mother

Another Sunday letter, and another Sunday at home, nobody has been called for yet since I have come back and there is a big crowd of us waiting – I am still the only captain shown available. I am going to have my light fleece lining put into my British warm; that is to say provided I do not get orders this weekend! that will make a good warm garment for when we are out of the line. I have not got Tommy's cooker or harness yet but am getting them this week ready. I am very interested in all Father's news you gave me, specially as I have not heard from him for about 2 weeks![340] He seems to be being looked after by people around but I do not think the C.A itself seems very well organised, or they would look after their workers better. It is just splendid the work he is doing. I am sure though he must come back at the end of February specially if Ruth is going off somewhere. Allen Bratton

---

337. This may be just an amusing pleasantry, the Loudons mishearing Philip's name. However a letter of sympathy to Philip's parents from 2nd Lt Bulling refers to Philip as 'Peter' throughout, so it may have been his nickname among his fellow junior officers.

338. A pocket trench stove, consisting of a tin with three fins for legs: it burnt solid methylated spirit.

339. Prominent Norwich photographic firm, founded by Albert Edward Coe in 1883.

340. William Hewetson was in France until early February 1918, when he returned to Salhouse.

came down here for last night, he is on leave from the 1ˢᵗ but he made a very short stay & stopped with the Groves so we did not see much of him. I am going out to tea with the Liddells to-day & then Hugo & I will probably walk down to St Johns evening service. I have quite definitely decided never to apply for <u>any</u> sort of job myself so long as I am G.S. It seems to me that a job behind the line in France is no better than occupying a "funk hole" in England. If I did chance to be offered something when I had been out in the line some time that might be different. There is a very strong feeling now about this "getting jobs" – nobody who is G.S. should try for them I think & so do most people. However I am not going to move one way or the other, I'll simply go where I am sent – It has been a horrid week for weather & now it is raining – I wonder how the dance went off. We had the usual one here yesterday afternoon & evening, I keep on thinking the longer I stay here you never get your teeth done!

Much love Your v loving

Philip.

MC 643/9/6

217.   Thursday

My very dear Ruth

I hardly think I'll be able to fill this but still as there is no small pad I shall start on it at any rate. I am hoping to arrange some leave for when Father comes, I shall try for 3 or 4 days & Hugo & I will trot up to town for one night & try & meet Powys Jones who is at an Off. Cadet Bn³⁴¹ at Oxford & then if Father were coming thro' town we could meet him & come home with him next day, however it must all be very hazy depending on what leave we can get & whether I am here.

I rather think no officers are going out for a few weeks yet though we are told nothing officially, however it seems as if they do not want us at present. How's the inoculation? have you had it yet & have you any further news of yourself. I am having 2 or 3 busy days at present as the Travelling Medic: Board is here & all my Coy (400) have to go before it to be examined & I have to be there. If Father goes & comes the 1ˢᵗ weekend in March <u>&</u> Hugo & I <u>&</u> Amie where are we all going?? It would give Johnny & the village something to think about wouldn't it! no chunks for 3 months & then we come on the same day! Oh here's that money at last! I have got 2

341. See note 229.

hockey matches for this weekend, on Saturday v the Essex & Sunday v the Norfolks. I am having a regimental ground made, goalposts etc & goal nets all complete.

Much love

from Philip.

MC 643/9/7

218.   Janry. 27. 1918

My very dear Mother

This is to wish you many happy returns of the day, and an awfully happy year to follow. Next year we'll hope there'll be no nasty old war going on! and also I hope you will have left all those nasty old illnesses a very long way behind. Ruth has been appointed to select a present from us both so I hope she has made a good choice. I am feeling most tremendously "joie de vive-y" – it is a simply glorious day; this morning it was very misty & foggy but now the sun has come out & it is absolute spring time. I enjoy Felixstowe in this sort of weather & am not pining for my orders to-day. Here's another week gone & I am still here, there is a tremendous crowd of officers in the Garrison in the same boat now, all "awaiting" – Hugo & I are going to repeat our visit to St Johns evening service again tonight – It is a nice service & I think it is easier to go in the evening perhaps. at any rate there is never any thing much to do then while in the morning there is. I had another very jolly evening last night at the Felix, I got to the dance rather late 6 pm, but had dinner with the Loudons & danced afterwards too. If only we had known I was going to be here so long you might have put in a weekend here but now any week should be the last & so it is not worth it, as if we once made arrangements I should probably be gone next week! and at any rate you will be coming to Folkestone. We have just all been taking photo groups of each other in the garden, they'll be very interesting if they come out alright. My hockey match unfortunately fell through yesterday owing to them arranging another match but I hope to get one fixed up next Saturday. I wonder if Ruth knows any more yet, & what she is going in to. Hugo sends his love & says I am to tell you he is doing his best to look after me! no letter came this morning. I expect it will arrive tomorrow very much love

Your v loving

Philip.

MC 643/9/8

219.   Sunday 3-2-18

My very dear Mother & Father

Once again I can write to you both in the same letter, how splendid, it is quite like old times again. I am sure Father must want a real good rest, and to take things very easy, and to make a new habit and stay in bed for a few days. Isn't my writing horrible to-day, but I haven't got my fountain pen with me & I do not like this one at all. Since I last wrote I haven't been enjoying myself much, I've managed to pick up a nasty cold which has made me feel a bit off colour, however with the aid of cinnamon and some ammoniated quinine I think I have got it more or less in hand now. The weather too has been about the worst possible, the most awful blustering cold gale, howling & whistling & going right through you, most awfully cold. However thank goodness to-day it rained & blew too and as a result this evening the wind has dropped & it is warmer again. On Thursday we had a most boring afternoon as we sat in our trenches from 2–10pm. Only practice of course, my word we were glad when the order came to close. I have heard no more yet about my projected trip to St Leonards as they are waiting for further information, if I go midweek I shall ask permission to come on home for the weekend afterwards. Hugo is going up to town on Tuesday to the War Office to see about this job of his at an Officers Cadet Battn:. This morning we had a massed Church parade with all Coy. Commanders attending & afterwards some men were decorated with the Military Medal. It <u>was</u> cold standing on that parade ground but the General did not keep us waiting at all, he was before his time if anything. I've had a lazy afternoon, Sandie & I are going onto supper with the Groves. I did not dance yesterday owing to my cold. It looks as if the much talked about German push[342] is getting a bit nearer now with these big raids taking place. Our going out however seems to be no nearer! as far as we know at any rate.

Much love

Your v. loving Philip.

MC 643/9/9

---

342. With the collapse of Russia, the Germans were able to concentrate their forces on the Western Front: the anticipated offensive actually began in March 1918.

220. Sunday 10-2-18

My very dear Mother

Your letter this morning with Ruth's enclosed was full of news. I am very sorry Father is a bit run down, but I expect he has been at it awfully hard & doing splendid work & has not realised what a strain it has been. Of course winter is so different from summer out there. He mustn't decide he is going out again yet a while. Ruth's news interested me too very much. You know I am really very pleased. I never was very keen on the WAACs, most <u>certainly</u> not unless as an officer & even then I always thought other things should be tried first. I think this G.S.V.A.D idea sounds much better. It is a shame the H.Q Administrator ever advised a position as a N.C.O.

So far I have had quite a busy Sunday as I took Church Parade this morning, the parade is at 9.30 and then we march to Church behind the Band, I at the head with my clinking spurs etc! The padre gave us quite a nice service. This afternoon I have got up a good hockey XI to play the Suffolks & we are all greatly looking forward to the game. Yesterday I had tea with the Banks at the Felix. Nellie B is a very pretty girl now, with lots to say, she dances well too. They had a girl from Ipswich with them whom I had met there at tennis; I also once went over to tennis at their house at Ipswich. They are a very nice family & I am going over there on Tuesday for tea & impromptu dance. I also met a fellow named Calthorpe who was at Repton with me, in the cricket XI & afterwards a Cambridge cricket "blue" – He is in the R.N.A.S. here & I am going down to their mess for dinner on Wednesday; so I am doing quite well in meeting people. I expect Hugo & I will go down to St Johns again tonight, we always enjoy it and Sandie came with us too last week. There is no more news of us going to the war. Sandie & I have decided that if we are here much longer we had better take a house, settle down & marry!

Much love Your v. loving

Philip.

MC 643/9/10

221. Wednesday 9 p.m

My very dear Ruth

This is only going to be a very short note because I'm 'orrid sleepy. Hugo & I went up to town on Monday & came back yesterday. We couldn't go yesterday & come back to-day so we did that instead & Alick Plant went a day earlier than he expected to. We had a topping time, left here 2.40 train, got to town 6pm and came back yesterday by the 5.23 we stayed in a much nicer hotel than the Arundel – the Russell. We had a great time including lunch at the Piccadilly Grill yesterday where I got the orchestra by special request to play a tune which we had specially liked at the Alhambra on Monday night. We <u>were</u> a jolly trio. Today I've been very busy, a busy morning, an early lunch, a route march 1.15 to 5.15, a conference of Coy. commanders etc 6.30–7.45. To-morrow will be a horrid day, all day in the trenches, I hope it is nice & warm! I hope to have another trip soon – to St Leonards!! A corporal who was in my Coy & transferred to R.F.C there has got into trouble & wants some officer here to go & speak for him & I hope v much they'll send me, I'll manage a night or two there & a night in town on the way back I hope – a good piece of luck?! lots of love Philip

& so to BED! yawning!

MC 643/11/21

222.   Sunday 17-2-18

My very dear Mother

Just think it is February 17 – I had my Board on Dec 17, so it is exactly three months since I was passed fit again! So all my efforts to get back quickly have not come to much, and now I am feeling quite "Felixstowish" once more & quite enjoying the place & all the life here. I found out another branch of work Ruth could go in for if the V.A.D. fell through. I was talking to someone yesterday who is doing it herself. The organisation is the Women's Legion.[343] She says it is all "ladies". She is driving a car in London & that's what they seem to do – all you have to do is to say & be able to drive a Ford, which after all Ruth could easily do from Amis[344]. The superintendent is Miss Ellis, 14 Pall Mall East. What a splendid long talky letter you sent me to-day. I must certainly manage a few days when Father comes home <u>if</u> I am still here, that I should think would be quite a good enough reason for leave though it might be a very short one. Hugo suggested he should come too so I shall bring him along! if I come. I think it is just a splendid idea getting somebody to do the duty when Father comes back to that he can have a real rest. We are having simply glorious mild spring weather, lovely – This morning we had another of those massed Church parades & a presentation

---

343. See Introduction.
344. Alfred Amis of Wroxham, the local taxi-cab proprietor.

of medals to 2 men afterwards. I have had a good week this week & have
been out a good deal seeing people. It is all a good experience meeting them
all & I have some real friends down here now, both civilians & officers in
other regiments here. Bill Plant has been down here all this week but is off
again tomorrow. He has 6 months Home Service & is going to an Officers
Cadet Battn as an instructor. Hugo's last Board gave him permanent H.S
& I think he is applying for a job at an O.C.B. too, but I hope he won't go
till I do. Much love

Yr v. loving Philip.

MC 643/9/11

223. Thursday

My very dear Ruth

So you are going to make No.3: of the family who are going to la belle land
of France.[345] I don't think that is a bad record out of 4! do you! I quite
thought I was going to be the only one at one time. I can't quite make out
what you are going to do yet, specially as you are going out so quickly, you
won't be trained in anything particular will you, but I suppose you'll start
as a bottle washer or something. I think V.A D-ism is a jolly good thing
to have got in to. I went into Ipswich on Tuesday to the Maynes I went in
by a 4 train & got there at tea-time ish. Who <u>do</u> you think I met there??
When I had been there a few minutes eating a "standing-up-balance-the-
tea-cup" tea when people made a move into the dance room, & up from
sitting just in front of me with her back to me came Mrs "Jellyfish"![346]
"My dear Philip – where <u>have</u> you sprung from?!" She was surprised to see
me & I too. She sent all sorts of messages to you & Mother, & told me
she'd heard Geoffrey had gone quite off his head! Poor C. had been very ill
she said – she looked flourishing, rather fat. She asked keenly about Father
too. Much love fr Philip.

MC 643/11/5

---

345. Ruth was thinking that her membership of the V.A.D. would lead to her working
across the Channel: this did not in fact happen.

346. The nickname of an unidentifiable family friend, who apparently lives in Ipswich:
Ruth refers to her in letters 281 and 285. The people about whom she talks – 'Geoffrey' and
'Poor C' – are also unidentifiable.

224.   Sunday 23-2-18[347]

My very dear Mother

Another Sunday come round and from what I can hear I do not think there is any probability of any of us going out for some little time yet – I quite think I shall go out later in the year this time than I did last. Isn't it extraordinary how we are all hanging on here, everybody is the same, nobody being taken. Nobody ever thinks of getting their orders any day now, we seem stuck here, at first we thought every weekend would bring them now we never give the matter a thought at all. I quite agree with you that the 2nd week in March would be better to try for leave in as you say Father would be tired after the journey & as there doesn't seem any fear that I shan't be here we'll try for the 10th – I can let you know actual dates later. I am awfully interested about Ruth. I wonder where she'll get buzzed off to first & when! & what's the uniform like?? Is she likely to go abroad at once I wonder? You need not expect Hugo to seem a very bad cripple, he gets about all over the place quite alright, in fact was kicking a football about with us the other day. He expects to get a job at an Off: Cadet Battn very soon now, his brother has a job at one too. We are off to London for the day on Tuesday. Alick Plant is being invalided out of the service, at least not exactly invalided but is resigning his commission, it is <u>awfully</u> bad luck & we will tell you all about it when we come home. At any rate Hugo, Sandie & I have got 24 hours leave to go & see him off & we hope Jim Gemmel will come up to town & meet us, it will be a very jolly party, as long as the Huns do not hear of our trip. Hugo & I will be doing our usual trip to St Johns tonight. I have had a busy week in the Coy with all my men going before the Trav. Med. Board. & have spent the last 3 days watching men being examined, wounds, hearts, coughs heads etc etc!! all the results of visits to the war. We had a good game of hockey yesterday but were beaten 4–0, our game to-day is scratched.

Much love your v loving

Philip.

MC 643/9/12

225.   Sunday March 1918 [?*17 Mar.*].

My very dear Mother & Father

I have written letters to "the family" at different periods of its history to all

---

347. In fact Sunday 24 Feb.

sorts of places but this is quite new I think! You at home & now Ruth & I both away.[348] You will be feeling it very strange & lonely & will miss her. But she seems to have got to a nice place at any rate it sounds as if it should be, nice people I expect. I am perfectly sure she will get on most awfully well, she is just the sort that would. I really do not see how she could not, she makes such an awfully good "pal" as I discover <u>more</u> & <u>more</u> each time I come home. I got a letter from her written in the train. I was so sorry I could not get in to see her off but it was much too short notice, you see I only got the wire back on Friday evening and I had only got back on Tuesday night. I badly wanted to see her in her rigout, but it could not be "did". There was a great hum going on in the White Horse when I got back on Tuesday. You see four of us had been on leave for the weekend & we were all full of news & chatter when we got back. My old leg is a lovely colour now, rather like an autumn sunset, it has been a bit stiff all the week, chiefly owing to the scar rubbing on the breeches, but it is much better & was well enough to allow me to restart my dancing exercises & amusements last night. We had the most exciting cup tie semi final v the E. Surreys whom you remember beat us in the final before Xmas yesterday. They scored in the first minute, & held the lead till 20 minutes from time when we scored twice in 10 minutes amid the most <u>extraordinary</u> excitement among a huge crowd. The football was absolutely first class & all the 2nd half we played one man short. I nearly lost my voice shouting! Hugo & I will be going to St. Johns tonight and afterwards to supper at Mrs Liddell's. Alick Plant came back here again on Thursday, much to our joy, he is still waiting developments & as he could not go on being on leave indefinitely he was recalled.

Very much love

Your v loving Philip.

MC 643/9/13

226. Thursday

My very dear Father

I have been quite a traveller the last two days, I have had a trip to Portsmouth and back. I took a draft of 90 odd men there on Tuesday. I got very short notice to go, as I only [*heard*] at 10. am & the train went at 11, I had to collect a few things, get on parade & to the station & entrain the men. We got to town at 1.55 & I marched the men to the Bank & from there went

---

348. Ruth went to Fargo Hospital, Wiltshire, on 16 March 1918.

by underground to Waterloo. We left there 3.45 & got to Portsmouth 6.15. I stayed at Southsea the night, a very nice quite little hotel, the Grosvenor. I got up to town at 12 yesterday, had time to go to the Hippodrome in the afternoon & back here by 5.23. Quite an enjoyable little trip especially as all the travelling was of course on a free warrant, & I can claim for allowances for putting up at night. A tremendous number of office got orders last night, but no N.Lancs so far. However they've started at last! I shall enjoy looking at that book you sent, it got here this morning. I am going to dinner with the Masons tonight. Aren't we living in momentous times, things are more & more strenuous both at home & abroad. Will "Fwank" be under 50!! and I suppose the Dr really will go now, as I see they take doctors up to 56![349]

Much love yr v loving

Philip.

MC 643/11/12

227.   Wednesday

My very dear Father

In spite of the great offensive[350] we are still here & none of us have yet received any orders so it looks as if we must have big reserves the other side still which seems very hopeful. For with all the casualties we must have had it is so splendid that we have not yet had to call on reserves from here! Meanwhile of course we all feel we may get orders any day. I have been studying that paper about the Egyptian & Sudanese Civil Services, and Hugo & I have both come to the same conclusion. We both think the Sudan Civil is no good, for the climate is <u>bad</u> for Europeans & though the condition of being unmarried is waived now still they were so strong against it before the war that it is practically a certainty that one could not ever marry & I certainly do <u>not</u> intend to tie myself up with any conditions like that! Now the conditions for the Egyptian Civil seem in every way better, tho' the pay is less & Hugo has written off to some people he knows who used to live in Egypt to find out about expenses etc. If the answer is favourable I am thinking I ought at any rate to get further papers about it & perhaps enter for it. Furlough is good, 2 months in each year on full pay! & a 3rd month if you want it on ½ pay. Everything like that seems such a long way off now but still it is I feel a good thing to look ahead & I shall feel much more settled if I am definitely

---

349. The local doctor was Wilfrid Aldred of Wroxham.
350. The long-awaited German attacks on the Western Front began on 21 March 1918

entered for something, I could always withdraw if I did change my mind & Egypt is not nearly so far away as some places. I shall take your advice about taking some more War Loan, & wish I had done it before! I do not know the exact arrangements about Good Friday but I think it is treated just the same as a Sunday. Salhouse will be pleased to have you back again at Duty but don't go & do too much at first please!

Much love your v. loving

Philip.

MC 643/9/17

228.   Sunday 24-3-18

My very dear Mother & Father

I have am afraid been very lazy & never written to you midweek. As a matter of fact I have had a v. fairly busy week & what with not much news I let it slide. On Wednesday I was in charge of the battalion route march which lasted from 2 to 6pm and on Thursday we sat in the trenches for the same time. After each of these I went to my Coy. office for an hour and so my evenings have been fairly full. Then on Friday I was paying out my Coy. & doing various Coy: business from 5 to 7.30 pm. I got most awfully excited over the budget from the Oxford Apptmts Commtee. Hugo & I have been talking it over & have a great deal more to think over about. I really think it seems an excellent thing. Before the war you practically had to be a "Blue" to get in, I know of several who were in or going into it from Oxford. It is really just most awfully splendid of you Father to say you could allow me that £50 if I married, however I have not lost my heart yet <u>and</u> at present the Western Front usurps everything & all our thoughts. It is & will be a time of great trial and Faith but everybody is absolutely confident & waiting. Bill Loudon is home on leave & tells me my old Battn is at Doignies on the Bapaume-Cambrai Road & right in the thick of it. I wonder if they have captured St Aubin's C.A Hut yet! We had a great hockey match yesterday but were beaten as usual. The weather is simply "summer" & we now have coffee after lunch in the garden & yesterday had tea there too. I am sending Ruth's letters back now, you never sent one to-day but you mention it. I do hope you <u>both</u> are much better & getting weller & younger again every day! you do not say you are one or the other but don't forget to rest <u>lots</u>, please do. I am just as fit as anything; Hugo sends his love, we're just off to watch some footer Lots of love yr v loving Philip.

MC 643/9/14

229. 3rd L.N.Lanc: Regt Old Felixstowe

My very dear Father

I am writing to tell you that I am probably going out to the front very soon. Nothing definite has come through from the War Office but the adjutant who is now Capt. Henderson said to me to-day, "You know Hewetson, you will probably be going out to the front with a draft soon. The Colonel considers you are now fit." This means that my name with perhaps one or two others (I believe one other) has been sent to the War Office so I shall very likely go next week. I have just asked the Colonel about some leave and I am to go & see him tomorrow so I will wire to you. I hope to come home on Saturday for 48 hours perhaps. There is a draft ready to go & I daresay I shall go with it on Tuesday but nobody knows definitely yet. Mother's Sunday letter curiously never came till Tuesday morning. Thank you so much for the P.O. you sent me, I forgot to put it in my Sunday letter. We are having lovely weather and you may be quite satisfied and at rest about my health, I have hardly ever been fitter, we are having lovely weather & I have been enjoying myself thoroughly, & keeping very fit with lots of marching. Please get me some more underclothes & thick socks ready. Then I think I have everything but will go through my things to night. I feel very happy and "Trusting" about going out and it will be nice to spend Easter together if I get leave. If not Mother & Ruth must come here & you follow but I want to get leave if possible. Very much love

from Philip

We'll have a nice cheery time if I come home.

MC 643/11/1

230. Thursday

My very dear Father

"Ye old White Horse Inn" feels a bit desolate to-day. Our numbers have been reduced this week. Alick Plant went off for good on Tuesday. The Gazette simply announced "Lieut. C.A.P. resigns his commission d-28-3-18" – I don't know what will eventually happened to him – he says now that he is out of the Army he's going to fight his case, though of course one cannot tell if it will do him any good! Then this morning Hugo departed for a month's course at Berkhamstead before getting an instructor's job at an Officers' Cadet Battn. I shall miss them both here very much, & it will make the place a bit different. We have no definite news of either the 1st or the 9th Battn, it is however fairly <u>certain</u> that there can be <u>very</u> little left of the 9th at all; and to-day we hear rumours that the 1st have been in action too & had a bad time but that is only very much rumour yet.[351] We had a ½ holiday on Easter Monday & our Regimental XI played a team from the Garrison. We had 4 changes from our Final cup tie side but we were only beaten 2–1. In the evening we had a dance at the Felix & I had dinner there with the Peytons. When I was home on leave I left my cigarette holder in its case behind & I've always forgotten to ask you to look for it. Can you see is it is in my pockets anywhere, either in my brown suit or the old tweed one, probably in the waistcoat pockets. I do hope mother is better again & taking lots of care of herself! Not too much Girl Guides or gardening!! I daresay that with such lots to arrange & difficulties of getting L.T.[352] & summer coming at home & battle in France you may not get out again? Well if you did not you have certainly done a <u>tremendous</u> big "bit" already. Lots of love

Your v loving

Philip.

MC 643/9/15

Philip crossed the Channel on 19 April 1918, again travelling via Folkestone and Boulogne: he visited his aunts at Bayham House, Folkestone, and met his mother there. He rejoined his battalion on 23 April.

231.   Saturday 20.4.18 [353]

My very dear Mother

I'll send this to Folkestone as it may just catch you before you go. Well here I am in this well known land once more! and I know you'll be wondering lots of things – first of all I expect "how's m' tummy" – well not <u>too</u> bad & not too good! but better than yesterday morning, still some backache, but with the help of peppermints & bismuth I think I shall soon be alright – I <u>really</u> do. If I do not improve I will report sick. Now – I am pretty sure not

---

351. The 9th were one of the battalions bearing the brunt of the German offensive in the third week of March. Twenty-three men were killed and no less than 216 missing – either dead or prisoners of war. The 1st were stationed further north and were not in front of the German attack.

352. Locum Tenens, a person who temporarily fills the place of another. William's brother-in-law, Philip's 'Uncle L'Estrange', had acted in this role during William's previous stay in France, but was presumably not now available.

353. In envelope addressed to Mrs Hewetson at Bayham House, Folkestone.

to be here long, a day or so perhaps, I am going back to the 9th again with several others, so write there straight. I could not get you a telegram – I got a nice place on the boat & kept warm, it was quite calm, though we finished with a snowstorm! Sandie & I had time to get some tea before the train started. Then he & I & Leake made ourselves very comfortable in the luggage van, lying on top of all the valises. Oh! your chicken rissoles were welcome <u>&</u> the biscuits, & gave us a nice little mouthful to keep us warm before the end. We got here in quite good time & found we were expected, & were given lots of blankets & some sandwiches to go to bed with. I am in a tent with Prout & Leake, the other 2 captains, it was a bit cold <las> early this morning but we've got our valises tonight & will remedy that. To-day we've been busy getting <box> gas masks, we had a 3 mile walk to the place & started in a blizzard of snow but now it's beautifully warm & sunny. We finished the morning with a most splendid lecture to stir us up!! Now I am in the officers club, a splendid big place where we all flock. I've just had a splendid tea here. All the waiting is done by Waacs. Now, mother dear, don't worry, I don't intend to be "liverish" & <u>if</u> I am I am going to take care of myself!

Lots of love your v. loving Philip

It was just <u>splendid</u> having you at F. to see me off!

MC 643/10/1

232. B.E.F. Saturday 20.4.18 [*FSP*][354]

Just a line to show I am safely across here. I was at Bayham House till after lunch which was very nice. I am writing in the Officers Club which is a splendid place. Send your letters straight to the 9th Bn. as that's where I am going. We had a regular snow blizzard this morning, so cold. & now it's really sunny & warm. I'm in a tent! but have got a bed & lots of blankets. The journey here was quite good, not too long & greatly improved by some food provided by Mother –

Much love P.

MC 643/10/2

---

354. Addressed to Miss R Hewetson, Fargo Military Hospital.

233. [*FSP*] [*21 Apr.*][355]

Sunday

Just a short line. I shall find these p.cs very useful I think. I've been much better to-day, still a bit back achey but picking up again decidedly. I go up tomorrow morning to the old Battn: with <*word illegible*> some others. I had a letter from Hugo here yesterday. I hope my revolver is on the way by now. I will let you have lots of news when I've joined the Battn. Please send me a pair of braces, mine are just finished. We've got food for the train.

Much love P.

MC 643/9/16

234. B.E.F. Wednesday 24th [Apr.]

My very dear Mother & Father

Here I am once again, but surprises never cease and I have only been with the Battn. for 12 hours. We arrived at the Battn at about 10 p.m last night. We had broken the journey and stayed a night in a camp, a most unsavoury place, not from any fault of the enemy but from the fact that the field had I think not so long ago been a horse lines.[356] However we were quite comfortable and finished our journey yesterday. I found the Battn: absolutely changed as regards officers. The colonel is now a Brigadier of our Brigade. We were very ready for the meal they gave us when we arrived and all bundled into a hut for a good nights rest. I found Bill Loudon still here, also Hartley who remembers Father's visit very well last November. Marsh is still Adjt: but beyond that there are very few I know. There is a very nice major from another regt. commanding them. This morning I was told I was to be in charge of my old Coy again but I only had it for about 1 hour! The major took me across at once to see the Brigadier, ie our late Colonel C-H.[357] He gave me an awfully warm greeting, (as has everybody) & said straight away he was going to put me in charge of the Brigade Instructional Platoon. He said he did not consider that I was really fit enough to stand regimental work in the present sort of warfare, he said he knew there was something just a bit not quite right with me constitutionally & however good the spirit was he thought it better to give me this job. Of course I said I was now quite

---

355. Postmarked 22 April.

356. A field where an artillery unit had kept its horses.

357. Craigie-Halkett. He had been promoted to command of the Brigade at the end of March 1918: Major W. H. M. Wienholt replaced him in charge of the 9th Battalion.

fit, but he said he thought this was just the job for me as I was very good, excellent he said, at smartening men up & organisation. The name tells you what it is & does, & I think I told you about them when I was at home. It is a nice job though I am not with the Battn. I have various officers & men from the Battns in the Bgde under me, & we are a separate little force. You will be very pleased to hear of this for me, we do not have trench life though of course they were taking their share of stopping the Boche. Still generally speaking I shall be more comfortable etc than otherwise & shall of course often be able to go & see the Battn, & get to know officers in all the Brigade. For instance now I am only about ½ a minutes walk from the Battn. You must address all letters to Capt. H L-N-L 74th B.I.P. B.E.F. Do not send them to the Battn. Now you will be wanting to know how I am, well really I am practically absolutely well again. The old backache has gone & I am just on the verge of feeling quite myself again. Everybody is full of their experiences & the extraordinary & exciting & thrilling happenings of the past weeks. I have heard some wonderful adventures & yarns already & descriptions of the fighting. I have been very warmly greeted by several old friends. It was very nice seeing Poppet[358] in town just before I came away. We had an awfully good time & saw the Lilac Domino at the Empire.[359] I have got my old servant, Pilkington, looking after me again much to his delight. I have taken over this B.I.P. from a lieutenant,[360] an old ex-sergt major with something well over 20 years service, you know the type. He is still with me as 2nd in command & will be of great service to me in the work; a proper "old soldier" you have to know how to treat them! Well I shall be very happy here, & I know you will be very thankful to hear of the job I have got. The guns boom – & sound much the same as when I last heard them!! Very much love

Your very loving

Philip.

MC 643/10/3

---

358. Unidentified friend or relative: In his schoolboy letters Philip refers to a 'Poppet' as a companion at Woburn Sands School, but, as here, it is unclear if it is a nickname or an actual name.

359. Operetta in three acts by Charles Cuvillier, a flop when first performed in Germany in 1912, but an enormous hit in London, where it opened on 21 February 1918.

360. Not otherwise identified.

235. Wednesday 24.4.18[361]

My very dear Ruth

You have not been very well treated with letters so far but the letter writing possibilities are only just starting, as I only got "up the line!" about 10.30 pm, last night. I left the base early on Monday morning & we broke our journey on <Tuesday> Monday night. We had quite an easy trip up & were not in the train nearly all the time as we finished about 3 on Monday & started again about the same time yesterday afternoon. There are not many of the battalion as I knew it here now but I have had a very hearty welcome from everybody including the Brigade staff. I was given my old Coy back again this morning & then went across to see the Brigadier who is our late Colonel. He immediately said he was going to take me away from the Battn: & put me in charge of the Brigade Instructional Platoon. So I did not stay with the Battn: long! My new address therefore is Capt. H. L.N.L. 74th Bgde. B.I.P. B.E.F. Of course I shall often see the Battn but I shall not go into the trenches with them & should have a much more comfortable & a bit less strenuous time than with the Battn. He has really given me this job in view of the way I went sick last time out as he says this sort of warfare is extremely strenuous. I live quite separately from the Battn. with a little *side* show of officers & men on my own. Everybody has the most thrilling & interesting stories & adventures to tell of the recent fighting they have been in. The guns are thundering away not so far off, & still have the same old sound! It really does not feel as if I have been away at all. I wonder when I shall start getting letters, not for a few days I expect. I am awfully pleased I have got back to the old Brigade & I have really not got half a bad job now. I expect Mother has been worrying over my old tummy but this job should reassure her & I am now quite fit again. I am looking forward to seeing those photos of yours. I can't remember the "Lilac Domino" tune. Sandie has gone back to the 1st Battn –

Cheerioh Much love –

Philip.

MC 643/10/4

---

361. In envelope addressed to Ruth at Fargo.

236.   Friday 26-4-18

My very dear Mother & Father

I have had a very international afternoon, I have been for a walk with a Belgian officer on one side and a Frenchman on the other. They are the two interpreters attached to the Brigade & we went out scouring the countryside for some food. On the way we came across a convent of monks & went in & were shown round. It was quite interesting. Going away we signed the visitors book which was started with the war. In it were the signatures of our King, the King & Queen of the Belgians, & the Prince of Wales. There are hardly any English signatures in it except mine & His Majesty's! We had a tremendous tramp yesterday, & went 15 or 17 kilometres, the annoying part was that it was in the shape of a circle & we need only have gone about a third of the distance really. We are living in a hut camp at present & are part of B. Team. The B.I.P generally is. I do not suppose I shall get any letters yet awhile, as I expect you have sent my letters to the Battn, which may delay them a day or so as we are at present, however I expect they'll come tumbling along presently. Mine too might be a bit delayed as we never know nowadays what we will be doing. I think we know a very great deal less about the war in general out here than anywhere else as we never see a paper. I am absolutely quite fit again now so you needn't trouble about me at all. Last night we arrived here with nothing but what we carried, no food or bedding! however we got some eggs boiled in a cottage & a loaf of bread. We slept in our clothes in our coats & I lay on the wire bed with straw on it & shared it with someone else & really kept jolly warm. Things were a bit rough & tumble this morning but are straightening out now & we have got our valises so are very comfortable. There is an awfully nice officer with the B.I.P, a L.N.L a Scotch boy of about 19,[362] awfully nice fellow, unfortunately he's going away for a week tomorrow for a rest & then I believe rejoins the Battn

Much love fr v loving Philip.

MC 643/10/5

237.   Sunday evening April 28

My very dear Mother & Father

I am really feeling much more established now for the first landmark in this trip to France has been reached. Namely your letters have started to arrive

---

362. Morison: see letter 242.

& I expect you have now got some from me so our lines of communication are established once more! I have had two so far, both forwarded from the base, one written on the 19th one on the 21st, so as they have been there & to the Battn: before coming to me I think they have done jolly well. We are still settled down in our little hut camp, & are really very comfortable. It is very very quiet & there is nothing to do but sleep, eat, read & write letters. I shall start parades tomorrow so far I have done very little as the first day no rations turned up till midday & we've been a bit disorganised. I say it is quiet – but just at present the guns are literally thundering away in the near distance. This quiet time is really just what I wanted on arrival to set me up. We mess very well & I am getting long nights in bed. My new boots I am delighted to say are a great success. I was afraid they were going to hurt my feet, but that's gradually wearing off & they are getting more comfortable each day. They are very strong too. Just think I have not seen a paper since Tuesday! Will you order the D.Mail for me to come direct each day from the publishers. If they send it direct from there it gets here the next day. I feel I must make some arrangement for a permanent paper as I am not with the Battn, & I miss the news & casualty lists. My companion officer enlisted in '89! he is a good hearted fellow & can spin all sorts of yarns, he got a commission about 18 months ago. He left the Army after the S.A. War[363] but re-enlisted at once in '14 & has been out ever since! We get on well together. I am still hoping for my revolver & have written to Felixstowe about it. I was interested in Julian's[364] letter & photo, he seems to have tumbled on his feet alright. Have Cox's sent the receipt for my £100 war loan to you yet I wonder. That French money I brought out was most welcome as you can't always get any at once. Bill Loudon is on B team & in this camp too wh: is nice.

Ever so much love

Yr v loving Philip.

MC 643/10/6

---

363. The South African War (fought against the Boers), 1899–1902.

364. Julian Tyndale-Biscoe was in Egypt: in the first four months of 1918, he was at the Imperial School of Instruction at Zeitoun, Cairo; served with General Staff Intelligence; and visited the battle line near Jericho where he captured one German and five Turkish prisoners. He describes these escapades, with typical modesty, in chapters 17 and 18 of *Gunner Subaltern*.

238.   Tuesday [*30 Apr.*]

Just a line to show you I'm still going strong. Today I got a letter written on 24-2-18 from you direct to Battn. We are leading a very gipsy picnic sort of life, just one place then another. Now we are in tents but very comfortable, though when we turned up last night there was absolutely nothing. I saw yesterday's paper to-day so am bit more up to date now. Have not brought another revolver, imposs: to do so, no need at present. Those peppermints will be most welcome! Living well – boiled fowl for lunch to-day v. tough! all food picnic fashion, lots of eggs. Slept in 6 camps in 10 days. Much love

P.

MC 643/10/7

239.   May 2 Thursday

My very dear Mother & Father

I have had a regular influx of 7 letters to-day, one from Hugo, one from Ruth & 2 from you Mother. Also the braces peppermints & pills <u>and</u> the revolver! So now I am quite happy & well set up. I will certainly use the pills & peppermints, but am feeling quite different now, though I still feel my back very slightly at times. Otherwise I am <u>quite</u> alright & in fine spirits. This is the seventh camping ground I have been in since I came back so you see I have not exactly stuck still so far. I am getting into the work as O.C. B.I.P, & shall like it I think. It will probably keep me out of the trenches as long I have the job. I am getting quite used to sleeping in a tent in my valise & manage to keep beautifully warm. We got splendidly comfortable in our last camping ground with tent boards & a table which we found in an empty neighbouring camp & then of course we had to move. We've got a table made of ammunition boxes now, and we sit round for meals on our valises, divan fashion. I like my "old Soldier" companion, he's a real old army veteran & we get on famously. He makes me roar the way he tells his yarns, he loves to "reminiss" over the good meals he has had!

Much love yr v loving

Philip.

MC 643/10/8

240.   Saturday May 5

My very dear Father

This is just a short line. I got a splendid long letter from you to-day, only written on Wednesday so that is very quick. It was quite like old times to see it written on C.A. paper. I am keeping very fit. I saw the Battn again to-day, and had some very interesting chats with them. Three of those who came up with me are already kitted. It is nice having Bulling in the Battn and Loudon, and I shall always enjoy going across & seeing them, and others there. I am afraid I cannot pay that debt of yours. I should like to have seen Clayton & Phillips if I could but I very much doubt if they are there now. I tell you what I shall like out here, and that is a book occasionally, I have nearly finished the one I am reading & I think I shall find a good deal more time for reading now. Nights are a good deal noisier than they used to be and some of the bombardments are simply terrific even though you are well behind, they shake the whole place, though I've been near nothing. The weather is getting warm & envelopes all stick together! I am getting quite used to living in a tent.
News is scarce.

Much love

Your v loving Philip.

MC 643/10/9

241.   Monday May 7

My very dear Ruth

Letters are splendid the way they are arriving now, I have got yours to-day which was only written on Friday so that's quicker than usual. Your photos are splendid. I like them ever so! they fit in very nicely in that case you've stuck them in & will be very easy to carry about. I had I think the most energetic day yesterday that I have had ever since I came out. We started with breakfast at 7.30 as we had to get the tents packed & our stores, then we set out on a march at 9.30 which we did not finish till nearly 4pm, we went about 18 kilometres; as it was raining most of the time & the roads were in a fearful state we were quite glad when we had finished. On arriving I found the B.I.P. were to sleep in a barn & they were very comfortable. We officers were going to pitch a tent but as the ground was much too sodden after a fine display of French by m'self the old man of the farm allowed us to sleep up in a sort of loft full of straw. We put our valises down on the

straw & it made a topping bed. They also gave us the use of a room for a mess, and as none of our mess kit turned up till late gave us a fine meal of fried eggs, fresh bread & butter & coffee. All this a very nice change as I have not been in a house since I landed & have had no fresh milk or butter either. Another change we appreciated was to be out of earshot of the <u>terrific</u> thunder of the guns all night long. The B.I.P. certainly has both ad- and disad-vantages. There are only 3 officers at present including myself. One is as I told you a man of 45 who enlisted 4 years before I was born in the ranks & who got a commission a year ago, a very good fellow who left the army after the S.A. war & has since been a storeman or something on the Midland Rlwy & a very amusing & capable man (farmer class) but though we get on <u>very</u> well – hardly a companion. He is very good at organising games & gets things going, he is a thorough "old soldier." The other aged 27, looks about 18, has been rejected several times and is out here for the first time, has been out almost 2 months; a weedy specimen, book worm, v. quick (temper), or rather takes offence! asks the most absurd questions, & generally is a bit of a trial but I rag him a lot; tho' at times he's quite alright. He however is only here for the course (2 weeks) & will I hope soon return to his regt. There is a third; away at present but he should be back soon, an awfully nice Scotch boy aged about 20. I am looking forward to his return. You have obviously got hold of the right Nichol, all particulars are correct, he is now in the R.F.C. It's a topping day to-day & we've had some football going & now the "old soldier" has got them all playing rounders in the orchard. Must stop now
much love from

Philip
You might send this home as the descriptions may interest them.

MC 643/10/10

242. Tuesday May 7

My very dear Mother & Father

I don't know when this will get to you as I rather think I shall not be able to get any letters away to you for a few days, but you need not worry I shall be quite alright and not near the war at all. Picture me now sitting in a farm house clothed in slacks & shoes, the first time I have put them on since I came out again. I have just finished a game of football with the men & being hot & muddy I had a good sponge down in a canvas bucket in my tent & now am as fresh as anything. The men all had a bath & clean change to-day for the first time for some weeks & were also paid put so you see we are a bit more civilized now! (pen run dry) I got yr. Thursday's letter on Monday so that's good, also one with Ruth's photos in I think they are splendid she looks so awfully nice in those V.A.D things. We had a full day on Sunday, as we were marching from 9.30 am to nearly 4 p.m. and it was raining most of the time, however we landed up in quite a nice farm at the end so settled down well. Yesterday evening Morison the Scotch boy came back to the B.I.P. I am very pleased as I think I shall get on very well with him. Isn't it splendid how well this Division has done, it always does, everybody has got their "tails up". I should love a cake & some soup tablets, but don't send anything else as rations for us are very good and we are part of Brigade Headquarters, also we can still buy things, though I think it a very good thing Father's not in his old place.

Yes Ruth must certainly have my Gramophone & records, it will make a big difference to her. My command is more like a company than anything else with platoons of each regiment in it. Have you sent orders for the Daily Mail to come to me, if it comes straight from the printers it gets here within 24 hours, otherwise I never see a paper, except by chance sometimes. Also I shall be glad of my other wrist watch[365] if & when it can be mended, this one is alright but I like to feel I've something to fall back on. Brig. Gen C.H.[366] now has a Bar to his D.S.O. This farm is in a filthy state it has been pouring with rain lately. Though we are a longish way from the line now the whole air & ground have been trembling & shaking all day. There has been a thundering & terrific bombardment going on somewhere without a pause for hours & hours. It is like a tremendous rolling thunderstorm never never stopping. Very much love I'm glad to hear you still stay in bed for breakfast

Yr v loving Philip.

MC 643/10/11

---

365. Early watches were mainly designed for the pocket. The wearing of wrist watches became common amongst soldiers during the First World war: service watches had unbreakable glass and luminous dials. From 1917 the British War Department began to issue wrist watches and soon almost every man at the front was wearing one. Precise timing was vital for 'pushes' over the top and when working closely with artillery barrages.
366. Craigie-Halkett.

243.   Monday May 13

My very dear Mother & Father

I got your letter d. May. 7. yesterday & hope that by now you will have got some of my letters as you say my last was dated April 26. but posts I expect would naturally get disorganised then, & there was & often is no method of getting letters away even if you can write them. I am writing from the same camp from which I last wrote & we are likely to be here a good few days yet, we are well away from the line too. I am on parade each day with my B.I.P from 9 to 12–20 & 2–4. I do not do much instructing myself as I have special instructors but I am always there supervising. At present our living quarters are quite comfortable, all in huts. The country is too is [*sic*] pretty, hilly & wooded; though so far we have not seen it in its best light as there has been a lot of rain & the camp as a result is very muddy. The cutting you sent me about the L.N.L. cricketer being killed is interesting as he came up from the base in the train with me to this Battn! I have not met Jack Marriott this time as our old Brigadier got a Division & M. went with him on his staff. I am interested about Gobagger's move but cannot see the necessity of it! I am looking forward to that cake arriving which you mention. We are of course quite a separate little unit – What I shall much enjoy sometimes will be a book, as I think I shall have a good deal more time to read on this job than with the Battn: Uncle Joseph is very welcome here, please thank him for me I will write some time. The Battn is only about 30 yards from us here so I can see a good deal of them. Have you sent in my papers for the Egyptian Civil yet, I think it is a splendid thing as I think it over. Our French interpreter who messes with us is very useful as the people hardly speak any English.

Much love yr v. loving

Philip.

MC 643/10/12

244.   Tuesday May 14[367]

My very dear Ruth

Quite your turn for a letter I think, I think it must be nearly a week or quite since you got one. We are very comfortable at present, we are a long way from the line and in a topping French hut Camp; you have probably seen

---

367. In envelope addressed to Ruth at Fargo, Philip's last letter to her.

the old division mentioned a good deal in the papers lately & indeed it has done splendidly & been in all the fighting up to now. There is nothing much to do in the evenings here after dinner & I usually turn in to bed soon after 9 pm however tonight I am sitting & scribbling by candle light. (pen run out!) I hope you have got the old gramophone by now & the records, you certainly must have them, mother said something about it. I am <u>so</u> sorry, she writes to-day & tells me she is having dreadful attacks of pain again, but seems to think the Dr. has got more idea of what to do now. Last week we had a big, railway journey & spent two nights in the train, we did jolly well though & time passed quite quickly. We had a march of about 5 hours to the train and when we got out about 3 hours march to our present camp. I quite like my present job, we do parades from 9 to 11.30 and then two hours in the afternoon. The only trouble is that the men are continually changing. Mother writes & tells me that the village has quite married "me to Amie!" however she has assured them it is not so, so I hope they now will find some one else for me – I knew they'd be gossiping. The rest of them (in here I mean) are threatening to blow out my candle & I am assuring them of dreadful things in return so there'll be a rag in a minute I'm sure. I'm always wrestling & ragging nowadays.

Much love

Philip

MC 643/10/13

245. Thursday May 16

My very dear Mother & Father – Such a splendid parcel to-day. thank you ever so much the books I shall enjoy, I can read a good deal out here now and this writing pad is the very thing, no bother about envelopes, in this weather they are always a nuisance sticking together – As for the cake, well – of course that goes without saying everybody in out little mess was loud in its praise. I am sure no history of war will be complete without a mention of "Cook's Cakes" – we are having simply glorious hot weather, really hot, I enjoy it like that. We are five officers in the mess at present, they will not however be permanent I expect but keep changing & other come in their place & the same with the men. I am getting my little command more in hand now, I naturally felt my way somewhat gradually at first, but now feel at home & know the work & my instructions etc. Things are being done my way & as I always ran my Coy. in the Battn – In my opinion things wanted organizing & putting together a bit, they wanted a bit of method, I am enjoying gradually seeing where my ideas are altering the general running of things. Today as well as the parcel I got Punch from Uncle Jos: & a letter from Father written on 11-5-18. I like the idea of that book Good Stories from Ox & Cam:[368] which you mention: I wonder if Uncle Henry is still with his old Divn. I haven't heard or seen anything of them; but if I knew which Divn he was still with if I came across it I would make an effort to see him. The country round here is awfully pretty, hilly & woody. A Padre attached to another Battn looks after us. It's bed time now – Mother I do hope you are better you must take lots of care of yourself Yr very loving

Philip

I'll write to Harold[369] – Yes do get him a present – does he smoke? Sure to – Good cigarettes holder – or ash trays??

MC 643/10/14

246.   Sunday May 19 8pm[370]

My very dear Mother & Father. We seem to be having a regular heat wave just at present, the weather is absolutely boiling. Today has been a rather unsatisfactory one & I think I shall have a bit of a "grouse" to you now just to ease off a bit!! It started wrong as for some reason or other when I got up I felt rotten & sick & was not up to more than dressing. This has now passed off but this morning as a result I did not go to Church parade but kept quiet. It was only after Church that I discovered it was "WhitSunday" I do not know why but it had never entered my head that it was so near; I thought it was a Sunday or two off still. I know in one of your letters you said something about it but somehow I never connected it with today. As a result I was a bit fed up that I had missed all services! Then this weekend 40 of my men & officers have gone back to their Battns: & others come to-day in their place this makes things a bit changed, but will be happening regularly. So I shall used to it. But it is the big drawback to this job that officers & men are continually changing & only here temporarily. Your parcels are just too splendid!! Soup & honey came yesterday – & we have been feeding splendidly we had some asparagus this week & rhubarb & are really doing well. Don't worry about my sickness this morning, another officer in BIP was the same later in the day. There was a <u>lot</u> of chloride of

---

368. *Good stories from Oxford and Cambridge; the saving grace of humour*, edited by T Selby Henrey (1918).
369. Philip's cousin Harold Tyndale-Biscoe.
370. Philip's last letter to his parents.

lime in the water yesterday & that may have done it. I have been greatly enjoying that book of Temple Thurston's[371] very much there are such nice ideas in it. We are still miles from the line & likely to be yet a while I hope – I have just been re reading your nice letter written last Sunday all about Whitsuntide & I am so annoyed with myself! – 10 pm. I had dinner by myself tonight but Morrison [*sic*] (Scotch lad) & the others who both left BIP today & another L who is coming to BIP have been in talking for the last hour so I'm cheery again! Much love Philip.

MC 643/10/15

---

371. Ernest Temple Thurston, playwright and novelist (1879–1933),

The Letters:
Ruth Hewetson

247.   Fargo Military Hospital Salisbury Plain[372]

7.15. [*16 Mar. 1918*]

My very dearest Mother & Father.

Here I am!!! I'll start from when I left Father. I had a nice journey down
– the country was so pretty – I hardly read at all & I managed the change
quite easily. When I arrived at Amesbury a Corporal touched me on the
shoulder & said "Are you for Fargo" so I said "Yes"; he collected all my
belongings & took them & me out to a Red X van (labelled "for infectious
cases only") put us all in behind & set off. We're 6 miles from the Station
& I had a very jolly ride feeling most amused at myself. When I arrived
there was no formality at all – I went almost immediately into the kitchen
& had a lovely tea while all other G.S. Members dropped in & out. They
are so nice & nearly all very Irish. (so Mother, do tell me about my Irish
relations & tendencies!) Since tea I've unpacked. We are in a sort of hutment
camp. I'm in a hut divided off into <u>dear</u> little cubicles by curtains. With a
passage w' stoves in round wh: we sit. (I'd like a small vase – then later you
can send me a few flowers now & then.) The photos & silver dressing table
things look so nice. It is a beautifully warm hut. I think I am here for a
year – so that will please you. Evidently it does not sound like "abroad" yet.
My <u>Work</u> is a hut like this used by 11 Sisters who are on night duty, I get
up at <u>5.30</u> (!!!!). have an early small breakfast & get their rooms done by 9
when they come in to go to sleep. I am entirely responsible but all I do is

---

372. See Introduction. Fargo Hospital closed in 1918, and was used as married quarters
for RAF officers at nearby Rolleston until 1931. It then fell into disuse and by the late thirties
most of the buildings had gone.

slops(!) dusting & sweeping (please send a few hints re proper way of doing a washstand!).

abbreviations / = of; \ = the[373]

<Piggo> Two awfully nice girls have just been talking to me. They are both 18 & Irish – names Piggot & Bates, keen on tennis (wh: we may get in the Summer). They told me they were the babies of the establishment – then after a few minutes talk one said "I think we might all be taken for the babies" so I think perhaps I'll make a trio to a very jolly pair (But hush! these are only rumours). Now I'm going to bed & one of them is to bring me my supper as it's my first night. I shall want some big rough overalls (of anything you like) dark blue or anything to cover myself with when doing my rooms, as soon as you can.

We get 2½ or 3 hrs off per day. ½ day per week & one day per month. On such occasions you bike (hurrah for mine) to the nearest village & have tea in a cottage! the only alternative is to go to a cinema of wh: there are 3 somewhere. Church is I think tomorrow in the dining room wherever that is! There's 'o' near here but military camps.

There seems no need to bother about dress – everybody is ever so nice & I am very happy. I've not yet seen a single "Authority". I may have to wait at table sometimes.

Please send this to Philip, then I won't have to repeat to him. I'll write tomorrow if I get a chance.

I hope Father had some tea. "Good night & God bless you" both very, very much dear love from Ruth.

Everybody is so nice because its my 1st time away fr: home. They say "How brave"!!

MC 643/16/1

248.   Sunday 11 a.m [*17 Mar.*][374]

Just a card to go by the same post as last night's letter. I've done my 1st mornings work – it will be longer later I think. I find we have a week in wh: to decide whether we sign on here for a yr: or not. I hope to go to Church tonight. I was up by 6.15 but am not at all tired I shld: like my dressing gown, a dark blue overall, a few more pictures (snaps we've taken, there are some on my wall – Xenia's the G. Law[375] as you suggest) also my blue jersey

---

373. See Introduction.

374. Written on blank postcard, postmarked 18, month illegible, but presumably Mar. [1918].

375. For Xenia Muriel see Introduction. The painting was probably called 'The Good

– they wear any colour here <also shoe cleaning apparatus>. I think we're rather in No Man's Land w' regard to churches, lodgings etc: but I'll find out soon. I loved getting yr: letter this morning – I'll start the diary today. How about a nice pillow case & a towel or 2 to supplement my one a week? On 2nd thoughts my wall is not strong enough for frames. So my G. Law wh: I have will be best. My arm is not v. comfortable but not v. bad – a neighbour has just done it up for me.

Very much love

Ruth.

MC 643/16/2

249. Fargo Military Hospital, Salisbury Plain [*18 Mar.*]

My very dearest Mother & Father.

Yesterday was certainly a very strange Sunday for me (so used to a different dress, a best hat, Church & S. School & lots of hymns) – I was up by 6 cleaning my hut – and by 8 I was thoroughly grubby & glad of a wash & breakfast. This was my 1st public meal & I won't deny I was rather terrified especially as sugar & marg: were not doled out till Tues & I had to rely on other people (therefore I got more than I wld: otherwise I expect!) but luckily I was hungry & all goes cheerily. I was on duty all morning but as I did not quite know what to do I was finished early & stood about feeling a bit dull. However after dinner I found 2 friends & now I'm quite happy. They are the 2 Irish babies of 18 & ever so nice (they will <u>not</u> however make up for *Amie*[376]) Bates is hugely fat (I call her the hippopotamus already!) dark, so Irish I can hardly understand her, & jolly, she rags me & I her – she came & sat on my bed last night & told me I "looked about 3" (!) Pigott is fair, slender, v. sweet & I think likes me quite. We are going to make a good trio. In the afternoon I was <off> "on duty" w' 'o' to do so I wrote & read. In the evening I was glad to hear a voice at – door of the hut "Anybody going to Church." so I went w' a G.S member I did not know before, Miss Martin.[377] She's v. nice, been in Norfolk, about 28 (perhaps or more?) & so

Law', no doubt on a religious/biblical theme, perhaps based on 1 Timothy 1.8: 'but we know that the law is good, if a man use it lawfully'.

376. Amie Evershed: see Introduction.

377. Emily Martyn. She kept in touch in later years, writing to Ruth during the Second World War, at which time she was living in Truro. Her letter said 'I don't forget my little friend of Fargo days.' [NRO, MC 643/42/17].

kind. We had Service (shortened evensong) in the Officers' Mess across the road. I wish there were a Church.

Tuesday (3.10) It would be so much nicer if there were, as it hardly seems Church-yfied but the House Sister (Sister Linton who looks after us, our work & well being) said as I had a bike I might be able to get to one of the village Churches sometimes. However I mean to manage well about my Services scurry thro' my work and then go. I expect on Easter Day I'll get to H.C at 6.30, it is also at 9 but I'm working hard then. To-day is my half-day so as it is wet I'm writing letters in our nice big sitting room w' a lot of others. I am getting on quite well & now I think I am quite at home. Someone has just told me I seem to have settled down very quickly & am getting on well. I had extra work today as someone has left so I shared hut w' my nice Sun: friend Miss Martin. I like her very much & she seems to have taken charge of me. Last night there was a farewell party to Asst: Matron (who is going to Salonika) & a lot of Med: Off came in. Oh dear!!! I shan't get married here. We had games & singing. We (as the "Maids") were allowed in 1st to watch, later we joined in. It lasted till 11. They were not the sort of Officers we approve of. But still there's no need to have anything to do w' them.

I do like P: she's a very sweet girl I think. Irish you know. With her Mother dangerously ill, one brother, & no father. I'm going to try later to change my work so that we can have times off together; not just yet tho' I've only just come!

I am really very happy – getting quite at home – I like nearly all the G.S.M's & I'm getting into my work. The meals are v. good – brkfast: this morning porridge (only twice a wk:) bacon, bread & marg: someday if you've any to spare I'd love a wee pot of homemade jam or marmalade (only a small one because I carry it in & out to meals & don't want to be too conspicuous!) We have tea in our own kitchen, make our own toast – have a sort of picnic meal wh: is v. jolly. We have meat 2 or 3 times per day.

Your letter just come, You know I'm in a much nicer position than you, it is you Mother dear who have to bear all the brunt – for loneliness is one of the worst things to fight against, I think.

You must not do Guides unless you're quite well again. I know they'll all love to have you – I cld: see it in their faces when I told them. I don't think O Bell means to slack – she can't let Ida take her place.[378] I wrote a

---

378. Salhouse Girl Guides: Olive Mary Bell, born Salhouse 1904, her mother the local schoolteacher; Ida Burton, born Salhouse 1903, daughter of the village butcher.

p.c. to Mrs Raikes[379] telling her I'd gone and that you were not at all well so perhaps you'll hear.

I wear mufti if I like when I'm "off" so I've got on white blouse & blue skirt now. <u>About you coming</u> :- I've not found out much but this is all I've gathered. We can have a "female friend" to stay in Hosp: for 2 nights if we like. There's Amesbury 5 or 6 m: away & this other village 2 or 3 m: away. Only everywhere is miles fr: a station. We're in the Back of Beyond you know & there's no chance of much dissipation – but I think I'll sign on for the yr: because, they all say we're lucky in freedom fr: strict rules re everything; I like the work & the life ever so already – & I know 2 (at any rate nice girls) who'll be here all the Summer. What d'you think. Of course the winter's bad but I think by then I shld: know all about doing for myself & cld: well stick it. I shld: get 14 days leave in Sept: if I sign for a year.

P's letter <cheer> makes me quite bubbly – I love to be appreciated by my brother.[380] I also had a sweet one fr: A. yesterday.

I feel it is just as imp: work here as abroad – they are understaffed & find it v. difficult to get people because of loneliness (wh: I'm used to after all) so I know it is worth stopping.

Goodbye, very dear love from Ruth.

I simply long for post & letters it is my chief excitement in life[381]

MC 643/16/3

250. Fargo Military Hospital Salisbury Plain

My very dearest Mother,

I got your lovely budget this morning – it <u>was</u> nice! I am <u>very</u> happy here & getting to know more & more about it. I shld: like to stay the year personally & I'll tell you all the pts: in favour. I really am wanted – they are short of G.S.M's & we are all kept very busy – it is just as good work as abroad I am feeling, altho' of course I wanted to go v. much. Pigott, Bates & several other nice ones will be here all the time & in any other place I might not get decent companions (G.S.M's are <u>not</u> all "quite quite"!). We have an extraordinary amount of freedom – V. little discipline – a House Sister looks after all our well being & we are not much bothered about

---

379. Postcard. Mrs Raikes was Commissioner of Eastern Division, Taverham District, of the Girl Guides, under which Salhouse came.

380. Philip's letter of praise (225) had presumably been sent on to Ruth.

381. Inserted at head of letter.

clothes etc: Then yesterday I found the sweetest village w' a shop or two, 2½ m: away Shrewton(?)[382] where everybody goes shopping or for tea. If you cld: get there it wld: be lovely, you'll just have to motor fr: Amesbury, it is probably about *4 or* 5 miles. It is a nice place w' 1000 people, and shops; so you wld: not be dull & I cld: get over everyday, as I am off always either from 2–4.30 or fr: 4.30–7.30. I am going to Church there whenever I'm off on Sunday evening & that is every other Sunday fr: 5–8. As for talking to Officers – that is perfectly all right – (they come here to parties) Any V.A.D person can do what she likes that way – no restrictions!

The work I enjoy (altho' it is hard) the "slops" only consist of basins(!). Yr: list will be useful but we've no time to work in such detail. I've 9 rooms, corridor & lavatories all alone you know & all must be done by 11 really, because they go to sleep.

It will be lovely here in the Summer, especially w' a bike. Bates & I are going to ask Sister Linton (the H.S) if we may have 2 little plots of ground outside the hut, if so I'll want seeds, roots etc: (a very few of each). I don't want to stay if you & F don't want me too but I rather think I'll do well here – I'm getting real friends with P. & B. (& I think I'm quite popular amongst all the G.S.M's – only don't say I said so!) and well – it will show you how happy I am if I tell you I've got "bubble & squeak" today badly.

<u>4.30</u>. Sister says she'll be delighted for us to <have a> take the "garden" in hand! Hurrah!! We're quite thrilled about it. Soon perhaps you cld: send me a few nice bedding out things – nothing big it's a v. small plot (carnations?) things that will give nice flowers for picking & also will grow up fairly quickly; you'll know best. Perhaps we'll get a few seeds.

<u>6.30</u>. Oh I am so happy! I'm just back fr: a most gorgeous bike ride, I went to the village & had tea in the upstairs room of the nice tiny shop. I had a dainty tea, thin bread & marg: & jam & biscuits. It will show you my appetite is all right if I tell you I'd already had my tea here (a huge round of toast & an equally big one of bread!). We really have excellent food. For brkfast: porridge 2 a week, & always bacon or fish (herrings etc:). dinner= nice meat & veg: & very good puddings (2 helps) cup of tea if you like (I don't). tea= as much bread & dripping or jam as you like. We have it in the kitchen because it's cosier & you can eat more. All other meals are in the Mess. A nice big room w' 2 <u>long</u> tables, Sister Linton at top of one, Matron the other (only she's very ill w' irresipilis (?? can't spell it) since Sat: For supper we have either fish or cold meat, then bread & cheese or jam, w' coffee & cocoa alternate

---

382. The question mark is Ruth's: her spelling is correct. Shrewton had a population of 611 in 1911.

nights. There, Mother dear, I know you like all details. Tell me do I tell you what you want to know, if not ask questions & I'll answer them.

Now about Services etc: I was pleased, this morning a Welsh girl Bowen by name to whom I talked yesterday, was talking to me today about playing & singing & she said "you must play some hymns on Sun: for me". Then she asked me to go to H.C w' her at 6.30 saying she'd help w' my work (wh: must be done early) was not it nice? On Easter Day I'm planning to hurry up all of my work, go at 6.30 to H.C, if possible at 11 too, & then perhaps to Evensong at the village (if there's someone to go w', if not I'll go here). The 11 may not be possible as I'm supposed to be on duty. But I'm finding quite a lot of keen Church people – wh: is nice. The Chaplain to Hosp: is new but I liked him on Sunday; I don't know his name. Father might write to the man at Shrewton if they're nice I'd go to tea w' them. I went into the Church yesterday – it is sweet both outside & in. I thought it might be open so I tried & it was. But I don't want him to call on me here, he can ask me there if he likes!!

I heard fr: Philip yesterday,

Now please:- Don't bother about more than one overall, I've got one to go on w'. And I've not much wall room so can only fit a few photos etc: A vase I'd like (small).

I also wld: love my camera, & the 2 dark slides wh: are with it (Coe[383] has the other 4 – I'll ask Given to send them, as she's going to send me the snaps). I must have 3 changes of underclothing because the washes overlap, can you get them soon, as I can't send combies, d'you think I need have thick linings I don't – but a thick bodice I'll want.

I must stop now. My arm is much better. I had it done up in the Sick ward yesterday! V. much love to both you & Father (I'll write to him next time).

From Ruth.

MC 643/16/4

251. Fargo Military Hospital Salisbury Plain

Thursday 3p.m.[?*28 Mar.*]

My very dearest Mother & Father.

I can't remember when I wrote home last – have not I written since Sunday – surely I have – no I don't believe I have. I did enjoy the lovely packet Mother sent on the other day & oh I was relieved to hear you expected me

---

383. See footnote 339.

to sign on. I am more & more convinced that it was the best thing to do. On Monday I got Mother's parcel (I've not tried the overall yet – I don't wear a white collar w' it but I think I can manage it all right, I'll try when I have to fit it on) and also my coat & skirt from Abram Browne.[384] It is very nice &, as far as I can judge, a perfect fit. Everyone said at once "oh it's tailor made" (!) So I'm delighted that it is satisfactory. Now – I know Mother is longing to see it! Well I think she'd be sure to be pleased.

On Monday I biked to Shrewton, went on to another dear little village w' the sweetest wee Church, then came back to Shrewton & had tea in my cottage, & came back again in time to be on duty by 4.30 and have another tea.

Tuesday was my half day – I went for a walk w' Bates over the plain to a big camp at Lark-hill – a huge place, WAAC's & all sorts, we went to buy things in the 3 "shops" they have there – (just sort of canteen places). I love the open plain – it is simply – huge & exhilarating – & just increases my "bubble & squeak" until I feel as if I were walking in air! In the evening I went up to the Aerodrome across the Plain & thro' a dear little wood of fir trees & grass paths w' a Miss Burgess (the funny nice little person) I go out w' her nearly every day. Then I had a hot bath & went to bed (in my nice dressing gown & rug) & Bates brought me a huge supper. That's what ½ day people generally do.

Next Tuesday is my whole day, so I am thinking of going to Salisbury having my hair shampooed, my photo taken (? in Uniform) & going over the Cathedral. Then coming back to Amesbury & going to tea w' my "friend" whose letter I'll send to you. Is she the Vicar's wife I wonder. I've written to her to ask her if I may come then. I am only "off" on Wed: fr: 2–4.30. wh: is an awkward time.

I'm longing for post-time & some letters – I just love getting them! Mother's are lovely – & betw: you you just keep me in them splendidly. I enjoyed all Father's bits of village gossip – fancy them still remembering my "Maiden Speech"!

Good Friday[385]

I got Mother's letter this morning & I was pleased as there is only one post today. I've made a rush w' my work & been to Church twice so don't think it has been just like an ordinary day. I went to 6.30 to Antecommunion & Intercession w' Bowen (the one who asked me last Sun:) I did not know she was going till I was ready. We were 5 in all. Afterwards the Chaplain spoke to me – he had got Father's letter last night – & he asked me if I "came fr:

384. A fashionable provincial tailor, based in St Peter's Street, Norwich.
385. Good Friday in 1918 was 29 March.

Norwich" so we had a little conversation – he was quite nice. Then I went again at 11 w' Bates & Miss Burgess, – a fairly big Service w' nice Good Fri: hymns. Now I'm sitting on my bed (as Mother suggests) all wrapped up in Father's lovely rug writing letters & reading.

I am longing for the parcel, especially the flowers.

I hear a lot from Amie lovely, long talk-y letters. I am so glad she'll come over & help w' the Guides. I've not had time to write any messages to any one except you & Philip & Amie – it keeps me busy to write that many. My letters are not a bad size on the whole are they?! I've not finished the first pot of jam yet – so I'm well off for Easter.

People here are all so nice.

Someone told me last night she knew as soon as she saw me <I> my Father was a clergyman & some one else standing by said the same. Is not it funny! I wonder what's the distinguishing mark. Most people who see my photographs (the Family) say I'm just like Father because I've got his expression & look. (in that nice khaki photo of his). They all admire P's eyes & say he is very like Mother. Have we any L'Estrange relations near Dublin – Pigott knows a Dr L'E w' 2 married sisters. I do want to know what part of Ireland my relations live in. I am going to try to go to Shrewton Ch: on S. evening. Have you written to the Vicar there yet.[386]

With very much love

from

Ruth.

MC 643/16/6

252. [1 Apr.][387]

This is just to say I'll be writing a long letter tomorrow (my whole day). Yesterday was a very nice Easter Sunday. Lovely parcel on Saturday. Sun:= H.C at 6.30 for a splendid Easter Service. In afternoon played & sang hymns for 1½ hr: w' another. Tomorrow I stay in bed for breakfast & lunch too if I like. Go to Amesbury Vicarage in the afternoon. Now just off for a walk w' Piggot. Getting happier each day!!

Much Love Ruth.

MC 643/16/8

---

386. The vicar was Allen Wilfred Bull, who took orders in 1894 and served in several Dorset and Wiltshire parishes. He was vicar of Shrewton between 1914 and 1923.

387. Written on plain postcard, postmark 1 Apr. '18: Easter Sunday in 1918 was 31 March.

253. Tuesday 8 p.m. [*2 Apr.*]

Bed(!)

My very dearest Mother & Father

Oh dear, oh dear, I meant to write crowds of letters to-day wh: I ought to write & instead I went to Salisbury so I've been out all day! I've had a simply lovely time!! I had brkfast in bed at about 7.45 then I dressed all in my best (white silk blouse, cvat & skirt) & biked to Amesbury, where at 10 am I caught the train to Salisbury (2nd Class Section 3/7 ½ – 3rd is 'o' but Tommies & <u>not</u> advisable) I arrived at 10.45, it shower-ed most of the day but I'd borrowed a mac: (I'd like my own very much) I wandered about – had my hair shampooed & did all sorts of shopping; had a nice lunch in a restaurant (beef steak pudding & apple tart = 2/5) & caught a 2.40 back to Amesbury where at 3.45 I presented myself at "Mrs March". They're the Doctor's people & <u>so</u> nice. A girl of about 20 & a nice Mother.[388] I talked to the girl nearly all the time, had a nice cosy sit down-tea looked over the garden, they've got a lovely tennis court & she's very keen Hurrah, hurrah, hurrah!! I'm to go whenever I like – <they're> there Father 'o' venture 'o' have!!

Do try the Shrewton Vicar now. Then I biked home & found my nice new underclothes & a letter fr Amie 9 pages back & front! I finished up this delightful whole day w' a lovely hot bath & supper in bed so now I'm well set up till the next one (the first Tues: in May you see). I'm so sleepy now I must stop – I'll send this off tomorrow early & write again in afternoon about Sunday & yr: lovely parcels. This I'll send now because I've not written for a few days now. V. much love fr:

Ruth.

MC 643/16/52

254. Fargo Military Hospital Salisbury Plain

Wednesday [?*3 Apr.*]

My dearest Mother & Father.

Now I'll begin another letter, wh: I'll try & get off tomorrow. I think I told you most about yesterday in my last night's letter didn't I? So I'll start w' the

---

388. The family lived at Comilla House, Amesbury: Joseph March, doctor, his wife Grace, with their daughter Violet: she was born in 1898 so Ruth's guess as to her age was accurate.

parcel – it arrived on Sat: afternoon & I was excited while I waited to open it. The flowers <u>were</u> (& are) sweet – they soon revived in warm water & they make my room ever so nice. I sent one to a G.S member in the Sick Ward (Miss Browne – Cook, who is very nice) & she was ever so pleased. The grt: surprise was those lovely chocs: & toffee – we have been enjoying those & I take surreptitious bites every time I go to my room – they're lovely. The nightgown is a pretty one – the shoes I find most useful, & the camera arrived quite safely & will be a joy when the weather gets better again.

<u>Thursday</u>
Sunday was quite Easterfied. There were about 30 of us at the 6 o 'c: & as they were all Sisters, the white caps gave quite the right effect & we had some beautiful flowers. In the afternoon I sang & played hymns in our anteroom to Bow<u>e</u>n (not Bowers Mother!) I was supposed to be on duty but there was nothing to do.

The Shrewton Service was ever so nice. I biked there alone – (no-one else who was 'off' wanted to go so far). The Church was packed, obviously the Vicar had made a lot of it before-hand as a Festival Service, & they had a military band – several officers & men in the Choir & an officer to read the lessons, processional & recessional hymns & an anthem (!). I got home about 8:15 & as I was "excused supper" I had it brought to me in bed by Bates. I've just got Mother's letter – I am grieved she's got a temperature again – do stay in bed, & get really better before you start the Guides.

I shall be thinking of you this weekend, it seems <u>so</u> funny that Amie shld: be at MY HOME without ME! Oh I'd love a wkend at home. But Mother dear so far I am very happy & don't feel miserable at all – I <u>will</u> tell you if I do.

Poor Pigott heard today that her Mother is dying (she has <u>v.</u> bad cancer & the child was sent away). I heard her crying so I went in & tried to sympathise; the only thing to do is to hug and caress people on such occasions I think & she is such a child. However she told me all about it – shewed me the letter & gradually calmed down. Tonight we've been for a walk & she seems much happier – but I want to take her any telegram when it comes – I don't think she minds crying (poor child) in front of me.

Oh yes I have my hut entirely to myself. I manage it all right generally. Nobody gives me any directions; I just have to keep my eyes & ears open & use my own common sense; it is rather funny to think of me (your undomesticated untidy little Missie) keeping that grt: place nice is not it – I'm awfully proud of meself today I began work at 5 past 6!!

I am as you say "on my own w' a vengeance" & to tell you truth I quite enjoy it! I wonder how my character is getting on – it is rather early to tell yet I think!

I believe we may wear white Panamas in Summer – if so I shall really have to embark on one. Oh yes, we wear our brown dresses all day then, & go out in them. Even now we go out (to certain places nearby) in our white caps w' our greatcoats if it's nice enough. I've got over £2.10.0 at present & in about 10 days I ought to be paid. Then I'll be rich as I get £4 for Uniform also – shall I keep that then you need not send me any? I'd love cake – but the only thing is I'd have to share it w' the others who have tea w' me wld: not I – there are only 5 tho' we have it in shifts you see. & they probably refuse it; (as Miss Martin said the other day "Yr: Mother did not send that jam for me to eat my child" – she is very dear – her house was absolutely destroyed at Margate[389] by Zepps & so she's come to W.Work. It is awfully plucky of her – she must be about 35 or more & she's always jolly & ready to laugh w' us younger ones *however tired she may be* she is quite a Mother to us all!)

A few little buns now & then to eat when I get up wld be nice anyhow. I'll give you a list of G.S people & a little about them – I expect you'd like to know them all.

Miss <u>Martin</u> (you know, she's Matron's maid)

Miss <u>Browne</u> (Hd: Cook, 50ish nice as far as I know, been in Sick Ward lately)

Miss <u>Grubbe</u> (cook, about 30, pretty, quite nice – has dropped calling me "Miss H"!)

Miss <u>Allsopp</u>[390] (Hd: Mess Maid. Clergyman's daughter I think I shall like her <u>v.</u> much when I Know her better; she's on leave now. V. nice to me when I came – about 30. One of the really "nice" ones).

Miss <u>Tottenham</u> (Mess Maid) oldish perhaps 32. <u>Not</u> popular – sarcastic (& bitter against the Sisters.) Rather a snob – but quite nice to me she sleeps next to me & wakes me every morning).

<u>Piggot</u> (Mess Maid)

<u>Bates</u> (Hut)

<u>Bowen</u> (Hut) (Welsh, good churchwoman, very conceited but likes me(!) Perhaps because I sit on her or nag her all day!)

---

389. Margate and Ramsgate, Kent, were badly damaged in a Zeppelin raid on 6 December 1915.

390. Later references make it clear that she was one of several daughters of Revd Richard Allsopp and his wife Harriet: Richard died in 1907 and in 1911 Harriett was living in London with two unmarried daughters, Dorothy and Margaret. The younger, Margaret is the most likely: she would be 37, rather than 30 as Ruth estimates.

<u>Silk</u> (Hut) (her friend, lately married, v. jolly & quite a friend of mine. They both go in 3 weeks).

<u>Miss Burgess</u> (Hut work) Very nice – I often go out w' her. I believe she's over 30. Rather queer but quite a dear.

<u>Mrs Jones</u>. (quite "impossible" but very kind & good natured. Late Tight Rope Dancer! Aren't I horrid?!)

<u>Miss Campbell</u> (a good hearted type of Irish shop girl – very kind).

<u>Mrs Bawdon</u> (fr: Norfolk, an apprentice at Caley's[391] – called "my Norfolk friend" by anyone who wants to annoy me!)

<u>Miss Silverlock</u> the latest – uppish, flirty annoying vulgar, 18 yr: old millinery apprentice! Tries to keep us all up to our work fr: the 1st day – Ugh!!)

2 others who don't matter they work in another part. I really must stop or this won't catch you.
I wrote to Philip yesterday.
I am sending Amie a note w' this.
Very very dear love to you both & please get well quickly Mother
From

Ruth

(Tell Amie about my companions – it will probably amuse her too!)

MC 643/16/7

255. Fargo. Thursday. 11th [*Apr.*]

My very dearest Mother & Father,

I'll start this now & finish it whenever I've time as I shall be going out soon I think.

I have enjoyed your last few letters the parcel & the Mags: The bit about Guides is splendid Mother, & I do envy you going to meet Lady B-P.[392] I can just picture you in my costume. I'm sorry O-Bell is such a little self-satisfied person but she means well I suppose! At any rate Annie Waters will be a grt standby I'm sure.[393] Yr account of their work is just splendid & exactly what I was wanting them to do – You've not been enrolled yet have you?

---

391. A large Norwich business, manufacturing drinks and chocolate, including 'Caley's Marching Chocolate'. Chapelfield Shopping Centre stands on the site of the factory.
392. Lady Olive Baden-Powell, (1889–1977), Chief Guide for Britain from 1918
393. A Salhouse Girl Guide, born Salhouse 1902, lived with her aunt a shop-keeper in the village.

The Laundry that does our Uniform is simply awful – everything is almost ruined – this week is especially bad (aprons ironmoulded first time of washing too! – caps dirtier than when sent). I hear complaints have been made but the difficulty is they have to be paid for, & so we send them free to an Army Laundry. Is not it a shame – I think we're going to complain again.

Do you remember Silverlock the latest arrival? Well she's an awful nuisance, fearfully "bounder-ish" & will talk late at night. All dislike her – especially the "old G.S.M's" (who've been here some time). I sleep in between her & Miss Tottenham (who is quite a friend of mine now – altho' she is very keen on being "quite-quite" while noone else is!). Yesterday I was talking to Miss Tot: about the ceaseless conversations wh: go on & I said she was lucky in only hearing voices I heard every word etc: finally I told her it was often disgusting filthy talk as well as endless "men men men". Well she told Miss Brown (Hd Cook) who told Sister Linton!! She came & asked me about it today. "Very sorry this shld: happen indeed, Matron & I always very particular that our own G.S.M's shld: be *as* happy & comfortable among each other as at home – Miss S. made a grt mistake does not know how a VAD shld: behave etc:". I told her it was not the sort of talk I was used to hearing – She was ever so nice (she always is to me) & awfully annoyed saying it wld: be stopped. Of course I never meant to complain to her but last night too the girl was v. rude to Miss Allsopp & so they evidently told of that too! Miss Tot. is rejoicing because she thinks Silverl: will "get the Sack". Matron will probably interview her anyhow. You see they look after us well – Sister L. was quite apologetic to me. I cld: not think what she meant when she called me to come & speak to her!

I am having the Daily Mirror (can't get Graphic) & sharing it w' Pigott)

I do like Miss Allsopp; & we're always off at the same time too. I had such a nice walk w' her the other day – we talked hard & found we had lots of likes & dislikes etc: in common. Of course she's much older than I am. I expect I'll go to Shrewton Ch: on Sunday nights w' her – I hope so.

We've two new G.S.Ms this week one quite nice (Hardy) one stolid & fat w' no aim in life but her work (Bridges). Silk leaves tomorrow I am sorry as I really like her v. much. She's only been married about a month & is wild to get off! I biked to Amesbury w' her the other day – everyone is sorry she's going.

Oh dear this letter sounds very grumbly but I'm not a bit really. I like the people more & more – (especially Miss Allsopp, Martin, Pigott, Bates, Burgess <Browne> also Miss Brown – Grubbe & even Miss Tot: whom I thought I'd hate I like quite now!)

Matron is on duty again – but this does not affect us, we hardly even see her. My watch is broken wh: is an awful nuisance – can't get it done in Salis: suppose must send to Norwich? It is a dreadful nuisance being w'out one.

I had such a nice letter fr: Miss Wise[394] the other day (I wrote to her) signed "Your affectionate friend" enquiring after you all.

I've also heard fr: Aunt Ruth, I'll try & write soon but we get so little time.

It pours nearly every day now but I've never missed going out since I came. Nor by the way have I missed my 2nd help of pudding at dinner – it is beginning to be a joke by now – altho' lots of others are just as bad!

I hear every morning (fr: my hut people Sisters & V.A.Ds) of deaths overnight. They seem to be pneumonia chiefly & of course flying accidents, 3 of our Sisters went to London for the big Service yesterday.[395]

My feet are all right now – I hear they are often bad the first wk: then recover. I must go now.

Much dear love to you both

Ruth.

MC 643/16/57

256.   Fargo[396] [19 Apr.]

I got back quite safely & don't feel at all tired today. I've been thinking of all of you all the time & I wonder if P. has sailed?[397] It was a lovely peep of you both. I got the hat satisfactorily in the end – had tea & got a nice seat. I eat [sic] 2 buns & a fishcake! We had one change. There was no Ambulance so I walked to Amesbury village (about 10 mins) & got a taxi – 8/- When I got back I got such a warm "Welcome Home" (!) fr: all who were still up; & while I eat my supper I told them all about everything – then tumbled into bed & found no difficulty in getting up this morning. I've just had my pay for March 16 – 31 (19/6)! Very dear love from Ruth. I can't use my pen!

MC 643/16/9

---

394. Ruth's headmistress: see Introduction.

395. A Memorial Service was held on 10 April 1918 at St Paul's Cathedral for nurses who had fallen in the war: it was attended by Queen Alexandra.

396. Written in pencil on plain postcard, postmark (Fri.) 19 April '18. The postcard is addressed to Mrs Hewetson in Folkestone.

397. He sailed on 19 April, the day she wrote, or at least posted, this card.

257.   Fargo. Wednes: [?*24 Apr.*]

My dearest Mother & Father.

I am writing this w' the new pen wh: arrived today: What a lovely surprise
& what a beauty it is! Oh Thank you ever so! Now I need not bother about
getting the other done in a hurry. I also got Mother's card & one from
Philip written on Sat: fr: an Officers' Club & telling me he was going to the
9th.[398] He'll like that best won't he? The new stockings will be lovely & I'll
send home the others either today or tomorrow (they are not so very bad
yet). I'm also sending sugar in a biscuit tin, I hope it will be safe. My overall
is getting rather dirty but that does not really matter (that's what it is for!)
However I want to send it to the wash soon, as at present the dye is liable to
come out. I'll answer M's questions before I go any further.

Our Hut is a very big one – it is really two – the original one, the two
small rooms then another. There are 18 of us altogether 10 in my part.[399]
This is a rough plan & here is mine enlarged. There is not that ingenious! I
sleep w' my window right down now – it is lovely! You see I'm rather lonely
up there but I don't mind a bit – it is far the nicest hut – lighter & more airy,
also quieter now. I thought at 1st it wld: be lonely w'out P. or B. but now I
like it. I like Miss A also Miss G. & Miss Tot: & I like to go to sleep once
I'm in bed, wh: I shld not do if I were w' Bates etc. I know! D'you know I
think I'm going to be like P. & get on well w' or prefer the Society of people
older than myself – <so> of course Pigott is much younger than I am, &
she palls now a bit – Bates is more like me – sensible! It is extr'ordin'ry how
easily I've fitted in to all these strangers – I never thought I wld: Yesterday –
(my ½ day) I had a good tidy up in my room, then "dressed up in me best"
& cycled to Amesbury had tea w' the Marches – ever so nice. Mrs improves
on acquaintance I thought her rather cold at first. But now I like her – very
practical I shld think.

They gave me some lovely wallflowers for my room & 28 sweet pea
seedlings wh: are looking lovely in the gardens. I planted them out last night
& Miss Grubbe saved me soot from the Kitchen this morning.

I've also put in lettuces, radishes cress & Bates has done a lot of flower
seeds, so we're coming on. Sister Harris[400] (the new Home Sister who's ever
so nice) has just been w' me admiring them. I got back last night about 7;
had a <u>gorgeous hot</u> bathe & got into bed w' a book – Pigott brought me

---

398. See letter 232, dated 20 April 1918.
399. Ruth has drawn the layout of the hut and a plan showing the layout of her room.
400. Ethel Mary Harris. Ten years older than Ruth, she married William Suffolk in
July 1918, after which date she is naturally referred to in the letters as 'Sister Suffolk'.

a

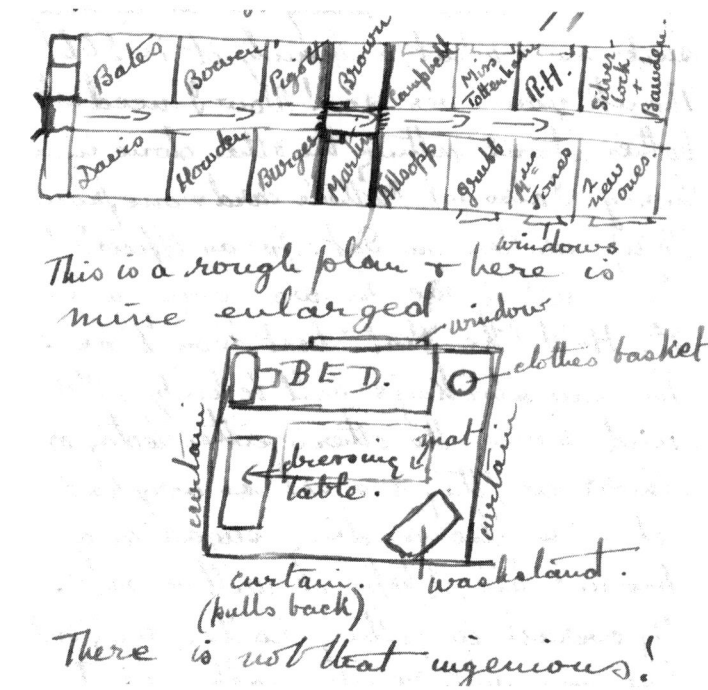

9. Drawing by Ruth from letter 257

lovely supper. (<the> fish pie, huge help of jam tart, bread & cheese & 2 cups of coffee!) Then I slept! & now I feel perfectly renewed & happy; for to tell the truth (wh: I know you like) I've been feeling a bit "dumpy" for the last 2 or 3 days. It is a disease one gets for a short time after having been here about 6 wks: (just bored w' life & fearfully sleepy & tired) but once you get over it you're all right. So I had a <u>very</u> short dose – no one else knows I had it!! Today I'm quite different. We really get a lot of fun out of life I seem to laugh (& eat) all day long. I'm sitting out in the sun writing now – sheltered fr: the wind by the hut. What d'you think of my Salary. 19/6 for a fortnight! I get much more next month as I hope for my uniform £4.

I'm thinking of sending to Garrould[401] for a summer hat (navy blue straw w' hatband 6/11) I've just seen one & they look so nice. It will soon be hot enough for one. Those caps are <u>not</u> for warm weather.

Can you (sooner or later) send my tennis racquet for me – just in its press w' a label I think; won't that do? Also I think I ought to have a pair of

---

401. Store in Edgware Road, London, specialising in clothing for nurses.

good white tennis shoes somewhere(?). I think we shall be able to play at the March's very soon – that will be simply splendid.

I heard from Uncle L E yesterday so must try & write to him. I'm also writing to Philip today.

So now I must stop.

Very dear love from

Ruth.

I don't know when the new stamp date begins; so I'll risk 1d: only today anyhow.[402]

MC 643/16/11

10.   Postcard of Amesbury sent by Ruth (letter 258)

258.   Thursday [25 Apr.][403]

this just gives you a vague idea of Amesbury, it is all more or less like this, & some of the shops are not bad. I'm expecting my photos but they've not

---

402. Inserted at head of letter. Postage rates were raised on 3 June 1918: the price for letters went up from 1d to 1½ d, for postcards from ½ d to 1d. As this letter was written at the end of April, she was worrying unduly.

403. Written on back of postcard with view of Amesbury High Street; date from postmark.

yet arrived. It is lovely sitting out in this weather. Cld: you send me the Latin bk: G. sent me; it is "Via Latina"[404] dark red; either in shelf in dining room cupboard or in cupbd in my room. Also in bottom shelf for my bk case "Oliver Cromwell" I don't want to rust! O now it is hot shall have time to sit out & read. Love fr Ruth.

MC 643/16/10

259. Fargo Military Hospital Salisbury Plain [*?27 Apr.*]

Saturday

My very dearest Mother

Just a wee line – I got your most welcome letter this morning sometimes they turn up on Sats: sometimes on Sundays. It was a nice talk – I'm just longing for that parcel, I love getting them! I finished the jam this morning, so it has done me well – chiefly brkfasts:

I am sorry about O.Bell but some how I've always felt happier about the other 2, & Ida will make a <u>good</u> Leader – tho' whether she shld: be permanent or not, I can't tell – the chief reason against wld: be that O.B might not come any more and I never want them to go off?! I'll be writing to them all tomorrow if I can.

I am sending off sugar & 2 pr stockings now – I hope they'll arrive safely.

Did I tell you Matron inspects every Sat:? Well today she did as usual & as a result <u>I</u> have been given more work so that someone else can do hers better! Now I have all (i.e 8) bathrooms & my hut. Jolly eh? I don't really mind as I can do them easily w' Monkey Brand[405] provided I do them regularly. But I presume the 4 I do now must have proved satisfactory so I'm given more.

The first seeds are up in the garden hurrah – Alyssum! I'm <u>ever</u> so pleased.

Tomorrow I'm going to a Concert in the evening by a regimental string band – This is a change for me on Sundays, but I've thought it over well, & come to the conclusion that as I am going to Church 2 in the morning & if I went in the evening again cld: only go for ½ service at Shrewton (wh: is a long walk) & we can't even stay for the Sermon – I think it is also the same sort of thing as P. playing hockey etc at Flxstowe – good music is something to take you away fr: everyday life & give you a different sort of atmosphere wh: is what I try to get on Suns: What d'you think? I am going w.' Miss

---

404. 'The Latin Way'.

405. Brooke's Soap Monkey Brand, a cleaning and scouring product produced by Lever Brothers from about 1910.

Allsopp. It is in aid of Work among the WAAC up here. Last night we had an awfully distracted night, as one of the new people (who is really crazy) persisted in talking (grumbling at everything) having a light & carrying on in a simply crazy fashion till about 12 o' c: or more! "battles" ensued & peace was not declared till about 2 o'c:!! Then of course we are up by 6!! I've survived wonderfully – but Miss Tot: had to go to bed w' an awful head (she's been disturbed by her before). The creature is going to be sent to Sick Ward tonight if she'll go!!!! She'll probably be sent home as "Medically Unfit.

(I enclose Commands for Guide <u>Drill</u> in case you'd like them.) you know it is good for us to have a bit of hardship like that I <just think> thought of P w' no sleep at all often probably & was thankful for my 3 or 4 hrs:

Tennis next wk: oh hurrah, I'll want my white skirt & the nice pique blouse wh: goes w' it (the new one you know) at any rate for Amesbury & here too perhaps.

Miss A. has just written about Panamas if we may wear them, I'll get someone else to buy my blue straw.

Very much love from

Ruth.

MC 643/16/47

260. "Fargo". [*29 Apr.*][406]

Monday.

It is a simply gorgeous afternoon & I've just come out behind the Hut to laze for an hour or two. I had quite a nice Sunday yesterday. Church at 6 w' Bowen & Pigott & at 11 w' Miss A. The concert was <u>very</u> good & I thoroughly enjoyed it. You know P. said I cld have the gramophone if I liked – well since I came back I've found a place where I cld: keep it safely, & it wld be just lovely.[407] We long for some decent music – it wld: make <u>all</u> the difference. What do you think abt it? I am here for a year you see. It cld: come to Amesbury & then up in an Ambulance, & w' cases of records wld: be quite safe in a packing case. I shld: keep it locked up & allow <u>no</u> one else to use it but myself. Do you think it possible? The photos have not come yet! I'm longing for that parcel.! Ruth.

MC 643/16/12

---

406. Written on back of plain postcard, postmark 30 April.

407. Ruth's parents presumably wrote to Philip after this letter, asking if Ruth could have the gramophone. See letter 242 for his reply.

261. <u>Fargo</u>. Sunday [*5 May*]

My very dearest Mother & Father

Oh what a lovely parcel & how quickly it came! I was simply delighted & ever so surprised to see it. I hurried to carry it to my room as it arrived at a very busy time yesterday; but as soon as I cld: I made my bed & last night I just enjoyed it thoroughly – they say I turned over & over! that was to get the very best out if it you see. The biscuits, jam etc: are too lovely. I emptied the jam into pots. It came at a very opportune moment too as we've had 'o' for 2 or 3 days except our marg: wh: as you can imagine is running short more quickly than usual. Some had some of the Rhubarb for tea (only 6 of us not the whole lot) It was just delicious! Then too I had 2 biscuits & one of those nice nougat things at 6 am this morning oh so good!

I am very happy & enjoying life tho' of course I do get tired sometimes. For instance (I know you want to know) yesterday was an exceptionally busy day. I had my own hut, the 8 baths, & another Hut (to do roughly as someone had a day off). Added to this Matron inspects on Saturday! However I got thro' by 11.30 (starting at 6). Of course I was tired, but I revived <by> after a good dinner. Then in the evening I had a simply lovely time. The Tennis Courts were opened & I went up at 4.30 – 7.30. It was quite fun but I did not play w' anyone very brilliant!

<u>Monday</u> Yr: other parcel just come – the overall & white skirt. Thank you ever so. I'm rather thinking the latter is a wee bit long now, but perhaps not. I've not grown since last yr: really.

Today I've been up to Tennis & had two quite good singles w' Miss Grubb – I beat her 6–1, 6–2 but w' practice she'll be good. I seem to be going to be quite good this year. And it is just delightful having it. The Sat: affair is always a party w' visitors (officers chiefly!). So I'll want my white. Now I want several other things tho' I've not much room to keep them! First, have I a straw hat to wear w' my white – I don't quite know whether that red one wld: do for Tennis & I've forgotten what else I have!? 2) White stockings <u>please</u>! 3) I think I must have one cotton frock – it is going to be hot, & I'm beginning to like getting into mufti now.

I'm going to play tennis as much as I can it makes such a difference & gives you "joie de vivre" however tired or bored you were before. I've not played at Amesbury yet – I very rarely find time to go – it is a bit far & I've never time to do ¼ I want to go here! Time flies when you're off – it's only 2–3 hrs: per day you see.

As for my work I can really do as much or as little as I like – I plan it all myself you see & no-one even looks at it officially! If I feel slack I don't do anything extra but only the bedrooms.

Our new Home Sister (Sister Harris) is <u>very</u> nice & grt: fun. She saw us having tea in the garden the other day & said "<Just> Has not that child got a bonny fat face"!! Today she said to me "Miss Hewetson I can see you getting fatter every day", "I am so glad there's someone keeping me Company", so you see I'm looking well. I talked to Matron quite a lot at the Tennis on Sat. It was rather funny she was so nice because a few days ago I had to go to her Office & be rowed for something (forgetting to return an Amb. pass) she was very Red Tape-y then! She's the real Army you know.

I wld: love a Counterpane! The Rug is heavy for the Summer & I use it out of doors a lot now. Cld: I have one, it wld: make my room <u>so</u> nice. Also something to cover my coat & skirt w' when hanging up. I'm glad you like the photos. Here they say they're "sweet"! Some like one, some another Miss Allsopp likes the outdoor because it shows more character & other "looks as if you did not talk much" (!) So you see I'm not shy here.

MC 643/16/48

262.   Wednesday 7 pm [*8 May*]

My very dearest Mother,

Father's letter has just arrived & I am very anxious about you. Another of those bad attacks – oh dear what a nuisance – I hate being away w' you ill again. Now someone <u>must</u> tell me all & exactly about you. I am relieved that Aunt E. Green is coming – it will be nice to have her w' you, as I know you must feel very poorly & anxious.

I don't believe I finished my *last* letter I had to do it up in such a hurry & then I missed the early morning post – I expect you thought it was never coming.

Don't bother about those things I asked for there's no hurry for them really.

I am getting my time filled right up & now Tennis has begun life is much more worth living. I'm hoping to play almost every day! I've got white for Sat: & I may borrow a hat if it is very hot!

Next week I'm going to change my halfday, & go w' Miss Allsopp right away as far as we can fr: huts & camps. We do get "out of conceit" with the place & people sometimes. She is very nice & I go out w' her a good lot; we two have tea in the "garden" together every day. Do you know I think I am really quite popular here. Miss Allsop I *really* like & I think she returns it. Miss Tottenham is very nice (she thinks I am "quite-quite" I suppose).

Miss Brown (Hd: Cook) is awfully nice; (Irish you know) so sympathetic (& I think I am quite one of her favourites). She came & sat on my bed & talked for quite a time last night. Miss Martin too is very sweet, & I go out w her fairly often, Pigott, Bates are a wee bit infantile, & pall occasionally!

Now Mother dear get better, & don't think I'm unhappy if ever I grumble in my letters or I'll stop!! Very dear love from Ruth

I go to H.C. at 6.30 tomorrow morning.[408] P.S. I shld: <u>love</u> the gramophone, let me know!

MC 643/16/13

263. Fargo – Monday [*13 May*][409]

My very dearest Mother & Father.

Oh, how time flies – I never seem to get a minute. We've been fearfully busy the last few days but now perhaps there won't be such a rush. Today the Hospital has been inspected by the Matron-in-Chief (of the Army I suppose?) & all our own Huts had to be as perfect as possible.[410] I've been having a regular Spring clean on my own. You'd have laughed if you cld have seen me at 6.30 the last two or three mornings black-leading my stoves & myself into the bargain! (By the way I'm going to send off whatever I've written tonight & the rest tomorrow, it's the only way). Well, today I was told to be ready by 9.30 as she wld: do the Night Hut as soon as she arrived. It really was nice lavatories, cupboards & passages positively shining, also tops & door knobs, & the rooms were better than they'd been for a long time. It had given me a good rush to get done so early. Then – she saw the Night people in the drawing room & as far as I know so far never went in the Hut!!! She went in my baths tho' wh: I only did properly on Saturday. You'll be pleased to hear I spoke to Sister & told her 8 were too many so Silverlock does the others again now (They were a pig sty & the only thing remarked upon – Matron is furious!) The last parcel has arrived & I just had time to put the counter pane on, when about 10 mins: after round came Matron & the Grand Lady! My room looks ever so nice as the Curtains are a dark red just like the bed spread.

I'm getting ever so thrilled about the gramophone. What about records. I'd love the large case & the small one w' dances in if possible – at any

---

408. To celebrate Ascension Day, 9 May in 1918.

409. *Next page to follow* inserted at head of letter, sent in two parts.

410. Matron-in-Chief (Queen Alexandra's Imperial Military Nursing Services): her name was Emma Almey.

rate we want Selections from the Plays. If you send the large case cld: you change the last 2 or 3 records for Messiah ones (I don't want Bubbly selections, Someday I'll make you love me wh: are both in it. Also a few of the Fox Trots might be changed for some songs (Eileen Alannah, Kath: Mavourween & anything else you think. [411]

Tuesday 7.30 am I've just sent off the first page so that you'll know the rest is coming! By the way last week I was paid, & at first I got too much so I went back & told them & we had quite a joke about it (Matron & all the rest of them). In the end I got £5.19.5½ !! £4 Uniform allowance wh: will do for April & May allowance won't it? £1.17.5½ April salary & 2/- Gratuity (because I've signed for at Home or Abroad & therefore belong to the Mobile Force). So now I've got:

£1.19.5½	April Salary
4.0.0	Ap & May allowance
19.5½	March Salary
16.0	In Hand

£7.14.11!!!!

I'm going to do my best to save fr: my actual salary but Laundry is a good lot & there is not time or place to do it oneself.

3.15 p.m Another scrap of time!
The white skirt was quite all right & on Sat: I thoroughly enjoyed myself. I went up as soon as I cld: 5 o' c: I was hailed before I got on the courts, almost, to play in a four wh: was quite a moderately good one – then at once, (as I was retiring to watch a while) I was asked to play in a 4 w' the 2 best M.O's & Matron (who is quite a General to a Private to me!!). We had a jolly good set – she's the best lady here. (I'm thinking I cld: beat her in a single but then of course she's not exactly young!). After that I had tea & then two more sets till 7.30. It is such a change for me to be a celebrity over Tennis & that's really what I am. – I hear people in Mess saying "Oh, Miss H she's very good" etc:!! I really am playing fairly well. It is ever so nice. I'm making lots of new friends<.> *with* Nearly everyone I wait on at dinner I've got some common topic to talk of. Sister Harriss the House S. is awfully sweet – she likes me I think. She laughs at me about my fat face & all the

---

411. *Eileen Alannah*, a song by E S Marble and J R Thomas, recorded by John McCormack in 1913; *Kathleen Mavournween*, an Irish song popular in the American Civil War.

meals I'm forever eating, & now she's asked me to teach her to play tennis! I'm getting to like Miss Allsopp & Miss Brown far the best here. Miss A is ever so nice. We go out for strolls after 9 o'c in the evening to get away fr: the crew of undesirables (I'm fast picking out the only nice ones). (I'm just aching for the gramophone – please don't forget the NEEDLES! They are inside it I think?) Miss Browne is a dear too – she simply spoils me – I get all the nice tit bits, & (w' Miss A) I have to eat them when no-one else is looking – otherwise jealousies & grumblings! However I'm favoured! I went w' her to meet her brother in law's brother the other day, & so I suppose I'll get to know some officers now.

I want cotton socks badly. The blue check & pink will be nice. I'd like brown shoes & stockings but really have no room to keep everything. I hear fr: P about once a week but do send his to you (I'll be very careful of them) & they're much more newsy than mine.

Wednesday 7.30 am
This really is the only way to write letters here. Did you get my Guide letter – I thought perhaps you'd read it out loud. Oh do you know I just love being liked! It is not conceited to know when you are popular *is it?* cos I really think I am! This life is such a change to me, I just enjoy it to the full, & even the boring annoying times I think afterwards are all an experience aren't they?

Half day today, I do hope it is fine. I'll order more of those photos as you're going to have some.

Very much love & please tell me how Mother is really. from Ruth.

MC 643/16/14

264.   Friday. 7.30 a.m.[?*17 May*]

I had a simply lovely afternoon on Wed: Miss Allsopp & I took out tea out & had it on a hayrick – we were out from 2.30 till 8.30, & we thoroughly enjoyed it. Now I've asked if I can change my ½ day permanently to the same as Miss A. This is almost unprecedented & an awful bother to arrange but Sister Harris is very sweet to me, & she says she'll try to arrange it! It wld: make all the difference; at present I've no one to go out with. My watch came back yesterday. Good! also more photos wh: I'll send to you for the Family (Gobagger has one).

I shall soon send back winter clothes in that sack – it is fearfully hot. <I think> I'd love that green-y skirt it wld: be the very thing w' the yellow jersey (I'll return others). Have we still that cream straw hat w' blck: band? One or 2 pr: brown stockings & <strap shoes> 1 pr: brogues that's the best costume for here, as it's always a bit windy. I always go to Ch: at 11 on Sun: & at 6.30 every 2nd. Therefore last Sun: walked to Shrewton in evening. Don't care for Vicar. Our Chaplain quite allright.

Much love from Ruth.

MC 643/16/53

265.   Sunday [?19 May]

My very dearest Mother & Father I got Mother's letter yesterday and today I had one from Philip, that's the 2nd in about 4 days so it was a surprise.[412] Oh that gramophone will be lovely, & I'll manage about the box somehow. I quite thought I put "Don't send too many F.Trots etc" however as I'm having the three cases I don't mind a scrap – as there's sure to be a good selection anyhow. I do hope it'll come soon. It must have been a dreadful bother packing it – oh thank you ever so – I get such a lovely lot of parcels, & as for the letters I just seize them when they arrive, & a day w'out is quite miserable!

It is so hot – we simply melt all day the only time for any proper work is before brkfast – after that it is very hard (especially bath cleaning!) However – Hut Girls have a better time than those in the Kitchen poor things.

Wednesday
The gramophone arrived yesterday (only 4 days!) & we were simply wild w' delight. You shld: have seen us at 5 (as soon as we were off) sitting on grass outside the Hut with it. Miss Allsopp & I stayed there till 7 just revelling in music – & many others were there on & off. This hot weather is rather trying & you want a thorough change whenever possible, that's what we got! I got yr: Monday's card on Tues: evening wh: was good, & now I'm looking forward to the parcel.

I hope to send you some snaps *soon*. I took a lot the other day, some on my camera some on Sister Harris' (she is awfully sweet). I hope they'll come out.

Mother wants to hear about food – well we have for brkfast either – boiled eggs, lovely cold fat bacon, kipper or scrambled egg; with porridge twice a week. Dinner (11.45) more often fish than meat w' potatoes & 2 or 3 times a wk: vegetables (so far turnip tops, cabbage or lately leek). Tea

---

412. Letters 241 and 244, the last two she was to receive.

(wh: I always have outside w' Miss Allsopp, as a sort of "unallowed treat" it is supposed to be in the Mess.) We have lots of bread & jam *cake or bun 2 a week* & Miss Browne gives us lovely cream (like Devonshire) wh: we eat instead of butter. Some luxury!!! It is off the milk wh: is all sterilised now. Supper coffee or cocoa & fish or meat pie, & bread & jam or cheese or treacle. If we wait however we have a much nicer meal after as we finish up all the cold puddings *etc*. I do this twice a week.

Friday 5.45 A.M! Must send this off now. Today I go to Salisbury w' Miss A & Miss Brown. Parcel arrived yesterday lovely – especially lemonade! Will return P's in next letter too early to send it now – awful hurry to catch 6 o 'c: post.

Much love to both Ruth.

MC 643/16/16

266. [?*21 May*][413]

Gram: arrived, played it in garden fr: 5–7! Too lovely for anything!! Letter tomorrow, not finished now. Space betw' pegs for hanging bag 12–14 inches. Lovely weather. Salisbury in mufti on Friday. Dear love fr: Ruth.

MC 643/16/15

267. Fargo Sunday [?*26 May*]

My very dearest Mother & Father

I was grieved when I got Father's letter on Friday evening to hear that Mother was ill again. I do hope Dr Aldred[414] is taking more trouble, & doing some good – if not can't you find someone else? I am glad Aunt E. Green is there (please thank her for P.C; I'll send the book tomorrow – I've no time to use it after all!). But I do wish I were at home or cld: even run over just to see you.

Now I know you'll be wanting to know about me & my clothes & parcels. I was so delighted to get them, & now I'm well set up. The shoes & stockings look too inviting for anything – the cotton frock is sweet,

---

413. Written on back of postcard of Amesbury High Street. Ruth started writing letter 266 on Sunday, looking forward to the gramophone. It arrived on Tuesday and she sent this postcard acknowledging it. On Wednesday she continued the letter she had started on Sunday, but now thanking her parents for the gramophone.
414. See note 349.

<but> skirt jersey & all I wanted. <u>But</u> I look a perfect sight in the hat! However I went to Salisbury & indulged in a dear little biscuit straw (of same sort of shape as my red one) for 7/11. As I don't need the Uniform straw – I shall sell it if I can & so I can afford this. It goes beautifully w' my jersey & skirt.

I will send my thick & dirty clothes home as soon as I can; also some things to be washed. Our Uniform is done so badly that we've all complained to Matron. But it has had a good effect on me – I have brought an iron (1/8!) & yesterday started doing my own caps & sleeves etc: but this all takes time wh: is very precious.

I have got some quite good snaps wh: I will send as soon as I have enough – The demand for them is great, so I'm going to do my own printing to save money & charge 4d or 5d each. Now Father do you think you cld: find my two <u>large</u> printing frames in the wicker cupboard in my room, <& if there is one a developing> <u>No!</u> & send them to me. Sometime too I want another Guide badge as mine is broken (I left 6 in an envelope w' other G things). I see heaps of G G in Salisbury, & on Friday I gave & received a Salute – you've no idea how pleased I felt! I'm going to talk to them if I get an opportunity.

<u>Later</u> Just back from Shrewton Church where I went w Allsopp & Grubb. Typical village Service, drawly choir <u>long</u> hymns & pompous Vicar! I'd like some decent book for Sundays. Something dealing w' Epistle & Gospel perhaps <w' some definite>, or a book on the Creed (dealing w' each clause?) I shall rust if I don't have something!
Must stop to catch post

Much love from Ruth

<u>photo</u>
= me & Bowen (now left) w'our Kitchen in background
Please return.

MC 643/16/51

268. Fargo Tuesday [*?28 May, morning*]

My very dearest Mother,

I was so grieved to hear from Father yesterday about you – I was beginning to hope you were just getting better fr: the last attack, & now you've had another. I wish I were at home, even tho' I know I can't do much to help. I long for the post & for news I suppose it is a good thing that they have at last decided what causes all that awful pain – that Dr B-F must be feeling jolly small.[415] It _is_ a good thing Aunt E.G is with you – she'll be such a tremendous help I know.

Tell Father just a p.c to me if he is very busy – as long as I have something. I'll be writing to P. today, & I wrote on Sat: so he'll get a nice lot of letters.

I am very well – I enjoy my "tub" at 5.45 every morning – & the work is getting more interesting as I get better at it. I must go to it now.

With very dear love, & I'm longing to hear good news of you Ruth.

_MC 643/16/55_

269.   Tuesday [_?28 May, evening_]

My dearest Mother

I'm just delighted at your lovely long letter tho' I rather suspect you tired your self by writing it?!
Now I'm just going to tell you tons –
Yr: questions first
1) I have no deck chair _but_ free use of Miss Tottenhams (personally I prefer my rug) so _don't_ send one.
2) The Daily Mail & Bystander (Weekly) is in our sitting room but I wld: rather like the E.D.P.[416]
3) Yes, I'll send washing home but there won't be v. much. I only wear mufti on ½ days & for tennis.
4) We go about in indoor uniform to the Post, Canteen or Tennis Courts or anywhere near (caps & aprons).
5). I went to Salisbury in Uniform Coat & Skirt & Cap (wh: everyone says suits me so well).
6). Of course our 11.45 meal is a real good dinner – twice a week _soup_ meat & pudding – (meat or fish you see) Always 2 helps of pudding. Wh: are excellent – milk, fruit & suet!!
7). Everyone has 7oz marg: per week dealt out on Tuesdays – I rarely use all mine especially now we have marmalade for brkfast. (_&_ cream for tea!)
8). I have 4 baths to do. I find them the nicest part of my work, & none too heavy! I do them w' Monkey Brand & I love them when they're clean!! I don't need to do them every day. "Every other" does.

---

415. Dr F W Burton-Fanning (1863–1937), consultant at the Norfolk and Norwich Hospital: a believer in 'fresh-air' treatment for tuberculosis, he established sanatoria on the Norfolk coast.

416. _Eastern Daily Press_, then – and now – the leading daily newspaper for Norfolk and East Anglia.

9). When "off" there are 2 or 3 nice wee woods near by, & often I just sit outside the Hut on the grass – it is quite shady.

10). We all lend each other bks: If I felt it wld: be worth it I'd join Boots Library in Salisbury but I can always borrow.

11). 10 mins: before yr: letter came we were watching Miss Brown cook asparagus for Matron & envying it. If you sent some so that I got it for a Friday – I have my supper in my room then & Miss Allsopp & I wld: enjoy it together – oh lovely!!

About yr: plans for future – I believe I might be able to transfer – in fact I've been wondering w' Miss A. whether we cld: not go to Italy together after 6 months (!!) but I'll find out. I know there's lots to do at <u>home</u>, but do you know, I have now tasted other atmospheres, & I do <u>not</u> want to go to <u>College</u>! Perhaps it is because I'm loving this sort of life at present or why it is I don't know, but my outlook on life seems different at any rate <at present> now I <shld> I don't think I cld: go & read & learn & do Essays & play hockey! <u>I am changeable are not I?!</u>

I do often wonder what's going to happen in the future but somehow I'm more content to live day by day than I ever was before. As for the superiority of other W. Works over this well all I can say is I hear that before G.S.M.'s came here they had maids & everything went wrong – place filthy, cooking bad, stealing etc:. They all say how much decent girls are needed here *& in all Hospitals*. Of course it does not use our education exactly except that that comes in when it comes to keeping yourself happy, busy & contented (wh: I find quite easy tho' others, especially the servant type, grumble a lot).

Matron has been splendid lately spending all her spare time over our Games Club (run by Mess Friends) we have Tennis, Clock Golf & Croquet. On Sats: we invite the Officers & then get quite good Tennis.

Tomorrow starts a series of weekly Tournaments to be held on Wednesdays. (I hope to win many!).

We can go up anytime & play – it is a shame more don't support it. Miss B, & Miss A. & I are meaning to go every Sat: (we're off from 4.30–7.30 so it is nice & cool) but very few of the Sisters play more than patball. However 1 or 2 of the M.O's <u>are</u> good.

I am grt: friends w' Miss Allsopp (however after Aug: she <u>hopes</u> got a Transfer near to London & then abroad perhaps Italy) we go out together every day practically. ½ day together on Fri's; evening stroll always when work is done, <u>or</u> gramophone. Ch: on Suns: together. W'out her I shall not <u>be <u>so</u></u> happy here but my 6 months ends in Sept.

I'd love you to be able to see the place if you're strong enough to come down. I may have a Visitor for 2 or 3 days (female) living in the Sisters Quarters – meals in the Mess & everything. How wld: that do – you'd see me really at work then – oh lovely eh?

I'm now quite accustomed to early rising & wake w'out being called – Soon I have a whole day & I'm looking forward to a brkfast in bed, as I missed last month's you know. So I am quite due (7 weeks w'out one!).

Don't think I've written this on purpose to cheer you up. I have not – only I don't think I've told you enough about our <u>daily</u> life here – it is not all bliss certainly but the experience of getting on w' others – that's what I call Life! AND I DO GET ON WITH THEM ALL! Probably I'll get on much better w' village work etc: after this what d'you think I'll think over all your suggestions what about a Hospital near home I'd thought of that already – Oh if I cld: have Wrox: Guides as well as my own – I love to hear how splendidly mine are doing – they are worth a lot of trouble I know. It is only that I don't know yet relish Norfolk dumplings again but after 6 months have gone I'll be wanting them perhaps. Other people <u>are</u> so different. What a muddy talk! Do you understand it all. I'm going to Tennis w' Miss Allsopp now – more later.

<u>Wed: morn: early 7.30.</u>
I'll finish this & send it now.

you know I've never mixed w' anything but Norfolkers since I was 10, & it is such a joy to me to find other different types (altho' lots of them are pretty bad). I believe absolute change of people will give me a sort of "filip" up in my outlook on life. It <u>is</u> so interesting. I love people! (even the annoying ones)! By the way I may try to change work & get into the Mess soon – I'm not sure tho!

Yes I hear fr: A. fairly regularly she's just going in for Schol: again, <u>if</u> she fails it may mean War Work but what???

Tell the Guides they none of them have written to me please Father!

Dearest love from Ruth.

MC 643/16/5

270.   Fargo Military Hospital Salisbury Plain Monday [*2 June*]

My dearest Mother

I've just had a letter from Father saying you are doing satisfactorily – oh I've been longing for news & I was so delighted when this came.

I had rather a lonely weekend but I'm cheered up again now. On Sunday I was dumpy (my dumps are <not> very few & far between but I know you like to know when I have them). On Saturday I had nice Tennis, & I wore my blue muslin (which looked sweet)! It had arrived the day before in a lovely bundle fr: home w' jam, asparagus & (oh joy) clean corsets! & lots of other useful things.

On Friday Miss Allsopp heard that her brother had been killed – a wire came while she was out & I undertook to give it to her but was relieved when Sister Harris came in first, so she cld: break the news.[417] She got two days, & so was away for Sat: & Sunday. I missed her, as I do most things with her now. I biked to Shrewton in the evening but the Service is not particularly inspiring. Why can't clergy preach practical Sermons – I've not heard one since I left home.

We're going to have a spell of wet weather now I suppose – well it must be badly needed.

I'm awfully anxious for news of Philip Father'll let me know as soon as you hear won't he?

Tuesday
It has been a lovely hot day again today & I'm enjoying my free time – halfday. I am liking reading a nice book again now either on my bed or in the garden. I've not read much *here* until lately but I'm beginning to find I want it – it rests & satisfies one; but of course there's very little time – what w' letters, mending etc & going out.

Tomorrow there's a Tennis Tournament wh: I hope to play in; it is Ladies Doubles so not very exciting – but anything for a change here!

By the way we have quite a good library.

Now what d'you think of this – when Miss Allsopp goes the Assis: Cook wants to go in to the Mess & so her place will be vacant. Miss Browne is willing to have ME(!) as 2nd in the Kitchen – I told her I knew nothing, but she says she'll teach me. Now wld: not it be lovely & such good experience. You see Miss B likes me & I'm very fond of her, she is a very good Cook; I want to get out of the Huts; & the Kitchen is far the best place in the Winter – also Hut work is very lonely & Kitchen is very sociable. I shld: feel then too that I was learning something really useful as well as working – what d'you think. Of course it is only a plan & has to pass House Sister & Matron's approval.

Pay day again yesterday – I've plenty so keep June & July's allowance for underclothes bill!

---

417. Jerome Boileau Allsopp, born West Lavington Wilts,1879, served in South African War; killed in action serving with South Lancashire Regt in France 27 May 1918; he was 38 years old. He left a widow, Gertrude, living in Lavington.

Now I'm going to have a lovely time Miss Allsopp has lent me the Times; what a treat.

Goodnight very dear love fr: Ruth.

MC 643/16/26

271. Fargo Military Hospital Salisbury Plain <u>Thursday</u> [*?6 June*]

My dearest Father

I got your <u>very</u> welcome letter yesterday, also a short one from Mother wh: was a great surprise. I was interested to hear about the farmyard – it is getting huge – I shan't know the place when I come home in September. I do hope you're better now – what a horrid time those old teeth seem to have given you – just when Mother was ill too. I am longing for news of Philip – we've not been so long w'out any before have we. The War news is awful is not it – I shld: think Gobagger is feeling very thankful she's moved, as Dover will be none too nice a place if the G's get Paris & thence Calais, will it?[418]

I expect you will see my last letter to Mother – what do you think of me becoming a Cook – it is just the sort of experience I want.

The Tournament we were going to have yesterday never came off as enough people did not enter. They are so slack – still I think most of them thought they were too bad to play in Tourn: (& so they are really!)

I am sending home that basket affair tomorrow – probably I will put full directions inside it for Cook.

Do you think either you or Aunt E.G cld: find me my paint box (I long to do some sketching if possible). It is small, & may be in a yellow card-board cover or in a black case I made for it – it is inside my wicker work cupboard.

We go in very much the same old way here day after day – the part of living wh: is really Life is the getting to know other people – all the individual characters, especially their good points I think.

The asparagus was <u>lovely</u> – I've not enjoyed anything so much for a long time. Miss Allsopp – Sister Harris & I eat it between us.

<u>Friday.</u> I must stop this now & post it.
Just got another letter from Mother & Cook too (does that mean another parcel – hurrah!? Mine goes off tomorrow it's ready.

Much love from Ruth.

MC 643/16/54

---

418. German advances seemed to open the way to Paris in the first days of June 1918: the American 2nd Division played an important role in halting the advance.

272.   Fargo Military Hospital, Salisbury Plain, [?*10 June*]

<u>Monday afternoon</u>
My very dearest Mother,

I got your welcome parcel on Sat: & as I had no clean blouse for Tennis that evening you imagine how pleased I was to find that nice pretty one; also to get a letter from <u>you</u>.

I expect you'll have got my lovely basket load by now? & Oh I've found lots more to send since then – it is no use keeping winter things here, & I left out such a lot. I shall keep the red hat I think.

Tomorrow is my whole day & I am greatly looking forward to the rest in bed – then perhaps I'll take my dinner & a book up to the little wood near by. The March's have asked me to Tennis in the afternoon wh: is nice – they remembered it was my "day off".

You know how pleased I was that I'd got my ½ day w' Miss Allsopp – well evidently there's been jealousy, grumbling etc: about it, *& other things* overheard, for on Sat: Sister Harris sent for me, & explained this to me saying in future there would be no more privileges of that sort. She was awfully nice & said "I am very annoyed at this spirit – <u>you</u> are not one of the offenders. I am so sorry Miss H. I wanted you to have Friday & I did my best to give it to you". Of course I said I knew she had & it was awfully nice of her – but now I have to have Tuesday as usual. However if the March's start asking me to Tennis I'll find something to do, & we <u>hope</u> to arrange one day together when we can go to Miss A's home – by hook or by crook! Of course it was a disappointment but fortunately we're always "off" together, so it <u>was</u> rather greedy to want ½ days too!

I had lovely Tennis on Saturday – 4 sets, 3 against Matron – 2 with 2 nice good M.O's. Capt. James a dear fatherly jolly man (he's 45) who takes quite an interest in me ("I have not played w' little Miss H today" he said "come along") He is going to take me to a nice house near by who throw open their house every Sunday. In the Summer for Tea, Tennis & Supper & in the Winter for Cosy musical evenings. Rather nice it will be, & such a change. The other is younger I think – Mr Fuller – good at Tennis I often play w' him v. Capt James & Matron, & it makes a splendid game. All the MO's here are crocks you know – wounded 2 or 3 times some of them. Those are the only 2 decent ones.

Our Sundays here are very different fr: home ones certainly – you see we have different periods "off" from other days – & this makes a chance of getting into a different atmosphere wh: we really do want occasionally. I always go to 11 o'c Service, & also to H.C at 6.30 every 2nd Sunday – then if

I have the evening off I try & get away. In the afternoon we generally write letters & picnic in the wood near by. This is done alternately you see.

Next Sunday we (4 of us) have the evening & we're going right away fr: Fargo & its prison walls (i.e grey palings & fences!) in a Car (fr: a Garage near by) to some lovely woods 12 or 15 miles away. It will be lovely; we' going to get late Leave (if allowed) & not get back till about 10 – leaving here at 5 or 4.30 if possible. Miss Allsopp Miss Grubb – Pigott & I are going.

Do you know it is funny how many people one meets knows someone you've known or seen before. Miss Browne's grtest friend (almost) is Frances Rowell! They trained together at a Poultry College. Miss B. wrote to her & heard back "Of course I remember Ruth Hewetson – her brother was my 1st love"! She's married just lately. I told Philip.

MC 643/16/46

273. Tuesday [?*11 June*]

In the middle of a <u>lovely</u> day.
Slept till 8.15!
Brkfast: (brought by Bates = lots of cold fat bacon, tea, toast, marmalade, <u>butter</u>! present fr: Miss Martin). Read & played gramophone & had people popping in all time till 11.30
<u>Bath</u>. mufti – brown costume
Now off to lunch in wood
Then Amesbury in white.
Much dear love,
Longing for news, of you. Is the operation tomorrow
I'm thinking of you all the time.
Ruth.

MC 643/16/49

274. Fargo Wednesday [?*12 June*]

My dearest Mother,

I am just longing to know how everything has gone – how I wish I could pay you a flying visit in your Nursing Home[419] & cheer you up by all my gossip & news. Oh – would not it be just too lovely! Won't I talk in September do you know I've been here nearly three months, & I'm sure I must be improving (no, I mean opening out & developing) in many ways;

---

419. At Hill House Road, Norwich, see note 426.

probably I'm degenerating in others too. You did not say anything about what you thought of my veering round in my ideas about College? Oh I am hopelessly at sea now as to the future. What is to happen – I don't know & yet somehow it does not prey on my mind & worry me like it used to. So I just wait.

By the way do you see any change in my writing or is it merely my fancy which makes me think it is more forward & decisive?!

Yesterday I had a lovely day; I had my dinner out in the garden & then sat & read & lazed till 3.30 – then I dressed up in my nice white – had a cup of tea & biked off to the March's; there I had a nice tea & then 5 sets of "ripping hard" tennis (meself playing really well!) on a lovely court w' two men & 2 other girls. I got back here by 8 not a bit too tired & after supper went up to the Courts to play w' Matron, Miss Brown & Sister Harris (absolutely the elect!) We played 2 sets – then bed, after a lovely whole day! When I got home I found yr: most welcome letter & one fr: Amie (I wonder if there is <u>any</u> chance of her coming <u>here</u> if she fails in her Schol?!)

(Oh oh oh why will that dreadful person play Home Sweet Home – it is <u>not</u> exactly for Fargo – where is her sense of humour! I'm roaring with laughter at her!). By the way a lot of new rules & restrictions came out yesterday wh: made us all grumble & say we were in a Convent – but we're recovering now. However don't send <it> me any <u>more</u> mufti we may only wear it now by permission (wh: will probably only be given on ½ days & for Tennis) I'm lucky in having a Uniform coat & skirt. Many have only a big coat. I'd love some more jam – Miss Allsopp & I always have our tea out & alone so we can eat our own things w' comfort.

Today I'm going over to have tea in the Hospital Kitchen w' Mrs Howden (the Cook) She is quite nice (& <u>very</u> much so to me) She is a clergyman's daughter but I think her people must have been of the "strait laced type of religion" as she is <almost> a sort of nothing at present. She says I'm just like what she was once, but tho' she teases me she is <u>not</u> sceptical & I <don't> like her. (She swears too much but so do so many here & I <u>always</u> stop laughing if she does it to me). (Miss Tot once told me that made her do it more – she's awful at times – Miss A & I are thoroughly annoyed about this failing).

Mrs H I like because she's very sort of open – & awfully kind – & I think she respects me for "sticking to my guns" & yet being fun (Now that's a "Mother's confidence").

I like to hear what you & Father are thinking about P. Somehow I'm sort of out of it here & don't exactly piece things together – unless you tell me your thoughts too. He writes me such jolly letters – I had been thinking perhaps he was in dangerous places now but I did not think he'd be as near as you say. Send me news as soon as you can <u>please</u>.

Much dear love fr: Ruth.

MC 643/16/17

275. Sunday 3pm [?*16 June*]

My very dearest Mother,

Another welcome letter from you this morning – how I love them & long for them – but how disappointed I was to hear 'o' of Philip – Oh I know how terribly anxious you must be – I am – & I'm in the same sort of position as you; no one to talk it over with. I ought not to say that really *tho'* – Miss Browne is always asking me every post if I have news & she & Miss A. are both ever so sympathetic about you too. They loved your message wh: I gave to them! (your love you sent). Still they're not "The Fam'ly" are they? I'm glad you got the book – I'm going to get you another as soon as I can. How splendid that you shld: be able to sit up – it is soon for that is not it? Shall I ask Matron if there's any chance of me getting home permanently after my 6 months:- at any rate then I'd know. I'm rather afraid I'll have to do the year – they're getting very strict here now – you see we are quite "Army" not the same as Aux: Hospitals. That's why we're so bothered with rules & regulations.

Sometimes it seems a little bit difficult to understand why we are Guided to certain moves does it not. Because you know <it was> how we asked for Guidance as to what I was to do, & then it seemed as if this work was Sent, & yet now – well I wonder if I'd ever have come away if I'd known how you'd need me – (perhaps after all I was meant to come & so I was not shown?) Now I'm asking for <Help> guidance again as to what I ought to do.

"God moves in a mysterious way" that just came into my head because that's what I've been thinking a lot lately. Do you understand me? Talk to me about it please in your next letter.

Now about my change of work –

There are two alternatives:-

1) <u>Kitchen</u> to work under Miss B, (who is very fond of me – she told me so last night – & I of her) learn <a certain amount of> "mass-cooking (I call it) – (have the cleaning of one large range).

2) Be 3rd in the <u>Mess</u> I prefer Mess Work – but <u>but</u> Miss Tottenham is going to be Head of the Mess – she's already started planning all her alterations

(awfully bad form as Miss Allsopp's nowhere near going yet) & I shall sure to be annoyed by her. We do quite like each other & I wld: not stand being put on by her – <u>but</u> she's very <u>hard</u> & rather nervy.

The thing is I like Mess Work (as now under Miss A) (waiting, cleaning, ante room to clean etc: pantry work) but what about "Tot": also Miss Browne is an absolute dear & "wld: adore to have" me – it <u>is</u> hard work in the Kitchen but Miss Tot: was heard to say "I'm going to make the Mess Girls work *really* hard". I almost think I'd rather slave for Miss B. than for the other. Except that I like Mess work best – then Cooking wld: be more useful after wld not it – So there I'm feeling rather doubtful but must decide during this week I think. What d'you think?

This is a very bad photo, but you can just see it is me – I'll send more soon.

I'm feeding on home made Jam, ginger breads & asparagus! Lovely!!!

My laundry & thick clothes go tomorrow I've not been able to send them before or really needed to. It is a big thing to get to the post for one thing – I wait until really full. Please ask Father for tie-on labels can't get them here. Not worn new skirt yet – too cold lately or wet – looks very nice tho:

Our uniform Laundry is done very well lately so I'm always clean now – also I'm about properly set up in all necessities. I bought two nice pretty thin nighties 7/11 & 9/6 – as I knew I had none quite thin & it is very hot here. Miss B. choose them for me in Salisbury – they're really awfully nice. My hat too is a grt: success!

Lovely tennis yesterday – played a Single w a quite good M.O while <u>all</u> the Staff (Matron etc:) watched! He only won 7–5, & they applauded all the time – Matron kept scoring. (She's very keen on Tennis).

<u>5.30</u> Miss A. & I have just had our tea up in the Tent at the Courts, cream, jam bread, cake & gingerbrds:!!

I think I've practically settled on the Kitchen – we shld: come to blows in the Mess (!) & I'm <u>really</u> fond of Miss Browne.

I am surprised about Mr<s> C-H[420]. I must write to Amie – it must have happened just in her Scholarship week – I suppose it may make a huge change in their lives but I don't exactly know. I wish she could come here! I hope Mrs E. comes to see you soon she is <u>so</u> nice. I ought to write to lots of people but really beyond The Fam'ly & Amie I have no time.

Did you hear Miss Wise had been operated on for appendicitis I wonder

---

420. Mr (or Mrs) Cozens-Hardy, from whom the Eversheds had rented The Plantation, Earlham Road, Norwich, since 1908: see Introduction.

how she is. I never hear any Norwich news, – Xenia & Mary wrote 2 or 3 times but not lately.[421]

I wrote to the 3 Guide Leaders the other day – is not this rather nice of Olive Bell's?!

I also send the last 3 letters of P's wh: I've had. Please keep for me.

Now I ought to go & wash up.

I'm awfully well,

well fed,

sleep well,

healthy life generally I consider, so much fresh air too.

Now Goodbye

With very dear love

from Ruth.

MC 643/16/27

276. Fargo. Tuesday [*18 June*]

My very dearest Mother & Father,

I hardly know what to say – I know how terribly sad you both are, & I long to be with you to talk it over. Oh it is such a long time – I shld have thought they'd have told us sooner – all that time to find out that he was missing – I don't understand. Do you know, I have a very strong presentiment that they have been taken Prisoners somehow I do not & cannot believe any thing worse – can you? [422]

I waited to write till Father's letter came in case it said anything more; I suppose as he was not with the Regiment it made it more difficult to trace him? but surely a small body like that could not fight – they'd just have to surrender?

I asked about Leave at once but Matron said Wait till I heard fr: you. I think they might give it me if you want me – how long I don't know. Pigott is willing to change Leaves with me; hers is due on Friday but I don't know whether they'd allow that or not. *& I hardly like to let her?* <Wire if>

421. For Xenia, see Introduction. Mary is probably Ruth's school friend [Agnes] Mary Glen, daughter of a Scottish-born Presbyterian minister: the family lived at Chester Place in Norwich, very close to the Eversheds. Mary helped Ruth edit the school magazine, in which she recorded the melancholy news of the death of her own brother Alec [David Alexander Glen], Royal Flying Corps, on 29 December 1916; aged nineteen.

422. Philip was missing from 27 May 1918, the telegram officially announcing the fact arriving at Salhouse Vicarage on 16 June.

What do you think – when will Mother be home – cld: I come now instead of Sept:?

<Matron said> Everyone here is awfully kind but then of course we want to be with our family in such occasions, don't we to talk it all out. Will you let me know what you think; & <if you> I can ask accordingly. Only I don't know – everything is so uncertain is not it – we don't know <whether> how long or short time it will be before we hear more.

Sister Harris <was> brought me the wire (by the way she is very anxious about her fiancée, & I think she'd had a fright & thought it was bad news for her) & went off at once to Matron for me – Matron said Wait for the letter – when she asked about Leave. The news came about 4 – I did not go on duty till about 5 but then I thought it wld: be best to stick hard at work & keep at it. Miss Browne has *been* is so nice (also Miss Allsopp) she cheers me up & lets me talk to her whenever I want to.

I want to know just everything you are thinking, & especially how Mother is – don't you yourselves think that our dearest Philip is more likely to be a Prisoner than anything – If so it wld: be just awful if he were wounded as well & yet if not well <as> it may be proved to be a way of answering our prayers for his safety. Some of the Camps are not as bad as others are they? Oh for a talk – you can't write things-

I feel for most things I'd love my Leave now, but it wld: then leave 9 months more on here. <I think I> You say what you think won't you –

I'm thinking of you both & longing to know your thoughts too.

I<'m> suppose it is no use <writing>advertising in the Times – 2 in today "Missing since May 27" will you try?

Very dear love – surely our Prayers may be being answered even now? Ruth.

MC 643/16/18

277.   Friday [?21 June][423]

I do hope you've got my letter by now – I never thought you'd be able to get home so soon – it is splendid. I asked about Leave this morning, & Matron is going to do her best to give me my fortnight so don't bother to write. I have to apply myself you see. I don't know how soon it will be or even if possible as we are one short, & also they have bad flue [sic] down here[424]

---

423. Written on a plain postcard, postmark illegible.
424. The 'Spanish' flu epidemic spread across the world in 1918 and 1919, killing as many people as died in battle during the First World War.

so are very busy but I mean to get it – I want it. Then we'll discuss Future. Why not advertise in Times?[425] I'd like to see letters etc: I will come home. Just going on duty – <No> Letter later

Much dear love Ruth.

MC 643/16/37

278.   Saturday Fargo [?*22 June*]

My very dearest Mother & Father

I just don't know what to do I am so wild w' fury & grief because of this letter business. I cld: not understand your wire because of course I wrote as soon as I got Father's letter on Tuesday evening but I sent it to the Nursing Home never dreaming you'd be home so soon.

I addressed it without a qualm or misgiving to The Nursing Home 1 Mill Hill Road, as I did the one before – I can't think why, that address just came to me as I wrote & I never doubted it being right – now I've been searching for your letter w' the address I find it shld: be Hill House Rd:[426] oh has it got to you yet & whatever are you thinking if not. No letter from me at a time like this – oh how awful. I'm going to try & send this an Express letter. It is just hateful having to write home – I want to talk & I want it more every day. I've applied for Leave & hope to get it very soon – I may have to wait 10 days, as we're short already but be sure I'm coming the very minute I can.

I can't believe the worst about our dear Philip I feel sure he is a Prisoner – otherwise why did we all have that feeling of Assurance when he went out?

Very very dear love from Ruth

I pray that this will reach you on Sunday for I know how miserable you'll be if you don't hear.

MC 643/16/19

---

425. *The Times* carried advertisements from families seeking information on missing men like Philip.

426. Hill House Road and Mill Hill Road are both streets in Norwich so the mistake is understandable: the nursing home was actually in Hill House Road.

279.   Fargo Sunday 2.30 [?*23 June*]

My very dearest Mother & Father.

You will have got my wire & express letter by now, so I'll go straight & tell you any news I have.

First. I went to Matron again and she said of course I could have Leave at once but as Pigott is away & we *are* one short I must wait till she comes back. Then (July 4th) I get my fortnight – thanks to Miss Browne who is going to change with me; I wish it could be sooner but it is evidently impossible. You see there are really 6 more to come before me but as Miss Browne has offered to change I can have the next fortnight. Just at present we're fearfully busy because there's a very bad outbreak of the "flu" on the Plain – it has been in London & is supposed to come fr: Spain. The Hospital is crammed – 2 or 3 new wards opened & today men lying out on the grass waiting for beds! The Nursing Staff have been recalled from Leave etc: & now number over 100 w' only 14 of us – so we are busy especially as the meals are all irregular w' lots of ones & twos always coming in late etc. Some of the Staff have got it now – luckily it only lasts 3 or 4 days, but is quite bad then I gather.

I do want to get home to talk things over – it is impossible in letters but don't think that I'm not always turning over future possibilities in my mind & pondering them well – I had a nice talk w' Matron yesterday she was very nice – what can she have said to Mrs Harker[427] & why ever did she write to her? I am pleased – that must mean my work is satisfactory(?) Sister Hariss [*sic*] has been most awfully sweet & kind to me all this week. She is pleased the wire came thro: her & told me to tell you so (she thought I'd told you not to send to her because of her fiancée but I did not did I). She caught me just after I'd got your 1ˢᵗ letter – when I was very sad & she was so nice; I could never have got on without her & Miss Browne who is just as kind. The best thing for me to do till I can get home is to work as hard as I can I find – but I am terribly worried about you getting no letter fr: me. I got your wire early on Sat: & Sister let me go down immediately after breakfast to answer it – I do hope you got that & the letter soon. I long to see all the letters & to hear every scrap of information or hope you get thro Hugo etc,

427. Margaret Harker (1880–1935) was an important figure in the Norfolk Red Cross, commanding the Blofield section from 1910 and later County Controller. She ran the VAD Auxiliary Hospital at Brundall Hall from October 1914 until it closed two years later. Margaret Harker died in 1935: memorials in stained glass in Blofield and Thorpe St Andrew parish churches include nursing scenes. See Barbara Pilch, *Windows on a Life: Margaret Gordon Harker* (Blofield, Norfolk 2006).

(What a sweet extract you give fr: his letter) are you going to advertise in the Times I've seen several adverts about men "Missing since May 27"? I've got a really strong feeling that our dear Philip is a Prisoner, & I don't believe we shall never meet again as a whole family – somehow that feeling is there & I don't lose it.

I see the Times now – only a day late but that is better than not at all. Miss A & I have got Matron's Maid to bring us hers always & we <u>do</u> enjoy it.

The bread is grtly: improved this week we're employing a baker in Shrewton I believe & supplying him with "Penny" Flour. Also our supply of vegetables & fruit seems very good lately.

I shall get ½ my Fare paid home – also be provided w' sugar, meat & margarine tickets – I have plenty of money w' me. I had a sweet little letter fr: Ida Burton yesterday – so nice.

The posts here have been horribly awkward. The one at 2pm: is about impossible because of work & the next does not go till <u>next</u> morning! I am sending a Wire tomorrow about my Leave on the Reply form wh: only arrived today so I had to pay for yesterday's! Now very very dear love from your Ruth.

MC 643/16/20

280. Fargo Military Hospital Salisbury Plain

Tuesday 8pm.[?*25 June*]

My very dearest Mother & Father.

I don't know whether Matron is writing to you or not or not but she sent word to me through Sister H<arriss> *ariss* about your letter & told me to tell you she was doing her very best about my Leave but she cld: not manage it till July 5 when Pigott returns owing to the excess of work because of "flu" (as I told you); 8 more members of the Staff have been sent for & we think it is only owing to their scarcity that we have not another G.S.M or two. To add to all this one of us has gone Sick & *as* she happens to be my "relief" I am doing double work. I manage very well on the whole & you really wld: be amused to see me how I've "buckled to" yesterday & today! Up at 5.45 start in my own hut at 6.15 – get <it done> most of it finished (all rooms & mats swept, crocks washed & dust) by 7.45(!) besides calling 18 people in the other hut. Huge breakfast; after which finish own hut (passage lavatories etc:) & then go & do the other one & as many of the 8 baths as possible till 11.45. (Bates has been helping with the baths). I like it really but I think the sick one will be back tomorrow. It is a good thing for me to be <u>really</u> busy until I can get home – don't you think so. I shall be busy then too I expect – a fortnight will be a nice long time & we shall be able to discuss everything thoroughly & make our new plans, but I do wish I were with you now Mother dear – there <u>is</u> such lots for me to do I know.

I heard from Amie yesterday – she says they'll be leaving Norwich soon – is not that sad. Also she says this wh: is news to me "Girton & Newnham are going to excuse Entrance exams to Girls who have done 6 mnths: War Work" – I think it is quite right that they should don't you. Amie is going to Girton whether she gets a Schol: or not – an Uncle is going to send her. I have not seen Philip's name in the Casualty list yet, but I saw another Capt: Hewetson[428] – Missing in the Staff: Regt: did you see it? People here say that if he is a Prisoner we shld: not be likely to <u>hear</u> under 6 weeks after the first news of "Missing". The parcel <u>was</u> nice – & such a surprise – I never thought you'd have a minute to think of that sort of thing w' all <your> that this trouble means on you. But the underclothes (especially lovely nightie (?!) are most welcome, & the bread we enjoyed for tea yesterday – but ours is quite nice again now. We had a HUGE photo of the whole staff taken today – I hope we are able to get them for ourselves.

With very, very dear love your very loving Ruth.

MC 643/16/21

281.   Fargo Military Hospital Salisbury Plain

Thursday 6pm [?*27 June*]

My very dearest Mother & Father

Mother's letter has just arrived quoting Captain Loudon[429] oh, how hopeful it sounds, & how splendid to be able to get <u>that</u> much first-hand information. You know I feel sure he is a Prisoner & even tho' that may be very awful yet it is at any rate far better than the worst possibility; & there are Prisons <u>&</u> Prisons even in Germany I suppose. When I told Miss Browne she said at once "Thank God. I knew he was a prisoner". What I do want to know

---

428. Captain John Dixon Hewetson of 8th S Staff Regt. In fact he died of wounds 30 May 1918: he is buried at Terlincthun British Cemetery, Wimille.

429. Loudon could supply first-hand information as he was the officer in command of 'A' Company of the 9th battalion during the German attack on 27 May. He was also a friend, mentioned in several of Philip's letters. He had met Philip's uncle Arthur Langdale-Smith on 28 June: see Introduction.

is how did Capt: Loudon escape – did he tell you? What a sweet letter from "Mrs Jellyfish"[430]. I know she always was fearfully affectionate and I used to like her ever so (except at the time of the Geoffrey episode!). We had some grt: fun with her too – d'you remember how fearfully interested she was in Philip & Mollie? I am as well as anything – this life <u>does</u> suit me. Everyone one remarks on my cheery, fat, brown, healthy etc: looks! The flu epidemic is passing over I think; at any rate none of us have it, so that's alright. Still I suppose the Staff are only just beginning – I believe 4 have it now. We have 4 American Nurses down here temporarily – they seem very nice. I am not really making any plans until I get home. <u>Then</u> we can <u>talk</u> it all over, & that will be the only way to come to any satisfactory decision I think.

I can't imagine Norwich without the Eversheds – <they> won't it make an awful difference – oh will it mean that Amie & I get quite separated. I know I've made "new", & in two cases at least "lasting", friends, but that does not mean she is not still "Amie" to me. What do you & Father think of Cambridge & its "War entries" – <u>I</u> really do not know what I'm meant to be or do – I just love each sort of life I take up (I've only had 2 selections so far, so that's rather a sweeping statement perhaps!) Undoubtedly I have fitted in here better than a good many would, & can't help knowing that I am popular. I know <u>all</u> G.S.M's like me & I have lots of friends among the Nursing Staff – of course I enjoy it to the full! By the way we hear <that tell> that G.S.M's now who join are nearly all of the Servant Type; so we feel glad that our staff here is fairly permanent (altho' of course it is not completely desirable!) I long to tell you all about everything – won't I talk – I'll outdo Father when he came home I expect!

My Fare is paid I believe. I'd <u>like</u> to manage the journey on my own – can't I? I'm capable, nearly 21 & in Uniform – I'm sure the experience in town wld: be good for me only means Lunch & then Tube across. Tell me what you think (Pigott went to Ireland alone!) Uniform makes all the difference you know, & I <u>am</u> capable!!

It may be Friday but Sister said Saturday – it depends when Pigott gets back.

Now will take this to Post <u>across</u> the Plain. Dear love from Ruth.

MC 643/16/22

---

430. Clearly the nickname of a friend of the family, she is also mentioned by Philip: see note 346.

282.   Fargo Military Hospital Salisbury Plain

Sunday 4:15pm [*?30 June*]

My very dearest Mother & Father

Such a lovely lot of letters as I get nowadays & how I love them. Father's letter with the news about Philip came on Friday – I think it is just too splendid to think of that little band <u>led by him</u> fighting all on their own for all that time – and oh I do think it really does sound as if he were a Prisoner.[431]

We can't understand about having to provide such a lot of food – it seems most extraordinary, what a lot it will cost – I was delighted to hear too about Mother – you must be getting on quite well if you can walk or even sit up so soon – must not you.

I am beginning to get ever so excited – I can now say "This time next week" –"! Just fancy a whole fortnight – it really is a lovely time. But Mother dear why say "have good food for a change". <I> Of course I know it will be lovely & homemade & a change but *what I mean to say is* we <u>do</u> have <u>good</u> food here (except for the bread that month, wh: is alright again now). I eat a tremendous lot, as I can always get tit bits from Miss Browne if I want them (& often *even* if I don't)! Shall I be bitten to bits by mosquitoes I wonder I quite miss their "humming" here – but they are well made up for by earwigs wh: simply swarm. Everyone advises me to avoid heavy luggage if possible because of scarcity of porters, & I have been offered a suitcase; <as> so I may bring that leaving everything else packed in my trunk – don't you think so? I shall certainly catch the 3:10 down & perhaps I'd better write to Aunt E[432] – I'll think of it anyhow. I'll find out all about trains from here.

Monday 2 o'c:[433]
I am coming on <u>Friday</u> by the 3:10 or 20. I'll get there early & so be all right. Hurrah!!!

I'm not having my whole day tomorrow but it is being tacked on to my fortnight, so I'm supposed to be back on Friday the 19th. [*July*]

Very dear love from Ruth

This must catch post so in pencil.

MC 643/16/23

---

431. It would appear that the letter from her mother had quoted what Langdale-Smith had written [see Introduction]: probably William then saw or heard from Loudon himself and obtained more details about Philip's last battle.

432. Probably 'Aunt' Ethel Biscoe at Godalming, a convenient place to break a journey between Fargo and Norwich.

433. Added in pencil.

Ruth was on leave at Salhouse for a fortnight 5–19 July

283. Fargo 9.30 pm [*19 July*][434]

Here I am – not a scrap tired – crossed London easily & got tea. Rather bored with my own Company, but lovely blow on Ambulance cheered me up.

Nice new room Hurrah! But <u>all</u> work <*word illegible*> remains the same until S. Harris returns, but that's only 10 days, so I'll <arrange> manage.

<u>Great</u> welcome fr: <u>every</u> one! Miss Allsopp away – her Mother died.[435] Flowers lovely also currants.

Good-night – <u>dearest</u> love

Ruth.

MC 643/16/33

284. <u>Wednesday</u> – <u>Fargo</u> [*24 July*][436]

I'm having a very busy time writing all my birthday letters. On Monday Uncle L 'E sent me 42/- & Amie a most beautiful little writing (attaché) case, all fitted up & initialled!

My room looks ever so nice & is both tidy & cosy. Yesterday, my ½ day I went out for a walk w' Miss Howden then to tea in her Kitchen – then tidied room, wrote letters – Supper in bed w' gram: & book. Nice!

Change of room is a huge success.

Awful letter fr: Mollie wh: I will send on soon. Also <u>most</u> appreciative but absolutely "inactive" one fr: Mrs Raikes.

Ought I to get a proper Mackintosh w' Uncle's £2.2.0? <u>If</u> I stay here I'll need one & probably should anywhere. A Big Black thing I mean!

Sister Harris is supposed to be back on Sunday so we hope to change work early next week. I told S. Hughes I might want transfer but I've not said anything definite as to whereabouts <u>yet</u>.

Please address letters to "Sisters' Quarters. Fargo etc" because there are new Women's Quarters for Ward Maids, & they might go there first otherwise. They are sort of G.S people – but!!!! I. F.[437] might like it. Cake a huge success!

---

434. Written on a plain postcard, postmarked 19 July '18.

435. Harriet Allsopp died 16 July 1918.

436. Written on a plain postcard, postmarked 24 July '18.

437. Probably Ida Farman of Salhouse, born c.1893, daughter of Arthur Farman, thatcher, and his wife Susannah: she may have been thinking of joining the V.A.D.

Very dear love Ruth.

MC 643/16/34

285.   Sunday 7.15pm [?*28 July*]

My very dearest Mother & Father,

You'll have got my hurried P.C & be wanting to know more about the Camb: plan I expect. Well it's nothing at all definite yet but things are beginning to work at any rate in our minds.

<Tuesday> Monday. I'd no time to finish this as there was a great rush at work in the evening & very few people on duty, as is usual every 2nd Sunday. We had such a nice "hymn sing-song" just before bed. Lots of V.A.D's began it – & Miss A & I went & joined in.

We mean to manage this transfer. We've just been round to see the G.S.M Administrator in the Women's Quarters. She is a Mrs MacDonald, not over us (as Matron is) but always ready to give advice & of course knows all our rules & regulations. She is a nice person, really a "lady" (I must call them that, there's no other word!). She says she's almost sure I cld: get a transfer to another Military Hos: & so you see as Miss A is already allowed one we're getting on. But we're determined not to go separately because of the style of G.S.Ms in many places.

We think Camb: because 1) it's near my home. 2) Miss A's sister at Bury S.E's wants her to be near her 3) it's such a change after here 4) I have friends there. But if there are no vacancies & London is possible that wld: be as good wld: not it?

Our programme at present is to wait & see if there are Mil: H's & G.S.M's at Camb: – then to apply for my transfer – tell Dev: H[438]. Miss A. wants to go to Camb: & we want to be kept together, & if it were possible get some Matron to apply for us. But this is all hazy at present.

However in the meanwhile I'm getting on well & most happily here. Sister Harris comes back tonight so we hope to change work very soon. I shall be awfully pleased to see her again. I'm rather tired of the Hut certainly – but on Sat: I was cheered up because Matron came round to inspect & did it much more thoroughly than usual. She told me my baths were "very well kept indeed" & as you remember last time they were the

---

438. Devonshire House, Mayfair, London. Headquarters of the Red Cross: the House was owned by the ninth Duke of Devonshire who allowed the Red Cross to use the ground floor during the war. Devonshire House was sold by the Duke in 1918 and demolished in 1924.

cause of a scolding you'll conclude I've been working at them! Well they did look nice, baths & floors spotless & brasses all shining too. I had 10/ from Aunt Ruth <now> yesterday. I'm thinking of buying Certificates I've got £4.2.0 clear birthday[439] – & you see I came back w' over £2 & have last month's salary untouched & this months to come. By the way I hear we get 24/- per wk: board & lodging when we're on Leave so I'll send you that(!!). Aren't I getting independent in money matters.

This week I've changed my half day & Miss Allsopp & I are planning to go to Salisbury together on Friday by the bus & get Late Leave so that we can have a nice time there. A sort of birthday flare-up for me!

Of course there's sure to be a little delay about my transfer but if I get it by "before the winter" that's what we want is not it? You see they'll have to get someone to replace me first, & now that is always a none too short proceeding.

One of the new members is being sent away again because of ill-health – she (the Xtian Scientist[440]) is an absolute bag of bones w' heart disease & a few other things – how she was ever passed we can't think.

My room is sweet & grtly admired – I've a nice looking glass – cretonne on it – the gramo: stand & wash stand (used as a writing table) it's only drawing pinned on at present, but I've had <u>no</u> time, & it looks nice!

Miss Browne comes back on Friday – I'll be delighted to see her.

We've found a hole in the camera wh: accounts for all trouble I hope – I take it to Salisbury to be mended.

One dear fat motherly old Sister *has* found another name for me – she calls me Cupid because of my "fat jolly face". "More potatoes for me Cupid!"

Many in the night hut call me Topsy! So my names are many.

On Saturday I played tennis 1st with Matron v: Capt James – then Singles w' Capt J, as he is very good & coached me this was excellent practice – I felt very "select" we were the only 3 up there!

Was not this a nice letter from L. Buckley – I've answered it.

D'you think you cld: find out fr: Mrs Jellyfish whether there is a Mil: Hos: at Ipswich or where else wld: be nice Flixstowe or Harwich – tell me. ½ past 4, must go on duty.

Very dear love from

Ruth.

MC 643/16/31

---

439. Ruth was 21 on 21 July 1918.

440. Christian Science, a philosophic system developed by Mary Baker Eddy, includes the view that sickness is an illusion caused by mistaken beliefs.

286.   Wednes: <u>9.30 pm</u> [*31 July*][441]

I am wild w' delight. There is now a Camp of G.S girls who work in the Wards, chiefly working class. I hear today Mrs Macdonald the Administrator wants all sorts of interest for them – she has been told I am a Guide Capt: & is very keen to start them – I must go & see her tomorrow. There are 70 of them & they'll "go under" here unless they have an interest. Senior G.G's wld: be the very thing!

Supposin' she asks me to run them!

S. Harris is back & so altogether I have joie de vivre badly!!

Parcel arrived, many thanks

Dear love

Ruth.

MC 643/16/35

287.   Sunday 2.30pm [*4 Aug.*]

My very dearest Mother & Father.

This is really being a Red Letter Sunday here. I'll tell you all about it. Last night 2 of my V.A.D. friends asked me if I wld: call them early for Ch:, so I got up at 6 & went to 2 or 3 rooms (not my Hut) & woke them – got dressed myself & went w' Miss Martyn & Pigott to such a nice Service – about 20 there we had 2 hymns, & special prayers. Then I went at 11 again – crowded Church, chiefly men, but a good number of us <u>and</u> Matron was there. Sister Hughes was there early too. We had short sermon & special Intercessions I was thinking of you – Father in Wroxham & Mother I knew in her room – this day has never meant so much to us before has it[442] – Surely we must hear something soon, & yet if they say letters are being kept back that makes it just a little more possible that news will come in time.

---

441. Written on a plain postcard, postmarked 1 Aug '18, second postmark Leamington Spa 2 Aug '18 and word 'Norwich' added in pencil.

442. Ruth's letter is undated: the probable reference is to 4 August, the anniversary of the outbreak of war, which was a commemorated as a Day of Remembrance and Prayer. Its importance to the family, and the public as a whole, is shown in the fact that William Hewetson held four services that day in Wroxham church, with 65 people receiving Holy Communion instead of the usual 15–20. The money from the collections was for 'Prisoners of War'. [Wroxham service register, NRO, PD 390/18].

I had such a budget too this morning Mother, Amie, The Magazine[443] & another thing.

Now such a lot has happened this week I hardly know where to begin.

First & foremost Amie's letter – I think it seems <an answer again> a lovely idea I'll quote *roughly* "Mum has induced me to ask you do you think by any chance Mrs Hewetson wld: care to take her & Baby[444] as paying guests at any rate for next term? We are in a dreadful fix no house in or near Norwich & we must leave this – I go to Camb: but Mum wants Baby to finish at N.H.S & she has a certain amount of work there too. We hope you won't think us rude but Mum knew Mrs H. wld probably be glad of a companion". What d'you think of that???

It wld: be in Sept: I suppose. Baby to do endless messages etc, Mrs E. is a dear you know so fond of & interested in <u>both</u> of us. Will you tell her what you think.

2). I'm getting ever such friends with w' the G.S Administrator Mrs MacD: she wanted me to start Guides but I have suggested a social Club, as they're rather old, & I am undertaking 2 evenings a week (w' other people fr: these quarters if I can get them). She has mentioned to Matron the necessity for interest for them to keep them straight, & M. agrees w' her – Mrs M. said she's heard there was a girl who was keen on that sort of work & M. said at once "I shld: think it must be Miss H.! So now we're going to get her to be President!

There will be 70–90 girls there soon! Please give me some ideas. Fancy little me out of all that huge Staff being the one to do this w' Mrs M. Sister Hughes talked to me about it & was ever so interested.

It is lovely having Sister Harris (now Suffolk) back again but poor thing she is awfully sad altho' she keeps up the whole time. He came down for 2 days & then went back to France. She is <u>so</u> nice to me I'm awfully fond of her – I go all her special messages & go & talk to her whenever I get a chance – I think she's really fond of me too – I've seen lots of her presents already.[445]

I am also very fond of S. Hughes (the Asst: Matron) & she must like me because honestly (its not conceit to tell the Fam'ly these things) those two don't treat any other of the G.S M's like they do me. Of course I always talk

443. Probably either the *Church Family Magazine*, which the parents certainly sent to Philip, or the local parish magazine, which contained details of Philip's last battle.
444. 'Baby' is Stephanie Gwen Evershed, Amie's sister, at this time sixteen and a pupil at Norwich High School. Given the closeness of the friendship between Ruth and Amie, that between their mothers appears much more distant.
445. Ethel Mary Harris married William Henry Suffolk in Greenwich on 20 July 1918.

to them & "cheek" them when I get a chance! Now there is this – I hear on all sides that in no other place wld: the G.S people be allowed to associate w' the Nursing Staff probably, so as we are treated so well here, & I certainly find the people I'm really fond of among them – I probably shld: find an awful difference if I went any where else, & as you say the class of GSM is deteriorating – so I must <u>know</u> <u>where</u> I go if I move.

I've made 3 or 4 more real friends since I got back – Miss Tribe the Senior V.A.D I told you about is very nice, & also 2 Asst: Nurses Barber & Evans I seem to get on w' very well. Misses T. & B. are both really nice & E is grt: fun & so good natured – I go & pay calls on them in their rooms after supper sometimes.

8.30. I've been for a walk w' Miss Grubbe across the Plain – It is just lovely – we brought back huge bunches of heather & I've been distributing mine, & in consequence having more conversations w' nice people. You see altho' none of the other G.S.M's make friends outside their co-workers I mean to – it is much better to get a change & I've found <u>many</u> nice girls; I think it is good for one don't you.

Yes I'll send a sub: to G.G's. We're having very little jam at present, in fact none the last 2 days but perhaps it'll come in again soon. I have <u>not</u> that little basket – I think it's in the room into the bathroom. Yes I wrote to Mrs Chitty – day after your letter came. I'm wondering whether I'll take a Postal Course from the Art School – it is very good, I sent a sketch up <from> for a criticism, <u>but</u> it is rather expensive.

Hampstead sounds nice – tell me about it please. On Friday I went to Salisbury w' Mrs Howden (Miss A. went to meet her brother who had leave so did not come). We had a lovely time, she is a dear thing. I did shopping for S. Hughes, S. Harris, several others, myself! Then we had a lovely tea.

Tuesday is my "day-off" I stay in bed, wash my head(?) & then I'm going out to tea w' Mrs Gabbutt. I am delighted its an invitation I've coveted.

The only people who go are Matron, S Hughes, S Harris & Miss Browne so far! I <was in> went to S Harris' room the other day when Mrs G. was there & she said she'd wanted me 2 or 3 times but I'd been away – She's the one who lives in a dear wee hut at Rollestone w' a sweet wee boy – her husband is an Engineer here. I got to know them at Tennis By the way I had real good Tennis yesterday w Matron, MO's & visitors. The next place I want to go to is Mrs Cole's – the Sunday rendezvous I told you of.[446]

---

446. The most likely family is that of Herbert Cole, farmer, and his wife Kate, of New House Farm, Shrewton Road, Chitterne All Saints, but their return in the 1911 census does not include the two boys Ruth refers to in letter 300: perhaps they were nephews or family friends rather than sons.

And about 3 people have already promised to take me so I hope to go soon. Mrs H. is also going to take me to friends of hers.

You'll think this is 'o' but my pleasures & praises but I know you're interested. Of course I have blck moments but I manage to forget them pretty soon – I think if you make up yr: mind to be happy & like people you can, & I always tell people the other way round is just as true especially in a place like this.

Our garden furnished all the flowers for Church today was that not nice? Sweet pea & alyssum.

Now I must stop & write to a few other people

dearest love & tell me what you think about future plans

your very loving Ruth.

MC 643/16/36

288.   Sisters' Quarters, Fargo Military Hospital, Salisbury Plain

My very dearest Mother & Father,

I was glad to get Father's letter this morning – but every time I see one from home I wonder if it is going to contain news of Philip – & then I always see "Still no news". It is a dreadfully long time. If he had been with his regiment we shld: sure to have heard something by now from some of those who were with him *surely*. It must be because they were such a lonely isolated little body that no news gets through – also I suppose there <u>were</u> no survivors except this one Officer – why can't he be of some use I wonder?

I am longing to know what you thought of my Sunday letter & the "Evershed suggestion" I sent a card to Amie to say I'd passed it on to you at once.

Things here are becoming rather interesting & yet complicated just at present. <A> They had a visit from the D.D.M.S etc, sent by Dev: House[447] last week especially to look into G.S.M conditions of life. There's jealousy betw; Mrs MacD's "ward orderlies" & us! (on their side) So yesterday Matron interviewed all her G.S people in the Kitchen. She spoke most awfully nicely to us saying that we were members of the Sisters' Mess & therefore ranked as Officers. This was now the exception & wld: be found in very few Hospitals but she had always done it w' great success & intended to continue it if we wanted to. (of course we said we did). Then she pointed out the new rule about being allowed to associate w' Tommies & said as

447. See note 438.

Members of the Sisters' Mess this wld: <u>not</u> apply to us – of course only while under these conditions. Evidently Matrons decide themselves whether we are to be "privates" or "officers". (She then turned to me – said she'd heard Mrs McD had asked me to help – but <u>as</u> this difficulty of jealousy had arisen there cld: not be any social intercourse betw' us <u>unless</u> we wld: like to be "Tommies" ourselves – of course as we are an "Army Mess" this is absolutely understandable). I don't really mind Mrs M was beginning to show she wanted every minute of my free time – I'd rather devote myself to a few up here (who are already keen).

We're making enquiries about Camb: & so far have heard there are no resident G.S.M's & a girl who used to be here says "they are <u>not</u> of the class you wld: want to be with". It <u>is</u> difficult is not it? Of course several of these are "servant type" (& Matron told Miss Martyn she was going to try & get rid of them & get nicer ones – at least implied it) but there <u>are</u> a good many nice girls.

On Tuesday I had a lovely whole day – I stayed in bed till about 2.30 – read, wrote & talked – there was someone in my room nearly all the time! Then I dressed myself nicely – little blue muslin – blue jersey & the nice red hat & went to tea w' Mrs Gabbutt – she is <u>so</u> nice quite young & I <u>did</u> like her. They have the sweetest little boy, Tony; he's about 3 – just like Bubbles[448], not a bit shy & talks away – we made great friends. He comes up to our Tennis Club on Saturdays so I knew him before. After he had gone to bed (6.30) I came back & after a little time went to the Pictures w' Duchess[449] – we could not stay long as we had to be back by 10. So I had a very successful day. There's an awful lot of bitter feeling among some of the G.S.M's because Miss Browne has had an extra week for sick leave. It is ridiculous – she was absolutely "done up" & now they say of course she always meant to get 3 wks & is a fraud. It is all jealousy really because she's popular w' those in authority (due to her own sporting nature & <goo> never failing cheeriness). As I'm a friend of hers they make a point of saying nasty things in front of me. However I ignore them & I've only flared up once when I told 2 malcontents to "get out of my room if they were going to talk like that" – I wish I had not, it is really wiser not to – but still they knuckled under at once. As a matter of fact they know I profess to be a friend of hers so wld: respect me more I suppose. (If I were not fairly

---

448. The John Everett Millais painting, originally entitled 'A Child's World', became world-famous as 'Bubbles' when it was used in advertising for Pears soap.

449. The staff nickname for the Matron. Twenty-five years later, Emily Martyn recalled, 'She was a jolly soul, wasn't she'. [NRO, MC 643/42/17].

popular – they cld: easily <go> be jealous of me *& some are* because Sister Hughes & Suffolk both take more notice of me than any other G.S.M except Miss B).

I'm going strong w' several friends among the Nursing Staff – especially Miss Tribe (she <wants> suggests me <to take> taking up nursing <u>rather</u> than more G.S.M.ing) but of course not unless I felt drawn that way. I'm gradually learning to typewrite as I go & watch her whenever I like.

<u>9pm</u>. Since I was writing this I've biked to Shrewton w' Miss A & Pigott & we've had our photo taken, p.c. size, outdoor uniform, 7/ the dozen – just for fun!

Also since supper Sister Harrison (another friend of mine – such a nice person) dressed me up in all her full Army Sister Costume & I've been visiting all of my special friends. Sister Suffolk simply died w' laughing at me – I was so "fetching" that they said I was to do it again & be photographed for you! They all spoil me thoroughly. Sister Suffolk calls me "her little Ruth". It <u>is</u> nice to be so sort of "at one & jolly" with so many people – you know it is because I was never popular at School that I so enjoy every bit of appreciation I get now – don't you think so.

Today week I go into the Mess – wh: I suppose I'm looking forward to – I am certainly tired of the Night Hut & Baths.

I wish you could see me now – sitting up in bed in my cosy little room writing this by candlelight surrounded by 5 other cheery friendly people – who don't mind how late I have a candle or how often I turn over! I washed my hair yesterday & dried it in the sun so it's nice now.

We've got some jam again now, but we do run out like that occasionally, so it's good to have some "in stock".

Miss Browne is supposed to come back tomorrow I hope she does – the atmosphere of the Kitchen is too "thundery" w' out her.

The Watch goes beautifully – I've a shield for it now wh: I wear when working.

I've had a certain number of squabbles w' people lately, but we always get over it, & I suppose they're good for me on the whole. I'm getting more "fiery & then done w' it" than I used to be – I'm still very much a creature of moods – one day up – one down – but it is chiefly "up" wh: triumphs.

If I don't stop now I shall never wake up in the morning.

Miss A's transfer is no nearer much to my joy, she's very doubtful if she dare risk another Hosp: now unless she knows its quite all right on good authority.

I enjoyed Father's letter all about Sunday – what a splendid Service at Wrox: Did not you think I had a nice Sun: too?

With very dear love to you both.

Ever your very loving

little Ruth. (Missie, Father)

MC 643/16/30

289. Sisters' Quarters, F.M.H.

Sunday 4pm [*11 Aug.*]

My very dearest Mother & Father,

I was so pleased to see a letter from Mother in the rack this morning especially as I'd had a little note w' those other letters yesterday. The jam arrived yesterday afternoon too – it had spilt a little on the blouse but luckily it is only on the part which is covered by the skirt. No, I don't think either of those letters about other Hospitals sounds very promising – it is a nuisance that after all our care in choosing my work (rejection of WAAC etc) I shld: have landed in something wh: seems none too satisfactory – but still I suppose I shld: meet w' the same difficulty in any Body of Women nowadays. Everything seems very difficult, but I shld: not be surprised if there is a drastic change of some sort here sooner or later – of course to all extents & purposes we go on as usual but I believe Matron is very worried about her GSMs since these others came down. So "we wait & see".

You will be surprised to hear I went to Sister yesterday & resigned my application for the Mess. The reason being that <sinc> while Miss Browne has been away Miss Tot: has been the "ringleader" of an awful lot of bitter feeling about her, & I cld: not help showing my disgust, so – that coupled w' the fact that I am a favourite of S. Hughes & Suffolk (both of whom she hates) has shown me I could not work under her, nor with Grubbe (whom she leads by the little finger). Also since I came back I've loved Hut work & the freedom one gets, and as my Hut has been praised lately I'm very keen about it & don't much want to leave it.

Monday I've been fearfully busy today – real hard work from 5.50 till 11.30! Preparing for a detailed inspection of my Hut & equipment at 8.30 tomorrow morning by Matron; & also doing ½ Bates' work, as she's gone for her fortnight. So now I'm "flopping" on my bed for the afternoon as it is so fearfully hot & I've not a lot of energy left.

Sister S. was v. nice about changing work again & said she quite knew what I meant & thought it far wiser of me.

Did you write to Mrs Evershed – I am sorry you don't think it wld: work.

I am so sleepy that I think I'd better not write any more, or else I'll be too tired tonight for work. I shall be thinking of you both & dear Philip on Wednesday.[450] Yes I'll write to Hugo as you suggest.

Dearest love from Ruth

This hot weather is lovely but it is not <u>good</u> for hard work – very many people get the "grumps" badly, so it is a bit of an effort to keep cheery always – still we do our best & I manage better than most!

MC 643/16/56

290. I've just found these so I'll send them for you to see.[451] The others ought to be here tomorrow I hope. No time for more.

How lovely about Philip.

Love Ruth.

MC 643/16/60

291. Fargo Friday [*16 Aug.*][452]

Your letter came yesterday evening & I seized it greedily as you can imagine. What an awful time that card took to come. How soon is there a chance of an exchange & will he have to go straight to a Hospital – I suppose he may be in one for ages – (is not Roehampton[453] the place)? We'd all want to be near him then. Yes, I went to S.Hughes last night (Matron is away for 3 weeks); she says I <'ve a> can make a strong case – but she's afraid I'm bound to give a month's notice! I suppose by law I am. She is going to find out all possibilities for me & let me know as soon as she can, so that's <u>one</u> step as <u>my</u> authorities are nice. I hope for more news soon. Can I have a clean u-gown please?! No more jam necessary. Linen follows at earliest possibility. Squabbles die down, & *real nice* friends are going strong – lovely weather. I'm in a real joie de v. humour! Very dear love to both. Ruth

---

450. The reference is to Philip's birthday, Wednesday 14 August (Ruth could not know that her brother had died in captivity some weeks earlier: it was another two months before his death was revealed to the family).

451. Two (now faded) photographs enclosed.

452. Written on a plain postcard, postmarked 17 Aug. '18.

453. Queen Mary's Convalescent Auxiliary Hospital in Roehampton House specialised in the fitting of artificial limbs, and in training men to use them.

I can do no more till I hear fr: Dev: H thro' S.Hughes I suppose. Anyhow she's going to work it for me.

MC 643/16/24

292.   Fargo, Monday [*19 Aug.*]

My very dearest Mother & Father

My Sunday letter this week will be a day late I'm afraid. Yesterday I got Father's, & was most interested in all the different plans. I had not thought before that Philip was likely to be <u>kept</u> in Switzerland[454] – I thought it was only a sort of junction? That card must have been delayed a terrible long time before it was posted – why just think, we might have got it weeks ago. Surely very soon we ought to hear from him again with his address on. Is not it awful not being able to write off at once to him. Father tells me how nice everyone is – oh, I know they will be – & what a tremendous difference the news of him being alive has made on our outlook on life – has not it – When I saw the telegram for me I hardly dare open it for one second as I was with others but then – I sent a wire to you straight off; everyone here has been genuinely nice too. Miss B told me she's prayed for him everyday. She is a dear, so interested in my Fam'ly; & my <u>best</u> friend here – at least she's always ready to help me & give me advice over anything. She wept when I told her I was going to resign. I've heard no more about that yet, but S. Hughes promised she'd find out for me – of course it is sure to be a bit of bother. However in the meanwhile I'm going on as usual i.e enjoying Life. Father says "don't bother about yr: letter" why shld: I? You'll let me know exactly what you're thinking & I'll act upon it. What is Southport[455] like residential? Oh I do hope we get a move. Is Gobagger w' you yet? Please give her my love & tell her I'm a horrid niece not to write to her more often. But do you know, as it is I don't go out enough I'm sure, for walks I mean – it's awful I never have time for anything. We are 3 short now – 2 on leave 1 sick – it makes a fearful lot of extra work. I'm doing *an* extra hut as well as my own & the baths! but I've never felt fitter, & altho' lots of people last week suffered fr: the food I'm perfectly all right. My appetite is huge! I work <u>hard</u>,

---

454. By international agreement, wounded or sick prisoners of war from all countries might be interned in Switzerland: by the end of the war, nearly 68,000 men had been brought there. These men were not at liberty to leave until the war was over: however, after 1917, men who were considered too badly wounded to rejoin the forces might be repatriated.

455. Lancashire seaside resort: William Hewetson may have been thinking of taking up a clerical vacancy there.

but even if dead tired by night I'm never tired when I start again next day. I've just been weighed & I weigh 10 stone 2lbs!! This is an increase of more than 1½ stone in a year – yet I feel most well! Is not it awful? I'm no fatter than when I was on leave so I suppose it's bone & muscle? This life & work evidently suits me. Yesterday I went, at last, w' Miss B. to Mrs Cole's. We got off early 3.30 & biked right over the Plain for about 4 miles to a lovely big old fashioned farm house w' lovely garden. Put up our bikes, walked straight in, upstairs, took off hats etc: & down to tea, w' about 20 in all – half us – half Officer's fr: Camps around!

Most hearty welcome fr: Mrs C to me – so good & kind. After tea – 3 lovely sets of real good tennis on a beautiful court. Then sat about, walked round garden. One very nice Engineer Officer I played w' I liked quite.

At about 8:15 had supper – home cured ham, salad etc: etc:--!! Then biked home in the moonlight over the Plain – simply wonderful – all the Camp lights shining all round, aeroplanes buzzing overhead. Back by 10 (late leave). The Cole's have done that for 2 or 3 years now every Sunday – absolutely open house – is it not good of them

Mr & Mrs & 2 nice boys, about 15 & 16. She asked me all about myself & Fam'ly, <& was> so as "to remember you next time you come". I shall go again whenever I can. I went & played tennis a good lot here last week in the evenings chiefly w' S. Harris, Miss Tribe & someone or other else. Then on Sat: I always get almost a ½ day because I go up to the Courts in the afternoon when on duty & help get the tea. S. Harris, Miss B & S. Hughes are always there S. Hughes is very nice. They all are most awfully nice to me. S. Hughes says "I'm not at all fond of Miss Hewetson you know" – well now why shld: the Assistant Matron be fond of the Housemaid *I ask you?!* <Yet she>. Today I'm simply bubbling over w' joy – I very often am here – I love Fargo – & lots of the people & the Plain.

One poor girl (Evans, who I like very much) has just lost her fiancée – he was S. Harris' husband's grt: friend – so she too feels it v. much. It must be awful for her – they only had a week's honeymoon & then he went back. She is most awfully brave because she's not like so many people nowadays – she <is> is one of those <girls> who love w' their whole being – & to have to come back to this work & have all the anxiety must be dreadful for her I think. Yet she's nearly always cheery. Of course I am more fortunate (I consider) than lots of the G.S.M's (they might not say so) because I'm fond of & therefore get on w' S. Harris, Hughes etc: but they all could if they liked.

Matron is away for 3 weeks so S Hughes "carries on". I'm very rich – £3.19.5 this month. This includes board & lodging for my leave (<24/->

22/- per week) so shld: I sent you back one of my cheques (Uncle L 'E's £2.2.0 its crossed & enclosed so I'd have to register it wld: not I?) Next month we get 30/- for our Overcoats, also I'm due for another £1 towards Uniform & we've all our Laundry to be paid back sometime! Miss Allsopp is still here – transferring & getting away together are rather lengthy jobs so it is well to set to work sometime before needed I think. Miss B & I have <applied> invented "We are Seven"[456] as a Title for the really nice people here i.e S.Hughes, S. Harris, Miss Tribe, Mrs Howden, Miss Allsopp, Miss Browne & myself! Of course there are lots of others very nice but this is our "inner circle"; at least, in the opinion of "Rita & Ruth". Pigott is very nice at present – & I like lots of the V.A.D's & nursing staff ever so too.

Miss Tot: is fast becoming a joke, she goes so far in her bitter sayings that no one minds them now – in fact we save them up merely as jokes – she is an extraordinary woman. She not worry me tho' – we never even speak to each other.

You said you liked the gossip Mother so there – I've given it you. Could you in my next bundle of linen let me have one of those photos of me taken at Coe ("in mufti") I'd love to show it to people here? <Also I sen> I'll send off dirty clo's tomorrow, my ½ day. I've got the 5/- P.O for the Guides & will send it to Amie. – how are they I wonder – quite capable I am sure.
Now it is time to work

With very dear love to you both

Ruth.

                                                                        MC 643/16/25

293.   Tuesday. [*?20 Aug.*]

Please I'm longing for a night gown – I've only the two you see.

Today we are 4 G S M's short out of <15> 14 altogether!

Two from the Kitchen sick. So on my own I worked in the Kitchen this afternoon, & then Sister said "Miss H. it is your half day" & caught me in the act! Also Sister Hughes came in & Miss B "split on" me. However they were both awfully nice & Sister H insists on making it up to me later altho' I told her I don't want her to. Still we had a very strenuous day. I got up early did my hut before brkfast & then after I helped in Kitchen & scullery. Poor Miss B. is simply worked to death – 2 in that huge Kitchen & scullery is awful.

---

456. The title of a poem by William Wordsworth, first published in 1798.

It is a heavenly evening so I'm going out for a blow – at any rate there's always a breeze on the Plain – wh: is lovely.

Dear love

from Ruth.

MC 643/16/50

294.   Sister's Quarters Fargo Sunday 2.30 [?*25 Aug.*]

My very dearest Mother & Father,

It is a pouring wet afternoon & I am off duty till 5, so I've tucked myself up on my bed in my nice rug: & my "bunk" looks so cheery & comfy with all the cretonne everywhere, & flowers fr: our garden on dressing & writing tables (the latter is really a washstand!).

Mother's & Father's letters both <u>full</u> of interest (even tho' M. did say she had no news!) How nice to have P's Brig: etc at Cromer & for F. to see them – Surely it is disgraceful that 100 men shld: be sent to a gap of 3 miles?!!?[457]

I <u>am</u> glad people are all being so nice. It shows that they're really fond of you all the time but it takes a <u>great</u> deal to make a Norfolk-er show his feelings – don't you think?

Now about myself! – I'm sending a letter to Matron (& thence to Dev: H) asking to be allowed to be released when necessary at <u>very</u> short notice. I am explaining all circumstances – It is written & pronounced an "excellent letter" by Miss A. & Miss B. – so do you think that's the thing to do – it is what Mother suggests is not it.

Tomorrow I start work in the Kitchen! Now is not that a coincidence; I never mentioned that I'd like it to anyone & yesterday S. Harris told me she wanted me to do it! Miss B. is pleased, I'm delighted! It may be because I turned to when the others were ill – one of them goes to my Hut – Oh I shall like it. I'm to be 3rd in there – so no ranges – a certain amount of cleaning, & cooking! You see Sister knows I'm fond of Miss B. & she of me.

How do you like the photos of me – don't I look huge – S.Hughes said "you're looking very worried about your family of 12 Miss H" they all tease me dreadfully about being so fat! Sister Hughes & S. Harris both seem to get nicer to me every day – of course I'm exceptionally fortunate. S. Hughes is really a very clever woman *& one* of the most amusing people I've ever met.

---

457. The Brigade was at Cromer in late-August: William Hewetson visited them, but missed seeing Colonel Craigie-Halkett. See Introduction.

There is very bad epidemic of dysentery in the Hospital – in fact all leave for the Staff has just been stopped. Men are coming in fast (48 last night!) & there have been several deaths.

Some of us have had slight attacks – of course not the same I suppose. I was rather wretched all Friday & in the evening Miss B. reported me & Miss Martyn (who was much worse). Sister Hughes came & talked to me & was awfully nice – we were both dosed drastically & now I'm thoroughly cured. Of course I was tired & shaky yesterday but I got off very lightly – Miss M. was ill for 3 days or more. I only one. They're very careful you see & S. Hughes gave us all sorts of things that night & the Night Sister came in to look after us. Now please don't worry about me – I am quite better now only I knew you wld: not be pleased if I did not tell you. Of course yesterday I looked quite washed out & tired but today I'm looking & feeling quite fit again.

I hope to go to the Coles again next Sunday – I'm so glad it is wet today as it's my short Sunday, there's more chance of fine weather next week. Mrs C. must be somewhere about 40 I shld think – a fearfully capable farmer's wife (she showed us lovely home made cheeses & all sorts of things) & also such a hostess.

Hurrah, no more old baths to clean! And I was complimented on them again yesterday, this time by Sister Hughes (who found me out when they were not – you remember) – she said they were beautiful! – there now – at any rate I've left Huts with a good name.

As leave is stopped we shall soon be fearfully busy w' a full Staff, especially if they start recalling those already gone – I shld: almost think Matron will have to come back.

The heather round here is gorgeous I'll try & send you some sooner or later.

I took some quite good photos this week, & oh joy! they came out, so the man in Salisbury did something effective to the camera – when they're printed I'll send you them. Did I leave all my Fargo ones behind me – if you've seen them cld: you send them please!

I think I must have sent all my stockings home – I'm extraordinarily short!

Very dear love

From Ruth.

MC 643/16/28

295. <u>Thursday 9.30pm</u> [*29 Aug.*][458]

Yes I am quite all right now today I've not been in the least un-happy after my meals – my attack really only lasted 2 days – I'll tell you all in my next letter Mother. The epidemic is raging <u>furiously</u> in the Hospital. Men in 20s & 30s from all over the Plain. 6 Staff borrowed fr: other other Hospitals. All working w'out time off & late on into the night – new wards opened. Said to be <u>very</u> bad – I don't know the cause!

Added to this we have 200 German Wounded – awful cases – very young – only captured on the 23rd only allowed to be nursed by men – it seems very wrong to send here.[459]

My ½ day, Went to <u>Good</u> Lecture by Lord Denbigh[460] (War Aims) & then Theatre "Raffles" at Bulford[461] – a 5 mile ride.

Dear love <u>Ruth</u>.

MC 643/16/38

296. Fargo Monday 6pm [?*2 Sept.*]

My very dearest Mother & Father,

My Sunday letter is a day late again because yesterday we went to Mrs Coles' <a> and also I have no slack afternoons on duty now. Mother's letter arrived this morning – most welcome & newsy – also stockings & other clean clothes wh: I seem to be exhausting again! I have all ready to hand (ie box & packing) for the gramo: How splendid that M. shld: be able to get into Nor: & back now!

I've such tons to tell you & time is so short that I'd better forge ahead (I wish we cld: write & read shorthand don't you?).

My new work is very nice – absolutely different, & honestly I don't consider anyone really works till they get in the Kitchen. It is not so much <u>hard</u> but <u>continuous</u> work. My duties as 3rd are very varied – I am entirely responsible for the boiler (in wh: now the milk is sterilised) must be lit &

458. Written on a plain postcard, postmarked 30 Aug. '18.

459. The Germans were now in retreat all along the Western Front: on 23 August a general advance was ordered, the Allies advancing across the 1916 battlefields of the Somme.

460. Rudolph Feilding, 9th Earl of Denbigh (1859–1939), a campaigner for full engagement in the war, gave many public meetings and spoke in the House of Lords.

461. *Raffles; the Amateur Cracksman*, a play by E. W. Hornung (1866–1921), first performed in 1906, filmed in 1917: possibly Ruth saw the film version at the Theatre.

clean by 6.30 – & then kept up all day, – then also I have charge of 2 larders & Sister's store room – passages betw' these too – they get filthy w' meat & fish & all food – those are regular undistributed duties then I do anything to help in the Kitchen (all vegs: except potatoes) any fruit cutting – salad etc. On Sunday we took 3½ hrs: to cut beans for 116 staff for midday!! today I did apples for puddings & then 4(!) cucumbers for salads. If "on" in afternoon (2 a week I am alone) there's often porridge – all kettles for lots of teas – milk & water to sterilize & things to prepare for supper. On Friday I had to <u>do</u> the Scullery alone (other girls day off) – that day I am quite proud of because I knew 'o' about it = Boiler lit by 6.30 wash up 1st Breakfast (plates & dishes – herrings for 50 people!), own brkfast – wash & dry up for 2nd brkfast (same thing). Now 8.30 – from then till 11.30 – scrub potatoes for 116 Staff! – scour 5 large milk buckets – clean pots & pans from all previous cooking (their name = Legion!) Afternoon off – evening more washing up & potatoes. That day of course an exception – I see plenty of the cooking & shall learn a good deal. Miss B. I believe really finds me useful, at least she tells everyone so. I must say my hands are <u>not</u> improving but at least they are "honourable scars"!

The epidemic is not much better – all the Staff are recalled & even Matron has curtailed her holiday – They say it is awful – so violent I shld: think perhaps 6 or 10 deaths – all the Staff look dead tired – they're working often with no "off duty" time – then of course all G. Prisoners must add to M.O.'s work hugely – now some Sisters are allowed in for dressings – there are 200 of them some <u>aw</u>fully bad (one w' both legs off I heard – another 'o' arms) D'you know when I came the Staff = 67 now it is 116, & there is no increase in G.S.M's, is not extr'ordinary?

I go out as much as possible in off time now, as I am not in & out when on duty. I am quite well now by the way!

Yesterday I cld: not get to Church for the 1st Sunday since I've been here (that was only because of those beans!) – we had a fearfully busy morning & there is no "scamping" work for a day in the Kitchen, like the Hut Girls can. But in the afternoon I was able to get thoroughly clean – put on nice white & go to Mrs C's w' Miss Browne. It was such a lovely change & I thoroughly enjoyed it – nice tennis & nice people.

We biked home about 10 of us by moonlight.

<u>9.30 pm</u> Such a busy evening & as I am to be first down tomorrow I must to sleep otherwise I'll never get up in time – I'm responsible for fire etc: in the early morning you see.

So I'll finish this tomorrow afternoon.

I'm really happy, but I have a bit of a rush, & not much time to myself however now I feel I'm really doing proper W. Work

Dearest love Ruth.

MC 643/16/29

297. Thursday 6pm [?*5 Sept.*]

My very dearest Mother & Father.

This is the first opportunity I've had of "sitting down" to letters since the half I wrote you. You see I get so grubby in the kitchen, *so* I spend a lot of my time washing & resting! Mother's nice parcel arrived yesterday – what lovely chocs:! I <u>am</u> enjoying them – we can't get any sweets round here just at present. Sister Hughes has <u>just</u> told me that Dev: House has accepted my letter & agreed to let me go as soon as a substitute can get here for me (i.e 3–4 days I suppose) – so that's splendid! It was rather a good letter I must say.

We're getting quite gay here – the new Colonel is <u>very</u> keen on entertainments & sports we hear. We've had 2 quite good concerts & a Lecture in the last 10 days & there's another Concert tonight. Last night the Colonel & M.O's came up here after supper to call on Matron & the Mess. It was a sort of introduction for him I suppose – they stayed quite late 9–11 & we only knew ½ hr before – so had a rush to get coffee & sandwiches! Matron sent a special message to say she wished the G.S.M's to go in (obviously she is determined we <u>shall</u> hold the same position as all the others), & yet only 4 had the decency to go! It is disgraceful & so silly – of course no-one <u>wanted</u> to get clean & tidy at 9 o'c: but after all it was a sort of state occasion – they've no esprit de corps. We had games & music – such a pretty sight in the Ante room (all the Sisters in clean white, & red capes etc:- a lot of V.A.D's & a fair sprinkling of Khaki) The Padre kept the whole thing going – he's just a grt: big bouncing jolly boy, & absolutely invaluable on such occasions. Afterwards we 4 & S. Harris had to clear away & wash up, so were rather late in bed – but still I'm not tired, & I think it was only right to go don't you – Matron was annoyed too.

I rather think I'm going to be the Emergency member because at present I'm doing the work of someone on a holiday – & as I'm uncertain that's maybe what they'll do w' me (I'd like it because of the variety) but I shall ask.

Miss B. really finds me useful in the kitchen; she says she <u>does</u> hope I'll stay there. She said today she felt she cld: always trust me to be down early (there now Father!) when I'm responsible that is for a week at a time be down at 6 to see to fire & kettles. So far this week I've been punctual every morning – of course it is an effort but I go to bed early. Ought not Philip to be in the Casualty List at least as Unofficially Reported Prisoner & Wounded? surely the next news we get won't take so long to come through – unless of course if he's on the "move" then it may.

If I work as Emergency then I'll be in the Mess for my next fortnight – I shld: quite like that.

There's no peace here – I've had dozens of interruptions since I started this – you see w' only curtains round I can hear everybody outside!

The watch P gave me has just come back fr Dibdin[462] & is going well. Now I must go to supper.

Dear love

from Ruth.

MC 643/16/32

298.   <u>Wednesday</u> [*11 Sept.*][463]

Today I have started a fortnight's work in the Mess which I shall enjoy <u>ever</u> so – it is very different from Kitchen work – much cleaner.

We have a Concert here tonight to wh: I shall go as it is my half-day.

Don't be surprised to hear very shortly that I shall be home soon – big changes are going on here & everything is in a muddle – I'll write a letter as soon as we know anything definite.

Have you any of my blk: stockings at home – I <u>do</u> want some.

"All things work together for good".

MC 643/16/39

299.   Fargo [*15 Sept.*][464]

My very dearest Mother & Father,

I won't keep these cheques any longer, – I can't get them cashed here and I've plenty of money. So Father will you pay them in for me please? I've all my June & July pay still (i.e. £5.19.4) & we've just had Aug (£3.10.2 ½) so I've bought 4 War Certs: with that! I'm the only one here who saves.

---

462. Dibdin & Co, jewellers, Sloane Street, Chelsea, London.
463. Written on a plain postcard, postmarked 12 Sep. '18.
464. Sent by registered post, postmarked 15 Sept. '18.

[465]You'll be wondering what I meant on my post card. – Well Matron is being forced (by Mrs MacDonald we think) to start treating her G.S.M's as they are most of them treated nowadays – she has told, most of us – saying <u>how</u> sorry she is but can hold out no longer – therefore next week she goes to Devonshire House to see what can be done, but in the meanwhile most of us are resigning. I don't think Matron will make any difference in our position yet – She said she'd do it <u>very</u> gradually.

Everything is very uncertain but of course I can get away still under my original conditions only it – may – be sooner.

In the meanwhile I am still thoroughly enjoying this place. My work in the Mess is awfully nice – I like it best of any work I've ever done here.

The newspaper cutting interested me ever so – that's Tom Ketley[466] (the lame boy).

I'm glad the Eversheds are going to be in Norwich a little longer – I've not heard fr: 'A' for quite a time. I was too busy & tired when in the Kitchen to write letters. Will you thank Olive for her letter & tell her I'll try & write the questions out tomorrow. "The Best of Luck & Success to the Guides' Concert"!

If I ever joined VAD again I shld: want to be a Nursing Member (Matron suggested this to lots of us but not here straight on however she said to some of us she'd be delighted to welcome us back as N.M.s after a time!)

Now I must stop & get tidy.

Dear love from

Ruth.

MC 643/16/40

300. Wednesday [*18 Sept.*][467]

We have heard no more yet but still continue in the same old way (as I think we shall as long as <u>we</u> are here). S. Hughes has gone to Dev: H today It is my "day-off" & I am staying in bed till after dinner w' books & letters – oh so nice!

Then I mean to wash my head & tonight Miss B. & I bike to Bulford

---

465. The remainder of the letter is written in pencil.
466. Not identifiable. No one named Thomas Ketley appears in the 1911 census for Norfolk. There was just one family named Ketley in the county at the time of the census, that of Frederick Ketley of Thorpe Hamlet, Norwich: his two sons, Eric and Richard would have been 15 and 10 respectively in 1918.
467. Written on a plain postcard, postmarked 18 Sept. '18.

Theatre to see "Betty" (d'you remember P & I saw it with Xenia in March).[468]

I like the Mess ever so but we are fearfully busy w' more arriving every day! I shall soon start sending unnecessary clothes etc: back!

Dear love

Ruth.

MC 643/16/41

301. Sunday 3p.m. [?*22 Sept.*]

My dearest Mother & Father.

I got the parcel yesterday – it was most welcome.

I <u>do</u> think this letter is <u>most</u> hopeful – we may indeed have him in England quite soon. Where did you find this wounded repatriated officer – I don't quite understand why he wrote to you?[469] By the way have you sent P's photo to any picture paper as someone on Leave saw it but they don't say which paper?

S. Hughes has been to Dev: H. & they say we can go as soon as they get reliefs! Of course this is <u>very</u> vague & how it will all fit in we don't know, but at any rate it is granted. We continue on the same lines (very happy) at present except that we are not included in any outside invitations to the "Staff" for concerts sports etc: Later on it will mean a separate mess & sitting room & of course we shld: not be able to join in Xmas festivities wh: we were all looking forward to. But I don't think they'll make the changes until <u>we</u>'ve gone.

But we're fearfully uncertain as to the time we'll be here – it may be a month <u>or</u> a few days! On Wed: I change work again & go to my own old Hut – I'm sorry to leave the Mess – it is very nice work but I'll be glad to get back to my old times off again.

---

468. ?*Betty: A Musical Play* (c.1915) by Frederick Lonsdale and Gladys Unger.
469. The reference is to Lt E Lart of the Dorset Regiment: a letter he wrote to Mrs Hewetson survives in which he compares his own experiences to those of Philip (whom he did not know personally), offering her reassurance. Lart had been captured, had lost a leg – and had been repatriated: the Germans 'exchange all amputatation cases as soon as they can', and telling Mrs Hewetson that offiers in hospital received plentiful and good food. The surviving letter is dated 16 September 1918, and makes it clear that it was his second letter (the first does not survive – perhaps because it was forwarded by Mrs Hewetson to Ruth?) [NRO, MC 643/13/7].

Bed 10pm

I've been to Shrewton Church this evening so nice.

Just been introduced to Mr Suffolk (at Shrewton for week end), I met them at the gate. He has right arm like P. had his left. Finish this tomorrow

Good night

Dear love Ruth.

To be concluded. Monday.

Last night I biked to Shrewton Church – I felt I must go to a proper Service again. So I went alone. It was S.P.G Sunday & we had nice hymns & a very interesting original Sermon about the history of the Society[470]. Then I biked home w' a lamp. As I was going over to bed I nearly ran into S. Suffolk w' her husband & while I was escaping she called me back & introduced me as "my little friend Hughie"(!) He was down at Shrewton for the week end from hospital, w' his right arm just out of a sling. It is awful for her not being able to get proper leave – but no one is away at present, we're so understaffed.

Matron says we "may go tomorrow or in a months' time"! We don't know how it is all going to be arranged – who'll go first nor anything at present. I roared w' laughter over Mother's letter today which suggests that I'm getting too fat to fit my clothes – I hope I'm not quite as bad as that yet!! I do get teased here – you know I'm very much treated as a "baby" in many ways & yet I'm sure I'm much more capable etc: than I used to be – is not it funny? S. Hughes is forever telling me of the tonic she's going to give me – but even tho' they do "rag" w' me generally – I hope (& think) they realise that I can be quite "a sensible woman"! I think I <u>now</u> have my full share of "self-confidence" – you'll have to sit on me when I come home.

I don't think I've many plans for the future – it is no use making many till we hear more of P. is it? But I certainly think I ought to have some – not "career" but "definite job I <u>can</u> do" in view – don't you. I want to earn & bear my share in the Fam'ly's expenses. I don't know what sort of a pension P. will get, but Miss A's says her brother will get about £90 wh: does <u>not</u> seem very adequate.

Now another point – I do not want to resign entirely fr: the B.R.C.S if possible but only fr: my work here. I shld: very much like to join as a Nursing Member; at least – I don't really know – but I don't want <cast> break all connection w' Red X. work unless absolutely essential – of course I don't feel drawn towards local hospitals (except the Military ones) but I shall not resign entirely until I've talked things over after I get home fr: here.

---

470. Society for the Propagation of the Gospel.

I am so sorry about the Guides – poor children Mrs S.[471] is too severe – I want to take them on *properly* in many ways & yet I feel there is no real possibility of going ahead – & I don't know whether I cld: work w' all that sort of "leading rein or <strings> webs holding you in in every direction feeling." You see for the last 7 mnths: I've been living in an atmosphere where everyone is out to "get on w' it at all costs & never mind how" & it is so different from dumplings! It is difficult to explain in a letter but don't think I mean I never want to do my old works again it is not that a bit, it is just that I've seen how very different people can be from Salhouse See? How Mother & Father have stood them all this time I can't imagine you are two Saints. & shld: not be wasted on dumplings.

I want to turn Lady Gardener[472] altogether but then I'd have no time for anything else if I did it properly – I know how to work hard & stick at it now you see – Oh dear, oh dear – I don't think I shall ever do much unless I stick absolutely to one thing – do you know how I feel?

I heard fr: X[473] lately – her letter bores me thoroughly – why? – she's working – but still in the same old atmosphere – Oh I can never be thankful enough that you tore me up from it & spared me to come right away for a time.

Is not this a talk – I think a lot when I'm working but I must "get it off my chest" sometimes. (I'm afraid I've got lots of new expressions – but they <u>do</u> express so well!)

Miss Allsopp is going to see her sister at Bury S.E's as soon as possible after leaving here & wld: love to come on & see us I'm sure you'd like – she's so just like us & such a sweet natured girl. So I'm giving her an invite.

How can Mother manage w'out Louisa[474] – Oh dear – please don't cook much – <give> bully beef & salmon – awfully good. I'm aching to saw that wood Father – really honestly I am!

One of the sisters here I like best is seriously ill w' pneumonia – they've sent for her people – her name is Harrison – I think I've probably mentioned her before. I <u>do</u> hope she gets better but I'm afraid she's very ill.

I don't want those thin clothes back again – but have I any warm

---

471. Mrs Mildred Steward of Oak Lodge, Wroxham, Captain of the Wroxham Guides: according to the *Wroxham and Salhouse Church Magazine* of July 1918 she also captained the Salhouse Guides in Ruth's absence [NRO, MC 643/48/3].

472. Probably Ruth's parents had suggested that if she was not happy with her VAD work she could return to Salhouse and take charge of the Rectory garden, which was being used to grow food for the family and for villagers.

473. Xenia Muriel.

474. See note 95.

nightgowns instead – one wld: do almost I shld: think. It is not cold yet but maybe soon!

This photo was taken about a month ago – very good of us all – Please Keep

Dear love from Ruth.

MC 643/16/59

302. Fargo Sunday 8.15pm [*?29 Sept.*]

My very dearest Mother & Father,

Oh such a day! Pour-pour-pour – heavy unceasing rain since 9 o'c: a.m. Fargo is grey & desolate today. And it is so cold. I luckily, have the evening off so I've retired to bed, after a hot bath, w' a book & letters & a hot bottle & I'm very comfy – (I'm glad to have the warm nightgown Mother). But good gracious! We'll all be washed away if it doesn't stop soon – it's real heavy dashing rain.

I am enjoying those Gentlewomen – what a nice magazine.[475] People are loud in their praises of that photo of P., even tho' it is not a good reproduction of it d'you think? They all remark on his eyes (they are as Mother says so "soulful").

Well – I wonder what plans will be made for us during this week – something further I shld: hope. We start meals in our own Mess tomorrow – still that's no real handicap (of course I enjoy them in the Mess because of all of my little interests wh: I have created for myself, per usual, but that's a habit peculiar to myself – on the whole it will be better & certainly quicker for us: I shld: think we're sure to start going soon.

We've just got a Theatre <*word illegible*> opened at Larkhill about 2 miles away – & we're awfully pleased (it is the same Co that I saw before at Bulford, they're the N.A.C.B[476]). I've seen Raffles & Betty (again)[477] there on Friday I went here w' Miss A. to The Happy Day, a very good musical play.[478] Next week I'm going again. We can have 2 late evenings per week – our ½ day & one "Picture Leave" – so that we can see each play that comes if we like – its only 1/- so I'm making the most of opportunities! Yes – that B. Bennet idea is sound[479] – I am beginning to think I'd like Nursing – (even as a <Career>

---

475. *Gentlewoman: The Illustrated Weekly for Gentlewomen* (1890–1926).

476. Entertainment Branch of the Navy & Army Canteen Board, run by Capt. Basil Dean.

477. See letter 300.

478. *The Happy Day: a new musical play* (c. 1916) by Seymour Hicks.

479. An unclear reference, possibly connected to Uncle Bennett, or to some other family member.

permanent idea – or at any rate it is splendid experience is not it – we must see) – I've written to Mrs Harker today explaining things & saying I'd like to stay in BRCS at any rate at present.

Yes, please Father I'd like that £3.3.0 to go in to my P.O. account.

I'm getting quite a little picture gallery of my friends gradually & my own photos are disappearing too now. Sister Suffolk came in to see me tonight (I was pleased, she naturally does not visit <m>any G.S.M's except Miss B) <and see> & she asked for a photo so I demanded hers in return & I'm to have it too!

I've a snap of Matron which I'll get her to sign before I leave – they'll be interesting momentos in future.

Dev: House is certainly not thought much of here – oh I'll have tons to tell you when I get back – how shall I remember it all! Lots more of my own successes or otherwise – conversations – happenings – ideas results!!

I must send some parcels home – today I found a nice cardboard box, so must start tomorrow. Hands getting cold so will stop now Goodnight – Best love from Ruth.

* I wrote to Hugo today – at last! I am exceptionally well & fit just now.*

MC 643/16/42

303.[480]

... so many relatives of "Seriously Ill" men here that the Hostel overflowed & they had to sleep in our "Church": services were curtailed on Sunday! Is not it awful, they say they're dying everyday – quite boys most of them.

I enclose a 2nd letter fr: Mrs Harker – I have replied "There are no distinctions now, & I think you quite misunderstood my last letter" *Yes v: badly!* Isn't she the limit. – even if Lady A. does kick up a fuss Dev: H. knows all about it – but I'm very angry w' the woman.

[481]I can't find the letter it says (to be brief) she has shown my letter about the distinction betw' G.S.M's at Fargo to Lady Ampthill & she wants to know if she may mention my <name> letter if she shld: bring the matter up" silly idiot I told her all distinctions were now done away with.[482] The letter is marked "Private", I don't care, Dev: H knows all about the position, &

---

480. The first folio of this letter is missing.
481. Written in pencil from this point.
482. Emily Russell, Lady Ampthill (1843–1927), Chairman of the Joint Women's V.A.D. Department of St John and the British Red Cross.

Matron thoroughly appreciates us. At any rate Lady A. did not say I showed
a very wrong spirit. It is absurd – I'm going to show that letter to Matron
right eno:

By the way D.H. cld: not possibly keep me because of that letter – I shld
make a fuss if they tried that on!

I think Mother I must have some warmer underclothes, it is very cold &
sometimes & I have not eno' – the things they shrunk so at this Laundry
are what I want!

Now goodbye bestest love fr: Ruth.

MC 643/16/58

304.   Saturday [5 Oct.][483]

I've just sent off the gram: not carriage Pd: because I might not be able to
afford it. The strap round it is Bates', so cld: you return soon please. We're
starting to go – one today – 2 on Monday – but it is absolutely uncertain
as to who goes when! Everything & everybody here is in a hopeless muddle!
I was almost the last to come so dare not hope to go for a week at least
perhaps – Cld: you send me back the photo of Matron – just inside one of
those little red books – I want her to sign it. Letters follows – this is scribbles
just before dinner.

Dear love – Ruth.

MC 643/16/43

305.   Fargo Sunday 6pm. [6 Oct.]

My very dearest Mother & Father

I don't think there's very much news exactly – I've never imagined that I
could be in such an unsettled frame of mind – at least we've started moving,
but I can't tell you when I shall get off – noone knows from hour to hour
who'll go next – it just depends on what reliefs come down.

Monday. The rest of yesterday evening I was working unceasingly so could
not go on with this.

This place has not been the same since we started the new arrangements,
& we're all longing to get away!

Miss Allsopp – Miss Tottenham & Miss Grubbe leave to-morrow

---

483. Written on plain postcard, postmarked 6 Oct. '18.

– S. Suffolk goes on 3 weeks leave, & Miss Tribe also goes on leave – so there'll only be Miss B. left.

I shan't be able to tell you anything really definite until I wire time of arrival. It is no use wiring immediately we're told here because it is nearly always contradicted soon after!

How soon will you be able to get me food tickets I'll enquire here, but we've heard 'o' about it yet.

I change work again this week (I expect I'll still be here) into another hut. They say we're going to have 300 British Wounded sent here – I hope not, it is far too isolated for them – & the Hospital is already under staffed. There are arrivals of Germans (the last lot very bad) I believe here now. What do you think of this letter of Mrs Harker's – it made me <u>furious</u>. I was particularly careful when I wrote only to state the facts & say "Matron wished us to resign"

I call her letter "Norfolk & country" – she wld: not much care for her daughters (if she has any) to be living under the same conditions w' the same associated as we <have> are at present – I shall be able to tell you about it when I get home. Please keep the letter. I am answering very short & <u>not</u> rude (altho' I'd like to be).

I hope the gramophone gets back safely – it was hard work packing it!

Don't think from this letter that I'm miserable – it's not that yet because all the same people are still here, but certainly no one wld: want to stay on in the future.

<u>Later</u> I've just heard we <u>are</u> provided w' some sort of a ration book – so that's alright.

Also all leave is stopped again Poor S. Suffolk – she's been looking forward to this her first chance of a <Leave> Honeymoon ever since her husband came home wounded. The Army does not study feelings! It is hard – is not it.

It is getting late & no new GSM's have turned up so the 3 who are going to tomorrow are beginning to resign themselves to their fate – you see it is hopelessly uncertain!

I've got a digestive biscuit tin nearly full of sugar as well as what I sent home the other day – is not that good. Oh well there's one consolation the longer I stay the more sugar I get!

Here too are Olive's papers – I'm sending 2nd Class Cert: to Mrs Harker – I wonder did M. Booker & A. Curtis ever get their Badges, I sent for while at home?

Now I must go to my never ending labours!

Good night, Dear love

Ruth.

MC 643/16/44

306. Saturday [*12 Oct.*][484]

So far nothing more has come through about moving but I'm going to seize the <u>very</u> first opportunity. I thought you'd be annoyed w' that letter – I shall probably do as you suggest. Miss Allsopp went yesterday – I <u>am</u> so sorry – but I mean to keep her up – & she me too, I think. We're all very unsettled & shall be delighted to get away! S. Suffolk got her leave after all so we've another Home Sister. I enjoy my work thoroughly at present wh: is a good thing. I've sent everything but uniform & bedding so can manage well – I have the sack.

Letter tomorrow. Dear love

Ruth.

MC 643/16/45

---

484. Written on a plain postcard, postmarked 13 Oct. '18.

Army Weapons of the First World War, as mentioned by Philip

Rifles and machine guns: the Hythe School of Musketry investigated the use of rifles, machine guns mortars and grenades between 1908 and 1913. The conclusion was that volume of fire was much more important than skill: the marksman fell out of favour. The rapid rate of fire was set at twelve to fifteen rounds a minute, compared with only eight a minute in other armies 'although there was some loss of accuracy at the higher rate the destructive effect was far greater.'[1] The Maxim machine gun was rated as the equivalent of twelve men with rifles, the Vickers machine gun, introduced in 1912, the equivalent of forty riflemen: it was also lighter, weighing 38 pounds. In a trial at Hythe in 1910, two men after just two weeks' training used two machine guns to inflict 60% casualties on a group of advancing men – in just one minute! The School thought that the number of machine guns in each battalion should be raised from two to six, but this was not put into effect, the rate of fire by each rifleman being raised instead. On the Western Front, each division had only 24 machine guns, two per battalion.

Lewis guns: light machine guns, much easier to carry than the machine gun: three thousand were ordered by the British Army between August 1914 and June 1915. In July 1915 they were issued at a scale of four per battalion, which equates to one per company.

Grenades: 'the master-weapon in the trenches'[2], especially after the introduction of the number 5 Mills Bomb, which was heavier than the German egg grenade and so could not be thrown as far. Men needed training, with a typical course lasting nine days. Philip was involved in training men in the use of grenades, as his letters show.

---

1. Shelford Bidwell and Dominick Graham, *Fire-power: the British Army weapons and theories of war 1904–1945* (Barnsley, 2004) p. 27
2. Bidwell and Graham, *op. cit.* p. 124.

Artillery: field guns, howitzers and heavy guns, firing from out of sight a long way behind the lines, frequently mentioned by Philip; criticised by the infantry for hiding behind hills! Artillery was the dominating force in the First World War. Artillery fire on the Western Front killed more people than rifle and machine gun fire combined – 59% of wounds suffered by British soldiers were from shellfire, compared with 39% from bullets. Such wounds were also more likely to be fatal: a man was three times more likely to die from a shell wound to the chest than from a bullet wound to the same area. Philip shows how men soon distinguished shells that would harmlessly pass overhead from those that were dangerous, simply from the sound that they made as they approached. Each division had 76 guns, fifty-four 18-pounders, eighteen 4.5 inch howitzers and four 60-pounder heavy guns.

Mortars: heavy and medium mortars used by the artillery, infantry used the Stokes light mortar – a length of pipe with a cartridge at the base which would explode when the bomb was dropped on it hurling the bomb up to 400 yards – might be used in the front line trench or fired from behind it. Each mortar had thirty bombs with it: eight men were needed to carry these forward.

Aeroplanes: at the start of the war the Royal Flying Corps had just 63 machines. By the end, a separate arm, the Royal Air Force, had been established and had 22,000 aeroplanes. The use of aeroplanes clearly excited Philip. Planes might drop bombs upon trenches, but their most effective use was in taking photographs on which enemy artillery, carefully hidden from sight at ground level, could be identified. The Germans used both aeroplanes and airships – 'Zeppelins' – to attack coastal towns in England: these raids are mentioned several times in the letters. The British had airships too, those based at Pulham in south Norfolk being referred to as 'Pulham Pigs': Philip saw one while at Felixstowe.

Tanks: another new development, an armoured vehicle in which infantry could cross No Man's Land without being mown down by machine gun fire. They were first introduced in 1916. Philip was very interested in them and gave serious thought to enrolling in the Tank Corps, as his letters show.

The horse: played a vital part in the war, for, in 1914, the Army had just 80 motor vehicles. The guns and most transport were pulled by horse, while horses for the officers are mentioned by Philip. Each division of 18,000 men had 5,592 horses all of which had to be watered, fed and looked after.

Philip's army acquaintances

Alldred, Reginald Alan; 2ⁿᵈ Lt, 3 Bn LNLR, attached to 1 Bn in France summer 1916; wounded 25–8 September 1916. A company director in Kensington, London, after the war; married Marjorie Hickman, 1925; died in London, 3 May 1964.

Andrews, Charles Neville; son of Charles and Ellen Andrews of Ealing, London. Graduated from Pembroke College, Cambridge, 1913. 2ⁿᵈ Lt, 3 Bn LNLR, attached to 1 Bn in France, February 1915. Killed in action 24 March 1915: he was 22 years old.

Barker, Henry Arundel Keith, brother of Roly Barker [see below]; born 1890, educated at Rugby school. 2ⁿᵈ Lt, later Acting Captain, in 3 Bn LNLR. After the war worked for Egyptian State Railways.

Barker, Robert Alexander; joined 1 Bn, LNLR, as 2ⁿᵈ Lt in France, January 1915; wounded following up attack on a German post led by 2ⁿᵈ Lt Dawes 28 January 1915: 'A second attempt, led by 2Lieutenant R A Barker was made two hours later, and this party succeeded in entering the enemy trench: a very hot fire was then opened by the Germans occupying a trench running at right angles to the railway embankment, and Barker being also wounded, his men fell back, the second attack having thus also failed.' [Wylly]. Letters mentioning 'Barker' refer to this man. The other two Barkers, also with Philip at Felixstowe, are referred to as 'Roly' and 'Roly's brother' in the letters.

Barker ['Roly'], Roland Auriol; an Oxford friend of Philip. His father was a Church of England clergyman (vicar of King's Pyon, Herefordshire, where Roland was born in 1892, and rector of Sacome, Hertfordshire, from 1909). 2ⁿᵈ Lt, 1 Bn LNLR, seeing service in France; later Captain, Indian Army Gurkha Rifles. C.B.E., M.V.O. In later life lived at Englefield Green Surrey. Died in Kampala, Uganda, 12 April 1954.

Blackburn, correctly Blackburne, Revd. Harry William; chaplain to the forces (3ʳᵈ class) ranking as Major. M.A. from Clare College, Cambridge; a priest from 1901, including service in South Africa and India. Chaplain at Sandhurst Military College from 1913. Anglican chaplain for the Division.

Bleistein, Gordon James; a university friend of Philip; born Hampstead, Middlesex, 1894, son of Siegfried and Gertrude: his father, a skin merchant, by trade was a naturalised British citizen (originally from Germany). Went to Rugby School, Oxford University, joined Public Schools Battalion. Joined Middlesex Regiment in September 1914. In the army and after he took the name Gordon James Blyth. Married Nancy Sternberg in 1934. Died in Paddington, London, 6 June 1963.

Bratton, Allen Basil; one of thirteen 2nd Lts appointed to 3 Bn LNLR (on probation) on 15 August 1914; joined 1 Bn from 3 Bn October 1916. Later Captain, winner of D.S.O. and M.C. (*London Gazette* 23 April 1918: when one of his men was wounded, he went back for him despite heavy shelling and pitch blackness). Part of Army of Occupation in Germany 1919.

Brown, Major, *see* Monteagle-Browne.

Browne, Mgnr; Roman Catholic chaplain mentioned in letter 52. Not further identified: the Army List for 1915 has one R.C. Chaplain of the name, Father T. Browne. Another Browne, Father F. M. Browne, was appointed chaplain to the 1st Irish Guards in March 1916 (Timothy Bowman, *Irish Regiments in the Great War* (Manchester, 2003) p. 27).

Bulling, Albert Edgar; Cyclists Corps, then 2nd Lt, 1 Bn LNLR, in France from 18 August 1916; wounded in the battalion's attack at High Wood 18 August 1916. Wrote two letters of sympathy to the Hewetsons after Philip's capture [NRO, MC 643/13/2,3]. Remained in the army after the war: address on Medal Card, Fulwood Barracks, Preston.

Calthorpe, *see* Gough-Calthorpe.

Carr, C.; 2nd Lt, with Philip in Felixstowe May 1915; joined 1/5 Bn LNLR in France May 1916.

Clayton, John Wilfrid; 2nd Lt Suffolk Regt, later with Phillips in 1 Bn LNLR, 1918; in France from 5 August. Address on Medal Card (1922): Wisbech, Cambs.

Cowper-Essex, Colonel Thomas; accompanied 3 Bn LNLR to Felixstowe as Colonel, August 1914. Honorary Colonel of 3 Bn 22 March 1916; retired to the Lake District, where he bred sheep. Died 1925.

Cox [initials not known]; Philip's servant at Felixstowe. There are about 40 men named Cox in the LNLR in the Medal Cards.

Craigie-Halkett, Lieut.-Colonel Hugh Marjoriebanks; served with Egyptian

Army before the war. Took command of 9 Bn 1 December 1917 and commanded it until March 1918 when promoted to command of Brigade. Later with Highland Light Infantry. D.S.O. 1917, with bar 1918, second bar 1919.

Cramer-Roberts, Herbert Alexander; born c.1870, son of Revd Francis Cramer-Roberts, (Bishop of Nassau 1878–85, then assistant to Bishop of Manchester and archdeacon of Blackburn). Married Evelyn Muriell, an Australian, in 1893. Captain, 3 Bn LNLR Dec. 1914.

Curwen, Donald Reginald; one of thirteen 2nd Lts appointed to 3 Bn (on probation) on 15 August 1914. Served in France 1915. Later promoted Captain. Survived the war; later lived in Milnthorpe Westmoreland.

Curwen, John Spedding; twin brother of the above. One of thirteen 2nd Lts appointed to 3 Bn (on probation) on 15 August 1914. Served in France 1915. Later Captain, 1 Bn LNLR and awarded O.B.E. Survived the war; later also lived in Milnthorpe Westmoreland.

Dawes, Charles Edward; joined 1 Bn LNLR in France as 2nd Lt, January 1915; killed on 28 January 1915 leading a party of 30 men in an attack on a German machine-gun post: 'the attack was started at 2 am, ten men advancing with hand grenades and slung rifles, while another ten men followed with fixed bayonets, the rest of the party moving in rear carrying tools and sandbags. Dawes was almost at once mortally wounded, being shot through the chest, and this initial attack failed.' [Wylly].

De Blaby, Reginald Swithun; son of Revd W de Blaby of Kemberton Rectory, Shifnal, Shropshire, and his wife Selena. Went to King's School, Worcester. One of thirteen 2nd Lts appointed to 3 Bn LNLR (on probation) on 15 August 1914. In D Company of 1/4Bn, one of the leaders of an attack on a ridge held by the enemy on 5 and 6 August 1916. One of twelve Loyal North Lancs men killed on 8/9 August 1916: he was 22 years old. His promotion to Captain, backdated to 2 May 1916, was announced (after his death) in *London Gazette* 21 September 1916. His name is on the stained-glass window in Worcester Cathedral cloister commemorating the dead of King's School.

Debbitch, correctly Debbage, Samuel Henry; in the 1st Essex Regiment. Older than most recruits, he was 40 years old when he enlisted, a widower with two children. The family lived in South Walsham, a Broadland village not far from Salhouse.

Diver, Cyril Roper Pollock; joined 1 Bn LNLR as 2nd Lt in France March 1915; in hospital in summer 1915, returning to the battalion on 16 August and taking over the duties of Adjutant the following day; wounded at the Battle of Loos 25 September 1915.

Elkington, T. H.; 2nd Lt, 9 Bn LNLR from early 1917, wounded at the Battle of Messines 1917. Later a coastguard officer. Address on Medal Card: Custom House, London.

Etches, Charles Roger; born Coventry 1856, graduate of University of Oxford, served in Boer War. Emigrated to United States, returning to serve in the First World War. Joined 1 Bn LNLR in France as Captain, February 1915, left front line for Headquarters 30 August 1915. Later Major in 3 Bn Hants Regt. He returned to the United States after the war, dying there in 1922.

Evers, Mervyn Saxelbye; son of a Leamington clergyman. M.A. from Cambridge, ordained in 1913. Army chaplain. Awarded M.C. December 1916 for working continuously for 18 hours in No Man's Land caring for and carrying in wounded under heavy fire. Wrote letter of sympathy to the Hewetsons after Philip's capture [NRO, MC 643/13/4]. Worked for the Church Missionary Society after the war.

Fairbairn, Charles Osborn; born Victoria, Australia 1893. Cadet in O.T.C. One of thirteen 2nd Lts appointed to 3 Bn (on probation) on 15 August 1914. Promoted to Lieutenant with Philip, 6 September 1915. Promoted to Captain, also with Philip, 2 May 1916. Later promoted to Major. After the war, returned to Australia. Died Melbourne, 1959.

Faulknor, Robert Sylvester John; son of Lt-Col A Faulknor and his wife Laura: they lived in Jersey. Commissioned 2nd Lt, LNLR 1910; Captain, 1 Bn LNLR in France June 1915; killed at the Battle of Loos 25 September 1915, his body being found right up on the German wire; he was 27 years old.

Forbes, Alexander William; born Hastings, Sussex October 1889, son of William and Margaret Forbes (father born in India, described as 'law student' in 1891 census, by which time the family were living in Wembdon, Somerset); L/Corporal in 1 Glouc R, in France August 1914; commissioned 1 October 1914, Lt in 1 Bn LNLR. Addresses on Medal Card in Bromley, Kent and Bath, Somerset. Later in India, returning in 1936: address in England given as Imperial Bank of India, London.

Gardner, 2nd Lt J.H.; joined 1 Bn LNLR in France May 1915; one of two battalion machine-gun officers; wounded by gas while leading a machine-gun attack at the Battle of Loos 25 September 1915.

Garrod, Alfred Noel; son of Colonel Sir Archibald Garrod, professor of medicine at Oxford University, and his wife Elisabeth; in the Royal Army Medical Corps, killed on 25 January 1916, aged 28.

Garrod, Basil Rahee; brother of above, joined the R.A.F., killed on 4 February 1919, aged 21.

Garrod, Thomas Martin; brother of above; joined 1 Bn LNLR in France as 2nd Lt, January 1915. Killed in action at Aubers Ridge on 10 May 1915 (one of seven LNLR officers killed in the battle): he was 20 years old.

Gemmel, James Allison Burns; from Liverpool. Joined 1 Bn LNLR as 2nd Lt in France June 1915; understudied the Brigade wiring officer 31 August 1915; wounded in attack on German trench at Flers 25–9 September 1916.

Gilliland, Horace Gray: born 1886, son of John and Emma (John described as 'a professor', dead by 1911). Joined 3 Bn, LNLR as 2nd Lt on probation 15 August 1914. Joined 1 Bn in France October 1914, a prisoner of war from December 1914. Promoted to Lieutenant with Philip, 6 September 1915. Escaped April 1917 after jumping from a train while being transferred to another prison camp. Described his experiences in *Two German prisons* (London, 1918). Died on war service 7 July 1941, leaving a widow, Violet.

Goldie, Paul Francis; born 1894, son of Edward and Nathalie Goldie, lived in Kensington, London, and St Servan-sur-Mer in France (Edward was an architect, especially of Roman Catholic churches). A private with 28th London Regiment, serving in France from 28 October 1914. Joined 1 Bn, LNLR as 2nd Lt in France October 1915. Killed at the Battle of Loos (in the attack led by Col Sanderson) 25 September 1915: he was 22 years old. His mother, then living in London, applied for his medals.

Goldie, Robert George; cousin of above and like him a private with 28th London Regiment, serving in France from 28 October 1914. 2nd Lt, 1 Bn LNLR in France October 1915; wounded [Wylly wrongly says killed] at the Battle of Loos 25 September 1915; acting Captain while commanding a Company March-April 1917. Later, captain in Machine Gun Corps. Survived the war, afterwards lived in Streatham, London.

Gough-Calthorpe, Frederick Somerset; a school friend of Philip at Repton: he was there between 1907 and 1911. Son of 8th Baron Calthorpe, born 1892. Went on to St Catherine College, Cambridge; a cricket blue; joined 1st Staff Yeo (TF) October 1914; promoted Lieutenant 1916; lieutenant in R.N.A.S. 1918. Survived the war, in later life captain of Warwickshire XI. Died in 1935.

Greenhill, Captain Frederick William; accompanied 3 Bn LNLR to Felixstowe August 1914; joined 1 Bn in France March 1915; later a Major and an O.B.E.

Grove, George Edward; formerly L/Corporal, EA and M Rifles. 2nd Lt, later Captain with 1 Bn LNLR; wounded November-December 1917. Wrote a letter of sympathy to Hewetsons after Philip's capture [NRO, MC 643/13/5]. Medal card gives his address as High Wycombe.

Halsted, John Gregson; joined 1 Bn LNLR as 2nd Lt in France, January 1915; wounded when HE shell fell on battalion orderly room 26 January 1915. He was hurt in the arms and leg: at 9.30 am the officers of the battalion assembled in a paved yard which was acting as Orderly Room: a heavy explosive shell fell on the group, killing thirteen men instantly: another eighteen were badly wounded, one dying later in the day. The official War Diary records: 'The havoc was awful…. This is a terrible disaster and a very severe blow to the battalion.' Either this tragedy was deliberately kept from the men at Felixstowe, or Philip chose not to mention it in a letter home. Later Captain, and then D.A.A.G. 8th Corps.

Harrison, Aidan; 2nd Lt, 8th (Service) Bn, LNLR Sept. 1914; later Captain. Awarded D.S.O. Medal card gives his address as Blackpool, Lancs.

Harrison, P.W.; Colonel of the 3rd (Reserve) Bn, LNLR at Felixstowe throughout the war. Uncle of the above.

Hartley, W.S.; Captain; joined 9 Bn as 2nd Lt October 1916; wounded in the great German attack of April 1918 (one of 821 men of the LNLR killed or wounded). Awarded M.C. for 'the gallant way in which he re-organised and led his company in the counter-attack' on 10 April 1918.

Helm, correctly Helme, Richard E.; Sergeant, LNLR, commissioned 2nd Lt, LNLR 20 June 1915. Killed in action at the Battle of Loos 25 September 1915: commemorated on the Loos memorial.

Henderson, V.L.; accompanied 3 Bn LNLR to Felixstowe August 1914 as Lieutenant; Adjutant 1915; later Captain, Special Reserve, LNLR. Address on Medal Card: Hampstead, London.

Hill, W.D.; served in South Africa 1899–1902 as 2nd Lt, 1 Bn LNLR; joined 1 Bn LNLR in France as Captain March 1915; wounded in attack on Aubers Ridge 9 May 1915.

Howe [initials not known]; Sergeant in LNLR; with Philip at Felixstowe.

Laurie, Frederick Grieve; commanded 'A' Company of 9 Bn LNLR at the Battle of Messines, where he was wounded June 1917. Awarded M.C. (supplement to *London Gazette* 14 August 1917: although stunned by shell fire, he recovered to lead his men until the final objective was attained). Fought in Russia after the war. Address on Medals Card: Bombay, India.

Leake, Kenneth Harper; 2nd Lt, 1 Bn LNLR. Awarded M.C. for his work taking out a patrol and extinguishing an enemy post (*London Gazette* 20 Oct. 1916). Later captain in the Royal Air Force. Medal card gives addresses in Leamington Spa and New York. The 'Leake' of letter 119.

Leake, Russell Medley; son of James and Florence Leake of Altrincham, Cheshire. Joined 2 Bn LNLR in France as 2nd Lt September 1916; with 1 Bn, wounded November 1916; Awarded M.C. (*London Gazette* 11 May 1917: he made three gallant attempts to rescue a wounded officer). joined 1 Bn as Captain April 1918. Killed in action 18 September 1918: he was 24 years old. The 'Leake' of letter 231. His brother, Eric Gilbert Leake, was in the R.A.F: he also won the M.C., and was killed in action 31 July 1918.

Leonard, Hugh Bonhote; born in Timsbury, the family were living in Bedford at the time of the 1911 census. Went to France as 2nd Lt, LNLR in May 1918. Leonard survived the war, dying in Newton Abbot, Devon, in 1978 aged eighty.

Lindsell, John; graduated from St John's College, Cambridge, 1911; appointed 2nd Lt (on probation), 3 Bn LNLR 11 November 1914. Joined 1 Bn in France October 1915. M.C. (Supplement to *London Gazette*, 1 January 1917). Part of the Army of Occupation in Germany in 1919

Livesey, Alan George Hilton; born at Streatham in 1889, son of Frank and Georgiana Livesey; educated in Sevenoaks (where Hamo Sassoon, younger brother of Siegfried Sassoon, was a fellow pupil), and at Pembroke College Cambridge, graduating in Mechanical Sciences in 1911. Joined the regiment at the outbreak of war, appointed 2nd Lt (on probation), 3 Bn LNLR 3 October 1914. Killed at the Battle of Loos 25 September 1915, his body being found right on the German wire: he was 26 years old. His parents then lived at Pinhoe, Exeter.

Livings, Arthur; born 1894. Company Sergeant, LNLR, 1914; commissioned 2nd Lt, 1 Bn LNLR April 1915; joined 1 Bn LNLR in France May 1915; wounded at the Battle of the Somme 14 July 1916; M.C. for leading forward a party of bombers: also 'he has done consistent good work for many months' [Supplement to *London Gazette* 18 August 1916:]. Joined 1 Bn as Lieutenant May 1917, later promoted to Captain. Died 1955.

Loch, G.; Captain, LNLR 1912; accompanied 3 Bn to Felixstowe as Captain August 1914; promoted to Major 2 May 1916.

Loudon, William Francis ('Bill'); 2nd Lt and later Captain. Commanded 'A' Company of 9 Bn LNLR 10 April 1918, and at Second Battle of the Aisne 27 May 1918: witness to Philip's being wounded.

Marriott, John Charles Oakes ('Jack'); a school friend of Philip's at Repton:

he was there between 1909 and 1914. His father was Charles Marriott of 15, St Mary's Road, Cromer, secretary of Cromer Golf Club. Marriott joined the 1st Northampton Regiment in 1914, serving in France the following year. M.C. [Supplement to *London Gazette*, 3 June 1916] and D.S.O. After the war he was a captain in the Scots Guards

Marsh, John Miles; 2nd Lt, 4 Bn, Princess Charlotte of Wales (Royal Berkshire Regt) June 1916; Lt, 8 Bn LNLR June 1917. Awarded M.C. for leadinga party to capture of 'a most important stronghold' [Supplement to *London Gazette* 14 Sept. 1917]. Lt, 9 Bn, LNLR June 1917; T/Captain 9 Bn, LNLR March 1918.

Maynard, Frederick Harrison; joined 1 Bn LNLR as 2nd Lt in France January 1915; wounded at the Battle of Loos 25 September 1915. Medal card gives address as Long Morston, Stratford-on-Avon.

Monteagle-Browne; Major, later Colonel. Born 1878, served in South African War. Stood twice for Parliament. Second in Command 1 and 7 Bns LNLR 1915; took over command of 1 Bn 19 August 1915. Appointed C.O. of 9th Royal Munster Fusiliers, 1917. Dismissed from the Army in 1917, in circumstances raised in Parliament [see *Hansard* 27 November 1917 and 29 January 1918].

Morison, Daniel McKenzie; born Greenock, Scotland 1899, the son of John and Janet Morison; originally with Argyll and Sutherland Highlanders; commissioned 2nd Lt, 4 Bn, LNLR 28 August 1917. There is confusion as to the spelling of his surname: Philip incorrectly calls him 'Morrison' in letter 246, and he is probably the '2nd Lt Morrison' who, according to Wylly, was with 9 Bn LNLR at the Second Battle of the Aisne, May 1918, taking command of 'C' Company and organising his men to form a defensive flank at a critical moment. Morison joined 2 Bn, LNLR August 1918. Medal Card gives address as Greenock. Emigrated to Canada 1932.

Morris, not further identified. With Philip at Felixstowe February 1915. Wylly mentions three officers named Morris: Morris, T.S.; joined 1/5 Bn LNLR as 2nd Lt in France August 1916: Morris, H., Captain, killed at Ypres 25 November 1917: Morris, E.S., 2nd Lt, 9 Bn, LNLR, wounded April 1918.

Newman, Vernon William; born 9 May 1885, son of Olinthus and Mary Newman, nee Bodman, of Bath (father killed in a tram accident, 1918). With West Yorkshire Regiment (Prince of Wales' Own). Joined 1 Bn LNLR as 2nd Lt in France 17 August 1915, posted next day to 'D' Coy with temporary rank of Captain. Killed at the Battle of Loos 25 September 1915: he was 30 years old.

Newth, Robert Charles; born 1885, Annerley, Kent, baptised 1886, Lambeth, Surrey; son of Robert and Jane Newth, Robert a 'professor of singing'. Aged

16 in 1901, an apprentice to a milliner. 2nt Lt, Manchester Regt. Joined 1 Bn LNLR as 2nd Lt in France July 1916.

Nichol, Edward Frank; one of thirteen 2nd Lts appointed to 3 Bn LNLR (on probation) on 15 August 1914. Promoted to Lieutenant with Philip, 6 September 1915. Joined 1 Bn in France early 1916; wounded in an attack on High Wood 18 August 1916. Promoted to Captain with Philip, 2 May 1916. In Royal Flying Corps by May 1918 (see letter 241); later joined Royal Air Force.

Nicholls, Ernest James; son of Joseph and Margaret Nicholls of New Southgate, London, (Joseph a solicitor). Lieutenant with 8 Bn LNLR; killed in action during German attack of 21 May 1916: he was 35 years old.

Ostrehan, Duncan Haldane; son of J E D Ostrehan of Pinner, Middlesex. As Lieutenant commanded 'D' Company of 1/4 Bn LNLR at the Battle of Messines in 1917, where he was wounded.

Palmer, Joseph Sidney Herbert; 2nd Lt with 1 Bn 1916 LNLR; arrived in France 24 August 1916; killed in action 27 September 1916, commemorated on Thiepval Memorial. Medal Card gives address of S Palmer M.D., Oxford St, Liverpool, probably Joseph's father.

Parker, not further identified, with Philip at Felixstowe December 1916 (letter 132). The Army Lists for 1916–17 have three junior officers of the name in the LNLR: Parker, P.; 2nd Lt 4 Bn Nov. 1914; Lt Sep. 15; Captain June 1916, awarded the M.C. by 1916; Parker, A., 2nd Lt, 4 Bn Apr. 1915, Lt June 1916; Parker, W., Lt 1 or 2 Bn, Dec. 1915: according to Wylly the last was with the Mounted Infantry of 2 Bn in East Africa in Jan. 1916, where he was severely wounded.

Phillips, Noel Clive; Captain, later Colonel, joined 1 Bn LNLR in France as Captain July 1915; badly gassed at the Battle of Loos 25 September 1915, but took over command; led attack on High Wood 18 August 1916. M.C. [Supplement to *London Gazette*, 3 June 1916].

Pilkington, [not further identified]; Philip's servant: there are Medal Cards for more than fifty men named Pilkington in the LNLR.

Plant, Charles Alick; born Poulton-le-Fylde. D of L Yeo, later 2nd Lt then Lieutenant in LNLR. Served in East Africa and France. Resigned his commission 28 March 1918. Medal card gives addresses in Preston and Poulton-le-Fylde. Died at the age of 92 in 1985: buried in Lytham St Annes.

Plant, William J ('Bill'); 2nd Lt (on probation), 3 Bn LNLR Feb. 1915; acting Captain LNLR while commanding a Company 12 June 1917; relinquished his commission and granted rank of Captain 5 November 1920.

Popham, Reginald Francis; born London 1892, a school friend of Philip's at Repton: he was there between 1906 and 1911. Joined 6 Bn Norfolk Regiment (TF) in October 1914, promoted Captain in June 1916. He was an accomplished sportsman, playing for both Norfolk Cricket Club and Norwich City Football Club before the war. He survived the war and played cricket for Middlesex in 1919, then returning to play for Norfolk until 1924. He married Eileen Ruth Oliver Riddell in 1920. Popham died in 1975 in Surrey.

Powys-Jones ['P J'], Lionel; one of Philip's University friends. Born c.1894, spent most of his life in Rhodesia: his father, Llewyllyn Powys Jones, was Resident Chief Magistrate in Bulawayo. Served as 2nd Lt in King's Royal Rifle Corps; resigned commission in 1920, probably returning to Rhodesia: in the 1950s he was Secretary for Native Affairs and Chief Native Commissioner, Southern Rhodesia.

Prout, Frank Yabsley; formerly private in Honourable Artillery Company; T/Capt., 2/4 LNLR Feb. 1917. Awarded M.C. for work in consolidating the battalion front after a successful attack, 'showing complete self-possession and ability under a trying fire' [*London Gazette* 24 Aug. 1917]; Captain, 7 Bn LNLR, 1918.

Reed, Richard Wyatt; Company Sergeant-Major in King's Royal Rifle Company; served in South Africa (South Africa Medal with clasps for service 1901, 1902). In France from 13 August 1914; joined LNLR (*London Gazette* 23 October 1914); commissioned 2nd Lt Sept. 1914. Promoted from 2nd Lt to Lieutenant 12 August 1915 (*London Gazette* 25 February 1916). G.O.C. Machine Gun Training Centre, Grantham. Address on Medal Card: Folkestone, Kent.

Richardson, John Noel; at Repton School and Oriel College, Oxford with Philip. Son of Revd G. F. Richardson of St Paul's Rectory, York. At Repton 1907–1912, Oxford 1912–4. 2nd Lt, 6 Bn, Royal Berks Regt from Sept 1914. Awarded M.C. for taking command when his company commander was wounded (*London Gazette* 20 Oct. 1916). Promoted to Major, 1918. After the war joined Sudanese Civil Service, working in Education Dept in Khartoum.

Sanderson, William Denziloe; Lieutenant Colonel, 1 Bn LNLR. Returned to the battalion from leave 11 August 1915; took over temporary command of Brigade 19 August 1915; wounded leading out his men at the Battle of Loos 25 September 1915. C.M.G.; D.S.O.

Sandie, John Grey; joined 1 Bn LNLR as 2nd Lt in France July 1916; remained with them through the war, later as Lieutenant, acting Captain. Awarded M.C. for forcing his way into a burning dug-out to rescue a man [*London Gazette* 8 January 1918].

Satterthwaite, Francis Edmund Sheridan; 2nd Lt, 3 Bn LNLR. Died 3 December 1955, Buxton, Derbyshire, letters of administration to Maud Gertrude Satterthwaite, spinster, probably a daughter.

Scott, Maurice Douglas Guest; appointed 2nd Lt (on probation), 3 Bn LNLR 7 October 1914; with 1 Bn in France from 1 October 1915, later in Royal Flying Corps. Died in an accident 17 March 1918: his widow applied for his medals from Derby.

Shipp, Harry Jackson; 2nd Lt, 11 Bn LNLR 1915. Wounded at the Battle of Messines June 1917. Living in County Down in 1927, when he applied for his medals.

Smith, C.T.S.; formerly a master at Thame School, in the Public Schools Bn with whom he did 6 months in France as a Company Sergt Major. Commissioned 2nd Lt in 3 Bn LNLR, 25 September 1916, aged 40, joining them at Felixstowe. Captain of Officer Cadet Battalion, 1918.

Smyth, John George; an O.R. [Old Reptonian] contemporary of Philip; born 1893. Lieutenant Smyth won the Victoria Cross for his action in carrying bombs across exposed ground on 18 May 1915. Survived the war and went on to be a Major-General, a Member of Parliament and a baronet. Died in 1983.

Stone, Walter George; 2nd Lt, 1 Bn LNLR Aug. 1914; in France in 1916. Later fought in East Africa, promoted to Captain. Served in Ireland after the war.

Strong, ['Hugh', 'Hugo', 'HS'], Hugh William; Philip's friend at Oxford. Born in London, 1893, son of Frederick and William Strong. By 1891, his mother was a widow, the family living in Bournemouth. Went to Lancing School, Oxford University. In the O.T.C. with Philip. Appointed 2nd Lt (on probation), 3 Bn LNLR 7 October 1914; joined 1/4 Bn from 2/4 Bn 21 August 1915; as Lieutenant, wounded 9 September 1916. Later Captain. Served in South Russia 1920. Died in Somerset, 1974.

Stuart, Cyril E.; born 1892, fellow student at Repton with Philip. Went on to St John's College, Cambridge. Joined the Staffordshire Regiment. He was ordained in 1920, becoming a missionary and later a bishop in Uganda. Returned to England 1952, canon at Worcester Cathedral from 1954. Died 23 August 1982.

Swift, Harold Heyes; born 1890, son of Thomas and Katherine Swift of Prenton, Birkenhead; educated at Birkenhead School. 2nd Lt, 9 Bn LNLR, 1917. Killed in action 10 August 1917: he was 27 years old. The administration of his effects, dated 14 November 1917, gives his address as Hillside, Storeton Road, Prenton and Thomas' occupation as 'wholesale stationer'

Torbett, Francis Herbert English; born Grassington, Yorkshire, 1875. Joined the army in 1897. Accompanied 3 Bn LNLR to Felixstowe as Captain and Adjutant August 1914; joined 1 Bn in France from 3 Bn 27 August 1915, being posted to 'D' Coy. Later he became a major in the 24th Tank Corps. After the war he lived in Wareham, Dorset. Died 1950.

Trimmer, James; Sergeant in LNLR. Served in France 1914.

Tripp, Cyril Claude; brother of below, friend of Philip's at Felixstowe. 2nd Lt, 3 Bn LNLR, attached to 7 Bn, killed in action on 13 November 1916.

Tripp, Donald Owen Howard; son of Mr and Mrs C. Howard Tripp. A former rugby player. Appointed 2nd Lt (on probation), 3 Bn LNLR, 7 October 1914. Joined 1 Bn in France October 1915; wounded 26–8 February 1916 while holding a crater single-handed against an enemy bombing attack. Promoted to captain and winner of the D.S.O., Tripp was among 32 men of the 1st Battalion killed during an attack on the High Wood area in August 1916: he died on 18 August. Losses in the Battalion included an entire platoon, none of whom were heard of again: they were killed by advancing too soon into a British bombardment.

Wakley, Bertram Joseph; Major, accompanied 1 Bn LNLR to France August 1914; took over command of 1 Bn after Battle of Loos 1915; wounded in the trenches November 1915. He married into the nobility, his wife being the Hon Dorothy Henrietta Hamilton. Restricted to Home Service by his wounds, he died in London on 11 February 1917, aged 37.

Waterworth, Sidney; 2nd Lt, 1 Bn LNLR; served in France 1915. Later Captain. Awarded M.C. for consolidating a captured trench [*London Gazette* 20 Oct. 1916]. Address on Medal card: Blackburn, Lancashire.

Weber ['Reggie'], Reginald Otho; Philip's pre-war friend, born in London in 1894. Son of Frederick and Emily Weber. His father, a merchant, born in Germany, later worked for the Ordnance Survey in Southampton, the family later moving to Bromley, Kent. With 8 Bn LNLR 1917. Reggie Weber was killed in action on 5 September 1917: he was 25 years old. Buried at Lussenthoek Military Cemetery.

Wharton, Frank Hammond; son of C.H.T. and Edith Wharton of Paddington, London; graduated from Trinity Hall, Cambridge, 1909. One of thirteen 2nd Lts appointed to 3 Bn LNLR (on probation) on 15 August 1914. Joined 1 Bn in France 7 August 1915, posted to 'A' Coy; killed at the Battle of Loos 25 September 1915: he was one of four officers whose bodies were found right up by the German wire. He was 25 years old. Promoted to Lieutenant with Philip, 6 September 1915: the announcement in the *London Gazette* was 1 November 1915, after his death.

Wood, Arthur E.; one of thirteen men appointed 2nd Lt (on probation) 3 Bn LNLR, 15 August 1914. Promoted to Lieutenant with Philip, 6 September 1915. He is the 'Wood' mentioned in letters 25 and 79.

Wood, Henry George; Lieutenant, son of George and Claudine Wood of Birkenhead. Joined Public Schools Battalion on outbreak of war, gazetted to 3 Bn LNLR December 1914. Joined 1 Bn in France from 3 Bn 27 August 1915, being posted to 'D' Coy. Killed in action at Loos on 25 September 1915: he was 38 years old. He is the 'Wood' mentioned in letters 7 and 114.

Woods, J.M.; 2nd Lt, 1/5 Bn LNLR; wounded in France July-August 1917, when the Battalion lost eight officers and 150 other ranks killed, wounded and missing in attacks on the German trenches between 30 July and 4 Aug., as part of the 55th Division.

The Family

William Hewetson, Philip's father was one of at least nine children of John Hewetson and his wife Ruth (formerly Charlesworth). Several of William's brothers and sisters are mentioned as uncles or aunts in the letters, including:

Joseph Hewetson, born 1860, who succeeded his father as vicar of Measham in 1893. He and his 'family' are sometimes referred to collectively as 'Measham': a bachelor, he lived there with two unmarried sisters, **Ruth**, born 1864, and **Elizabeth**, born 1868: the former is mentioned several times, the latter is probably the 'Betsey' mentioned once by Philip.

John Hewetson, born 1859, a judge in India.

Henry Hewetson, born 1869, a professional soldier who was on the Western Front at the same time as Philip. Major, later Colonel in the Royal Army Medical Corps, he was in France from 27 August 1914, in charge of a Stationary Hospital. Awarded a DSO [*London Gazette* 1 January 1917]. 'Uncle Henry' is mentioned in several letters.

Mary Hewetson, born 1867: she married in 1897 but I have not been able to trace her after this: she could be the 'Aunt Mary' mentioned but there is another candidate among the many relatives on the other side of the family.

The Hewetsons' mother, **Kathleen** was of an Irish family: her mother, Frances Julia L'Estrange, had married Robert Bennett Burges, vicar of St Paul's Birmingham, both having been born in Ireland. They had no less than sixteen children between 1850 and 1872: five died young, those growing to adulthood included:

Julia, headmistress of Bayham House, Folkestone, a private school for girls. Aunt Julia is always referred to in the letters as '**Gobagger**', a family nickname that is never explained. It was a long-standing one, as Philip uses the name in letters written home from Woburn Sands School in 1902.[1]

Helen, assistant mistress at Bayham House. She and Aunt Julia are sometimes referred to collectively as 'Folkestone' in Philip's letters.

---

1. NRO, MC 643/1/9, 10.

Blanche, married Cecil Tyndale-Biscoe ['Uncle C', 'Uncle Cecil'], a missionary and teacher in Kashmir from 1891 to 1947: two of their children, **Julian** and **Harold**, cousins to Philip and Ruth, are mentioned in the letters.

Harriet Constalia, known as Aunt Connie, married Arthur Langdale-Smith, a clergyman: they continued the family tradition of large families by having nine children. The family lived in Holton, very close to Oxford, and is sometimes collectively known as 'Holton' in Philip's letters. One of their children, **Julia**, generally known as Julie, is mentioned in the letters.

Susan Almeda Catherine Burges: fifteen years older than Kathleen, by default she is probably the 'Aunt Lalla' mentioned by Philip.

Emily Burges: another unmarried sister, died in Croydon in 1916.

John Charles Walter L'Estrange Burges, a clergyman: he was assistant master at Srinigar school in India 1899 to 1902. He was curate at Coulsdon 1912–1915 and lived at Purley. He helped out at Salhouse when William Hewetson was in France. He is usually referred to as '**Uncle L'Estrange**'; unmarried himself, he may have taken a special interest in his nephews and nieces.

Frederick Augustine L'Estrange Burges ('Uncle Fred'), a Birmingham doctor, and highly-rated tennis player: he was five times Warwickshire champion. His wife **Mary** could be the Aunt Mary of the letters.

Bennett L'Estrange Burges, a Handsworth bank manager. There is no 'Uncle Bennett' in the letters but his wife **Edith** is probably the 'Aunt Edith' mentioned occasionally.

'Aunt E. Green' mentioned three times by Ruth, and 'Aunt Evelyn' mentioned by Philip, who may, of course, be the same person, remained unidentified. She was not an aunt in the strict sense, nor married to any uncle: the term 'aunt' was commonly used among the middle class of someone who was actually a more distant relative or even just a family friend.

The **Mollie** referred to by both Ruth and Philip was a more distant relative, a cousin of Julian's, mentioned by him as a young lady living in Godalming, Surrey and as being at school in Oxford (where she was probably in contact with Philip). Her real name was Ethel Mary Biscoe, born 1898. Her parents were Henry Biscoe, a brother of Cecil Tyndale-Biscoe, and his wife Ethel (nee Primrose): the latter was the 'Aunt Ethel' who held the notorious lunch party attended by Julian and Philip.[2]

---

2. Tyndale-Biscoe, *Gunner Subaltern* pp. 11, 65.

Index

The writers of the letters, Philip and Ruth Hewetson, and the recipients, their parents William and Katherine Hewetson, are not included in the index.